INTRODUCTION TO GREEK

Second Edition

CYNTHIA W. SHELMERDINE

Robert M. Armstrong Professor of Classics,
The University of Texas at Austin

Focus Publishing
R. Pullins Company

Introduction To Greek

Second Edition

Cynthia W. Shelmerdine

Robert M. Armstrong Professor of Classics,
The University of Texas at Austin

Focus Publishing
R. Pullins Company
www.pullins.com

Introduction To Greek, Second Edition

Focus Publishing/R. Pullins Company
PO Box 369
Newburyport, MA 01950

Corrections made in November 2011 printing.

ISBN 13: 978-1-58510-184-9

Also available as a PDF ebook (ISBN 978-1-58510-476-5)

Printed in the United States of America

12 11 10 9 8 7 6 5 4

1014BB

Table of Contents

Preface

This book was born of my experience over the last three decades teaching ancient Greek to American university students, who bear little resemblance to the audience (British schoolboys with some knowledge of Latin) for which most older textbooks were intended. College students appreciate an acknowledgment of the fact that they are coming to Greek at an older age and with wider interests. They find a new paradigm, for example, easier to remember if they understand the linguistic pattern behind it. At the same time they need some review of English grammar, and many have never taken Latin. Newer morphology-based textbooks address these needs, some in great detail. Another characteristic, however, of the students for whom it is intended is that they want results: they want to absorb the grammar and to start reading Greek, real Greek, as soon as possible. Retention rates suggest that many students are unwilling to invest two or even more semesters in a language if at the end of that time they will still be learning syntax, rather than reading the authors who inspired them to learn the language in the first place. To this end, I have tried to provide useful linguistic background, but also to focus on the basics and keep the book fairly short. The readings, drawn chiefly from Xenophon and Herodotus, are as close to the original as feasible, and increasingly so in later chapters. They seem to me to provide better practice and preparation than the invented passages of reading-based textbooks. The epigraphs which appear at the beginning of some chapters illustrate a point of grammar covered in that chapter. They are there for teacher and students to enjoy together if they wish; the vocabulary is not included in the glossary.

The starting point for the first edition was L.A. Wilding's *Greek for Beginners* (2nd edition, Faber and Faber Limited 1959), one of the best of the older texts. Wilding's selection of readings, practice sentences and vocabulary were appealing features. His assumption that Greek students already knew Latin was a drawback, however, and he provided little in the way of forms or grammatical explanations, referring students instead to a primer of Greek grammar. I created a full textbook based on Wilding's sentences and readings, including paradigms, explanations of morphology and syntax, chapter vocabularies, and so on. I also added material not in the original, like athematic verbs and conditions, and moved some syntactical sections earlier in the book. Grammar was explained with reference to English, not Latin.

The second edition carries these changes still further. The most significant modifications are the following:

1. The order of presentation has been further revised; for example, the perfect and pluperfect tenses and the numbers are deferred to near the end of the book, and athematic verbs have moved from the last chapter to chapter 23.

2. Some material omitted from the first edition has been added (e.g. the potential optative, accusative of respect, alternative verb forms).

3. Some longer chapters have been split into two.
4. Chapter vocabularies now distinguish between words in bold (to be learned, and recurring in future chapters) and words in regular type (appearing in the current chapter, but rarely if at all in future exercises, and never in English-to-Greek sentences).
5. Explanations have been revised and in some cases expanded. Increased use of bullets and outline format will, I hope, make information easier to find.
6. Syntactical presentations emphasize how to recognize a construction rather than how to form it. That is, they proceed from the perspective of a reader who is working through a Greek sentence, learning to use key words to predict what will follow and to recognize constructions. (The presentation of contrary-to-fact conditions in Ch. 12.6 exemplifies this approach.) Tables of reading expectations are provided for more complex constructions; these are repeated in Appendix 5. Those who like the traditional construction summaries, more useful when working from English to Greek than in reading, will find them in Appendix 6.
7. Exercises of various types are included, especially in earlier chapters, though the focus is still on Greek-to-English and English-to-Greek sentences.
8. Principal parts are emphasized more, and more consistently.
9. The focus is on Attic spelling (**ττ** for **σσ**), and Attic forms current in the 5th cy. BCE. Thus, for example, some extant but later principal parts are omitted.

These and other changes will, I hope, make the textbook more effective and easier to use. Many of them either echo or derive from comments by those who have reviewed the first edition and/or used it themselves. While I have not adopted every suggestion offered, I offer heartfelt thanks to all who have helped in this way and by catching errata to improve the book. They include my colleagues at The University of Texas at Austin Lesley Dean-Jones, Ben Henry, Tom Hubbard and Jack Kroll, colleagues elsewhere Simon Burris, Barbara Clayton, Brent Froberg, Jim Marks, Jeanne Neumann, Kirk Ormand, Gilbert Rose and Susan Shelmerdine, as well as the anonymous reviewers for Focus Publishing. U.T. graduate students Bart Natoli and Luis Salas assisted with proofreading. Finally, I would like to express once again my debt to many students whom I have taught with this book in earlier drafts and in the first edition. They are the best test of what works well and how to improve what does not; and they have given me the pleasure of shared discoveries which is one of the most rewarding aspects of teaching.

Cynthia W. Shelmerdine
New Year's Day 2008

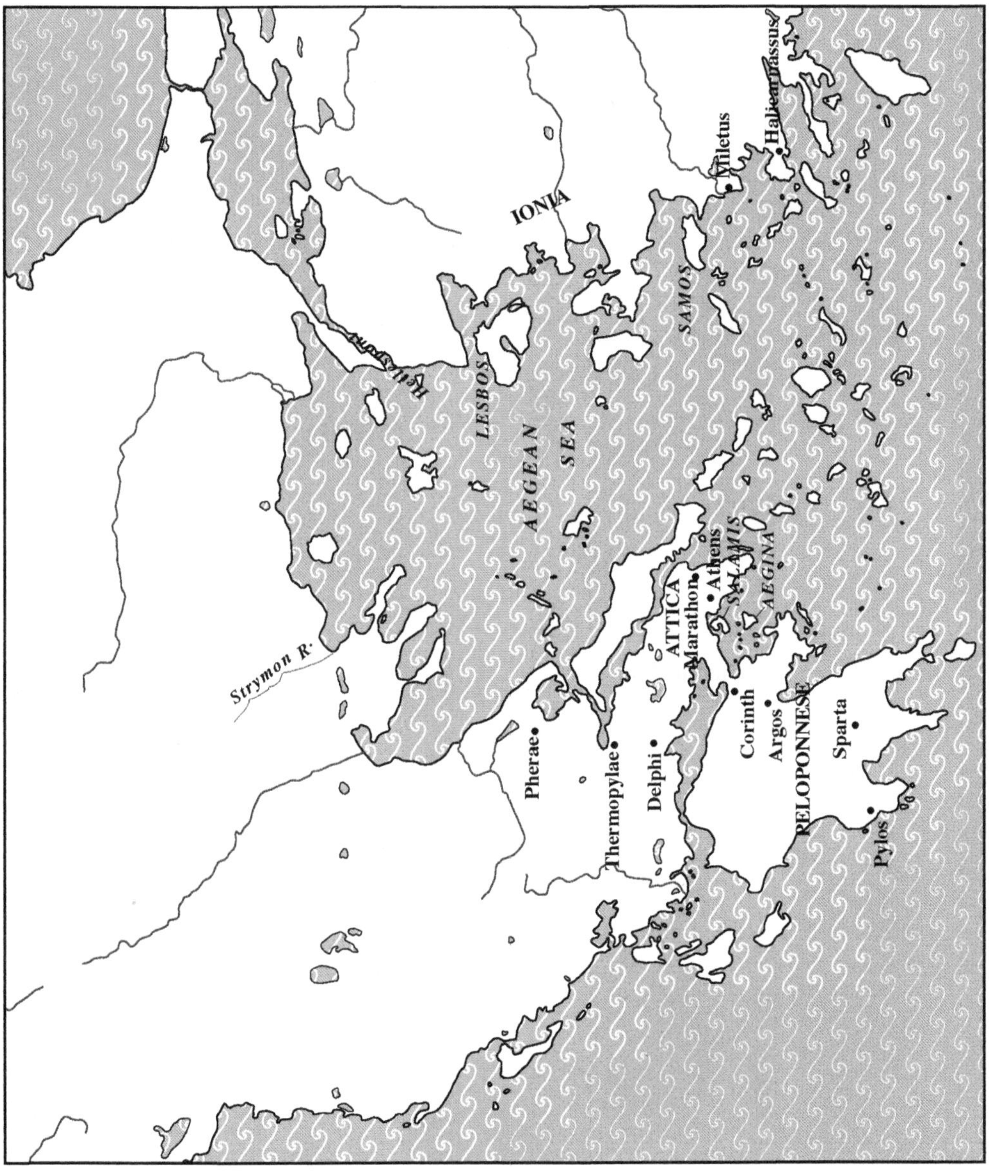

GREECE AND THE AEGEAN

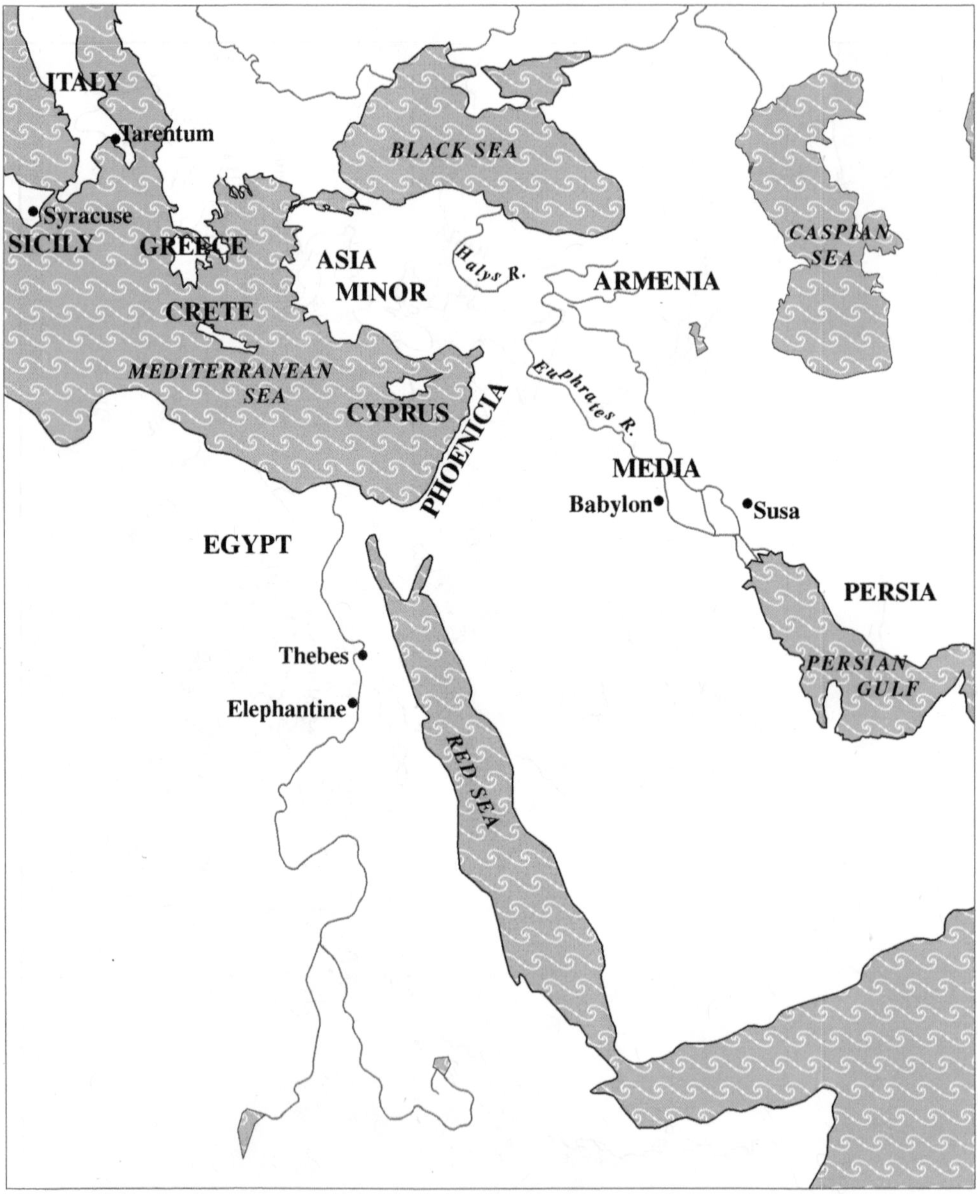

The Ancient World

CHAPTER 1

1. The Greek alphabet

Form	Name	Pronounced like
Α α	Alpha	short: second **a** in *drama*; long: first **a** in *drama*
Β β	Beta	**b**
Γ γ	Gamma	**g** in *good*
Δ δ	Delta	**d**
Ε ε	Epsilon (short e)	**e** in *bet*
Ζ ζ	Zeta	**sd** in *wisdom*
Η η	Eta (long a, e)	**a** in *man*, though often pronounced as in *hate*
Θ θ	Theta	**th** in *hothead*, though often pronounced as in *thick*
Ι ι	Iota	short: **i** in *hit*; long: **i** in *machine*
Κ κ	Kappa	**k**
Λ λ	Lambda	**l**
Μ μ	Mu	**m**
Ν ν	Nu	**n**
Ξ ξ	Xi	**x** (**ks**) in *hex*
Ο ο	Omicron (short o)	**ou** in *thought*
Π π	Pi	**p**
Ρ ρ	Rho	**r**; properly tapped or trilled
Σ σ, ς	Sigma	**s**
Τ τ	Tau	**t**
Υ υ	Upsilon	short: **u** in *put*; long: **u** in *cute*
Φ φ	Phi	**ph** in *hiphop*, though often pronounced as **f**
Χ χ	Chi	**kh** (**ch**); sound as in *backhand*
Ψ ψ	Psi	**ps**
Ω ω	Omega (long o)	**o** in *long*, though often pronounced as in *bone*

Gamma: when **γ** is followed by **γ**, **κ**, **χ** or **ξ** it is pronounced **ng** as in *angle*, *ankle*.

Omicron and Omega: the words describe the long and short vowels: μικρόν means 'small', and μέγα means 'big'.

Sigma: written **ς** at the end of a word, **σ** elsewhere in most books you will see. Another ancient option was the *lunate* sigma, **c**, used in place of both **σ** and **ς**. In the 1980's, Greek texts began to appear using the lunate sigma.

Latin spelling: Romans adjusted the spelling of Greek words, particularly proper names, to conform to the Latin alphabet. English frequently uses the Latinized forms.

c for **κ**: Σωκράτης becomes 'Sōcratēs'.

y for **υ**: κύκλος ('circle') gives us the word cycle.

ae for **αι**: Αἴσχυλος becomes 'Aeschylus'.

oe for **οι**: Οἰδίπους becomes 'Oedipus'.

A more recent practice has been to keep the Greek spelling as much as possible: Aiskhylos, Oidipous.

2. Consonant groups

The following table shows how consonants can be grouped according to how and where in the mouth they are produced. *Labial* consonants are produced with the lips, *dental* or *lingual* consonants with the tongue against the teeth (or the hard palate just behind the teeth), and *palatal* or *velar* consonants with the soft palate or velum.

	labial	**dental**	**palatal**	
stops:	π	τ	κ	unvoiced
	β	δ	γ	voiced
	φ	θ	χ	aspirated
	ψ	σ	ξ	+ σ
nasals:	μ	ν	γκ, γγ, γχ, γξ	

The table also shows another way of distinguishing consonants, as *unvoiced* (produced with no vibration from the voice box), *voiced* (produced with vibration) and *aspirated* (adding the sound **h**). The aspirated stops in ancient Greek were actually pronounced like the unvoiced stop accompanied by a puff of air, and the unvoiced stops were pronounced with no puff of air. Native English speakers do this inadvertently: 'spot' contains an unaspirated **p**, while in 'pot' the **p** is aspirated (put your hand in front of your mouth and try saying the words!). However, it is difficult for an English speaker to make the distinction voluntarily. For this reason, many English speakers settle for mispronouncing **θ** as **th**, **φ** as **f**, and **χ** as **kh** = **k**.

3. Vowel groups (diphthongs)

Diphthongs (δίφθογγοι) are two vowels combined into a single syllable. The second vowel is always **ι** or **υ**. They are pronounced as they look, with the sound of the first vowel followed by the sound of the second vowel.

αι, ᾱι as in *aisle* (θεαί, θεᾷ / θεᾶι)

αυ as in *plow* (ταῦτα)

ει, ηι as in *weigh* (Δαρεῖος, τιμῇ / τιμῆι)

ευ, ηυ as ε + υ, η + υ, though often pronounced as in *Europe* (Ζεύς, ηὕρηκα)

οι, ωι as in *boil* (οἶνος, οἴνῳ / οἴνωι)

ου as ο + υ, though often pronounced as in *boot* (Μοῦσα)

υι as in *sweet* (λελυκυῖα)

When **ι** follows a long vowel—**ᾱ**, **η** or **ω**—the **ι** is often written *subscript* underneath the long vowel. The **ι** may also appear *adscript*, written on the line. This is the rule when the long vowel is upper case, and in the 1980's, Greek texts began to appear using the iota adscript even after lower case vowels.

4. Accents

Greek has three accents: acute, ´, grave, `, and circumflex, ˜. They are part of the spelling of most Greek words. In ancient Greek the accents indicated pitch; the acute raised the syllable about a musical fifth above an unaccented syllable, the grave perhaps about a third, and the circumflex raised the syllable a fifth and lowered it again. For convenience, most English speakers treat the accents instead as stress accents, indicating which syllable of a word to emphasize.

An accent is written over a vowel; it appears on one of the last three syllables of a word. For each position, there is a rule for what form the accent must take. The following table shows all possible accents and their positions, using the following symbols.

○ = short or long syllable (length determined by length of vowel)

Ⓢ = short syllable: ε, ο; sometimes α, ι, υ; αι, οι when they end a word

Ⓛ = long syllable: η, ω; sometimes α, ι, υ; diphthongs (exception above)

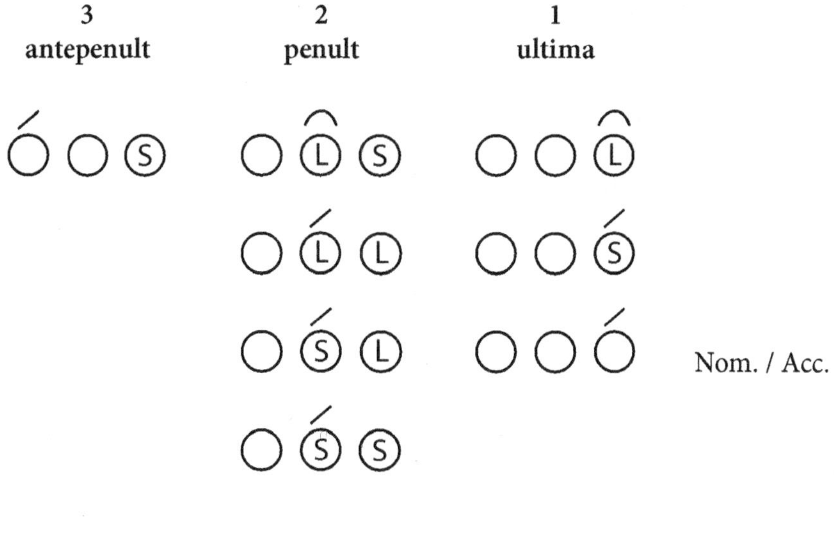

Position 3: accent on antepenult. Only acute, and only if **last** syllable is short.

Position 2: accent on penult. If penult is long **and** followed by a short syllable, accent is circumflex; otherwise, acute.

Position 1: accent on ultima. If ultima is long, accent is usually circumflex; if ultima is short, accent is acute.

EXCEPTION: accents on the nominative, accusative and vocative cases of nouns and adjectives, and on some other words, are acute / grave (unless the syllable is contracted; Ch. 19.6). "Nominative / accusative acute" is a good memorizing device.

Note: An acute accent on the ultima becomes grave when another word follows (unless that word is *enclitic*; Ch. 7.4).

Accents appear directly over a lower case vowel and to the left of an upper case letter: καλόν, Ἥρα. They appear over the second vowel of most diphthongs, but over the long first vowel **ᾱ, η** or **ω**: Ζεύς, τῇ θεᾷ, τῆι θεᾶι. For accents on vowels that begin a word, see below, sec. 5 on breathings.

5. Breathings

A breathing mark always appears on an *initial* vowel, diphthong or **ρ**—that is, one that begins a word. Like the accent, the breathing is part of the spelling of a word:

A *smooth breathing*, written like an apostrophe, is silent: ἐγώ ('eh-GO').

A *rough breathing*, written like a backward apostrophe, adds an **h** sound: ὕδρα ('HUdra').

Note: Initial **ρ** and **υ** always have a rough breathing.

A breathing mark appears directly over a lower case letter, and to the left of an upper case letter: ἐγώ, Ἥρα. The breathing is written over the second vowel of most diphthongs, but over the long first vowel **ᾱ, η** or **ω**: εἱρήνη, Αἴσχυλος, ᾗ, ἧι. If a syllable has both a breathing and an acute (or grave) accent, the breathing comes first; it stands underneath a circumflex accent: ἄγω, ἤ, ἦγον (for accents see above, sec. 4).

6. Punctuation and capital letters

Period, comma: as in English.

Colon, semicolon: a period written above the line: ἀγαθός·

Question mark: like English semicolon: ἀγαθός;

Capital letters: not used at the start of every sentence in Greek. They are used in proper nouns, to introduce quotations, and sometimes at the beginning of a paragraph.

Quotation marks: not used in Greek, although some textbooks occasionally add quotation marks for extra clarity.

EXERCISE 1. The following English words are Greek in origin. Write them out in the Greek alphabet; ignore accents, but include correct breathings. Follow *spelling* rules, not sound: what English letter corresponds to what Greek letter? Remember to convert Latinized spellings to proper Greek spellings. Long vowels **ē** (**η**) and **ō** (**ω**) are marked; plain **e** and **o** are short (**ε**, **ο**).

EXAMPLES: isoscelēs = ἰσοσκελης; hydrophobia = ὑδροφοβια

1. drama	9. genesis	17. calyx
2. rhinocerōs	10. mētropolis	18. rhododendron
3. nectar	11. thōrax	19. iris
4. sarcophagus	12. analysis	20. parenthesis
5. crisis	13. critērion	21. climax
6. canōn	14. basis	22. horizōn
7. paralysis	15. acrophobia	23. catastrophē
8. comma	16. cōlon	24. acropolis

EXERCISE 2. The following are all figures in Greek myths. Write in English, using Latinized spelling.

1. Ποσειδῶν	9. Ἀφροδίτη	17. Ἄρης
2. Ἄρτεμις	10. Προμηθεύς	18. Ψυχή
3. Ἑρμῆς	11. Ἥρα	19. Ἀθήνη
4. Κίρκη	12. Περσεφόνη	20. Ὀδυσσεύς
5. Κύκλωψ	13. Ἡρακλῆς	21. Ὑπερίων
6. Θησεύς	14. Ἀγαμέμνων	22. Ἕκτωρ
7. Μίδας	15. Ἀνδρομάχη	23. Χάρων
8. Δημήτηρ	16. Ἠλέκτρα	24. Ἄλκηστις

EXERCISE 3. The following are names of Greek people and places. Write them out in Greek letters (don't worry about accents). Long vowels are marked.

(a) 1. Dēmosthenēs	5. Nicias	9. Themistoclēs
2. Solōn	6. Cleisthenēs	10. Alcibiadēs
3. Leōnidas	7. Pythagoras	11. Hippias
4. Euripidēs	8. Xerxēs	12. Philocratēs

(b) 1. Argos	5. Olympia	9. Eretria
2. Dēlos	6. Naxos	10. Pylos
3. Mytilēnē	7. Chios	11. Phōcis
4. Samos	8. Thasos	12. Mycēnae

CHAPTER 2

1. Verb formation: principal parts

Like English, Greek has a number of *finite* verb forms; these forms indicate five specific features.

- **person**: 1st (I, we), 2nd (you), 3rd (he / she / it, they)
- **number**: singular, dual, plural. Singular and plural are familiar from English. The dual, used of two persons or things, is much less common, and is not covered in this book.
- **tense**: past, present, future. There are seven tenses in Greek. The past tenses are called *secondary* or *historic*; the others are called *primary*. The future perfect is rare and is not covered in this book.

primary	secondary
present	imperfect
future	aorist
perfect	pluperfect
future perfect	

- **voice**: active, middle, passive. The active and passive voices are familiar from English.

  active: the subject performs the verb action:
    'He stops (the boy).'

  middle: the subject performs the verb action on or for himself:
    'He stops (himself).'

  passive: the subject receives the verb action:
    'He is stopped (by the boy).'

- **mood**: The mood of a verb presents the action as a fact, command, possibility, etc. There are four moods in Greek; only the optative has no parallel in English.

  indicative: presents a fact as a statement or question:
    'He writes a letter.'

  subjunctive: presents a possibility or assumption:
    'What am I to do?'

optative: presents a possibility or wish:
'If I were you...' 'If only...',
imperative: presents a command:
'Come here.'

The two *non-finite* verb forms are the infinitive (a verbal noun: 'to come', also used as a gerund, 'coming') and the participle (a verbal adjective: 'coming').

The Greek verb has six *principal parts*; each is the basis for forming one or more tenses. A particular identifying marker distinguishes each principal part from the others. This lesson covers the present active indicative. The complete list of principal parts is as follows.

P.P.	regular marker	forms the following tenses	example	
1st:		present active, middle, passive	λύω	I loose
	augment	imperfect active, middle, passive	ἔλυον	I was loosing
2nd:	**σ**	future active, middle	λύσω	I will loose
3rd:	augment / **σα**	aorist active, middle[1]	ἔλυσα	I loosed
4th:	reduplication / **κα**	perfect active[1]	λέλυκα	I have loosed
	augment / redup. / **κε**	pluperfect active	ἐλελύκη	I had loosed
5th:	reduplication	perfect middle, passive	λέλυμαι	I have been loosed
	augment / redup.	pluperfect middle, passive	ἐλελύμην	I had been loosed
6th:	augment / **θη**	aorist, future passive	ἐλύθην	I was loosed

[1] This list shows the regular formation of the weak or 1st aorist and perfect tenses. Strong or 2nd aorists and perfects are formed differently (Ch. 11.5; 32.1).

2. The present active indicative of thematic verbs (1st principal part)

The present tense has several forms in English, for example 'I go', 'I do go', 'I am going'; 'I walk', 'I do walk', 'I am walking'. The present tense in Greek covers all of these meanings.

In English, person and number are indicated by a pronoun ('I', 'they', etc.). Greek is an *inflected* language: endings attached to the verb stem indicate person and number. The present active forms of *thematic verbs* all contain the *thematic vowel*, which appears in some forms as **ο** and in others as **ε**.

	Singular			Plural		
1st	(I)	-ω	o	(we)	-ο-μεν	o
2nd	(you)	-εις	e	(you)	-ε-τε	e
3rd	(he)	-ει	e	(they)	-ου-σῐ(ν)	o

We can describe a thematic verb as consisting of three parts: stem + thematic vowel + personal ending. Here is the present indicative active of λῡ́ω, 'I loose', 'I am loosing', etc. (The hyphens are not part of the spelling, but are inserted here to show the different components; in the singular and the 3rd person plural, the thematic vowel and the ending are combined).

Note: In a *paradigm* (table of forms) such as the following, the column of 'endings' includes the personal endings and the thematic or stem vowel.

		Stem λῡ-	Translation	Endings
Sing.	1st	λῡ́-ω	I loose	-ω
	2nd	λῡ́-εις	you loose	-εις
	3rd	λῡ́-ει	he / she / it looses	-ει
Plur.	1st	λῡ́-ο-μεν	we loose	-ο-μεν
	2nd	λῡ́-ε-τε	you loose	-ε-τε
	3rd	λῡ́-ου-σι(ν)	they loose	-ο-υσῐ(ν)

Note: The **-ν** in parenthesis on the 3rd person plural is added when the next word begins with a vowel, or when a punctuation mark follows (or for metrical reasons in poetry). Because it moves on and off the form as needed, it is called *nu movable* (*paragogic nu*).

3. Verb accents

The accent on a *finite* verb (one with person, tense and number; above, sec. 1) is *recessive*; that is, it always goes back toward the start of the word as far as accent rules (Ch. 1.4) permit.

- last syllable short: accent recedes to antepenult (must be acute)
- last syllable long: accent recedes to penult (must be acute)

Note: The verb accent always recedes, and the same rules always apply, so you should be able to reason out the correct accent for any verb form.

EXERCISE 4. Add accent and breathing, and translate (see chapter vocabulary):

1. φερει	4. γραφομεν
2. πεμπουσι	5. αγεις
3. κωλυετε	6. φυλαττω

EXERCISE 5. Translate (see chapter vocabulary):

1. κωλύεις	5. ἄγομεν	9. λύουσι
2. θύομεν	6. γράφεις	10. θύετε
3. λύει	7. πέμπουσιν	11. πέμπομεν
4. πέμπετε	8. κωλύει	12. γράφω

EXERCISE 6. Translate:

1. They lead	5. You (s.) loose	9. We are loosing
2. You (s.) hinder	6. They sacrifice	10. She sends
3. We sacrifice	7. I send	11. They hinder
4. He is writing	8. You (pl.) write	12. I lead

EXERCISE 7. Translate:

1. φυλάττομεν	5. διώκετε	9. φέρουσι
2. διώκουσι	6. φέρετε	10. ἔχει
3. φεύγει	7. ἔχεις	11. φυλάττεις
4. φέρω	8. φεύγουσιν	12. διώκομεν

EXERCISE 8. Translate:

1. They guard	5. I am fleeing	9. You (pl.) guard
2. We are fleeing	6. You (pl.) have	10. It is pursuing
3. He has	7. We carry	11. We have
4. You (s.) carry	8. She is pursuing	12. You (s.) flee

4. The negative οὐ

The negative used with main verbs appears as οὐ before consonants, οὐκ before vowels with smooth breathing, to ease pronunciation, and οὐχ before vowels with rough breathing, to show the aspiration (Ch. 1.2). It commonly stands just before the word it negates.

Note: οὐ is a *proclitic* word (from πρό, 'forward' + κλίνω, 'lean'), meaning it has no accent of its own. The lack of accent does not affect neighboring words.

5. Common conjunctions

καί, 'and, also, even', and ἀλλά, 'but' are common connectors. They are used and placed just as in English. They always connect items of the same kind: verbs with verbs, nouns with nouns, clauses with clauses, etc.

EXERCISE 9. Translate:

1. οὐ γράφει	6. We lead and carry
2. διώκομεν καὶ κωλύομεν	7. You do not loose
3. οὐ διώκει, ἀλλὰ φεύγει	8. He does not sacrifice
4. οὐκ ἔχομεν	9. They do not guard, but they flee
5. γράφουσι καὶ πέμπουσιν	10. You are not hindering

Chapter 2 Vocabulary

In the chapter vocabularies, words in bold will recur frequently and should be learned carefully. Other words may recur occasionally, but not in English-Greek exercises.

Verbs:

ἄγω	lead, bring	**λύω**	loose, set free
γράφω	write	**πέμπω**	send
διώκω	pursue	**φέρω**	carry, bear, bring
ἔχω	have	**φεύγω**	flee
θύω	sacrifice	**φυλάττω**[1]	guard
κωλύω	hinder, prevent		

Adverbs:

καί	also, even	**οὐ**, οὐκ, οὐχ	not

Conjunctions:

ἀλλά	but	**καί**	and

[1] The double -ττ- is a feature of the Attic dialect; other dialects use σσ: φυλάσσω.

CHAPTER 3

1. Noun formation

Like verbs, Greek nouns consist of a stem and an ending. These endings indicate *number* (singular, dual, plural). They also show grammatical *gender* (masculine, feminine, neuter)—whether or not the noun has a natural gender. Finally, the endings show the *case* of the noun, and thereby its grammatical function. Greek has five cases, with the following names and basic functions.

Case	Function	Example
Nominative	subject	*The goddess* writes.
	predicate	She is *a goddess.*
Genitive	possessive	The honor *of the goddess*;
		the goddess' honor
Dative	indirect object ('to' or 'for')	I sacrifice *to the goddess.*
Accusative	direct object	I worship *the goddess.*
Vocative	used in direct address	*Goddess*, I write.

2. The definite article

The definite article in Greek corresponds to English 'the'. The indefinite article, 'a', 'an' in English, does not exist in Greek; it is indicated by omitting the definite article.

The definite article is an adjective, and *agrees with* a noun. Agreement means it has the same gender, number and case. This chapter includes the feminine forms of the article, which agree with the 1st declension nouns introduced in the next section. (For the other forms, see Ch. 4.1.)

> **Note:** An adjective and noun that agree in gender, number and case do not necessarily have the same endings. Each uses the ending appropriate to its own paradigm.

3. Feminine nouns of the 1st declension

A *declension* is a set of noun or adjective endings. Greek has three declensions. The first comprises nouns and adjective forms whose stem ends in -**α** or -**η**. (To find the stem, remove the genitive singular ending; whatever is left is the stem.) There are four types of 1st declension feminine nouns. They are identical in the plural, but different in the singular.

- **type a**: τιμή type. Singular forms have the vowel -**η**. Originally this type ended in long -**ᾱ**. However, in the Dark Ages a change in pronunciation took place in some dialects, including Attic. This raised the **ᾱ** sound to **η**. This change, which did not affect short **α**, is called the *great vowel shift*.
- **type b**: χώρᾱ type. Singular forms have the vowel long -**ᾱ**, preceded by **ε**, **ι** or **ρ**. In Attic Greek, this letter protected the -**ᾱ** from the great vowel shift. The noun thus preserves its original form, with so-called 'pure' -**ᾱ**.

		Article	honor	country	Endings	
			a	b	a	b
Sing.	Nom.	ἡ	τιμή	χώρα	-η	-ᾱ
	Gen.	τῆς	τιμῆς	χώρας	-ης	-ᾱς
	Dat.	τῇ	τιμῇ	χώρᾳ	-ῃ	-ᾳ
	Acc.	τὴν	τιμήν	χώραν	-ην	-ᾱν
	Voc.	(ὦ)	τιμή	χώρα	-η	-ᾱ
Plur.	Nom.	αἱ	τιμαί	χῶραι	-αι	-αι
	Gen.	τῶν	τιμῶν	χωρῶν	-ων	-ων
	Dat.	ταῖς	τιμαῖς	χώραις	-αις	-αις
	Acc.	τὰς	τιμάς	χώρας	-ᾱς	-ᾱς
	Voc.	(ὦ)	τιμαί	χῶραι	-αι	-αι

- **types c, d**: θάλαττᾰ, γέφυρᾰ types. The nominative, accusative and vocative singular end in short -**ᾰ**. The genitive and dative singular endings are long, and were therefore affected by the great vowel shift. Thus the vowel in those cases appears as -**η** (type **c**), unless preceded by **ε**, **ι** or **ρ** as in γέφυρα, when it appears as -**ᾱ** (type **d**).

		Article	sea	bridge	Endings	
			c	d	c	d
Sing.	Nom.	ἡ	θάλαττα	γέφυρα	-ᾰ	-ᾰ
	Gen.	τῆς	θαλάττης	γεφύρας	-ης	-ᾱς
	Dat.	τῇ	θαλάττῃ	γεφύρᾳ	-ῃ	-ᾳ
	Acc.	τὴν	θάλατταν	γέφυραν	-ᾰν	-ᾰν
	Voc.	(ὦ)	θάλαττα	γέφυρα	-ᾰ	-ᾰ

		Article	sea	bridge	Endings	
			c	d	c	d
Plur.	Nom.	αἱ	θάλατται	γέφυραι	-αι	-αι
	Gen.	τῶν	θαλαττῶν	γεφυρῶν	-ων	-ων
	Dat.	ταῖς	θαλάτταις	γεφύραις	-αις	-αις
	Acc.	τὰς	θαλάττας	γεφύρας	-ᾱς	-ᾱς
	Voc.	(ὦ)	θάλατται	γέφυραι	-αι	-αι

Note: ὦ is not a form of the definite article, but a word that (usually) precedes a noun in the vocative. The literal translation of ὦ + vocative would be 'O goddess', etc. but since we do not use this interjection in English (we say 'Fred!', not 'O Fred!'), ὦ should not be translated. The vocative plural is always the same form as the nominative plural; in this declension the singular vocative and nominative forms are also the same.

If confronted by a noun in an *oblique* case (genitive, dative or accusative), you can find the nominative by the following rules.

Stem Ends in	Nom. Sing.	Example
ε, **ι** or **ρ**	long or short **-α** (type **b** or **d**)	ἀγορῶν from ἀγορά
σ, double consonant (**ζ**, **ξ**, **ψ**) or two consonants (**λλ**, **σσ**, **ττ**)	short **-ᾰ** (type **c**)	Μούσῃ from Μοῦσα
any other letter	**-η** (type **a**)	ἐπιστολαῖς from ἐπιστολή

4. Noun and adjective accents

Noun and adjective accents are *fixed* (*persistent*); that is, wherever the accent appears in the nom. sing., there it remains as long as accent rules permit, and follows the rule for that position (Ch. 1.4).

Note: When the accent is on Position 1, it is acute / grave in the nom., acc. and voc.—even when normal accent rules suggest a circumflex (Ch. 1.4).

5. Accents of 1st declension nouns

Accents can sometimes show you the length of a syllable.
θάλαττα: short ᾰ in ultima (note accent is on Position 3)
χώρα: long ᾱ in ultima (note Position 2 accent is acute).

Some accent rules affect individual cases.

- nom. / voc. pl.: short **-αι**
  αι and **οι** at the end of a word are counted short for accent purposes.

- gen. pl.: always -**ῶν**
  1st declension nouns originally ended in -**άων**. The **α** contracts with the **ω** of the gen. pl. ending: **α** + **ω** = **ω**. The accent remains on the contracted syllable, and follows the rule for Position 1.
- acc. pl.: long -**ᾱς**

6. Prepositions

Prepositions each take a particular case, sometimes a choice of cases depending on their meaning. Here are three common prepositions that take only one case. The genitive case typically describes motion *out of* or *away from*, the dative typically describes a stationary position, and the accusative typically describes motion *into* or *toward*.

Note: The following prepositions are *proclitic* (Ch. 2.4), and have no accent.

Gen.	ἐκ τῆς χώρας	out of the country	(where from)
Gen.	ἐξ οἰκίας	out of a house	(where from)
Dat.	ἐν τῇ χώρᾳ	in the country	(where)
Acc.	εἰς τὴν χώραν	into the country	(where to)

Note: When ἐκ is followed by a vowel, it is written ἐξ.

EXERCISE 10.

1. Give the acc. sing. of: τιμή, κώμη, θάλαττα, θεά, σοφία.
2. Give the gen. and acc. sing. of: μάχη, χώρα, πύλη, δόξα, στρατιά.
3. Give the nom. and dat. sing. of: οἰκιῶν, ἐπιστολῆς, ἀγοράν, γεφύραις.

EXERCISE 11. Translate the underlined words only:

1. The goddess <u>of the market-place</u>
2. I pursue <u>the army</u>.
3. <u>The Muse</u> has honor.
4. The army has <u>honor</u>.
5. I sacrifice <u>to the goddess</u>.
6. He flees <u>out of the house.</u>
7. We march <u>into the village</u>.
8. Will you remain <u>in the country</u>?

EXERCISE 12.

1. ἡ θεὰ πείθει τὰς Μούσας.
2. οὐ γράφει ἐπιστολάς.
3. φεύγομεν εἰς τὴν χώραν.
4. θύουσιν ἐν τῇ ἀγορᾷ.
5. θεραπεύετε τὴν θεάν.
6. στρατιὰν οὐκ ἔχομεν.
7. ἡ θεὰ φυλάττει τὴν κώμην.
8. διώκομεν τὴν στρατιὰν εἰς τὴν θάλατταν.

9. αἱ Μοῦσαι δόξαν ἔχουσιν.
10. θεραπεύεις τὴν θεάν; (; is a question mark; Ch. 1.6)

EXERCISE 13.

1. They send a letter.
2. The sea does not hinder the army.
3. We honor the Muses.
4. The army has glory.
5. You (pl.) are pursuing the army into the country.
6. Do they flee from the sea?
7. I am not carrying letters.
8. She sacrifices to the goddesses.
9. In the market-place they are honoring the goddess.
10. We do not pursue the army, but flee.

7. The future active indicative of thematic verbs (2nd principal part)

The future active ('I shall go', 'you will sacrifice', etc.) is formed from the 2nd principal part (Ch. 2.1). Like the present it is a primary tense. The regular marker for the future is the stem ending **-σ**. When the verb stem ends in a vowel, there is no problem. (Verbs whose stem ends in a consonant will be discussed starting in Ch. 11.) The future indicative uses the thematic vowel, and the personal endings are the same as those of the present.

		Stem λῡσ-	Translation	Endings
Sing.	1st	λύσ-ω	I shall loose	-ω
	2nd	λύσ-εις	you will loose	-εις
	3rd	λύσ-ει	he / she / it will loose	-ει
Plur.	1st	λύσ-ο-μεν	we shall loose	-ο-μεν
	2nd	λύσ-ε-τε	you will loose	-ε-τε
	3rd	λύσ-ου-σι(ν)	they will loose	-ου-σῐ(ν)

EXERCISE 14. Fill in the blanks:

1. ἡ θεὰ παύσει τ______ μάχ______.
2. φέρω τὴν ἐπιστολὴν εἰς τ______ κώμ______.
3. ἡ θάλαττ______ οὐ κωλύσει τὴν στρατιάν.
4. αἱ Μοῦσαι κωλύσ______ τὴν μάχην.
5. θύσομεν τ______ θε______ ἐν τῇ κώμῃ.

CISE 15.

1. θεραπεύσουσι τὴν θεάν.
2. οὐκ ἄγομεν τὴν στρατιὰν εἰς τὴν γέφυραν.
3. ἄγετε τὴν στρατιὰν ἐκ τῆς χώρας.
4. στρατεύσετε εἰς τὴν θάλατταν;
5. οὐ λύσομεν τὴν στρατιάν.

EXERCISE 16.

1. We will set free the village.
2. I shall not stop the battle.
3. Will you sacrifice to the goddess?
4. They will not march out of the country.
5. We will honor the Muses.
6. He is not writing the letter.
7. They are leading the army from the market-place.
8. You will worship in the country.
9. We shall not prevent the battle.
10. Will they stop the army?

Chapter 3 Vocabulary

Verbs:

θεραπεύω	honor, worship	**πείθω**	persuade
παύω	stop	**στρατεύω**	march

Nouns (noun entries include nominative, genitive ending and article):

ἀγορά, -ᾶς, ἡ	market-place	**μάχη**, -ης, ἡ	battle
γέφυρα, -ας, ἡ	bridge	Μοῦσα, -ης, ἡ	Muse
δόξα, -ης, ἡ	glory	**οἰκία**, -ας, ἡ	house
ἐπιστολή, -ῆς, ἡ	letter	πύλη, -ης, ἡ	gate
ἡμέρα, -ας, ἡ	day	**σοφία**, -ας, ἡ	wisdom
θάλαττα, -ης, ἡ	sea	**στρατιά**, -ᾶς, ἡ	army
θεά, -ᾶς, ἡ	goddess	**τιμή**, -ῆς, ἡ	honor
κώμη, -ης, ἡ	village	**χώρα**, -ας, ἡ	country

Article:

ἡ	the (feminine form)

Prepositions: (in parentheses, the case of the noun governed by the preposition)

εἰς (+ *acc.*)	into, onto, to	**ἐν** (+ *dat.*)	in, on, at
ἐκ (+ *gen.*)	out of, from		

ἐξ when followed by word starting with a vowel

Address:

ὦ	(used with voc. but not translated)

CHAPTER 4

1. The paradigm of the definite article

Here is the paradigm of the definite article (Ch. 3.2). The masculine forms agree with the 1st declension nouns introduced in the next section.

	Singular			Plural		
	M	F	N	M	F	N
Nom.	ὁ	ἡ	τό	οἱ	αἱ	τά
Gen.	τοῦ	τῆς	τοῦ	τῶν	τῶν	τῶν
Dat.	τῷ	τῇ	τῷ	τοῖς	ταῖς	τοῖς
Acc.	τόν	τήν	τό	τούς	τάς	τά

2. Masculine nouns of the 1st declension

There are two types of 1st declension masculine nouns. Type **a** corresponds in form to type **a** of the 1st declension; type **b** corresponds to type **b** (Ch. 3.3).

		Article	judge	young man	Endings	
			a	b	a	b
Sing.	Nom.	ὁ	κριτής	νεανίας	-ης	-ᾱς
	Gen.	τοῦ	κριτοῦ	νεανίου	-ου	-ου
	Dat.	τῷ	κριτῇ	νεανίᾳ	-ῃ	-ᾳ
	Acc.	τὸν	κριτήν	νεανίαν	-ην	-ᾱν
	Voc.	(ὦ)	κριτά	νεανία	-ᾰ	-ᾱ
Plur.	Nom.	οἱ	κριταί	νεανίαι	-αι	-αι
	Gen.	τῶν	κριτῶν	νεανιῶν	-ων	-ων
	Dat.	τοῖς	κριταῖς	νεανίαις	-αις	-αις
	Acc.	τοὺς	κριτάς	νεανίας	-ᾱς	-ᾱς
	Voc.	(ὦ)	κριταί	νεανίαι	-αι	-αι

Note: The voc. sing. of nouns in **-της** ends in short **-ᾰ**; most other nouns have long **-ᾱ**.

3. The imperfect active indicative of thematic verbs (1st principal part)

The imperfect is a past tense, also known as a *historic* or *secondary* tense. In English it has a progressive meaning: 'I was going'; its meaning in Greek is discussed below.

The Greek imperfect is formed from the 1st principal part of the verb (Ch. 2.1)—that is, it uses the present stem. The indicative has a set of past tense endings, and it also has an *augment*, like all secondary tenses. For verbs beginning with a consonant, the augment is the letter **ε** preceding the verb stem. (Verbs that begin with a vowel are augmented by lengthening the vowel; Ch. 11.2). The thematic vowel appears throughout, as in the present.

		Stem λῡ-	Translation	Endings
Sing.	1st	ἔ-λυ-ο-ν	I was loosing	-ο-ν
	2nd	ἔ-λυ-ε-ς	you were loosing	-ε-ς
	3rd	ἔ-λυ-ε	he / she / it was loosing	-ε-(ν)
Plur.	1st	ἐ-λύ-ο-μεν	we were loosing	-ο-μεν
	2nd	ἐ-λύ-ε-τε	you were loosing	-ε-τε
	3rd	ἔ-λυ-ο-ν	they were loosing	-ο-ν

The imperfect in English describes an ongoing or repeated past action: 'I was going', 'I used to go'. These are its two most common meanings in Greek also. It can also mean 'I tried to go' (the *conative* imperfect), because the action is incomplete.

ἡ στρατιὰ ἐδίωκε τὸν νεανίαν.
The army was pursuing the young man.

οἱ πολῖται ἐθεράπευον τὴν θεάν.
The citizens used to worship the goddess.

οἱ πολῖται ἔπειθον τὸν κριτήν.
The citizens tried to persuade the judge.

EXERCISE 17. Translate:

1. ἔθυεν
2. ἐπαύομεν
3. ἐκώλυον
4. ἔφερες
5. ἐπέμπετε
6. He tried to write
7. You (pl.) were sacrificing
8. I used to march
9. We were pursuing
10. You (s.) tried to stop

4. Some uses of the definite article

In Greek the article has several uses that go beyond its function in English. Among its common uses are the following.

- In place of a possessive adjective, when the context makes it clear who the possessor is.

  ἄγει τὴν στρατιάν.
  He leads *his army.*

- With nouns denoting a class or type in general.

  οἱ ποιηταὶ ἔχουσι τὴν σοφίαν.
  Poets have wisdom.

- With abstract nouns, especially when the noun is the subject of the sentence, or the topic of discussion.

  ἡ δικαιοσύνη φυλάττει τὴν εἰρήνην.
  Justice guards *peace.*

- With proper nouns, especially after the first time the person or place is mentioned.

  ἡ Ἀθήνη — Athena
  αἱ Ἀθῆναι — Athens

5. Verbs taking genitive or dative

Some verbs take an object in the genitive or dative, instead of a normal direct object in the accusative. Often one can see the logic behind the usage.

- Verbs of ruling take the genitive (be king *of*).

  βασιλεύει τῆς χώρας.
  He rules / is king of the country.

- πιστεύω 'trust, believe' takes the dative (put one's trust *in*, give credence *to*).

  πιστεύουσι τῇ θεᾷ.
  They trust the goddess.

Note: Verbs taking the genitive or the dative are always so noted in the chapter vocabulary.

EXERCISE 18. Fill in the blanks, and add accents:

1. οἱ ποιητ____ θεραπευουσι την Μουσ____.
2. ὁ κριτης την μαχ____ επαυ____.
3. οἱ στρατιωτ____ εφευγον εἰς τας Ἀθην____.
4. ἐθυετε ἐν τ____ κωμ____;
5. οἱ νεανιαι πιστευουσι τ____ ναυτ____.

EXERCISE 19.

1. τῷ ταμίᾳ οὐκ ἐπιστεύομεν.
2. οἱ κριταὶ τὴν δικαιοσύνην διώκουσιν.
3. ὁ Ξέρξης ἐβασίλευε τῶν Περσῶν.
4. στρατεύσετε, ὦ νεανίαι, εἰς τὴν χώραν.
5. οἱ στρατιῶται ἐκώλυον τοὺς ναύτας ἀπὸ τῆς κώμης.

EXERCISE 20.

1. We were not hindering the soldiers.
2. The young men were marching toward Athens.
3. Will Athena stop the battle?
4. The sailor flees to his house.
5. The sailor was not trusting Xerxes.
6. We used to train the young men in the village.
7. Poets will always honor Sparta.
8. Citizens, will you set free the soldiers?
9. The citizens tried to keep the soldiers away from the houses.
10. Are you king of the country?

Chapter 4 Vocabulary

Verbs:

βασιλεύω (+ *gen.*)	be king, reign	**παιδεύω**	educate, teach, train
κωλύω (ἀπό)	keep (someone) away (from)	**πιστεύω** (+ *dat.*)	trust, believe

Nouns:

Ἀθῆναι, -ῶν, αἱ	Athens	**Ξέρξης**, -ου, ὁ	Xerxes
Ἀθήνη, -ης, ἡ	Athena	**Πέρσης**, -ου, ὁ	(a) Persian
δικαιοσύνη, -ης, ἡ	justice	**ποιητής**, -οῦ, ὁ	poet
εἰρήνη, -ης, ἡ	peace	**πολίτης**, -ου, ὁ	citizen (long ῑ)
κριτής, -οῦ, ὁ	judge	**Σπάρτη**, -ης, ἡ	Sparta
ναύτης, -ου, ὁ	sailor	**στρατιώτης**, -ου, ὁ	soldier
νεανίας, -ου, ὁ	young man	ταμίας, -ου, ὁ	steward

Article:

ὁ, ἡ, τό	the

Adverb:

ἀεί	always

Prepositions:

ἀπό (+ *gen.*)	from, away from	**πρός** (+ *acc.*)	to, toward

CHAPTER 5

Ἐν ἀρχῇ ἦν ὁ λόγος, καὶ ὁ λόγος ἦν πρὸς τὸν θεόν, καὶ θεὸς ἦν ὁ λόγος.

— John 1:1

1. Masculine and feminine nouns of the 2nd declension

Both masculine and (less common) feminine nouns of the 2nd declension have stems that end in **-ο**. The pattern of long and short endings is the same as for the θάλαττα / γέφυρα types of 1st declension nouns (types **c** and **d**, Ch. 3.3): short in nom., acc. sing., voc.; long in gen., dat., acc. pl.

		Article	word	Article	island	Endings
Sing.	Nom.	ὁ	λόγος	ἡ	νῆσος	-ος
	Gen.	τοῦ	λόγου	τῆς	νήσου	-ου
	Dat.	τῷ	λόγῳ	τῇ	νήσῳ	-ῳ
	Acc.	τὸν	λόγον	τὴν	νῆσον	-ον
	Voc.	(ὦ)	λόγε	(ὦ)	νῆσε	-ε
Plur.	Nom.	οἱ	λόγοι	αἱ	νῆσοι	-οι
	Gen.	τῶν	λόγων	τῶν	νήσων	-ων
	Dat.	τοῖς	λόγοις	ταῖς	νήσοις	-οις
	Acc.	τοὺς	λόγους	τὰς	νήσους	-ους
	Voc.	(ὦ)	λόγοι	(ὦ)	νῆσοι	-οι

2. The aorist active indicative of thematic verbs (3rd principal part)

The *aorist* is the simple past tense, which corresponds to English 'I went', 'I watched', 'I did not watch', etc. Unlike the imperfect, the aorist does not imply that an action was ongoing or repeated, simply that it happened. The distinction is clear in English.

Imperfect	**Simple Past**
I was going	I went
it was happening	it happened
they were running	they ran

The aorist active is the 3rd principal part of a Greek verb, after the present and the future (Ch. 2.1). It is formed in one of two ways. In English, some verbs form the past tense by adding the ending **-ed** to the present stem ('I watch' / 'I watched'); these are called *weak verbs.* Other verbs change their stem instead ('I go' / 'I went'); these are called *strong verbs.* The same distinction applies in Greek: a verb has either a weak or a strong aorist (commonly referred to as 1st and 2nd aorist). The 2nd aorist will be presented in Ch. 11.5.

The 1st aorist tense stem ends in **-σ**, with a stem vowel **-ᾰ**; it replaces the thematic vowel of the present, future and imperfect tenses, except that the 3rd sing. aorist ends in **-ε**. The personal endings of the indicative are the same as those of the imperfect, except in the 1st sing. Like all past tense indicatives the aorist begins with an augment (Ch. 4.3).

		Stem λῡσ-	Translation	Endings
Sing.	1st	ἔ-λυσ-α	I loosed	-ᾰ-
	2nd	ἔ-λυσ-α-ς	you loosed	-ᾰ-ς
	3rd	ἔ-λυσ-ε(ν)	he / she / it loosed	-ε-(ν)
Plur.	1st	ἐ-λύσ-α-μεν	we loosed	-ᾰ-μεν
	2nd	ἐ-λύσ-α-τε	you loosed	-ᾰ-τε
	3rd	ἔ-λυσ-α-ν	they loosed	-ᾰ-ν

3. Aspect in the indicative

Greek tenses in the indicative mood (and in some uses of the infinitive and participle) carry time distinctions. In all moods the choice of tenses may also make the important distinction of *aspect.* The aspect of a verb indicates whether the action described is a single act or an ongoing or repeated one. In the indicative, the difference between the imperfect (ongoing) and aorist (single act) is one of aspect (above, sec. 2).

Many verbs may occur in either aspect: ἐστράτευον, 'they were marching'; ἐστράτευσαν, 'they marched'. Some verbs, however, naturally describe a single, simple act or imply completion of a process: ἔπαυσας, 'you stopped'. These verbs occur in the aorist much more often than the imperfect. Other verbs naturally imply an ongoing action: ἔμενες, 'you remained (were remaining)'. In Greek, such verbs occur more often in the imperfect, though the English translation may use the simple past tense.

EXERCISE 21. Give the following forms, <u>with article</u>:

1. Nom. sing. of: νήσῳ, δούλοις, ἡμερῶν, νεανίαν.
2. Gen. and dat. pl. of: οἰκία, λόγος, στρατιώτης, ἵππος.
3. Gen. and acc. sing. of: πολίτης, στρατηγός, εἰρήνη, ποταμός.

EXERCISE 22. Give the following verb forms:

1. He will march
2. I used to sacrifice
3. You (s.) will run risks
4. She tried to persuade
5. They hindered
6. We stay
7. They are writing
8. You were loosing
9. I stopped

EXERCISE 23.

1. ἐκωλύσαμεν τοὺς ἵππους ἀπὸ τῆς χώρας.
2. τὴν σοφίαν ἐδιώκομεν.
3. ὁ δοῦλος ἔγραφεν ἐν τῇ οἰκίᾳ.
4. οἱ νεανίαι εἰς τὴν Σπάρτην στρατεύσουσιν.
5. ὁ ἰατρὸς ἐθεράπευσε τὴν νόσον.
6. οἱ στρατιῶται ἐστράτευον πρὸς τὸν ποταμόν.
7. ἡ νόσος τὸν πόλεμον οὐκ ἔπαυσεν.
8. οἱ Ἀθηναῖοι ἔθυσαν ἐν τῇ νήσῳ.
9. οἱ στρατιῶται ἐφύλαττον τὴν ὁδόν;
10. ὁ Ξέρξης τὴν στρατιὰν ἄγει ἐν τῇ ὁδῷ.

EXERCISE 24.

1. We set free [*use aorist*] the slaves.
2. The Persians trained their horses.
3. The Athenians were pursuing not war, but peace.
4. You ran risks on the road, doctor.
5. The young men remained [*use imperfect*] on the island.
6. The soldiers believed the general.
7. We were fleeing toward Athens.
8. The soldiers marched to the village.
9. The doctors did not keep the plague from Athens.
10. We are leading the horses to the river.

4. Word order

In Greek the ending of a word, rather than its position in the sentence, shows its grammatical function. Thus word order is generally flexible. There is no rule that requires, for example, the verb to be at the end of the sentence. The most important point is that the order should be logical and the meaning clear. This flexibility has certain advantages. To emphasize a word, a Greek author may just move it from its natural place toward the beginning of the sentence; this gives it prominence, as underlining does in English. Sometimes, too, a certain word order will be chosen for its harmonious sound, or for variation.

Some situations, however, do require a particular word order; one of them is explained in the next section.

5. The possessive genitive

One of the most common uses of the genitive case is to indicate possession: τοῦ στρατηγοῦ, 'of the general'. There are two acceptable *constructions*:

- ἡ τοῦ κριτοῦ οἰκία = the judge's house
- ἡ οἰκία ἡ τοῦ κριτοῦ = the judge's house

Usually the genitive phrase is 'sandwiched' between an article and its noun (the *attributive* position, Ch. 7.2), as in the first example above. In the other construction the genitive phrase is still attributive, because the article of the noun it depends on is repeated, as in the second example. It is equally good Greek; authors used this construction both for emphasis and simply for variation.

EXERCISE 25. Translate the underlined words only:

1. The slave loosed the general's horse.
2. The steward of the house trained the slaves.
3. Do you trust the judges' words?
4. We value the wisdom of the sailors.

EXERCISE 26.

1. ὦ πολῖται, πιστεύσομεν τοῖς νεανίαις.
2. οἱ στρατιῶται ἐφύλαττον τὰς τῶν πολιτῶν οἰκίας.
3. οἱ τῶν Ἀθηναίων στρατηγοὶ ἐκινδύνευσαν.
4. ἡ στρατιὰ ἡ τοῦ Ξέρξου φεύγει.
5. ἐν τῇ ὁδῷ ἐκινδυνεύομεν.
6. ὁ Ξέρξης οὐκ ἐβασίλευσε τῶν Ἀθηναίων.

EXERCISE 27.

1. The soldiers were guarding the village.
2. We marched into the country of the Persians.
3. The generals of the Athenians tried to stop the battle.
4. Young men do not always pursue wisdom.
5. Xerxes did not trust his soldiers.
6. We will keep the Persians away from Athens.

Chapter 5 Vocabulary

Verbs:

θεραπεύω	heal, cure, tend	**μένω**	stay, remain
κινδυνεύω	run risks		

Nouns:

Ἀθηναῖος, -ου, ὁ	Athenian	νόσος, -ου, ἡ	illness, plague
δοῦλος, -ου, ὁ	slave	**ὁδός**, -οῦ, ἡ	road, way, journey
ἰατρός, -οῦ, ὁ	doctor	**πόλεμος**, -ου, ὁ	war
ἵππος, -ου, ὁ	horse	**ποταμός**, -οῦ, ὁ	river
λόγος, -ου, ὁ	word	**στρατηγός**, -οῦ, ὁ	general
νῆσος, -ου, ἡ	island		

CHAPTER 6

καὶ σὺ τέκνον.

— perhaps Julius Caesar's last words
(Suetonius, *de vita Caesarum* 82)

1. Neuter nouns of the 2nd declension

Neuter nouns of the 2nd declension have the same endings as neuter forms of the article, except that the nom., acc. and voc. sing. end in **-ον**. In neuter nouns and adjectives, the accusative and nominative forms are always the same. There is only one type of 2nd declension neuter noun.

		Article	gift	Endings
Sing.	Nom.	τὸ	δῶρον	-ον
	Gen.	τοῦ	δώρου	-ου
	Dat.	τῷ	δώρῳ	-ῳ
	Acc.	τὸ	δῶρον	-ον
	Voc.	(ὦ)	δῶρον	-ον
Plur.	Nom.	τὰ	δῶρα	-ᾰ
	Gen.	τῶν	δώρων	-ων
	Dat.	τοῖς	δώροις	-οις
	Acc.	τὰ	δῶρα	-ᾰ
	Voc.	(ὦ)	δῶρα	-ᾰ

Note: In Greek, if the subject is neuter, the verb is singular—even if the subject is plural. The English translation must use a plural verb if the subject is plural.

τὸ δένδρον ἔχει καρπόν.

The tree has fruit.

τὰ δένδρα ἔχει καρπόν.

The trees have fruit.

2. Some uses of the dative

- indirect object (Ch. 3.1).

  θύομεν τῇ θεᾷ.

  We sacrifice *to the goddess.*

  Note: In expressions of motion *to* or *toward* a place, the dative is not used. To say 'to the house' Greek uses a preposition with the accusative (Ch. 3.6).

- with the preposition ἐν (Ch. 3.6).
  - literally, place where:

    θύομεν ἐν τῇ ἀγορᾷ.

    We sacrifice *in the market-place.*
  - metaphorically:

    παιδεύομεν τοὺς νεανίας ἐν τῇ σοφίᾳ.

    We educate the young men *in wisdom.*

- *means* or *instrument* by which something is done.

  τὸν κριτὴν ἐκώλυες τοῖς λόγοις.

  You were hindering the judge *with your words.*

  ἐπιστολῇ πείθει τοὺς πολίτας.

  He persuades the citizens *by means of a letter.*

3. The present active infinitive of thematic verbs

The *infinitive* is a verbal noun, corresponding to the English infinitive: 'to loose', 'to write'. It is one of two non-finite forms of the Greek verb (the other is the participle, a verbal adjective, Ch. 21.1). The present active infinitive consists of the present stem (1st principal part) + the thematic vowel **ε** + the ending **εν**. The two **ε**'s contract to **ει**: λύ-ειν, γράφ-ειν.

Note: The accent on infinitives is not *recessive*, like the accent on finite verb forms (Ch. 2.3), but *fixed* (*persistent*), like those of nouns and adjectives (Ch. 3.4). For each form of the infinitive the position of the accent must be learned. The accent on the present active infinitive always stands on the last syllable of the stem (Position 2-penult).

As a verbal noun, the infinitive has some features of a verb, but in other ways it is like a noun.

- verb features:
  - tense (present, future, etc.)
  - voice (active, middle, passive)
  - it can have a subject and an object
- noun features
  - it can function like a noun, in different cases (Ch. 13.5)

- it may appear with the neuter article (the *articular* infinitive, Ch. 13.5)
- the accent is fixed (persistent), not recessive (Ch. 3.4)

4. The complementary infinitive

The infinitive often appears as a complement to a main verb. This *complementary* use is familiar from English: ἐθέλω πέμπειν, 'I want to send'. The negative used with this type of infinitive is μή, not οὐ. In general, the subject of an infinitive is in the accusative case, unless it is also the subject of the main verb. The infinitive can also take a direct object.

οὐκ ἐθέλομεν κόπτειν τὰ δένδρα.
We are not willing to cut down the trees.

ἐκελεύσαμεν τοὺς νεανίας φεύγειν.
We ordered the young men to flee.

πείθομεν τοὺς νεανίας μὴ κόπτειν τὰ δένδρα.
We persuade the young men not to cut down the trees.

5. Reading expectations

A verb like 'be willing' raises the expectation that an infinitive (complementary) will follow in the sentence.

ἐθέλω → infinitive = complementary ('I am willing to do x.')

Even if it is not the next word, you can predict and look out for it.

οὐκ ἐθέλομεν τὰ δένδρα κόπτειν.
We are not willing to cut down the trees.

Similarly, you can predict what will come after a verb like 'persuade' or 'order': 'I order *someone to do something*'. Learning to anticipate the possibilities will help you read Greek accurately, and with increasing speed.

6. The negatives οὐ and μή

There is no difference in meaning between the two negatives οὐ and μή. Of the constructions you have seen so far, οὐ is used with the indicative, and μή with complementary infinitives. With few exceptions, the negative for moods other than the indicative is μή, not οὐ.

EXERCISE 28.

1. ὁ κριτὴς ἐκέλευσε τοὺς πολίτας μένειν ἐν τῇ κώμῃ.
2. ἐλύσαμεν τὸν καρπὸν ἀπὸ τῶν δένδρων.
3. οἱ πολῖται ἐθεράπευσαν τούς τε ποιητὰς καὶ τοὺς στρατηγούς.
4. τὰ τῶν πολεμίων ἔργα βλάπτει τοὺς πολίτας.
5. οἱ δοῦλοι οὐκ ἐθέλουσι τῇ θεᾷ θύειν.

6. ὁ ποιητὴς οὐ τοῖς ἔργοις τὴν μάχην ἔπαυσεν, ἀλλὰ τοῖς λόγοις.
7. τὰ τοῦ ταμίου τέκνα θεραπεύσει τοὺς ἵππους.
8. ἐπείθομεν τοὺς πολεμίους μὴ πιστεύειν τῷ στρατηγῷ.
9. οἱ ποιηταὶ τὴν δόξαν παρέχουσι τοῖς Ἀθηναίοις.
10. ἐθέλεις βασιλεύειν τῶν νησῶν;

EXERCISE 29.

1. The judge educated the young men in justice and wisdom.
2. We will prevent a battle in the village.
3. The poet was writing among the trees.
4. The general will order the soldiers to run risks.
5. Gifts do not always persuade the goddess not to harm the animals.
6. Is it difficult to train the horses with words?
7. We are sending a letter to the general.
8. I ordered the slave to stay in the market-place.
9. They sacrificed to the goddess of the country.
10. The soldier persuades the young men to march.

Chapter 6 Vocabulary

Verbs:

βλάπτω	harm, injure, damage	**κόπτω**	cut, cut down
ἐθέλω	be willing, wish	παρέχω	provide, cause, produce
κελεύω	order		

Nouns:

δένδρον, -ου, τό	tree	**πολέμιοι**, -ων, οἱ	enemy (group)
δῶρον, -ου, τό	gift	σῖτος, -ου, ὁ	food
ἔργον, -ου, τό	work, deed	**στρατόπεδον**, -ου, τό	(army) camp
ζυγόν, -οῦ, τό	yoke	τέκνον, -ου, τό	child
ζῷον, -ου, τό	animal	φιλία, -ας, ἡ	friendship
καρπός, -οῦ, ὁ	fruit		
ὅπλα, -ων, τά	arms, weapons		

Preposition:

ἐν (+ *dat. pl.*)	among

Adverb:

μή	not

CHAPTER 7

πᾶν δένδρον ἀγαθὸν καρποὺς καλοὺς ποιεῖ.

— Matthew 7:17

1. 1st and 2nd declension adjectives

Adjectives exist in all three genders, so that they can agree with any noun. The masculine and neuter forms of most adjectives have 2nd declension endings (Ch. 5.1, 6.1). The feminine forms have 1st declension endings of the τιμή or χώρᾱ type (type **a** or **b**, Ch. 3.3). Thus most feminine singulars end in -**η**, but after **ε**, **ι** and **ρ** the long -**ᾱ** will appear.

		wise			**friendly**		
		M	F	N	M	F	N
Sing.	Nom.	σοφός	σοφή	σοφόν	φίλιος	φιλίᾱ	φίλιον
	Gen.	σοφοῦ	σοφῆς	σοφοῦ	φιλίου	φιλίας	φιλίου
	Dat.	σοφῷ	σοφῇ	σοφῷ	φιλίῳ	φιλίᾳ	φιλίῳ
	Acc.	σοφόν	σοφήν	σοφόν	φίλιον	φιλίαν	φίλιον
	Voc.	σοφέ	σοφή	σοφόν	φίλιε	φιλίᾱ	φίλιον
Plur.	Nom.	σοφοί	σοφαί	σοφά	φίλιοι	φίλιαι	φίλια
	Gen.	σοφῶν	σοφῶν	σοφῶν	φιλίων	φιλίων	φιλίων
	Dat.	σοφοῖς	σοφαῖς	σοφοῖς	φιλίοις	φιλίαις	φιλίοις
	Acc.	σοφούς	σοφάς	σοφά	φιλίους	φιλίας	φίλια
	Voc.	σοφοί	σοφαί	σοφά	φίλιοι	φίλιαι	φίλια

Note: The gen. pl. of the feminine is accented like the masculine and neuter, not as in 1st declension nouns.

2. Attributive adjectives

An *attributive* adjective simply defines a noun within a noun phrase: 'the good soldier', 'the wise king'. In Greek, as in English, it is normally placed between the article and the noun. Alternatively the article may be repeated, with the adjective following it. If there is no article, the word order is flexible.

οἱ σοφοὶ λόγοι λόγοι οἱ σοφοί οἱ λόγοι οἱ σοφοί the wise words	λόγοι σοφοὶ wise words

These same two options exist for any attributive word or phrase; you have already seen them for the possessive genitive (Ch.5.5).

ὁ τοῦ στρατηγοῦ ἵππος
ὁ ἵππος ὁ τοῦ στρατηγοῦ
the horse of the general / the general's horse

τὰ ἐν τῇ νήσῳ δένδρα
τὰ δένδρα τὰ ἐν τῇ νήσῳ
the trees on the island

The noun may be omitted when the context, and the gender of the article, make its meaning clear enough. This construction exists in English too, though it is less common: "...the land of the free and the home of the brave."

οἱ σοφοὶ
the wise (men)
ταῖς σοφαῖς
to the wise (women)
τῶν κακῶν
of the bad (men or things)

3. Predicate adjectives and nouns

A *predicate* adjective or phrase appears with a noun phrase and the verb 'be' (or another verb describing a state of being: e.g. 'seem', 'look', 'become'). The present 3rd singular and plural of εἰμί, 'be' (below, sec. 5), however, may be omitted. The *position* of the adjective distinguishes the predicate from the attributive: an attributive adjective always immediately follows the article, a predicate never does. The predicate adjective agrees with the subject noun it modifies.

ὁ λόγος σοφός (ἐστιν).
σοφός (ἐστιν) ὁ λόγος.
The word is wise.
ὁ ἵππος (ἐστὶ) τοῦ στρατηγοῦ.
The horse is the general's.
τὰ δένδρα ἐν τῇ νήσῳ (ἐστίν).
The trees are on the island.

Nouns can also be predicate. Because the verb 'be' states an equality or equivalency, the predicate noun, like a predicate adjective, is in the same case as the subject.

ὁ στρατιώτης (ἐστὶ) ποιητής.
ποιητής (ἐστιν) ὁ στρατιώτης.
The soldier is a poet.

Since the subject and the predicate in the sentence above are both nominative nouns, how do you know which is the subject? If only **one** of the nouns has an article, that is the subject; if both do, the subject comes first. An article always accompanies one noun or both.

ὁ στρατιώτης (ἐστὶ) ποιητής.
ποιητής ὁ στρατιώτης (ἐστίν).
The soldier is a poet.

ὁ ποιητής (ἐστιν) ὁ στρατιώτης.
The poet is the soldier.

EXERCISE 30. Translate the underlined material:

1. The wise poet has honor.
2. The poet (is) wise.
3. We found the foreigners in the village.
4. I ordered the foreigners in the village to fight.
5. He hates bad things.
6. The young men (are) brave.
7. They trust the strong horses.

4. Enclitics

An *enclitic* (from ἐν, 'on' + κλίνω, 'lean') is a word that has no accent of its own, but leans on the previous word for its accent. The effect is like adding a syllable to the previous word. An enclitic can never be the first word of a clause or sentence; if it were, there would be nothing for it to lean on. The verb 'be' is enclitic in the present indicative, except in the 2nd singular.

Enclitics can be one or two syllables long. The following diagram shows how accents work for a one-syllable enclitic (**e**) and for a two-syllable enclitic (**ee**). Generally you take care of the enclitic by adding an acute accent to the last syllable of the previous word, or in Position 1-acute by leaving the accent acute. The one exception is Position 2-acute.

Position 3	(ό ο ο):	ό ο ό e	ό ο ό ee	πόλεμός τις	πόλεμός ἐστι
Position 2	(ο ô ο):	ο ô ό e	ο ô ό ee	δῶρόν τι	δῶρόν ἐστι
	(ο ό ο):	ο ό ο e	ο ό ο eé or eê	λόγος τις	λόγος ἐστί, λόγων τινῶν
Position 1	(ο ο ό):	ο ο ό e	ο ο ό ee	σοφός τις	σοφός ἐστι
	(ο ο ô):	ο ο ô e	ο ο ô ee	σοφοῦ μου	σοφοῦ τινος

Position 2-acute: the effect of the acute accent only reaches the first syllable of the enclitic. In the other instances an acute accent could be added to the last syllable of the preceding word. Here, however, to avoid two acute accents in a row (a pronunciation problem with pitch accents), the second syllable of the enclitic carries its own accent—acute or circumflex as appropriate by normal accent rules.

Note: Suppose a sentence contains several enclitics in a row. Each has its accent on the previous word, thus: ποταμός τίς ἐστί σοι.

The accent for σοι is added to the last syllable of ἐστι.

The accent for ἐστι is added to τις.

τις is covered by leaving the accent on ποταμός acute.

5. The present indicative and infinitive of εἰμί, 'be'

The verb εἰμί, 'be' is an *athematic* verb in Greek (Ch. 23.1); it does not have the thematic vowel. It is also irregular, as this verb is in many languages.

Most forms of the present indicative of εἰμί are enclitic; only the 2nd singular has its own accent. By convention, acute accents are shown on the ultima of the enclitic forms; the accent would only be used if the previous word had a Position 2-acute accent.

INDICATIVE		
Sing.	1st	εἰμί
	2nd	εἶ
	3rd	ἐστί(ν)
Plur.	1st	ἐσμέν
	2nd	ἐστέ
	3rd	εἰσί(ν)
INFINITIVE		
		εἶναι

ἐστί and εἰσί often mean 'there is / there exists' and 'there are / there exist'. If the sense is not emphatic, these forms may be omitted altogether; when they appear, they are enclitic. If the sense is emphatic, these forms appear with an accent on the penult. Since the emphatic forms have their own accents, they can stand first in a clause or sentence—as is appropriate for emphatic words.

βάρβαρός ἐστιν ἐν τῇ οἰκίᾳ.
There is a foreigner in the house.
A foreigner is in the house. (not emphatic)

ἔστι δικαιοσύνη.
There *is* justice.
Justice *does* exist. (emphatic)

6. The dative of possession

The verb εἰμί, 'be' can be used with a dative of the possessor, in simple sentences of the following type, literally 'Y is to / for X'. Translate into good English: 'X has Y'.

ὅπλα ἐστὶ τοῖς στρατιώταις.
The soldiers have weapons.

τῷ νεανίᾳ ὁ ἵππος ἐστίν.
The young man has the horse.

EXERCISE 31.

1. ὁ σοφὸς κριτὴς πείθει τὸν νεανίαν μὴ κόπτειν τὸ δένδρον.
2. καλοί εἰσιν οἱ τοῦ ποιητοῦ λόγοι.
3. τῷ ποιητῇ καλοὶ λόγοι εἰσίν.
4. οὐκ ἐπιστεύομεν τοῖς τῶν κακῶν λόγοις.
5. δεινὰ ὅπλα ἐστὶ τοῖς Πέρσαις.
6. ὁ τοῦ δένδρου καρπὸς ἀγαθὸς τοῖς ἀνθρώποις.
7. ὁ δεσπότης καλὰ ἀγγέλλει τοῖς τῆς οἰκίας δούλοις.
8. τοῖς πολίταις πόλεμος χαλεπὸς καὶ μακρός ἐστιν.
9. οἱ βάρβαροι ἐκέλευσαν τοὺς στρατιώτας βλάπτειν τὸ στρατόπεδον.
10. οὐκ ἐθέλομεν δεινοὶ εἶναι, ὦ Ἀθηναῖοι.

EXERCISE 32.

1. The hostile foreigners hindered the soldiers.
2. Bad masters do not have good slaves.
3. Strong men are not always wise.
4. The goddess of the island is friendly to the Athenians.
5. You are a wise general.
6. The judge ordered the citizens to be brave.
7. The poet wishes to train the young men with his words.
8. There are beautiful trees on the island.
9. The soldiers' victories have honor among the citizens.
10. The Athenians have strong weapons.

Chapter 7 Vocabulary

Verbs:

ἀγγέλλω	announce, report	**λέγω**	say, speak, tell
εἰμί	be		

Nouns:

ἄνθρωπος, -ου, ὁ	man (human being), person	δεσπότης, -ου, ὁ	master (of a household)
βάρβαρος, -ου, ὁ	foreigner (non-Greek)	**νίκη**, -ης, ἡ	victory

Adjectives:

ἀγαθός, -ή, -όν	good	**κακός**, -ή, -όν	bad
ἀνδρεῖος, -α, -ον	brave	**καλός**, -ή, -όν	beautiful, fine
δεινός, -ή, -όν	strange, terrible, clever	μακρός, -ά, -όν	long
		σοφός, -ή, -όν	wise
ἐχθρός, -ά, -όν	hostile	φίλιος, -α, -ον	friendly
ἰσχυρός, -ά, -όν	strong	**χαλεπός**, -ή, -όν	difficult, dangerous, harsh

Adverb:

ἤδη	already

CHAPTER 8

Μῆνιν ἄειδε, θεά, Πηληϊάδεω Ἀχιλῆος...

— Homer, *Iliad* 1.1

Ἄνδρα μοι ἔννεπε, Μοῦσα, πολύτροπον...

— Homer, *Odyssey* 1.1

1. 3rd declension nouns

The 3rd declension is also called the *consonant declension*, because the stem of most nouns (and adjectives) belonging to it ends in a consonant. There is just one set of endings for masculine and feminine nouns of the 3rd declension, and one set for neuter nouns; genitive and dative are the same in both sets. The endings all have short vowels except the gen. pl.

		M/F	N
Sing.	Nom.	-ς or none	—
	Gen.	-ος	-ος
	Dat.	-ῐ	-ῐ
	Acc.	-ᾰ	as nom.
	Voc.	-ς or none	as nom.
Plur.	Nom.	-ες	-ᾰ
	Gen.	-ων	-ων
	Dat.	-σῐ(ν)	-σῐ(ν)
	Acc.	-ᾰς	as nom.
	Voc.	as nom.	as nom.

The 3rd declension endings are attached to several stem types, to be learned over the next several chapters. It is not clear from the nominative what the stem of a 3rd declension noun is; remove the ending from the gen. sing., and what remains is the stem. The following chart shows what happens when the consonant of the stem is followed by **σ**, as in the dat. pl. and sometimes the nom. sing. (Ch. 1.2).

labials:	π, β, φ	+ σ = ψ	palatals:	κ, γ, χ	+ σ = ξ
dentals:	τ, δ, θ	+ σ = σ	nasals:	μ, ν	+ σ = σ
				γγ, γκ, γχ	+ σ = γξ

2. 3rd declension nouns: stems in -κ, -τ

The following types are typical of 3rd declension nouns. κῆρυξ is masculine; σῶμα is neuter.

			herald		body
Sing.	Nom.	ὁ	κῆρυξ	τὸ	σῶμα
	Gen.		κήρυκος		σώματος
	Dat.		κήρυκι		σώματι
	Acc.		κήρυκα		σῶμα
	Voc.		κῆρυξ		σῶμα
Plur.	Nom.		κήρυκες		σώματα
	Gen.		κηρύκων		σωμάτων
	Dat.		κήρυξι(ν)		σώμασι(ν)
	Acc.		κήρυκας		σώματα
	Voc.		κήρυκες		σώματα

3. The present active imperative, 2nd person, of thematic verbs and εἰμί

Greek has four finite *moods*: indicative, imperative, subjunctive and optative. The *indicative* verb forms you have learned so far make a statement, or ask a simple question.

Imperative verbs express a direct command, in Greek as in English: 'Sit!', 'Stay!'. For thematic verbs, the 2nd person of the present imperative is formed by adding **-ε** (singular) or **-ετε** (plural) to the present stem: λῦε, 'loose!'; γράφετε, 'write!'.

The present imperative of εἰμί, 'be' is irregular in the singular: ἴσθι. The plural is regular: ἔστε. These forms are not enclitic.

> **Note:** The 2nd plural imperative and the 2nd plural indicative are identical in form. The context will make it clear which mood is intended.

The present imperative expresses a command when the action is ongoing or repeated. (Negative commands [prohibitions] referring to a specific occasion are expressed by the aorist subjunctive, Ch. 25.5.)

Singular	**Plural**	
μέν-ε	μέν-ε-τε	stay!
δίωκ-ε	διώκ-ε-τε	keep pursuing!
ἴσθι	ἔστε	be!

The person addressed is in the vocative case, usually preceded by ὦ (Ch. 3.3). The negative is μή (Ch. 6.6).

μένε ἐν τῇ κώμῃ, ὦ νεανία.
Stay in the village, young man.

μὴ πιστεύετε τοῖς κακοῖς ἀνθρώποις.
Do not trust bad people.

ἀεὶ ἀνδρεῖοι ἔστε, ὦ στρατιῶται.
Always be brave, soldiers.

EXERCISE 33. Fill in the blanks and add accents:

1. ὦ κηρυκ____, ἀγγελλ____ τὴν καλ____ νικ____.
2. μὴ πιστευ____ τ____ κακ____ ἀνθρωπ____, ὦ πολῖται.
3. ἴσθι χαλεπ____ τοῖς πολεμι____, ὦ φύλαξ.
4. διωκ____ τὴν δικαιοσύνην, μὴ τ____ χρημ____.

4. Connection

In English, a conjunction ('and', 'but') can connect two nouns, two verbs, and so on. It is also used to connect two main clauses within a sentence. In Greek, sentences too are usually linked by a conjunction, to show how the new matter is related to what went before. Conjunctions always connect two items of the same kind (nouns with nouns, clauses with clauses, etc.).

The commonest conjunctions are:

- coming first in its phrase, clause or sentence (Ch. 2.5):

  καί, 'and', 'also'
  ἀλλά, 'but'

- coming second in its phrase, clause or sentence (*postpositive*):

  δέ, 'and', 'but'
  γάρ, 'for', 'because'
  οὖν, 'therefore'
  τε, 'and' (enclitic)

Some conjunctions can be repeated or used in combination.

- καί and τε can be repeated, or used in combination, to mean 'both...and'. Because τε is enclitic it cannot stand first in its phrase. It may come second, or at the end of a phrase, right before καί.

καὶ οἱ στρατιῶται καὶ οἱ ναῦται
οἵ τε στρατιῶται οἵ τε ναῦται
οἵ τε στρατιῶται καὶ οἱ ναῦται
οἱ στρατιῶταί τε καὶ οἱ ναῦται
both the soldiers *and* the sailors

- ἤ, 'or' can likewise be repeated to mean 'either...or'.

  ἢ μένομεν ἢ διώκομεν τοὺς ἵππους.
  Either we stay *or* we pursue the horses.

  ἐθέλω εὑρίσκειν ἢ φίλον ἢ σύμμαχον.
  I want to find *either* a friend *or* an ally.

- the compound negative οὔτε...οὔτε (οὐ + τε) can be repeated to mean 'neither...nor'. If the proper negative is μή instead of οὐ, the compound is μήτε instead of οὔτε. This pattern holds for all compounds involving οὐ (Ch. 33.4).

  οὔτε οἱ Πέρσαι οὔτε οἱ Ἀθηναῖοι εἰρήνην ἔχουσιν.
  Neither the Persians *nor* the Athenians have peace.

  ἐθέλω μήτε διώκειν μήτε φεύγειν.
  I want *neither* to pursue *nor* to flee.

Note: As a proclitic οὐ normally has no accent (Ch. 2.4). οὔτε is accented thus to cover the enclitic τε. οὐ also carries an accent when it appears at the end of a sentence: οὔ.

5. μέν and δέ

μέν and δέ signal words or clauses that correspond to or contrast with each other. μέν signals the first part of the contrast, δέ the second part (and any subsequent parts). These two words are both *postpositive*; each comes second in the phrase or clause that is the point of the contrast. μέν shows that a correspondence or contrast is being set up; there is no need to translate it. As usual, δέ can mean 'and' or 'but'.

Like other connectors (e.g. καί, ἀλλά), μέν and δέ connect items *of the same type*: nouns with nouns, adjectives with adjectives, verbs with verbs, clauses with clauses.

ῥᾴδιον μέν ἐστι λέγειν, χαλεπὸν δὲ πείθειν.
It is *easy* to speak, but *difficult* to persuade. (adjectives)

ὁ μὲν ποιητὴς γράφει, ὁ δὲ κριτὴς παιδεύει.
The *poet* writes, and the *judge* teaches. (nouns)

ὁ ποιητὴς γράφει μέν, παιδεύει δὲ οὔ.
The poet *writes*, but he does not *teach*. (verbs)

ὁ ποιητὴς γράφει καλὰ μέν, μακρὰ δέ.
The poet writes *beautiful* things, but *long* ones. (adjectives)

Sometimes, rather than connecting two different nouns, μέν and δέ connect two sets of the same noun. In this case the noun is expressed in the μέν clause, but is not repeated in the δέ clause. In fact, any term that remains the same in both clauses is not repeated.

οἱ μὲν στρατιῶται ἐδίωκον, οἱ δὲ ἔφευγον.
Some soldiers were pursuing, and others were fleeing.

οἱ μὲν τῶν ποιητῶν πείθουσιν, οἱ δὲ οὔ.
Some of the poets persuade, but others do not.

When the contrast is between 'some (men)' and 'others', etc., no noun is necessary at all. The article gives the gender, and thus suggests the right pronoun (cf. Ch. 7.2).

οἱ μὲν τοῖς λόγοις πιστεύουσιν, οἱ δὲ τοῖς ὅπλοις.
Some (men / people) trust in words, others in weapons.

αἱ μὲν ἀνδρεῖαι, αἱ δὲ οὔ.
Some (women) are brave, but others are not.

ὁ, ἡ, τὸ δέ and οἱ, αἱ, τὰ δέ may start a sentence 'and he / they / etc.', but only when they refer to a preceding noun or pronoun in an *oblique* case (gen., dat., acc.). μέν does not serve as a link with what has gone before.

EXERCISE 34.

1. οἱ πολέμιοι ἐλάμβανον τούς τε φύλακας καὶ τοὺς κήρυκας.
2. οἱ στρατιῶται τὰ σώματα θώραξιν ὁπλίζουσιν.
3. σοφὸς ἴσθι, ὦ νεανία, καὶ πίστευε τοῖς τοῦ φύλακος λόγοις.
4. ῥᾴδιόν ἐστι διώκειν τοὺς βαρβάρους, ὦ στρατιῶται· οὐ γὰρ ἰσχυροί εἰσιν.
5. οἱ μὲν Ἀθηναῖοι ἐστράτευον, οἱ δὲ Λακεδαιμόνιοι ἔθυον.
6. καὶ οἱ Λακεδαιμόνιοι καὶ οἱ Ἀθηναῖοι ἐπὶ τοὺς Πέρσας ἐστράτευον.
7. ὁ κῆρυξ ἀγγέλλει τὴν νίκην ἐν τῇ κώμῃ.
8. οἱ μὲν συμμάχους ἀνδρείους εὑρίσκουσιν, οἱ δὲ οὔ.
9. ὁ δεσπότης οὐ πιστεύει τοῖς δούλοις· τῷ οὖν ταμίᾳ ἐστὶ τὰ χρήματα.
10. ἀγαθοί ἐστε, ὦ πολῖται, ἢ κακοί;

EXERCISE 35.

1. Neither the Persians nor their allies were fleeing.
2. The island has a beautiful name.
3. The herald is announcing a victory to the Athenians.
4. The general is leading his army to the sea.
5. The soldier finds both weapons and money in the army camp.
6. Flee from the village, citizens, for the enemy are pursuing.
7. Some of the trees are beautiful, others are not.
8. Be good, young men.
9. The sailor wants to be either brave or wise.
10. The horse is easy to catch, but difficult to train.

READING.

Note: The vocabulary for reading exercises is not given in the chapter vocabulary list, and it is not part of the material to be learned for tests. It will be found in the Greek-English vocabulary at the end of the book.

UNDERGROUND DWELLINGS

The Armenia referred to here lay to the southeast of the Black Sea.

οἱ δὲ Ἀρμένιοι τὰς οἰκίας ἔχουσι κατὰ τῆς γῆς· ταῖς δὲ οἰκίαις τὸ μὲν στόμα μικρόν, κάτω δὲ μεγάλαι. αἱ δὲ εἴσοδοι τοῖς μὲν ὑποζυγίοις ὀρυκταί εἰσιν, οἱ δὲ ἄνθρωποι καταβαίνουσιν ἐπὶ κλίμακος. ἐν δὲ ταῖς οἰκίαις εἰσὶν αἶγές τε καὶ ἄλλα ζῷα· οἱ δὲ Ἀρμένιοι τὰ ζῷα ἔνδον θεραπεύουσιν. ἐν δὲ ἀγγείοις ἐστὶν οἶνος· καὶ τὸν οἶνον εἰς τὸ στόμα μύζουσι καλάμοις.

Adapted from Xenophon, *Anabasis* IV.v.25-27

Chapter 8 Vocabulary

Verbs:

εὑρίσκω	find, find out	ὁπλίζω	arm
λαμβάνω	take, capture, catch		

Nouns:

θώραξ, -ακος, ὁ	breastplate	**σύμμαχος**, -ου, ὁ	ally
κῆρυξ, -υκος, ὁ	herald	**σῶμα**, -ατος, τό	body
Λακεδαιμόνιος, -ου, ὁ	a Spartan	**φύλαξ**, -ακος, ὁ	guard
ὄνομα, -ατος, τό	name	**χρῆμα**, -ατος, τό	thing; *in plur.*, money

Adjectives:

μικρός, -ά, -όν	small	**ῥᾴδιος**, -α, -ον	easy

Preposition:

ἐπί (+ *acc.*)	against, onto

Conjunctions:

γάρ	for, because (*postpos.*)	**μήτε...μήτε**	neither...nor
		οἱ μὲν...οἱ δέ	some...others
δέ	and, but (*postpos.*)	**οὖν**	therefore (*postpos.*)
ἤ	or		
ἤ...ἤ	either...or	**οὔτε...οὔτε**	neither...nor
καί...καί	both...and	**τε**	and (*postpos.*)
μέν	(*sets up contrast with δέ; postpos.*)	**τε...καί**	both...and
		τε... τε	both...and

CHAPTER 9

δὶς ἐς τὸν αὐτὸν ποταμὸν οὐκ ἂν ἐμβαίης.

— Heraclitus (Plato, *Cratylus* 402a)

1. 3rd declension nouns: stems in -τ, -δ, -θ

These nouns are generally formed the same way as those in Ch. 8.2. When the stem is followed by **σ**, the dental disappears (Ch. 8.1). Nouns with nominatives in **-ις** or **-υς**, unless accented on the last syllable, usually form the acc. sing. by dropping the dental and adding **-ν**. (However, in Homer, Herodotus and Attic poetry the acc. sing. of these nouns has the normal ending in **-α**.)

Most one-syllable nominatives like ὁ/ἡ παῖς, παιδός accent their gen. and dat. sing. and pl. on the last syllable. παῖς itself actually violates this rule in the gen. pl.: παίδων.

			torch		grace		child
Sing.	Nom.	ἡ	λαμπάς	ἡ	χάρις	ὁ/ἡ	παῖς
	Gen.		λαμπάδος		χάριτος		παιδός
	Dat.		λαμπάδι		χάριτι		παιδί
	Acc.		λαμπάδα		χάριν		παῖδα
	Voc.		λαμπάς		χάρι		παῖ
Plur.	Nom.		λαμπάδες		χάριτες		παῖδες
	Gen.		λαμπάδων		χαρίτων		παίδων
	Dat.		λαμπάσι(ν)		χάρισι(ν)		παισί(ν)
	Acc.		λαμπάδας		χάριτας		παῖδας
	Voc.		λαμπάδες		χάριτες		παῖδες

EXERCISE 36. Give the following forms:

1. Gen. sing. and dat. pl.: the long island, the worthy child
2. Acc. sing. and gen. pl.: the brave guard, the good hope
3. Nom. sing. and acc. pl.: the wise herald, the hostile exile
4. Dat. sing. and nom. pl.: the small shield, the strong body

2. αὐτός, intensive use

The pronoun αὐτός, -ή, -ό is declined like a regular 1st and 2nd declension adjective, except that the nom. and acc. neuter sing. end in **-ο**, not **-ον** (like the definite article). There is no vocative case.

		M	F	N
Sing.	Nom.	αὐτός	αὐτή	αὐτό
	Gen.	αὐτοῦ	αὐτῆς	αὐτοῦ
	Dat.	αὐτῷ	αὐτῇ	αὐτῷ
	Acc.	αὐτόν	αὐτήν	αὐτό
Plur.	Nom.	αὐτοί	αὐταί	αὐτά
	Gen.	αὐτῶν	αὐτῶν	αὐτῶν
	Dat.	αὐτοῖς	αὐταῖς	αὐτοῖς
	Acc.	αὐτούς	αὐτάς	αὐτά

One use of this pronoun is for emphasis: 'himself / herself / itself'. αὐτός has this intensive meaning when it appears either by itself in the nominative, or in the predicate position agreeing with a noun (in all cases). The predicate may either precede or follow the noun-article phrase. In the third example, the English sentence is ambiguous as worded (does himself refer to 'He' or 'the young man'?), but in Greek the ending of αὐτός makes the meaning clear.

ὁ στρατηγὸς αὐτὸς ἄγει τοὺς στρατιώτας.
The general himself leads the soldiers.

πέμπω τὸν κήρυκα εἰς αὐτὴν τὴν κώμην.
I send the herald into the village itself.

αὐτὸς ἐδίωκε τὸν νεανίαν.
He was pursuing the young man himself.

3. αὐτός as personal pronoun

αὐτός is also the personal pronoun 'him / her / it / them'. It has this meaning only when it appears alone in the oblique cases (gen., dat., acc.). The verb ending already indicates person ('he / she / it / they') in the nominative case, so if αὐτὸς appears in the nominative it is always emphatic (above, sec. 2).

πέμπομεν αὐτὸν εἰς τὴν κώμην.
We send him into the village.

ἔγραφον ἐπιστολὴν αὐτῇ.
I was writing a letter to her.

οἱ λόγοι αὐτῆς πείθουσι τοὺς πολίτας.
Her words [The words of her] persuade the citizens.

Oblique forms of αὐτός can refer to a noun mentioned earlier in the sentence, but not to the subject. The pronoun will have the same gender as the noun it refers to, but the case may be different. In the first example below, αὐτήν is feminine to agree with ἐπιστολήν, 'letter'. In the second example, 'her' is feminine to agree with 'goddess', but it is in the dative case after πιστεύσομεν.

γράφω ἐπιστολὴν καὶ πέμπω αὐτήν.
    I write a letter and send it.

θεραπεύσομεν τὴν θεὰν καὶ πιστεύσομεν αὐτῇ.
    We shall honor the goddess and trust her.

Note: The possessive genitive forms of this pronoun are always in predicate position; they are not sandwiched between article and noun like possessive adjectives.

4. αὐτός, attributive use

The other use of αὐτός is as an adjective, in the attributive position, meaning 'the same'.

αἱ αὐταὶ θεαί
    the same goddesses

τὸ αὐτό
    the same (thing)

Note: The difference in word order between the attributive and intensive uses of αὐτός is the same as in English.

ὁ αὐτὸς κριτής
    the same judge (attributive)

ὁ κριτὴς αὐτός
    the judge himself (predicate)

EXERCISE 37. Translate the underlined material:

1. The same heralds are coming.
2. I sent a horse to the general himself.
3. I ordered him to find the river.
4. I admire their weapons.
5. You will lead the same allies to the village.
6. The children themselves trained the horses.

5. Elision

Short vowels at the end of a word may be *elided* or cut off when the next word begins with a vowel. An apostrophe marks the deletion. The elision may have an effect on accent or spelling, as follows.

- When conjunctions and two-syllable prepositions (except περί) with an accent on the ultima (Position 1) are elided, their accent is lost with the elision.

  ἀπὸ αὐτοῦ → ἀπ' αὐτοῦ

  ἡ δὲ οἰκία → ἡ δ' οἰκία

  ἀλλὰ ὁ παῖς → ἀλλ' ὁ παῖς

- When other words with an accent on the ultima (Position 1) are elided, the accent moves back to Position 2.

  κακὰ ἔργα → κάκ' ἔργα

- When the syllable preceding a two-syllable enclitic is elided, the enclitic keeps its accent on the ultima (Position 1).

  κακά ἐστιν → κάκ' ἐστίν

- When the following vowel has a rough breathing, an unvoiced consonant (π, τ) will shift to its aspirated form (φ, θ).

  ἀπὸ ὧν → ἀπ' ὧν → ἀφ' ὧν

  τά τε ὅπλα → τά τ' ὅπλα → τά θ' ὅπλα

EXERCISE 38.

1. οὐ ῥᾴδιόν ἐστιν ἢ εὑρίσκειν τὴν ὄρνιν ἢ λαμβάνειν αὐτήν.
2. ὁ στρατηγὸς αὐτὸς ἀγγέλλει τὴν νίκην ἐν τῇ ἀγορᾷ.
3. ἐδιώκομεν αὐτὸν ἀπὸ τῆς χώρας.
4. οἱ μὲν τῶν στρατιωτῶν ἐφύλαττον τὴν κώμην, οἱ δ' ἔφευγον ἀπ' αὐτῆς.
5. οὐ θαυμάζομεν οὔτε τοὺς Ἀθηναίους οὔτε τοὺς Πέρσας.
6. τοῖς στρατιώταις εἰσὶ κόρυθές τε καὶ ἀσπίδες.
7. χάριν ἔχομεν τοῖς συμμάχοις αὐτοῖς.
8. κελεύσομεν τὰ τέκνα μὴ φεύγειν ἐκ τῆς κώμης αὐτῆς.
9. ἀνδρεῖοι ἔστε, ὦ στρατιῶται, καὶ ἄξιοι τῆς τιμῆς.
10. ἡ μὲν εἰρήνη καλή, ὁ δὲ πόλεμος κακός.

EXERCISE 39.

1. Some Persians are brave, but others flee from Greece.
2. The same boys find torches in the market-place.
3. The general ordered the soldiers to bring the exiles into the house.
4. The herald is announcing the victory to the Athenians themselves.

5. We want to pursue the enemy and capture them.
6. Both the exiles and the foreigners were staying in the same village.
7. Some admire money, others wisdom.
8. The goddess herself ordered the army to honor them.
9. Either the girls or the young men will sacrifice to the goddess.
10. The soldiers trust neither shields nor helmets.

6. οἷός τέ εἰμι

In the following reading passage from Herodotus you will see an idiomatic way to say 'I can / am able'. It has three components:

οἷος , οἵα, οἷον	adjective, fully declinable; literally 'of such a kind'.
τε	enclitic conjunction, meaning 'and'; not translated here. Before a vowel, usually elided to τ' (θ' before rough breathing).
εἰμί	enclitic verb 'be', fully conjugated.

Thus to say 'we are able', οἷοι must be plural, and ἐσμεν must be 1st plural present. Some more examples show how the accent is handled when the enclitic τε is elided.

οἷοί τ' εἰσί	they are able
οἵα τ' ἐστί	she is able
οἷός τ' εἶ	you (*sing.*) are able

READING.

CYRUS IS HELPED BY CAMELS

Croesus, king of Lydia (in Asia Minor, modern Turkey), after conquering most of the Greek cities east of the Aegean, invaded Persia in 546 B.C. in an attempt to crush the power of Cyrus the Great, king of the Medes and Persians.

ὁ δὲ Κροῖσος, ὅτε ἐβασίλευε τῶν Λυδῶν, ἐστράτευσεν ἐπὶ τοὺς Πέρσας. τὸ γὰρ μαντεῖον ἔπειθεν αὐτόν, ὡς ἐνόμιζε, καταλύειν τὴν τῶν Περσῶν ἀρχήν. πρῶτον μὲν οὖν ποταμὸν (τὸ ὄνομά ἐστιν Ἅλυς) διαβαίνει καὶ φθείρει τὴν χώραν, ἔπειτα δὲ τάττει τὴν στρατιὰν εἰς μάχην. *(This battle was indecisive.)* μετὰ δὲ τὴν μάχην, ὁ Κροῖσος φεύγει εἰς τὰς Σάρδις·[1] ἐθέλει γὰρ κήρυκας πέμπειν πρὸς τοὺς συμμάχους. (*Before the allies can arrive, Cyrus appears before Sardis with a large army.)* ἀνάγκη δ' οὖν τῷ Κροίσῳ ἐστὶν ἐξάγειν τὴν στρατιὰν εἰς μάχην. καὶ ὁ Κῦρος αὐτὸς ἀθροίζει τὰς καμήλους καὶ κελεύει στρατιώτας ἀναβαίνειν καὶ ἄγειν αὐτὰς πρὸς <u>τὴν τοῦ Κροίσου ἵππον</u> [*Croesus's cavalry*], τοὺς δὲ πεζοὺς τάττει ὄπισθε τῶν καμήλων, τὴν δ' ἵππον ὄπισθε τῶν πεζῶν· οἱ γὰρ ἵπποι οὐχ οἷοί τ' εἰσὶ φέρειν οὔτε τὴν ἰδέαν οὔτε τὴν ὀδμὴν τῶν καμήλων. ἐν δὲ τῇ μάχῃ αἱ κάμηλοι δεινὸν φόβον παρέχουσι τοῖς ἵπποις. οὕτω δὲ ὁ Κῦρος ἀναγκάζει τοὺς τοῦ Κροίσου στρατιώτας φεύγειν.

Adapted from Herodotus I.76-80

1 Sardis was the capital city of Lydia.

Chapter 9 Vocabulary

Verbs:

θαυμάζω	wonder at, admire	χάριν ἔχω	be grateful
οἷός τέ εἰμι	be able, can		

Nouns:

ἀσπίς, -ίδος, ἡ	shield	**παῖς**, -δός, ὁ/ἡ	child, boy, girl
Ἑλλάς, -άδος, ἡ	Greece	**πατρίς**, -ίδος, ἡ	fatherland, own country
ἐλπίς, -ίδος, ἡ	hope, expectation		
κόρυς, -υθος, ἡ	helmet	**φυγάς**, -άδος, ὁ/ἡ	exile (a person)
λαμπάς, -άδος, ἡ	torch	χάρις, -ιτος, ἡ	grace, thanks
ὄρνις, -ιθος, ὁ/ἡ	bird		

Pronoun:

αὐτός, -ή, -ό	self; him, her, it (in oblique cases)

Adjectives:

ἄξιος, -α, -ον	worthy (+ *gen.*)	**αὐτός**, -ή, -ό	same (*attributive*)

Preposition:

μετά (+ *acc.*)	after

CHAPTER 10

ὦ ξεῖν', ἀγγέλλειν Λακεδαιμονίοις ὅτι τῇδε
κείμεθα τοῖς κείνων ῥήμασι πειθόμενοι.

— Epitaph of the Spartans at Thermopylae
(Herodotus, *Histories* VII.228.2)

1. 3rd declension nouns: stems in -ντ, -κτ

The only form of these nouns that needs explanation is the dative plural of nouns in **-ντ**. The dental drops out before **σ**, and then so does the **ν**; because the series of consonants made for a long syllable, the vowel is lengthened to preserve the length of the syllable, and compensate for losing two consonants. This change is called *compensatory lengthening*. One-syllable nouns have gen. and dat. accents on the last syllable (Ch. 9.1). The proper name Xenophon has a contracted syllable (Ch. 19.6), so its accent pattern is different; there is no plural.

		giant	night	lion	Xenophon
Sing.	Nom.	ὁ γίγᾱς	ἡ νύξ	ὁ λέων	ὁ Ξενοφῶν
	Gen.	γίγᾰντος	νυκτός	λέοντος	Ξενοφῶντος
	Dat.	γίγαντι	νυκτί	λέοντι	Ξενοφῶντι
	Acc.	γίγαντα	νύκτα	λέοντα	Ξενοφῶντα
	Voc.	γίγᾰν	νύξ	λέον	Ξενοφῶν
Plur.	Nom.	γίγαντες	νύκτες	λέοντες	
	Gen.	γιγάντων	νυκτῶν	λεόντων	
	Dat.	γίγᾱσι(ν)	νυξί(ν)	λέουσι(ν)	
	Acc.	γίγαντας	νύκτας	λέοντας	
	Voc.	γίγαντες	νύκτες	λέοντες	

2. The future and imperfect indicative of εἰμί, 'be'

The future ('I shall be', 'you will be', etc.) and the imperfect ('I was', 'you were', etc.) tenses of εἰμί, 'be' are not enclitic. The future endings are those of the *middle* voice (Ch. 17), with an irregular 3rd sing. The imperfect is the only past tense of this verb.

		Future	Imperfect
Sing.	1st	ἔσομαι	ἦ / ἦν
	2nd	ἔσῃ / ἔσει	ἦσθα
	3rd	ἔσται	ἦν
Plur.	1st	ἐσόμεθα	ἦμεν
	2nd	ἔσεσθε	ἦτε
	3rd	ἔσονται	ἦσαν

3. The relative pronoun

The relative pronoun introduces a *relative clause*, a subordinate clause that refers to a noun (or pronoun) in the main clause. All forms except the nom. sing. masculine look like the definite article, with a rough breathing instead of the initial **τ-**.

		M	F	N
Sing.	Nom.	ὅς	ἥ	ὅ
	Gen.	οὗ	ἧς	οὗ
	Dat.	ᾧ	ᾗ	ᾧ
	Acc.	ὅν	ἥν	ὅ
Plur.	Nom.	οἵ	αἵ	ἅ
	Gen.	ὧν	ὧν	ὧν
	Dat.	οἷς	αἷς	οἷς
	Acc.	οὕς	ἅς	ἅ

A relative pronoun *agrees with* its antecedent: it has the same *gender* and *number* as the noun to which it refers. However, its *case* depends on its function in the relative clause. The relative clause is underlined in the following examples. Where does the relative pronoun come in the clause?

ὁ παῖς ὃν παιδεύω ἔχει ἵππον.

The child (whom) I teach has a horse.

(rel. pronoun is masc. sing., agreeing with 'child'; it is accusative as direct object)

ὁ παῖς ὃς πέμπει δῶρον ἀγαθός ἐστιν.

The child who sends a gift is good.

(rel. pronoun is masc. sing., agreeing with 'child'; it is nominative as subject) πιστεύσομεν τῷ παιδὶ ὃς ἀγαθὰ λέγει.

We will trust the child who says good things.

(rel. pronoun is masc. sing., agreeing with 'child'; it is nominative as subject)

ὁ παῖς ᾧ λέγω ἀγαθός ἐστιν.

The child to whom I speak is good.

(rel. pronoun is masc. sing., agreeing with 'child'; it is dative as indirect object)

ἡ κώμη ἐν ᾗ μένομεν μικρά ἐστιν.

The village in which we are staying is small.

(rel. pronoun is fem. sing., agreeing with 'village'; it is dative as object of preposition)

ὁ παῖς οὗ ὁ δοῦλος λέγει ἀγαθός ἐστιν.

The child whose slave is speaking is good.

(rel. pronoun is masc. sing., agreeing with 'child'; it is genitive as possessive)

Note: You may observe two things in the examples above:

- the relative pronoun is always the first word in the relative clause, unless it is the object of a preposition; then the preposition comes first, followed immediately by the relative pronoun.
- the relative clause is not split up; once it starts, it finishes before you get back to the main clause.

The relative pronoun is a key word that raises expectations about what will follow in the sentence (Ch. 6.5). When you see one, you can predict that a relative clause will come next.

EXERCISE 40. Underline all relative clauses, and translate:

1. οἱ φυγάδες οἳ μένουσιν ἐν τῷ στρατοπέδῳ οὐκ ἔχουσιν. ἐλπίδας μετὰ τὴν μάχην.
2. ἡ νῆσος ἐν ᾗ ἦν καλὰ δένδρα οὐ μικρὰ ἦν.
3. οὐ ῥᾴδιόν ἐστιν ἢ εὑρίσκειν τοὺς λέοντας ἢ λαμβάνειν αὐτούς.
4. ἡ κώμη ἐχθρὰ ἦν τοῖς βαρβάροις ὧν ἡ στρατιὰ ἐστράτευεν.
5. ὁ Ξενοφῶν αὐτὸς ἔπαυσε τὴν μάχην διὰ τὴν νύκτα.
6. αἱ Ἀθῆναι ἐλεύθεραι ἔσονται· οἱ γὰρ πολῖται ἐθέλουσιν ἀποθνῄσκειν ὑπὲρ τῆς πατρίδος.
7. οὐχ οἷοί τ᾽ ἦτε ἀποκτείνειν τὸν γίγαντα ὃς ἔβλαπτε τὰς οἰκίας;
8. οἱ μὲν νεανίαι ἰσχυροί εἰσιν, οἱ δὲ γέροντες σοφοί.
9. οἱ Ἀθηναῖοι ἐθέλουσι σῴζειν τούς τε γέροντας καὶ τοὺς παῖδας.
10. θαυμάζομεν τοὺς στρατηγοὺς οἷς πιστεύομεν· ἀνδρεῖοι γάρ εἰσιν.

EXERCISE 41. Underline all relative clauses, and translate:

1. Always honor old men, children.
2. Greece, which is their fatherland, will be both strong and free.
3. It will not be easy to teach the boys who are not willing to stay.
4. We were slaves, Athenians, but now we will be free, for we have worthy allies.
5. There were small trees on the island.
6. It will be good to have shields that are strong.
7. We will loose the same animals that we capture in battle.
8. Night stopped the battle that was keeping the Persians away.
9. The young men were pursuing the enemy, but the old men were fleeing.
10. The poet who honors peace does not wish to die in a war.

READING.

Note: Greek does not have quotation marks. The first word of a quotation is capitalized; context and common sense will indicate where the quotation ends.

THE BATTLE OF THERMOPYLAE

In 480 B.C. three hundred Spartans with their king, Leonidas, heroically tried to defend Greece against the invading army of Xerxes, king of Persia. The battle took place at Thermopylae, a narrow pass in the south of Thessaly.

ὅτε δὲ ὁ Ξέρξης ἐστράτευεν ἐπὶ τὴν Ἑλλάδα, οἱ Λακεδαιμόνιοι ἐφύλαττον τὴν ἐν ταῖς Θερμοπύλαις εἰσβολήν· καὶ πρὸ τῆς μάχης λέγει τις τῶν συμμάχων, Τοσοῦτός ἐστιν ὁ ἀριθμὸς τῶν βαρβάρων, ὥστε ἀποκρύπτουσι τὸν ἥλιον τοῖς τοξεύμασιν. Ἀγαθὰ ἀγγέλλεις, λέγει Λακεδαιμόνιος στρατιώτης, ὀνόματι Διηνέκης· ὑπὸ οὖν σκιᾷ ἔσται πρὸς αὐτοὺς ἡ μάχη, καὶ οὐκ ἐν ἡλίῳ. ὁ δὲ Λεωνίδας, ὅς ἦν ὁ τῶν Λακεδαιμονίων στρατηγός, ἐκέλευσε τοὺς στρατιώτας μένειν καὶ ἀνδρείους εἶναι.

ἐν δὲ τῇ μάχῃ αὐτῇ οἱ λοχαγοὶ τοὺς Πέρσας μάστιξιν ἐποτρύνουσιν· οἱ γὰρ βάρβαροι οὐκ ἀνδρεῖοί εἰσιν. οἱ δὲ Λακεδαιμόνιοι ἀνδρείως μὲν φυλάττουσι τὴν εἰσβολὴν ὑπὲρ τῆς πατρίδος, μάτην δέ· μόνον γὰρ τριακόσιοί εἰσιν. ὁ δὲ Λεωνίδας αὐτὸς ἐν τῇ μάχῃ πίπτει· καὶ νῦν ἐστιν ἐπὶ τῷ τάφῳ αὐτοῦ λίθινος λέων.

Adapted from Herodotus VII.223-226

Chapter 10 Vocabulary

Verbs:

ἀποθνῄσκω	die	**σῴζω**	save, protect
ἀποκτείνω	kill		

Nouns:

γέρων, -οντος, ὁ	old man	Ξενοφῶν, -ῶντος, ὁ	Xenophon
γίγας, -αντος, ὁ	giant	**ὁπλίτης**, -ου, ὁ	hoplite (heavy-armed soldier)
θεός, -οῦ, ὁ	god		
λέων, -οντος, ὁ	lion	**ὕλη**, -ης, ἡ	forest
νύξ, -κτός, ἡ	night		

Adjective:

ἐλεύθερος, -α, -ον	free

Pronoun:

ὅς, ἥ, ὅ	who, which, that

Adverb:

νῦν	now

Preposition:

διά (+ *acc.*)	on account of	**ὑπέρ** (+ *gen.*)	on behalf of, for

Conjunction:

ὅτι	because

CHAPTER 11

τοὐντεῦθεν ἤδη τοῦ ξένου (τὸ) θαῦμ' ὁρῶ·
λαβὼν γὰρ ἐλάτης οὐράνιον ἄκρον κλάδον
κατῆγεν, ἦγεν, ἦγεν ἐς μέλαν πέδον·
— Euripides, *Bacchae* 1063-1065

1. 3rd declension nouns: stems in -ρ

ῥήτωρ, 'orator' is an example of a regular 3rd declension noun whose stem ends in **-ρ**. The noun θήρ, 'wild beast' is declined like it, but follows the accent rule for one-syllable nouns (Ch. 9.1).

μήτηρ, 'mother' and πατήρ, 'father' have an **ε** vowel (long in the nominative and short elsewhere) in most cases; it is lacking in the gen. and dat. sing. and the dat. pl. The -**ρα**- in the dat. pl. represents an original *syllabic* **r**, which made for a whole syllable; this Indo-European consonant appears in Attic Greek as **ρα** or **αρ**.

The declension of ἀνήρ, 'man', 'husband' is similar, but the **ε** vowel is lacking except in the nom. sing. The **δ** appears simply because the combination **νρ** was hard to pronounce without it.

		orator	wild beast	mother	father	man
Sing.	Nom.	ὁ ῥήτωρ	ὁ θήρ	ἡ μήτηρ	ὁ πατήρ	ὁ ἀνήρ
	Gen.	ῥήτορος	θηρός	μητρός	πατρός	ἀνδρός
	Dat.	ῥήτορι	θηρί	μητρί	πατρί	ἀνδρί
	Acc.	ῥήτορα	θῆρα	μητέρα	πατέρα	ἄνδρα
	Voc.	ῥῆτορ	θήρ	μῆτερ	πάτερ	ἄνερ
Plur.	Nom.	ῥήτορες	θῆρες	μητέρες	πατέρες	ἄνδρες
	Gen.	ῥητόρων	θηρῶν	μητέρων	πατέρων	ἀνδρῶν
	Dat.	ῥήτορσι(ν)	θηρσί(ν)	μητράσι(ν)	πατράσι(ν)	ἀνδράσι(ν)
	Acc.	ῥήτορας	θῆρας	μητέρας	πατέρας	ἄνδρας
	Voc.	ῥήτορες	θῆρες	μητέρες	πατέρες	ἄνδρες

2. Syllabic and temporal augments

You have seen that when a verb stem begins with a consonant, it is augmented by adding the prefix **ε-** (Ch. 4.3, 5.2). This form is called a *syllabic augment*, because it adds a syllable to the verb. When the verb stem begins with a vowel, it is augmented by lengthening the vowel (a *temporal augment*). Sometimes the lengthening is obvious: **α → η**, **ε → η**, and **ο → ω**. Initial **ι** and **υ** also become long, but look the same. Initial **η** and **ω** are already long, and remain so.

present	imperfect
ἄγω	ἦγον
ἐθέλω	ἤθελον
ἥκω	ἧκον
ὁπλίζω	ὥπλιζον

Note: ἔχω has an unusual imperfect, εἶχον. The verb stem was originally ***σεχ-**, with a normal syllabic augment: ***ἐσεχ-**. The **σ** between vowels was weak, and eventually dropped out; the two vowels contracted: **ε** + **ε** = **ει**.

3. Augments of compound verbs

Sometimes a preposition is added to the verb stem as a prefix to form a *compound* verb: ἐκπέμπω, 'send out, εἰσάγω, 'lead into'. Prefixes were originally adverbs, not attached to the verb. The prefix therefore has no effect on the augment or accent of most verbs (enclitics are the exception; Ch. 12.3).

- The augment appears as usual right before the verb stem. The prefix stands in front of the augment.
- The accent only recedes as far as the augment. It does not normally appear on a prefix.

ἐκπέμπω	ἐξέπεμπον
εἰσάγω	εἰσῆγον

Several rules govern the combination of prefix and verb stem.

- Two-syllable prepositions ending in a vowel behave as in elision (Ch. 9.5):

most drop the final vowel	ἀπέπεμπον (ἀποπέμπω)
περί remains intact	περιέβαλλον (περιβάλλω)

- One-syllable preposition ending in a vowel:

contracts with the augment (**ο** + **ε** = **ου**)	προύπεμπον (προπέμπω)

- ἐκ-:

becomes ἐξ- as usual before a vowel	ἐξῆγον (ἐξάγω)
	ἐξέπεμπον (ἐκπέμπω)

- σύν-:

becomes **συμ**- before a labial (**π**, **β**, **φ**)	συμβουλεύω
becomes **συγ**- before a palatal (**κ**, **γ**, **χ**)	συγγιγνώσκω
becomes **συλ**- before **λ**	συλλαμβάνω
remains **συν**- before a vowel	συνεβούλευον

EXERCISE 42. From what verb does each of the following forms come?

1. ὥπλιζον
2. ἤγγελλον
3. κατέλυον
4. ἀπέθνῃσκον
5. προσέφερον
6. ἤκουον
7. ἐξέπεμπον
8. ἧκον
9. συνεβούλευον

EXERCISE 43. Give the 1st singular Greek form of the imperfect indicative active of the following verbs.

1. ἀγγέλλω
2. ἐθέλω
3. ἀναγκάζω
4. εὑρίσκω
5. ἐξάγω
6. εἰσβάλλω
7. ἀποφεύγω
8. προπέμπω
9. ἔχω

EXERCISE 44.

1. ὁ τοῦ Ξέρξου πατὴρ ἦν Δαρεῖος, ὃς εἰσέβαλλεν εἰς τὴν Ἑλλάδα.
2. οἱ παῖδες χάριν ἔχουσι τῇ μητρί, ἣ αὐτοὺς θεραπεύει.
3. ὁ πατὴρ ἔκοπτε δένδρα ὄπισθε τῆς οἰκίας;
4. οἱ Ἀθηναῖοι ἐθαύμαζον τοὺς λόγους οὓς ὁ ῥήτωρ ἔλεγεν.
5. κάμηλός ἐστιν ἐν τῇ κώμῃ πρὸς ἣν ἥκομεν.
6. ὁ στρατηγὸς τοὺς ἄνδρας ὥπλιζε θώραξί τε κόρυσί τε.
7. ὁ μῶρος ῥήτωρ οὐκ ἄξιος ἦν τῆς τῶν πολιτῶν τιμῆς.
8. ὁ γέρων αὐτὸς ἤκουε τὴν τῆς ὄρνιθος φωνήν.
9. διὰ τοὺς θῆρας χαλεπὸν ἦν τοῖς ἀνδράσι φυλάττειν τὸν ποταμόν.
10. μὴ πιστεύετε τοῖς θηρσὶ τοῖς ἐν τῇ ὕλῃ.

EXERCISE 45.

1. Evil men do not rule the Athenians.
2. The mothers were sending forth their boys to the war.
3. The men tried to escape from the wild beasts who were pursuing them.
4. The herald was advising the citizens not to remain.
5. I do not listen to the orator; for he is either bad or foolish.
6. We did not believe the words of the judge.
7. The mothers of the Spartans admire the brave.
8. It is not always easy for fathers to educate their children.
9. Will the poet himself educate the young men in wisdom?
10. We were wishing to destroy the enemy who were invading the fatherland.

4. Principal parts of palatal stem thematic verbs

The six principal parts of the Greek verb are the forms from which all the tenses can be generated (Ch. 2.1). You have learned active forms based on the first three principal parts.

- 1st: present and imperfect tenses (active, middle and passive);
- 2nd: future tense (active and middle); marker **-σ**
- 3rd: aorist tense (active and middle); weak aorist marker **-σ** with stem vowel **-α**

Up to now you have seen the future and aorist forms of regular thematic verbs whose stem ends in a vowel. In such verbs the tense markers follow the stem vowel with no problem. When the verb stem ends in a consonant, however, a consonant cluster is formed. You have already seen in 3rd declension nouns how various consonants combine with **σ** (Ch. 1.2, 8.1).

When a verb stem ends in a palatal consonant, the cluster of stem consonant + **σ** results in **ξ**.

$$\left.\begin{matrix}\kappa\\ \gamma\\ \chi\end{matrix}\right\} + \sigma = \xi$$

Here are the first three principal parts of the palatal stem verbs you have already learned, and the common irregular verb ἔχω.

1 Present	2 Future	3 Aorist (Active)
ἄγω	ἄξω	ἤγαγον[1]
ἄρχω	ἄρξω	ἦρξα
διώκω	διώξω	ἐδίωξα
ἔχω	ἕξω / σχήσω[2]	ἔσχον[1]
ἥκω	ἥξω	—
λέγω	λέξω	ἔλεξα
πράττω	πράξω	ἔπραξα
ταράττω	ταράξω	ἐτάραξα
τάττω	τάξω	ἔταξα
φεύγω	φεύξομαι[3]	ἔφυγον[1]
φυλάττω	φυλάξω	ἐφύλαξα

1 Strong aorist; below, sec. 5.

2 ἕξω means 'I will (go on) having'; σχήσω means 'I will (acquire and) have'. The difference is one of aspect (Ch. 5.3, 13.4).

3 For future conjugation see Ch. 17.2.

5. The strong aorist active indicative of thematic verbs (3rd principal part)

The aorist forms you have learned so far are all *weak* or *1st aorists*, with a stem ending in **-σ** (Ch. 5.2). Some verbs, like ἄγω, ἔχω and φεύγω above, have a *strong* or *2nd aorist* instead. This type uses the thematic vowel instead of the tense vowel **ᾰ**. It therefore has the same *endings* as the imperfect (Ch. 4.3), but the *stem* of the 3rd principal part is different from the present stem (1st principal part), which is the basis for the imperfect tense. Compare the strong aorist of ἄγω ('I led', 'you led', etc.) with the imperfect.

		Aorist Stem ἀγαγ-	**Translation**	**Imperfect Stem ἀγ-**	**Endings**
Sing.	1st	ἤγαγ-ο-ν	I led	ἦγ-ο-ν	-ο-ν
	2nd	ἤγαγ-ε-ς	you led	ἦγ-ε-ς	-ε-ς
	3rd	ἤγαγ-ε(ν)	he led	ἦγ-ε(ν)	-ε-(ν)
Plur.	1st	ἠγάγ-ο-μεν	we led	ἤγ-ο-μεν	-ο-μεν
	2nd	ἠγάγ-ε-τε	you led	ἤγ-ε-τε	-ε-τε
	3rd	ἤγαγ-ο-ν	they led	ἦγ-ο-ν	-ο-ν

Here are the first three principal parts of all the verbs learned so far that have strong aorists (compound verbs are given only when the simple verb has not yet been introduced).

1 Present	**2 Future**	**3 Aorist (Active)**
ἄγω	ἄξω	ἤγαγον
ἀποθνῄσκω	ἀποθανοῦμαι[1]	ἀπέθανον
εἰσβάλλω	εἰσβαλῶ[1]	εἰσέβαλον
εὑρίσκω	εὑρήσω	ηὗρον / εὗρον
ἔχω	ἕξω / σχήσω	ἔσχον
λαμβάνω	λήψομαι[2]	ἔλαβον
φέρω	οἴσω	ἤνεγκον
φεύγω	φεύξομαι[2]	ἔφυγον

1 For future conjugation see Ch. 20.4.

2 For future conjugation see Ch. 17.2.

EXERCISE 46. Fill in the blanks:

	Form	Person	Number	Tense	Verb
1.	διώξεις	______	______	______	______
2.	______	3rd	plural	future	φέρω
3.	ἦρξας	______	______	______	______
4.	______	1st	singular	imperfect	φυλάττω
5.	εὑρήσομεν	______	______	______	______
6.	______	2nd	plural	future	διώκω
7.	ἔσχε	______	______	______	______
8.	ἀπέθανεν	______	______	______	______
9.	______	1st	plural	aorist	φεύγω
10.	σχήσετε	______	______	______	______

EXERCISE 47.

1. ὁ πατὴρ αὐτῆς ἧκε εἰς τὴν ἀγοράν.
2. ὁ Ξέρξης οὐ σχήσει τὴν Ἑλλάδα.
3. οἱ παῖδες ἔπραξαν ἃ ἐκέλευσεν ἡ μήτηρ, ἢ οὔ;
4. ὅπλα ἠνέγκομεν πρὸς τοὺς φύλακας.
5. ὁ στρατηγὸς τοὺς συμμάχους ἔταξεν.
6. ἔλεξας ὑπὲρ τῶν φυγάδων οὓς ἐλάβομεν;
7. αἱ κάμηλοι ἐτάραξαν τοὺς ἵππους.
8. οἱ γίγαντες οἳ ἔμενον ἐν τῇ νήσῳ δεινοί τε καὶ ἰσχυροὶ ἦσαν.
9. ἠκούσαμεν τοῦ Λεωνίδου, ὃς ἦρχε τῶν Λακεδαιμονίων.
10. προυπέμψατε εἰς τὴν ὕλην τὸν θῆρα ὃν ἔλαβον;

EXERCISE 48.

1. The Persians will not throw them into confusion.
2. The old men found their camels in the market-place.
3. The same Athenians pursued the Persians into the sea.
4. Will you carry the letters to the judge?
5. Cyrus drew up his soldiers behind the camels.
6. Neither the old men nor the children wanted [*use imperfect*] to stay.
7. The exiles will be free now, because they have come [*use present*] to a fine country.
8. The good citizens always pursued justice.
9. The slave himself led the horses to the river.
10. The Spartans died, but they were protecting Greece from the enemy.

READING.

XERXES WHIPS THE SEA

The bridges referred to were built across the Hellespont between Abydos and Sestos and were nearly a mile long. This effort was in preparation for Xerxes' invasion of Greece in 480 B.C.; his father king Darius had died in 485 B.C.

μετὰ δὲ τὸν τοῦ πατρὸς θάνατον ὁ Ξέρξης ἦρχε τῶν Περσῶν. ὅτι δ' ἤθελε κολάζειν τοὺς Ἕλληνας διὰ τὰς ἀδικίας αὐτῶν,[1] ἐβούλευσε διαβαίνειν τὸν Ἑλλήσποντον καὶ στρατιὰν ἄγειν διὰ τῆς Εὐρώπης ἐπὶ τὴν Ἑλλάδα· ἐκέλευσεν οὖν Φοίνικας καὶ Αἰγυπτίους, οἳ σύμμαχοι ἦσαν τῶν Περσῶν, δύο γεφύρας κατασκευάζειν. ἐπεὶ δὲ τὸ ἔργον ἔπραξαν, χειμὼν μέγιστος κατέλυσε τὰς γεφύρας. ὁ οὖν Ξέρξης μάλιστα ἐχαλέπαινε καὶ ἐκέλευσε τοὺς ἄνδρας οὐ μόνον τόν τε Ἑλλήσποντον τριακοσίαις πληγαῖς τύπτειν καὶ δύο πέδας εἰς αὐτὸν βάλλειν, ἀλλὰ καὶ ἀποτέμνειν τὰς τῶν ἐπιστατῶν κεφαλάς. ἔπειτα δὲ ἄλλους ἐπιστάτας ἐκέλευσε κατασκευάζειν τὰς γεφύρας.

Adapted from Herodotus VII.34-36

1 Darius had wanted to punish the Greek cities of Athens and Eretria for helping the Greeks of Ionia (in Asia Minor) to revolt against the Persians in 499 B.C. His expedition had been defeated at Marathon in 490 B.C.; Xerxes thus had a further motive for his invasion in 480 B.C.

Chapter 11 Vocabulary

From now on the chapter vocabulary includes the first three principal parts of new verbs. A long dash means a principal part is not attested. Some forms will not be learned until later, but the principal parts are so essential to verb formation that it is a good idea to learn them along with the meaning of the verb.

Verbs:

ἀκούω, ἀκούσομαι, ἤκουσα (+ *acc.* thing, + *gen.* person)	hear, listen to
ἀναγκάζω, ἀναγκάσω, ἠνάγκασα	force, compel
ἀποφεύγω, ἀποφεύξομαι, ἀπέφυγον	flee away, escape
ἄρχω, ἄρξω, ἦρξα (+ *gen.*)	rule, command
εἰσβάλλω, εἰσβαλῶ, εἰσέβαλον (+ εἰς)	throw into, invade, flow into
ἥκω, ἥξω, —	have come
καταλύω, καταλύσω, κατέλυσα	destroy
πράττω, πράξω, ἔπραξα	do, manage; fare
προπέμπω, προπέμψω, προύπεμψα	send forth
συμβουλεύω, συμβουλεύσω, συνεβούλευσα (+ *dat.*)	advise
ταράττω, ταράξω, ἐτάραξα	throw into confusion
τάττω, τάξω, ἔταξα	draw up

Nouns:

ἀνήρ, ἀνδρός, ὁ	man, husband	**Λεωνίδας**, -ου, ὁ	Leonidas
Δαρεῖος, -ου, ὁ	Darius	μήτηρ, μητρός, ἡ	mother
θήρ, θηρός, ὁ	wild beast	**πατήρ**, πατρός, ὁ	father
κάμηλος, -ου, ὁ/ἡ	camel	**ῥήτωρ**, -ορος, ὁ	orator
Κῦρος, -ου, ὁ	Cyrus	φωνή, -ῆς, ἡ	voice

Adjective:

μῶρος, -α, -ον	foolish

Prepositions:

εἰς (+ *acc.*)	for (a purpose)	**σύν** (+ *dat.*)	with
ὄπισθε(ν) (+ *gen.*)	behind		

CHAPTER 12

οὐ γάρ ποτ᾽ οὔτ᾽ ἂν εἰ τέκν᾽ ὧν μήτηρ ἔφυν
οὔτ᾽ εἰ πόσις μοι κατθανὼν ἐτήκετο,
βίᾳ πολιτῶν τόνδ᾽ ἂν ᾑρόμην πόνον.

— Sophocles, *Antigone* 905-907

1. 3rd declension nouns: stems in -ν

In some **-ν** stem nouns the stem vowel is long (**η** or **ω**) throughout the paradigm; in other such nouns it is short except in the nom. sing. As usual in the 3rd declension, the stem is clear in the gen. sing.

		Greek	contest	shepherd	leader
Sing.	Nom.	ὁ Ἕλλην	ὁ ἀγών	ὁ ποιμήν	ὁ ἡγεμών
	Gen.	Ἕλληνος	ἀγῶνος	ποιμένος	ἡγεμόνος
	Dat.	Ἕλληνι	ἀγῶνι	ποιμένι	ἡγεμόνι
	Acc.	Ἕλληνα	ἀγῶνα	ποιμένα	ἡγεμόνα
	Voc.	Ἕλλην	ἀγών	ποιμήν	ἡγεμών
Plur.	Nom.	Ἕλληνες	ἀγῶνες	ποιμένες	ἡγεμόνες
	Gen.	Ἑλλήνων	ἀγώνων	ποιμένων	ἡγεμόνων
	Dat.	Ἕλλησι(ν)	ἀγῶσι(ν)	ποιμέσι(ν)	ἡγεμόσι(ν)
	Acc.	Ἕλληνας	ἀγῶνας	ποιμένας	ἡγεμόνας
	Voc.	Ἕλληνες	ἀγῶνες	ποιμένες	ἡγεμόνες

EXERCISE 49. Give the following forms, with the article:

1. Nom. sing. of: πατράσι, λιμένα, λεόντων, ἀγῶνας.
2. Acc. sing. and gen. pl. of: ἡγεμών, γίγας, ἀνήρ, ποιμήν.
3. Nom. and dat. pl. of: νύξ, γέρων, ῥήτωρ, χειμών.

2. More uses of the article

The article can be combined with other words to make a noun phrase. The noun itself can be omitted, when the context and the gender of the article make it clear. Two of these combinations have already been introduced.

- With an adjective (Ch. 7.2)

οἱ σοφοί	the wise [men / people]
τὸ καλόν	the good, beauty

- With μέν and δέ (Ch. 8.5)

οἱ μὲν καλοί, οἱ δὲ κακοί	some [people] are good, some bad

- With a genitive noun.

τὰ τῆς πατρίδος	the [affairs] of the fatherland
οἱ τῆς Ἑλλάδος	the [people] of Greece

- With a prepositional phrase or adverb

τὰ ἐν τῇ οἰκίᾳ	the [things] in the house
αἱ πάλαι	the [women] of old
οἱ ἐκεῖ	the [people] there

Note: The article never stands all by itself; it is always accompanied by another adjective, a noun, μέν or δέ, etc.

3. Compounds of εἰμί, 'be'

A verb accent normally only recedes as far as the augment; it does not stand on the prefix of a compound verb (Ch. 11.3), except in a few cases. However, enclitic verb forms, like most of the present tense of εἰμί, 'be', cannot carry their own accent. In compound verbs like ἄπειμι, 'be absent', therefore, the accent appears on the prefix in enclitic forms.

		Present	Future	Imperfect
Sing.	1st	ἄπειμι	ἀπέσομαι	ἀπῆ / ἀπῆν
	2nd	ἀπεῖ	ἀπέσῃ / ἀπέσει	ἀπῆσθα
	3rd	ἄπεστι(ν)	ἀπέσται	ἀπῆν
Plur.	1st	ἄπεσμεν	ἀπεσόμεθα	ἀπῆμεν
	2nd	ἄπεστε	ἀπέσθε	ἀπῆτε
	3rd	ἄπεισι(ν)	ἀπέσονται	ἀπῆσαν

Note: The future and imperfect tenses are not enclitic, so they are accented normally.

EXERCISE 50.

1. οἱ ἡγεμόνες ἤνεγκον τὰ ὅπλα πρὸς τὸν λιμένα.
2. κακὸς στρατηγὸς ἦρξε τῆς τῶν βαρβάρων στρατιᾶς.
3. εὖ ἐπράξατε τὰ τῆς πατρίδος ὑπὲρ τῶν πολιτῶν.
4. διὰ τὴν νύκτα ὁ ἡγεμὼν οὐχ ηὗρε τὴν ὁδόν.
5. ἢ ὁ στρατηγὸς ἢ ὁ Λεωνίδας αὐτὸς ἔταξε τοὺς Ἕλληνας εἰς μάχην.
6. εἰ αὐτὸς ἐπαίδευσας τὸν ἵππον, εὖ ἂν ἔπραξας ἐν τῷ ἀγῶνι.
7. οἱ στρατιῶται οἳ ἄπεισιν ἀπὸ τῆς μάχης οὐ σχήσουσι τὴν τιμήν.
8. οἱ νεανίαι εὖ ἔπραξαν ἐν τοῖς ἀγῶσιν.
9. οὐ κακῶς ἔπραξαν οἱ δοῦλοι· ὁ γὰρ δεσπότης ἀπῆν.
10. χαλεπὸν ἦν αὐτοῖς κωλύειν τοὺς Πέρσας οἳ εἰσέβαλλον· οἱ γὰρ σύμμαχοι ἀπέθανον.

EXERCISE 51.

1. We led the men on the island into the harbor.
2. We did not fare well after the contest.
3. The boys found a lion in the house.
4. The people there were faring badly, for they did not have allies.
5. The shepherds will guard their animals well.
6. Night will not stop the contest.
7. The generals were managing the affairs of Greece.
8. On account of the storm we will guard the harbor.
9. We ordered the (women) in the meadow to flee.
10. The guide himself falls in the battle.

4. Conditions

A conditional sentence describes the condition under which an action occurs, or may occur. A subordinate clause, the *protasis* or if-clause, expresses the condition. The *apodosis* or main clause states the outcome: 'If John thinks that, he is wrong.'; 'If it rains, we will stay home.'

There are several types of conditional sentences in Greek, each constructed in a particular way. Conditions using only the indicative are presented here (for other types, see Ch. 28).

> **Note:** The negative used in the protasis of any condition is μή; οὐ is used in the apodosis.

5. Simple conditions

A simple condition is the most basic type of conditional sentence. It may refer to the present or to the past, but not to the future. Simple conditions appear as follows.

Protasis	Apodosis
εἰ, 'if' + indicative (present or past)	indicative (present or past)
negative: μή	negative: οὐ

εἰ ὁ παῖς μὴ ἀγαθός, ὁ πατὴρ κακῶς πράττει.

If the child is not good, the father fares badly.

εἰ ὁ στρατηγὸς σοφὸς ἦν, οὐκ ἐπίστευσε τῷ ἡγεμόνι.

If the general was wise, he did not trust the guide.

Note: The apodosis may contain an imperative or other main clause construction instead of an indicative.

εἰ ὁ παῖς φεύγει, δίωκε αὐτόν.

If the child flees, pursue him.

6. Contrary-to-fact conditions

A contrary-to-fact condition describes what might be happening now, but isn't, or might have happened, but did not, because the necessary condition was not fulfilled.

If I were rich [but I'm not], I would be happy [but I'm not].

If it had not rained [but it did], I would have gone out [but I didn't].

In each case, both clauses describe a situation contrary to the known facts: I'm not rich, and I'm not happy; it did rain, and I didn't go out.

Contrary-to-fact conditions in Greek can only refer to the present and past (future facts are not yet known). The verbs are always indicative.

Protasis	Apodosis
εἰ, 'if' + indicative (imperfect or aorist)	indicative (imperfect or aorist) + ἄν
negative: μή	negative: οὐ

The conditional particle ἄν is not translated; it is a useful marker for certain kinds of clause. It is postpositive, like μέν and δέ (Ch. 8.5). It often stands second in the verb phrase, following the verb or a negative or other adverb. It usually precedes an enclitic verb.

If the verb is imperfect, the clause refers to the present. If the verb is aorist, the clause refers to the past. These are the only verb tenses used in contrary-to-fact conditions. The protasis and the apodosis are not always in the same tense.

εἰ δοῦλος ἦν, οὐκ εὖ ἂν ἔπραττεν.

If he were a slave, he would not be faring well. (present c.-to-f.)

εἰ τὸ στρατόπεδον ἐφυλάξατε, οἱ πολέμιοι οὐκ ἂν εἰσέβαλον.

If you had guarded the camp, the enemy would not have invaded. (past c.-to-f.)

εἰ μὴ κατελύσαμεν τοὺς Πέρσας, δοῦλοι ἂν ἦμεν.

If we had not destroyed the Persians, we would be slaves. (mixed c.-to-f.)

Reading expectations

εἰ + indicative ↗ indicative = simple condition
εἰ + indicative ↘ indicative + ἄν = contrary-to-fact

imperfect = present time
aorist = past time

Note: Tables like this one show graphically how a key word allows you to expect and predict what construction will follow in a sentence (Ch. 6.5, 10.3); often there are just two possibilities.

EXERCISE 52. Identify the types of all conditions, and translate:

1. εἰ ὁ χειμὼν χαλεπός ἐστιν, μένετε ἐν τῷ λιμένι.
2. ἔτι ἐν κινδύνῳ ἂν ἦμεν, εἰ ἡ θεὰ μὴ ἔπαυσε τὴν μάχην.
3. εἰ ὁ στρατηγὸς μὴ ἐκέλευσε τοὺς ὁπλίτας μένειν ἐκεῖ, οἱ πολέμιοι ηὗρον ἂν αὐτούς.
4. εἰ οἱ θῆρες ἐν τῇ κώμῃ εἰσίν, ἐθέλομεν λαμβάνειν αὐτούς.
5. οἱ πολῖται ἐπίστευον ἂν τῷ ῥήτορι, εἰ σοφοὶ ἦσαν.
6. οἱ Ἀθηναῖοι ἐθαύμαζον τοὺς πάλαι.
7. μῶροί ἐστε εἰ μὴ ἀκούετε τοῦ Ξενοφῶντος.
8. εἰ τὸν δοῦλον ἐφύλαξα, οὐκ ἂν ἔφυγεν ἐκ τοῦ λειμῶνος.
9. εἰ ὁ ναύτης τοῖς θεοῖς ἔθυσεν, δῶρα ἂν ἔπεμπον πρὸς αὐτόν.
10. εἰ τὰ χρήματα πείθει τοὺς παῖδας, μῶροί εἰσιν.

EXERCISE 53. Identify the types of all conditions, and translate:

1. If there is a camel in the house, do not stay!
2. If she had money, she would have carried it to the market-place.
3. If they did not stay in the harbor they were in danger.
4. If the storm were dangerous, we would not be marching out of Athens.
5. The Persians would be ruling Greece now if the Athenians had not stopped them.
6. If we were not brave, we would have fled away.

7. If the shepherds had not guarded the animals, the enemy would have captured them.
8. If the Greeks want to save their fatherland, I admire them.
9. If he had not died, he would be a general now.
10. The orator would have advised them if they had listened to him.

READING.

ADMETUS AND ALCESTIS

The following is the outline of the plot of the Alcestis, *one of the best known plays of Euripides* (c. 485-406 B.C.). *Pherae was a town in Thessaly.*

ὁ Ἄδμητος, ὃς ἐβασίλευε τῶν Φερῶν, ἦν ὁ τῆς Ἀλκήστιδος ἀνήρ· ἐπεὶ δὲ ἡ ὥρα ἧκεν αὐτῷ ἀποθνῄσκειν, ὁ Ἀπόλλων ἔλεξεν ὅτι διὰ τὴν πρὶν εὔνοιαν ἐξῆν αὐτῷ μὴ εὐθὺς ἀποθνῄσκειν, εἴ τις τῶν οἰκείων ἤθελεν ὑπὲρ αὐτοῦ ἀποθανεῖν. ἀλλ' ὁ Ἄδμητος οὐχ οἷός τε ἦν πείθειν οὔτε τὸν πατέρα οὔτε τὴν μητέρα· καὶ δὴ ἡ Ἄλκηστις μόνη ἤθελε σῴζειν τὸν ἄνδρα· ἐκέλευσεν οὖν χαίρειν τούς τε παῖδας καὶ τὸν ἄνδρα αὐτόν. μετὰ δὲ τὸν τῆς Ἀλκήστιδος θάνατον ὁ Ἡρακλῆς παρῆν εἰς τὴν οἰκίαν. ὁ δὲ Ἄδμητος ἐξένιζε μὲν αὐτόν, ἔκρυπτε δὲ τὴν συμφοράν· εἰ γὰρ ἔλεξε τῷ φίλῳ <u>τὰ ἀληθῆ</u> [*the truth*], ὁ Ἡρακλῆς ἂν ἔφυγεν. τέλος δὲ ὁ Ἡρακλῆς, ὡς ηὗρε τὰ περὶ τῆς Ἀλκήστιδος παρὰ τῆς θεραπαίνης, εἰς τὸν τάφον <u>ἦλθε</u> [*went*] καὶ ἔλαβε τὴν Ἀλκήστιδα <u>πρὸς βίαν</u> [*by force*] ἀπὸ τοῦ Θανάτου· ἔπειτα δὲ πρὸς τὸν ἄνδρα ἤγαγεν αὐτήν.

Chapter 12 Vocabulary

Verbs:

ἄπειμι, ἀπέσομαι, ἀπῆν	be absent
εὖ πράττω	fare well, manage well
κακῶς πράττω	fare badly
πίπτω, πεσοῦμαι, ἔπεσον	fall

Nouns:

ἀγών, -ῶνος, ὁ	contest, game	λειμών, -ῶνος, ὁ	meadow
Ἕλλην, -ηνος, ὁ	a Greek	**λιμήν**, -ένος, ὁ	harbor
ἡγεμών, -όνος, ὁ	leader, guide	ποιμήν -ένος, ὁ	shepherd
κίνδυνος, -ου, ὁ	danger	**χειμών**, -ῶνος, ὁ	storm, winter

Adverbs:

ἐκεῖ	there, in that place	**κακῶς**	badly
ἔτι	still, yet	πάλαι	of old, long ago
εὖ	well		

Conjunction:

εἰ	if

Particle:

ἄν	*conditional particle*

CHAPTER 13

ἐρωτηθεὶς τί δύσκολον, ἔφη, Τὸ ἑαυτὸν γνῶναι·
τί δὲ εὔκολον, Τὸ ἄλλῳ ὑποθέσθαι.

— Thales (Diogenes Laertius, *Vitae philosophorum* 1.36)

1. 3rd declension nouns: stems in -σ

In these nouns the **σ** drops out between the stem and ending vowels. The vowels then contract, as follows.

ε + ε = ει	ε + ο = ου
ε + α = η , ει (acc. pl.)	ε + ω = ω

The accent is placed before the contraction takes place; if the accented syllable is caught up in the contraction, the accent remains on the (long) contracted syllable. Hence the accentuation of the gen. pl. forms. Masculine and feminine nouns of this type are declined like τριήρης, neuters like τεῖχος (the gen. pl. accent on τριήρης follows the rest of the paradigm).

		trireme		wall	
Sing.	Nom.	ἡ τριήρης		τὸ τεῖχος	
	Gen.	τριήρους	(τριήρεσ-ος)	τείχους	(τείχεσ-ος)
	Dat.	τριήρει	(τριήρεσ-ι)	τείχει	(τείχεσ-ι)
	Acc.	τριήρη	(τριήρεσ-α)	τεῖχος	
	Voc.	τριῆρες		τεῖχος	
Plur.	Nom.	τριήρεις	(τριήρεσ-ες)	τείχη	(τείχεσ-α)
	Gen.	τριηρῶν	(τριηρέσ-ων)	τειχῶν	(τειχέσ-ων)
	Dat.	τριήρεσι(ν)	(τριήρεσ-ι)	τείχεσι(ν)	(τείχεσ-ι)
	Acc.	τριήρεις	(τριήρεσ-ας)	τείχη	(τείχεσ-α)
	Voc.	τριήρεις	(τριήρεσ-ες)	τείχη	(τείχεσ-α)

2. Principal parts of dental stem thematic verbs

The stems of these verbs end in **-τ, -δ, -θ.** Stems in **-ζ** also belong to this group, since **ζ** actually represents the consonant cluster **sd** (Ch. 1.1). When a dental consonant is followed by **σ**, the dental disappears (Ch. 1.2, 8.1).

$$\left.\begin{matrix}\tau\\ \delta\\ \theta\end{matrix}\right\} + \sigma = \sigma$$

Here are the first three principal parts for the dental stem verbs you have learned so far.

1 Present	2 Future	3 Aorist (Active)
ἀναγκάζω	ἀναγκάσω	ἠνάγκασα
ἐλπίζω	—	ἤλπισα
θαυμάζω	θαυμάσομαι[1]	ἐθαύμασα
ὁπλίζω	—	ὥπλισα
πείθω	πείσω	ἔπεισα
σῴζω	σώσω	ἔσωσα

1 For future conjugation see Ch. 17.2.

EXERCISE 54.

1. ὁ ἡγεμὼν ἠνάγκασε τοὺς βαρβάρους μένειν ἐν τῷ ὄρει.
2. οἱ στρατιῶται ἐθέλουσι μήτε μένειν μήτε φυλάττειν τὰ τείχη.
3. ὁ Λεωνίδας, ὃς τῶν Λακεδαιμονίων ἦρχεν, ἑτοῖμος ἦν κινδυνεύειν.
4. παρεσκευάσαμεν τὰς τριήρεις ἃς οἱ σύμμαχοι μένουσιν.
5. οἱ Ἀθηναῖοι ἐφύλαττον τὴν ὁδὸν μακροῖς τείχεσιν.
6. ἐπιστεύσαμεν τῷ Σωκράτει, ὃς εὖ συνεβούλευε τοῖς πολίταις.
7. σώσετε τὴν πατρίδα, ὦ πολῖται.
8. εἰ ἀγαθὰ ὅπλα ἦν τοῖς Ἕλλησιν, εὐθὺς ἂν ἠνάγκασαν τοὺς Πέρσας ἀποφεύγειν.
9. ὀλίγα ἦν τὰ ἐν τῷ λειμῶνι ζῷα μετὰ τὸν χειμῶνα.
10. οὐκ ἰσχυροὶ ἦσαν οἱ σύμμαχοι· ὀλίγαι γὰρ τριήρεις ἦσαν αὐτοῖς.

EXERCISE 55.

1. He compelled the sailors to remain on the island.
2. We persuaded those in the harbor to escape.
3. The general saved both the old men and the children.
4. If the Athenians had persuaded their allies to send triremes and sailors, they would not be in danger now.

5. The women in the house were training the slaves.
6. The children found few horses in the village.
7. The weapons that we are waiting for will be not be ready immediately.
8. Will the sailors save Greece with their triremes?
9. The storm kept the men away from the mountains.
10. The young men were listening to the words of Socrates himself.

3. The future and aorist active infinitives of thematic verbs

The future active infinitive consists of the future stem (2nd principal part) + **ειν**: λύσ-ειν. The accent falls on the last syllable of the stem = Position 2, penult (remember noun accents are persistent, Ch. 6.3).

The future infinitive has only a few specific uses.

- As a complementary infinitive after two particular verbs
  - ◇ μέλλω, 'intend' 'be about to'

    μέλλω θύσειν.

    I am about to sacrifice.
  - ◇ ἐλπίζω, 'hope', 'expect' when it refers to the future

    οὐκ ἐλπίζω πείσειν αὐτόν.

    I do not expect to persuade him.
- In indirect statement (Ch. 14.5)

The 1st or weak aorist active infinitive consists of the aorist stem (3rd principal part) + **αι**: λῦσ-αι. The accent falls on the last syllable of the stem = Position 2, penult.

The 2nd or strong aorist active infinitive (3rd principal part) has the same thematic ending as the present infinitive: φυγ-εῖν. In addition to having a different stem, however, the accent also differs, falling on the ending = Position 1, ultima.

Note: The aorist infinitive has no augment; augments occur only in the indicative mood.

Perfect infinitives are uncommon, and will be presented later (Ch. 31.5).

Form summary

present active inf.: present stem + **ε** + **-εν** = **-ειν** λύειν, πείθειν, ἄρχειν

accent: on the last syllable of the verb stem

future active inf.: future stem + **ε** + **-ε** = **-σειν** λύσειν, πείσειν, ἄρξειν

accent: on the last syllable of the verb stem

1st aorist active inf.: aorist stem + **-αι** = **-σαι** λῦσαι, πεῖσαι, ἄρξαι

accent: on the last syllable of the verb stem

2nd aorist active inf.: aorist stem + **ε** + **-εν** = **-εῖν** φυγεῖν, ἀγαγεῖν, λιπεῖν

accent: on the **-ε-**, producing **-εῖν** on the contracted syllable

4. Infinitive aspect

Aspect in the indicative mood has already been discussed (Ch. 5.3); the imperfect expresses ongoing or repeated action, while the aorist expresses a single, simple act. Aspect also exists in other moods (imperative, subjunctive, optative) and in the infinitive. In these forms, the present and aorist tenses indicate not time but aspect: ongoing action for the present, a single act for the aorist.

Note: Even word formation can reflect this difference of aspect. For example, you saw in Ch. 11.4 that ἔχω has two future forms:

ἕξω (present stem) = ongoing aspect: 'have (and go on having)'

σχήσω (aorist stem) = single aspect: '(acquire and) have'

Complementary infinitives (Ch. 6.4) show this aspect distinction: present infinitive for ongoing action, aorist for a single act. It does not matter what tense the main verb is. English does not show the same distinction, so aorist and present infinitives may be translated the same way; sometimes extra words in English may make the aspect clear.

Note: The negative used with complementary infinitives is μή (Ch. 6.4, 6).

ἐκέλευσα τοὺς ἀνθρώπους μὴ διῶξαι τὸν ἵππον.
I ordered the men not to pursue the horse. (single act)

ἤθελον τοὺς ἀνθρώπους ἀεὶ διώκειν τὴν τιμήν.
I wanted the men always to pursue (keep pursuing) honor. (ongoing action)

οὐκ ἐθέλει στρατεῦσαι.
He does not want to march. (single act)

ἐθέλει μὴ στρατεύειν.
He wants not to march (go on marching). (ongoing action)

5. The infinitive as a verbal noun; the articular infinitive

In addition to its complementary use, the infinitive can also be used as a verbal noun or gerund, treated as a neuter singular. The negative used with it is μή.

The infinitive may be the subject or predicate of a sentence, as in 'To hear is to obey', 'Seeing is believing'. The Greeks would use an infinitive in both these sentences, even though the second sentence does not use an infinitive in English.

The infinitive can also function in other cases. When it is in the genitive or dative case, and when it is the object of a preposition, the definite article must be used with it (in other circumstances the article is optional), and it is called the *articular* infinitive. Since the infinitive is thought of as neuter singular, the article and any associated adjectives must also be neuter singular.

χαλεπόν ἐστι <u>μένειν</u> ἐν τῇ κώμῃ.

To stay in the village is dangerous.
Staying in the village is dangerous.
It is dangerous *to stay* in the village.

πείθει τὸν νεανίαν <u>τῷ λέγειν</u>.

He persuades the young man *by speaking*.

διὰ <u>τὸ μὴ φυγεῖν</u> ὁ στρατιώτης εἶχε τὴν τιμήν.

On account of *not fleeing*, the soldier had honor.

EXERCISE 56.

1. εὑρήσετε τὸ καλὸν τῷ ἀεὶ διώκειν αὐτό.
2. μέλλεις διώξειν τοὺς Πέρσας ἐκ τῆς Ἑλλάδος;
3. πείσομεν τοὺς συμμάχους ἀπαγαγεῖν τὰς τριήρεις.
4. ἑτοῖμαί εἰσιν αἱ τριήρεις ἃς οἱ σύμμαχοι ἔμενον;
5. ῥᾴδιον μὲν συμβουλεύειν ἐστίν, χαλεπὸν δὲ πρᾶξαι.
6. χαλεπὸν αὐτοῖς σῶσαι τοὺς γέροντας οἳ ἐν κινδύνῳ εἰσίν.
7. τοὺς μὲν ἠναγκάσαμεν φυγεῖν, οἱ δὲ ἀπέθανον ἐν τῇ μάχῃ αὐτῇ.
8. εἰ ἠθέλετε εἰρήνην σχεῖν, οὐκ ἂν κατελύετε τὰς οἰκίας αὐτῶν.
9. ἀγαθὸν ἦν τοῖς νεανίαις τοῦ Σωκράτους ἀκοῦσαι;
10. εἰ τὸ ὄρος ὑψηλόν, κελεύσω τοὺς ὁπλίτας μὴ μένειν ἐκεῖ.

EXERCISE 57.

1. Few of the leaders were ready to march to the high mountain.
2. We ordered the generals to lead the army away from the country of the Persians.
3. Leonidas himself was not able to bring back the soldiers.
4. By pursuing the young men, the lion forced them to flee into their village.
5. The enemy intended to force the Athenians to destroy their walls.
6. Did you advise the hoplites to save the children?
7. If the orator had not spoken well, the young men would not be admiring him now.
8. Admetus was not able to persuade his father to die.
9. If night hinders them, they stop the battle.
10. We hope to have peace by persuading the enemy not to invade.

READING.

THE WOODEN WALL

Between the two Persian invasions of 490 and 480 B.C. a rich vein of silver was discovered in Attica. It was used to develop the Athenian navy, which fought first against the people of Aegina (an island southwest of Attica, and a strong naval power), and then against the Persians, especially in the decisive victory off Salamis in 480.

ἦν δέ ποτε ἀνὴρ Ἀθηναῖος ὀνόματι Θεμιστοκλῆς· διὰ δὲ τὸ εἶναι χρήματα οὐκ ὀλίγα ἐν τῷ κοινῷ, οἱ μὲν ἤθελον ἕκαστον τῶν Ἀθηναίων λαβεῖν δέκα δραχμάς. ὁ δὲ Θεμιστοκλῆς ἔπεισεν αὐτοὺς παρασκευάσαι διακοσίας τριήρεις εἰς τὸν πρὸς τοὺς Αἰγινήτας πόλεμον· καὶ οὕτως ἠνάγκασε τοὺς Ἀθηναίους ἀριστεύειν κατὰ θάλατταν.

ἐν δὲ τῷ πρὸς τοὺς Πέρσας πολέμῳ οἱ Ἀθηναῖοι ἔπεμψαν ἄνδρας εἰς Δελφούς· ἐν γὰρ μεγίστῳ κινδύνῳ ἦσαν. καὶ ἡ Πυθία, Εἰ μέλλετε σώσειν τὴν πατρίδα, ἔφη, πιστεύετε τῷ ξυλίνῳ τείχει. ὁ δὲ Θεμιστοκλῆς ὧδε συνεβούλευσε τοῖς πολίταις· Ὁ θεὸς τῷ ξυλίνῳ τείχει οὐ τὴν ἀκρόπολιν σημαίνει, ἀλλὰ τὸ ναυτικόν, καὶ κελεύει τοὺς πολίτας ταῖς τριήρεσι πιστεύειν. οἱ δὲ πλεῖστοι ἐπίστευσαν αὐτῷ, καὶ οὕτω ἔπεισε τοὺς Ἀθηναίους καὶ ἄλλο ναυτικὸν παρασκευάσαι. καὶ δὴ εἰ μὴ ἔσχον ναυτικὸν καλόν, οὐκ ἂν κατέλυσαν τοὺς Πέρσας.

μετὰ δὲ τὴν ἐν ταῖς Θερμοπύλαις μάχην, οἱ μὲν Πελοποννήσιοι ἐφύλαττον τὸν Ἰσθμὸν τείχει, οἱ δὲ Ἀθηναῖοι ἐπόρευσαν τά τε τέκνα καὶ τοὺς οἰκέτας ἐκ τῆς Ἀττικῆς, τοὺς μὲν εἰς Τροιζῆνα, τοὺς δὲ εἰς Αἴγιναν, τοὺς δὲ εἰς Σαλαμῖνα, καὶ οὕτως ἔσωσαν αὐτούς. οἱ δὲ Πέρσαι εἰσέβαλον εἰς τὴν Ἀττικὴν καὶ κατέλαβον τὰς Ἀθήνας καὶ ἔκαυσαν [*burned*, from καίω] τὴν ἀκρόπολιν, ἐν ᾗ ἦσαν οἱ ὀλίγοι οἳ οὐκ ἐπίστευσαν τῷ Θεμιστοκλεῖ.

Adapted from Herodotus
VII.141-144, VIII.41, 53

Chapter 13 Vocabulary

Verbs:

ἀπάγω, ἀπάξω, ἀπήγαγον	lead away, bring back
ἐλπίζω, —, ἤλπισα (+ *fut. inf.*)	hope, expect
μέλλω, μελλήσω, ἐμέλλησα (+ *fut. inf.*)	be about to, intend
μένω, μενῶ, ἔμεινα	await, wait for
παρασκευάζω, παρασκευάσω, παρεσκεύασα	prepare

Nouns:

Ἄδμητος, -ου, ὁ	Admetus	**Σωκράτης**, -ους, ὁ	Socrates
Δημοσθένης, -ους, ὁ	Demosthenes	**τεῖχος**, -ους, τό	wall
		τριήρης, -ους, ἡ	trireme
ὄρος, ὄρους, τό	mountain		

Adjectives:

ἑτοῖμος, -η, -ον	ready	ὑψηλός, -ή, -όν	high
ὀλίγος, -η, -ον	little, few		

Adverb:

εὐθύς	immediately, at once

CHAPTER 14

ἄνδρες γὰρ πόλις, καὶ οὐ τείχη οὐδὲ νῆες ἀνδρῶν κεναί.
— Thucydides, *Histories* 7.77.7

1. 3rd declension nouns: stems in -ι, -υ

These nouns appear irregular in some forms, and must be learned carefully. Most **-ι** stems and some **-υ** stems show an alternate stem vowel **-ε** in many cases. πόλις, 'city', πρέσβυς, 'elder' and ἄστυ, 'town' are examples of this type. ἰχθύς, 'fish' keeps the **-υ** throughout.

		city	elder	town	fish
Sing.	Nom.	ἡ πόλις	ὁ πρέσβυς	τὸ ἄστυ	ὁ ἰχθύς
	Gen.	πόλεως	πρέσβεως	ἄστεως	ἰχθύος
	Dat.	πόλει	πρέσβει	ἄστει	ἰχθύϊ
	Acc.	πόλιν	πρέσβυν	ἄστυ	ἰχθύν
	Voc.	πόλι	πρέσβυ	ἄστυ	ἰχθύ
Plur.	Nom.	πόλεις	πρέσβεις	ἄστη	ἰχθύες
	Gen.	πόλεων	πρέσβεων	ἄστεων	ἰχθύων
	Dat.	πόλεσι(ν)	πρέσβεσι(ν)	ἄστεσι(ν)	ἰχθύσι(ν)
	Acc.	πόλεις	πρέσβεις	ἄστη	ἰχθύας, ἰχθῦς
	Voc.	πόλεις	πρέσβεις	ἄστη	ἰχθύες

Note: The accent on the gen. sing. and pl. of πόλις seems to violate normal rules. The gen. sing. form was originally πόληος, with the regular ending. However, the length of the last two vowels was switched from **ηο** to **εω** (a process called *quantitative metathesis*). The accent was not adjusted to the new form; the gen. pl. copies the gen. sing.

2. Principal parts of labial stem verbs

The stems of these verbs end in **-π**, **-β**, **-φ.** When a labial consonant is followed by **σ**, the result is **ψ** (Ch. 1.2, 8.1).

$$\left.\begin{matrix}\pi\\ \beta\\ \varphi\end{matrix}\right\} + \sigma = \psi$$

Here are the first three principal parts of the labial stem verbs you have learned so far.

1	2	3
Present	**Future**	**Aorist (active)**
βλάπτω	βλάψω	ἔβλαψα
γράφω	γράψω	ἔγραψα
κόπτω	κόψω	ἔκοψα
κρύπτω	κρύψω	ἔκρυψα
λείπω	λείψω	ἔλιπον
πέμπω	πέμψω	ἔπεμψα
πίπτω	πεσοῦμαι[1]	ἔπεσον

1 For future conjugation see Ch. 20.4.

EXERCISE 58. Fill in the blanks:

	Form	Person	Number	Tense	Verb
1.	ἔλιπε	______	______	______	______
2.	______	1st	plural	aorist	πέμπω
3.	πείσετε	______	______	______	______
4.	______	2nd	singular	aorist	ἀναγκάζω
5.	κόψομεν	______	______	______	______
6.	ἔσωσαν	______	______	______	______
7.	______	2nd	plural	future	γράφω
8.	______	3rd	singular	imperfect	κρύπτω
9.	ἔβλαψαν	______	______	______	______
10.	γράψεις	______	______	______	______

EXERCISE 59.

1. εἰ ἐπέμψαμεν πρέσβεις εἰς τὴν πόλιν αὐτῶν, εἰρήνην νῦν ἂν εἴχομεν.
2. οἱ πολέμιοι οὐ βλάψουσιν οὔτε τοὺς παῖδας οὔτε τοὺς γέροντας.
3. ἐθέλομεν εὐθὺς παῦσαι τὸν πόλεμον ὃς καταλύει τὴν πόλιν.
4. διὰ τὸ χρήματα μὴ ἔχειν, οἱ ἐν τῷ ἄστει κακῶς ἔπραττον.
5. οἱ δ᾽ Ἀθηναῖοι ἔγραψαν τὰ τῶν στρατιωτῶν ὀνόματα ἐν λίθῳ.

6. τοῖς συμμάχοις οὐκ ἦν ῥᾴδιον καταλιπεῖν τὰ ὅπλα ἃ ἔλαβον.
7. ὁ στρατηγὸς αὐτὸς ἤθελεν ἐπιστολὴν γράψαι περὶ τῆς νίκης.
8. μέλλομεν πέμψειν πρέσβεις εἰς τὸ ἄστυ αὐτῶν.
9. ἐλίπομεν τοὺς μικροὺς ἰχθῦς ἐν τῇ θαλάττῃ.
10. ἔπεσεν ὁ μῶρος νεανίας ἀπὸ τοῦ τείχους;

EXERCISE 60.

1. The child left the old man behind in the market-place.
2. The Persians will damage the city, but they will not be able to destroy it.
3. The men whom the general drew up will hit the enemy with stones.
4. Did you order the ambassadors either to send or to carry letters to the Athenians?
5. Did the citizens listen to Themistocles?
6. The elder was advising the young men about wisdom.
7. The sailor found a fish and he will send it to her.
8. The Athenians sent their allies' children out of the city.
9. Those on the wall were running risks for their fatherland.
10. The Spartans had few towns.

3. νομίζω and φημί

νομίζω, 'think' and φημί, 'say' commonly introduce indirect statements (below, sec. 4-5). νομίζω is a dental stem verb; the present and aorist are regular in form, but the future will be learned later (Ch. 20.4).

φημί is an athematic verb, like εἰμί, 'be'; that is, in the 1st principal part it does not have the thematic vowel. Also like εἰμί it is enclitic in the present tense. For the past tense, the imperfect is regularly used, and is often aorist in meaning. These two tenses are formed as follows.

INDICATIVE		Present	Imperfect
Sing.	1st	φημί	ἔφην
	2nd	φῄς	ἔφησθα / ἔφης
	3rd	φησί(ν)	ἔφη
Plur.	1st	φαμέν	ἔφαμεν
	2nd	φατέ	ἔφατε
	3rd	φασί(ν)	ἔφασαν
INFINITIVE			
		φάναι	

Note: The negative οὔ φημι means 'I deny', 'I say...not...'. 'I do not say' is expressed by other verbs: οὐ λέγω.

4. Indirect statement

A *direct* statement is like a quotation: it gives a person's words or thoughts in their original form. An *indirect* statement reports the original words or thoughts at second hand.

Direct	**Indirect**
They are coming.	I think that they are coming. He said they were coming.

In Greek each main verb that introduces an indirect statement takes one of three particular constructions. After most verbs of thinking and some verbs of saying, the verb of an indirect statement is in the infinitive. νομίζω, 'think' and φημί, 'say' are two common verbs of this type. (For other constructions, see Ch. 27.6-7). When you see such a verb, you can predict that an indirect statement will follow, and you can expect to see an infinitive.

> **Note:** The negative in indirect statement is usually οὐ, though a few exceptions occur (e.g. after verbs of hoping and promising).

5. The infinitive in indirect statement

If the subject of the main verb (the reporter) is also the subject of the infinitive, it does not have to be repeated before the infinitive. Any modifiers must be nominative. In the following examples, the general is the reporter.

ὁ στρατηγὸς νομίζει σοφὸς εἶναι.
The general thinks he is wise.

ὁ στρατηγὸς οὔ φησι αὐτὸς σοφὸς εἶναι.
The general says that he himself is not wise.
The general denies that he himself is wise.

If the subject of the infinitive is different from the reporter, it appears in the accusative, and any noun or adjective modifying it must also be accusative.

ὁ στρατηγὸς νομίζει τὴν θεὰν σοφὴν εἶναι.
The general thinks the goddess is wise.

The infinitive expresses time relative to the main verb of thinking or saying. The tense of the main verb itself has no effect on this relative relationship.

present infinitive:	same time as the main verb
future infinitive:	later time than the main verb
aorist infinitive:	earlier time than the main verb

The Greek system is thus different from the English system, where changing the tense of the main verb also changes the tense of the verb in the indirect statement.

νομίζω τὸν στρατηγὸν <u>πέμπειν</u> συμμάχους. (same time; *present* inf.)
I think (that) the general *sends / is sending* allies.

ἐνόμιζον τὸν στρατηγὸν πέμπειν συμμάχους. (same time; *present* inf.)
I thought (that) the general *was sending* allies.

νομίζω τὸν στρατηγὸν οὐ πέμψειν συμμάχους. (later time; *future* inf.)
I think (that) the general *will not send* allies.

ἐνόμιζον τὸν στρατηγὸν οὐ πέμψειν συμμάχους. (later time; *future* inf.)
I thought (that) the general *would not send* allies.

νομίζω τὸν στρατηγὸν πέμψαι συμμάχους. (earlier time; *aorist* inf.)
I think (that) the general *sent* allies.

ἐνόμιζον τὸν στρατηγὸν πέμψαι συμμάχους. (earlier time; *aorist* inf.)
I thought (that) the general *had sent* allies.

The tense of the infinitive corresponds to the finite verb tense of the original direct statement (an imperfect finite verb becomes a present infinitive).

- In the first two examples above, the original statement was "The general *is sending* allies." The infinitive in the indirect statement is likewise in the present tense.
- In the third and fourth examples, the direct statement was "The general *will send* allies"; thus the infinitive is future.
- In the last two examples, the direct statement was "The general *sent* allies"; thus the infinitive is aorist.

EXERCISE 61. Translate, and write out in English the direct form of each statement:

1. They say that the men will train the horses.
2. He said that he would train the horses.
3. We think that we ourselves speak well.
4. We think that the orator spoke well.
5. The sailor thought the slave had taken the money.

EXERCISE 62.

1. ὁ κῆρυξ ἔφη τοὺς πολεμίους ὀλίγους εἶναι.
2. ἐνομίζομεν τοὺς Πέρσας οὐκ εὐθὺς καταλύσειν τὴν πόλιν.
3. ὁ Σωκράτης οὐκ ἐνόμιζε σοφὸς εἶναι.
4. ὁ μὲν ἡγεμὼν φησι σώσειν τοὺς γέροντας· οἱ δὲ πιστεύουσιν αὐτῷ.
5. οὐκ ἔφαμεν πέμψειν στρατιώτας ἐπὶ τὴν Ἑλλάδα.
6. εἰ οἱ πολῖται εὖ ἀκούουσι τῶν πρέσβεων, σοφοί εἰσιν.
7. ἡ παῖς ἔφη αὐτὴ λαβεῖν τὸν ἰχθύν.

EXERCISE 63.

1. The soldiers said that the enemy were fleeing.
2. We think that the orator is not wise.
3. Did they think that the elders had managed the affairs of the city well?
4. The wise men were not intending to harm the animals.
5. Do you think Themistocles will save the city?
6. The Athenians said that they themselves would prepare triremes.
7. Even the Persians thought that the Spartans were brave.

You have now learned three uses of the infinitive: the complementary use (Ch. 6.4), the infinitive as a verbal noun (Ch. 13.5), and the infinitive in indirect statement (this section).

EXERCISE 64. Identify the use of the infinitive, and translate:

1. ὁ δοῦλος ἐκέλευσε τοὺς παῖδας μὴ βλάψαι τὰ δένδρα.
2. οἱ μὲν παιδεύονται τῷ λέγειν, οἱ δὲ τῷ γράφειν.
3. ὁ Σωκράτης ἔφη ἀκοῦσαι τοῦ θεοῦ.
4. οἱ πολῖται μέλλουσι παρασκευάσειν τὴν στρατιάν.
5. τὸ ἀεὶ εὖ πράττειν καλὸν μὲν τοῖς ἀνθρώποις, χαλεπὸν δέ.

EXERCISE 65. Identify the use of the infinitive, and translate:

1. Some persuade by doing, others by speaking.
2. The general thought that the triremes were ready.
3. It was difficult for them to find their father's money.
4. The citizens said that they did not trust the orator.
5. To be king is not easy.

READING.

THE TEN THOUSAND REACH THE SEA

In 401 B.C. *Cyrus the Younger rebelled against his brother Artaxerxes, king of Persia, with the aid of Greek mercenaries. Cyrus was killed at the battle of Cunaxa, not far from Babylon. Xenophon, who was chosen as one of the leaders of the Greeks, describes their return to the sea.*

μετὰ δὲ τὸν πόλεμον ὁ Ξενοφῶν ἤγαγε τοὺς Ἕλληνας διὰ [*through,* with gen.] τῆς Ἀρμενίας. ἧκον δ' εἰς χώραν καλήν, ἧς ὁ ἄρχων τοῖς Ἕλλησιν ἡγεμόνα ἔπεμψεν. καὶ ὁ ἡγεμὼν ἔφη πέντε ἡμερῶν [*within five days*] ἄξειν τὴν στρατιὰν πρὸς ὄρος ὅθεν ἡ θάλαττα ἔσεσθαι [fut. inf. of εἰμί: *would be*] φανερά. εἰ δὲ μή, ἐθέλειν ἔφη ἀποθανεῖν. οὐ μέντοι διὰ τὴν πρὸς τοὺς Ἕλληνας εὔνοιαν ἦγεν αὐτούς· ἡ γὰρ ὁδὸς ἡ τῆς στρατιᾶς ἦν διὰ χώρας ἣ πολεμία [*hostile*] ἦν τῷ ἄρχοντι. ἔπεισεν οὖν τοὺς Ἕλληνας αἴθειν καὶ φθείρειν τὴν χώραν. ὁ δ' ἡγεμὼν τέλος ἤγαγεν αὐτοὺς εἰς τὸ ὄρος, ὀνόματι Θήχης. τότε ἔσπευδον οἱ στρατιῶται· ἐπεὶ δὲ οἱ πρῶτοι ἦσαν ἐπὶ τοῦ ὄρους, ὁ Ξενοφῶν ἤκουσε κραυγήν. ἀναβαίνει δ' οὖν ἐφ' ἵππον καὶ ἀκούει τὴν βοήν, Θάλαττα, θάλαττα. ἐπεὶ δὲ οἱ στρατιῶται ἧκον ἐπὶ τὸ ἄκρον, περιέβαλλον ἀλλήλους καὶ στρατηγοὺς καὶ λοχαγούς, καὶ ἐδάκρυον. καὶ οἱ στρατιῶται ἔφερον λίθους καὶ κολωνὸν παρεσκεύαζον. τῷ δὲ ἡγεμόνι παρέσχον δῶρα, ἵππον καὶ φιάλην ἀργύρου καὶ σκευὴν Περσικὴν καὶ δαρεικοὺς δέκα, καὶ αὐτὸν ἀπέπεμψαν.

Adapted from Xenophon, *Anabasis,* IV.vii

Chapter 14 Vocabulary

Verbs:

καταλείπω	leave behind
κρύπτω, κρύψω, ἔκρυψα	hide
λείπω, λείψω, ἔλιπον	leave
νομίζω, νομιῶ, ἐνόμισα	think
τύπτω, τυπτήσω, —	strike, hit
φημί, φήσω, ἔφησα	say
οὔ φημι	say…not, deny

Nouns:

ἀνδρεία, -ας, ἡ	courage, bravery	λίθος, -ου, ὁ	stone
ἄστυ, ἄστεως, τό	town	**ναυτικόν**, -οῦ, τό	fleet, navy
Θεμιστοκλῆς, -έους, ὁ	Themistocles	**πόλις**, -εως, ἡ	city
		πρέσβυς, -εως, ὁ	elder
ἰχθύς, -ύος, ὁ	fish	πρέσβεις, -εων, οἱ	ambassadors

Preposition:

περί (+ *gen.*)	about, concerning

CHAPTER 15

Ἄριστον μὲν ὕδωρ. ὁ δὲ χρυσὸς αἰθόμενον πῦρ
ἅτε διαπρέπει νυκτὶ μεγάνορος ἔξοχα πλούτου.
— Pindar, *Olympian* I.1-2

1. 3rd declension nouns: stems in diphthongs

The long nom. pl. ending of the βασιλεύς type is the result of a contraction. That type underwent the same process of quantitative metathesis as the πόλις type (Ch. 14.1).

		king	**ox**	**old woman**
Sing.	Nom.	ὁ βασιλεύς	ὁ βοῦς	ἡ γραῦς
	Gen.	βασιλέως	βοός	γρᾱός
	Dat.	βασιλεῖ	βοΐ	γρᾱΐ
	Acc.	βασιλέᾱ	βοῦν	γραῦν
	Voc.	βασιλεῦ	βοῦ	γραῦ
Plur.	Nom.	βασιλεῖς / -ῆς	βόες	γρᾶες
	Gen.	βασιλέων	βοῶν	γρᾱῶν
	Dat.	βασιλεῦσι(ν)	βουσί(ν)	γραυσί(ν)
	Acc.	βασιλέᾱς	βοῦς	γραῦς
	Voc.	βασιλεῖς / -ῆς	βόες	γρᾶες

EXERCISE 66. Give the following forms, with article:

1. Nom. sing. of: πρέσβεσι, Σωκράτη, ἱερέας, ὄρη.
2. Gen. and dat. sing. of: τεῖχος, ἱππεύς, ἄστυ, γραῦς.
3. Nom. and acc. pl. of: πόλις, τριήρης, βοῦς, ἰχθύς.

2. The present and imperfect passive indicative of thematic verbs (1st principal part)

So far all the verb forms you have learned belong to the *active voice*, where the subject performs the action. In the *passive voice*, the subject of the verb is the object or receiver of the action.

ACTIVE	PASSIVE
The boy writes.	The boy *is taught*.
The horse was running.	The horse *was being ridden*.

Most Greek verbs have a set of passive as well as active endings for most or all tenses. The present passive indicative has both a simple and a progressive meaning: 'I am loosed', 'I am being loosed'.

Present: Like the present active, the present passive is formed from the 1st principal part, and uses the thematic vowel. It has the same endings as the future tense of εἰμί, 'be' (Ch. 10.2). These are the primary personal endings for the passive voice (and the middle, Ch. 17.2).

		Stem λῡ-	Translation	Endings
Sing.	1st	λύ-ο-μαι	I am loosed	-ο-μαι
	2nd	λύ-ῃ / λύ-ει	you are loosed	-ῃ (-ε-σαι)
	3rd	λύ-ε-ται	he / she / it is loosed	-ε-ται
Plur.	1st	λυ-ό-μεθα	we are loosed	-ο-μεθα
	2nd	λύ-ε-σθε	you are loosed	-ε-σθε
	3rd	λύ-ο-νται	they are loosed	-ο-νται

Imperfect: The imperfect passive has a range of meanings similar to the imperfect active (Ch. 4.3): 'I was being loosed', 'I used to be sent'. Like the imperfect active, it is formed from the 1st principal part, and uses the thematic vowel. Like all past tense indicatives it has an augment. The endings are the secondary personal endings for the passive voice (and the middle, Ch. 17.2), except for the aorist passive (below, sec. 5).

		Stem λῡ-	Translation	Endings
Sing.	1st	ἐ-λυ-ό-μην	I was being loosed	-ο-μην
	2nd	ἐ-λύ-ου	you were being loosed	-ου (-ε-σο)
	3rd	ἐ-λύ-ε-το	he / she / it was being loosed	-ε-το
Plur.	1st	ἐ-λυ-ό-μεθα	we were being loosed	-ο-μεθα
	2nd	ἐ-λύ-ε-σθε	you were being loosed	-ε-σθε
	3rd	ἐ-λύ-ο-ντο	they were being loosed	-ο-ντο

Note: The 2nd singular endings are the result of contractions. In the present tense, **σ** is weak between the thematic and ending vowels and drops out; **ε** + **αι** = **ῃ** (a similar process affects some 3rd declension nouns, Ch. 13.1). However, to avoid confusion with the subjunctive, which also ends in **-ῃ**, **-ει** is often used in the indicative. In the imperfect, also, the **σ** drops out; the contraction **ε** + **ο** = **ου**.

3. The genitive of personal agent

The person or *agent* responsible for the action of a passive verb is expressed in Greek by the preposition ὑπό and a genitive noun or pronoun (a dative of personal agent appears with the perfect and pluperfect tenses; Ch. 31.4). The thing or *instrument* used is expressed by the dative without preposition; this is the dative of means or instrument (Ch. 6.2).

genitive of personal agent	**dative of means**
τυπτόμεθα ὑπὸ τῶν πολεμίων. We are being struck *by the enemy.*	τὸ τεῖχος τύπτεται λίθοις. The wall is struck *with stones.*
ὑπὸ τοῦ κριτοῦ πείθεται. He is persuaded *by the judge.*	τοῖς λόγοις πείθεται. He is persuaded *by the words.*

EXERCISE 67.

1. οἱ δὲ στρατιῶται τάττονται ὑπὸ τοῦ βασιλέως.
2. ὁ Ξενοφῶν χάριν εἶχε τῷ ἡγεμόνι· ηὗρε γὰρ τὴν ὁδόν.
3. ὁ στρατηγὸς ἔφη τοὺς ἱππέας ἐλαύνειν τοὺς ἵππους ἐπὶ τοὺς πολεμίους.
4. τὰ δὲ ζῷα ἃ ἐδιώκομεν ἔφευγε πρὸς τὴν κώμην.
5. ταῖς τριήρεσι ἐλπίζομεν τὴν νίκην σχήσειν.
6. εἰ οἱ πολέμιοι λίθοις τύπτονται, οὐκ οἷοί τ' εἰσίν μένειν ἐπὶ τοῦ τείχους.
7. πέμπεσθε εἰς τὰς νήσους, ὦ παῖδες;
8. οἱ δοῦλοι ἤλαυνον τοὺς βοῦς εἰς τὸν λειμῶνα.
9. τὰ τῆς πόλεως ἐπράττετο ὑπὸ τῶν στρατηγῶν.
10. διωκόμεθα ὑπὸ τῶν βασιλέως[1] ἱππέων.

1 βασιλεύς without the article means "the king of Persia"; see chapter vocabulary.

EXERCISE 68.

1. The oxen are being set free by the boy.
2. Ambassadors are being sent by the Persians concerning peace.
3. The king whose army was being pursued by the Greeks destroyed the town.
4. The old woman intends to hide the money.
5. If their country is ruled by a giant, I do not advise they stay.
6. The cavalry were being led by a good guide.
7. The enemy said they would not harm either the old men or the children in the city.

8. The house of the ambassadors was being guarded by soldiers.
9. Themistocles sent a letter to the king of Persia.
10. The cavalry whom we were pursuing left their horses in the forest.

4. Irregular 3rd declension nouns

Some 3rd declension nouns are irregular, though they mainly have normal 3rd declension endings. Ζεύς exists only in the singular, of course.

		woman	ship	water	Zeus
Sing.	Nom.	ἡ γυνή	ἡ ναῦς	τὸ ὕδωρ	ὁ Ζεύς
	Gen.	γυναικός	νεώς	ὕδατος	Διός
	Dat.	γυναικί	νηΐ	ὕδατι	Διΐ
	Acc.	γυναῖκα	ναῦν	ὕδωρ	Δία
	Voc.	γύναι	ναῦ	ὕδωρ	Ζεῦ
Plur.	Nom.	γυναῖκες	νῆες	ὕδατα	
	Gen.	γυναικῶν	νεῶν	ὑδάτων	
	Dat.	γυναιξί(ν)	ναυσί(ν)	ὕδασι(ν)	
	Acc.	γυναῖκας	ναῦς	ὕδατα	
	Voc.	γυναῖκες	νῆες	ὕδατα	

5. The aorist passive indicative of thematic verbs (6th principal part)

The aorist and future passive are both formed from the 6th principal part (Ch. 2.1; the 5th principal part will be presented in Ch. 31). The aorist passive is a simple past tense ('I was loosed'). As with the aorist active (Ch. 5.2, 11.5), some verbs have weak stems and others have strong stems. The endings are the same for both.

- **1st (weak) aorist passive.** In the indicative, the 1st (weak) aorist passive stem ends in **-θ**, with a tense vowel **-η**. It uses the *active* set of secondary endings.

		Stem λῠθ-	Translation	Endings
Sing.	1st	ἐ-λύθ-η-ν	I was loosed	-η-ν
	2nd	ἐ-λύθ-η-ς	you were loosed	-η-ς
	3rd	ἐ-λύθ-η	he / she / it was loosed	-η-
Plur.	1st	ἐ-λύθ-η-μεν	we were loosed	-η-μεν
	2nd	ἐ-λύθ-η-τε	you were loosed	-η-τε
	3rd	ἐ-λύθ-η-σαν	they were loosed	-η-σαν

Note: When two successive syllables contain an aspirated consonant, one of them will lose its aspiration (Grassmann's law). In the aorist passive, the marker stays intact and the preceding stem consonant is deaspirated.

θύω ἐτύθην

Some verbs with consonant stems have 1st aorist passives, with various effects from the cluster of the verb stem consonant + **θ**. The result cannot always be predicted, but there are a few consistent patterns.

◇ Verbs with dental stems (including –**ζ**) have -**σθ**-.

ἀναγκάζω ἠναγκάσθην
πείθω ἐπείσθην

◇ In verbs with labial or palatal stems the verb stem consonant is aspirated.

διώκω ἐδιώχθην
λείπω ἐλείφθην

- **2nd (strong) aorist passive.** The 2nd (strong) aorist passive stem has its own consonant, instead of -**θ**.

		Stem βλαβ-	**Translation**	**Endings**
Sing.	1st	ἐ-βλάβ-η-ν	I was harmed	-η-ν
	2nd	ἐ-βλάβ-η-ς	you were harmed	-η-ς
	3rd	ἐ-βλάβ-η	he / she / it was harmed	-η-
Plur.	1st	ἐ-βλάβ-η-μεν	we were harmed	-η-μεν
	2nd	ἐ-βλάβ-η-τε	you were harmed	-η-τε
	3rd	ἐ-βλάβ-η-σαν	they were harmed	-η-σαν

6. The future passive indicative of thematic verbs (6th principal part)

The future passive ('I will be loosed') is formed from the stem of the aorist passive (6th principal part). To the aorist passive stem and stem vowel -**(θ)η**- is added the -**σ**- marker of the future tense. The endings are the regular set of primary passive endings (above, sec. 2).

		Stem λῠθησ-	**Translation**	**Endings**
Sing.	1st	λυθήσ-ο-μαι	I will be loosed	-ο-μαι
	2nd	λυθήσ-ῃ / -ει	you will be loosed	-ῃ (-ε-σαι)
	3rd	λυθήσ-ε-ται	he / she / it will be loosed	-ε-ται
Plur.	1st	λυθησ-ό-μεθα	we will be loosed	-ο-μεθα
	2nd	λυθήσ-ε-σθε	you will be loosed	-ε-σθε
	3rd	λυθήσ-ο-νται	they will be loosed	-ο-νται

For consonant stem verbs, the future marker **σ** is likewise added to the aorist passive stem.

ἐγράφην	γραφήσομαι
ἐδιώχθην	διωχθήσομαι
ἐλείφθην	λειφθήσομαι
ἐπείσθην	πεισθήσομαι

EXERCISE 69. Copy the following verb chart and fill in:

1. For στρατεύω in the 3rd singular.
2. For διώκω in the 2nd plural.
3. For λείπω in the 3rd plural.

	Present	Imperfect	Future	Aorist
Active				
Passive				

EXERCISE 70.

1. ἡ ναυμαχία ἐπαύθη ὑπὸ βασιλέως.
2. ἡ ναῦς ἐκωλύθη τῷ χειμῶνι.
3. οἱ Πέρσαι οἳ ἔφυγον οὐκ ἐκωλύθησαν ὑπὸ τῶν Λακεδαιμονίων.
4. ὦ πολῖται, πέμπετε τάς τε γυναῖκας καὶ τοὺς παῖδας ἐκ τῆς πόλεως.
5. οἱ νεανίαι παιδευθήσονται εἰς τὸν πόλεμον.
6. οἱ ἱερεῖς ἦσαν ἑτοῖμοι θῦσαι τὸν βοῦν τῷ Διΐ.
7. οἱ Ἀθηναῖοι ἐπείσθησαν ὑπὸ τοῦ Δημοσθένους εὐθὺς πέμψαι τριήρεις.
8. οἱ νεανίαι οἳ ἐπαιδεύθησαν ὑπὸ τοῦ Σωκράτους σοφοί τε καὶ ἀγαθοὶ ἦσαν.
9. εἰ ὁ Ἄδμητος μὴ ἔπεισε τὴν γυναῖκα ἀποθνῄσκειν, αὐτὸς ἂν ἀπέθανεν.
10. οἱ βόες ἠλαύνοντο πρὸς τὴν κώμην ὑπὸ τοῦ γέροντος.

EXERCISE 71.

1. Was the slave set free immediately?
2. The women said that the children had hindered them on the journey.
3. The horses that were trained by the cavalry are good in battle.
4. Those on the mountain will not be driven away by the Spartans.
5. Did the soldiers find water on the island?
6. The god whom the Greeks used to worship was Zeus.
7. Admetus was set free from death by his wife.
8. The ships will not be hindered by the storm.
9. Themistocles was trusted by the Athenians.
10. The cities sent earth [γῆν] and water[1] to the king of Persia.

1 A traditional symbol of surrender.

READING.

THE CUNNING OF ARTEMISIA

The following episode took place at the battle of Salamis, where in 480 B.C. *the Greeks defeated the Persian fleet.*

παρῆν δ' ἐν τῇ ναυμαχίᾳ ἡ τῶν Ἁλικαρνασσέων[1] βασίλεια, ὀνόματι Ἀρτεμισία. ἐπεὶ δ' αἱ τῶν Περσῶν νῆες ἐπιέζοντο καὶ ἐβλάπτοντο ὑπὸ τῶν Ἑλλήνων, ἡ τῆς Ἀρτεμισίας ναῦς ἐδιώκετο νηῒ Ἀττικῇ. ἡ δὲ βασίλεια οὐχ οἵα τ' ἦν διαφυγεῖν (ἔμπροσθε γὰρ αὐτῆς ἦσαν ἄλλαι νῆες φίλιαι)· ἐκέλευσεν οὖν τοὺς ναύτας ἐμβάλλειν νηῒ φιλίᾳ. ὡς δὲ κατέδυσεν αὐτὴν, εὐτυχίᾳ ἡ βασίλεια εὖ ἔπραξεν. ὁ μὲν γὰρ τῆς Ἀττικῆς νεὼς τριήραρχος ἐνόμισε τὴν ναῦν τὴν τῆς Ἀρτεμισίας Ἑλληνικὴν εἶναι, ἢ τοὺς ναύτας αὐτομόλους εἶναι ἐκ τῶν βαρβάρων. οὐκέτι οὖν ἐδίωξεν αὐτήν, ἀλλ' ἐνέβαλλεν ἄλλαις ναυσίν· καὶ οὕτως ἡ Ἀρτεμισία ἐκ τῆς μάχης διέφυγεν.

τὸ δὲ τῆς βασιλείας ἔργον φανερὸν ἦν τῷ Ξέρξῃ· βασιλεὺς γὰρ αὐτὸς ἐν ὑψηλῷ θρόνῳ ἐπὶ τῆς ἀκτῆς ἐκάθιζεν. ἔλεξε δὲ Πέρσης αὐτῷ· Δέσποτα, ἡ Ἀρτεμισία ναῦν τῶν πολεμίων κατέδυσεν. ὁ δὲ Ξέρξης πρῶτον μὲν οὐκ ἐπίστευεν αὐτῷ, τέλος δ' ἐπείθετο· μάλιστα δ' ἐθαύμαζε τὴν τῆς βασιλείας ἀρετήν. Οἱ μὲν ἄνδρες, ἔφη, νῦν εἰσι γυναῖκες, αἱ δὲ γυναῖκες ἄνδρες.

Adapted from Herodotus VIII.87-88

1 Herodotus was born in Halicarnassus, a city in Caria, in Asia Minor.

Chapter 15 Vocabulary

Verbs:

ἀπελαύνω			drive away, march away
ἐλαύνω, ἐλῶ, ἤλασα			drive, march

Nouns:

βασιλεύς, -έως, ὁ	king	**θάνατος**, -ου, ὁ	death
βασιλεύς *without article*	the king of Persia	ἱερεύς, -έως, ὁ	priest
		ἱππεύς, -έως, ὁ	cavalryman
βοῦς, βοός, ὁ/ἡ	ox	ἱππεῖς, -έων, οἱ	cavalry
γραῦς, γραός, ἡ	old woman	**ναυμαχία**, -ας, ἡ	sea battle
γυνή, γυναικός, ἡ	woman, wife	**ναῦς**, νεώς, ἡ	ship
Ζεύς, Διός, ὁ	Zeus	**ὕδωρ**, ὕδατος, τό	water

Prepositions:

ἐπί (+ *gen.*)	on, upon	**ὑπό**	by (+ *gen.* of personal agent)

REVIEW OF PRINCIPAL PARTS

You have now learned four of the six principal parts of the Greek verb (Ch. 2.1), the basis for forming the following tenses:

- 1st: present and imperfect tenses (active, middle and passive);
- 2nd: future tense (active and middle); marker -**σ**
- 3rd: aorist tense (active and middle); weak aorist marker -**σ** with the tense vowel -**α**; strong aorist marked by stem change
- 6th: aorist and future tense (passive); weak marker -**θ** with the tense vowel -**η**; strong aorist marker -**η**

Here are all the principal parts for the verbs introduced so far for which you are responsible (bold in chapter vocabularies). Compound verbs are included only when the simple form has not yet been introduced. For completeness, the list includes the 4th and 5th principal parts, covering the perfect and pluperfect systems (Ch. 31.2-3, 32.1, 3), and some other forms you will learn later on.

From now on, chapter vocabularies will include all six principal parts for new verbs. Appendix 1 is a complete list of principal parts.

	1 Present A/M	2 Future A/M	3 Aorist	4 Perfect A	5 Perfect M/P	6 Aorist P
announce	ἀγγέλλω	ἀγγελῶ	ἤγγειλα	ἤγγελκα	ἤγγελμαι	ἠγγέλθην
lead	ἄγω	ἄξω	ἤγαγον	ἦχα	ἦγμαι	ἤχθην
hear	ἀκούω	ἀκούσομαι	ἤκουσα	ἀκήκοα	—	ἠκούσθην
force	ἀναγκάζω	ἀναγκάσω	ἠνάγκασα	ἠνάγκακα	ἠνάγκασμαι	ἠναγκάσθην
die	(ἀπο)θνήσκω	ἀποθανοῦμαι	ἀπέθανον	τέθνηκα[1]	—	—
kill	(ἀπο)κτείνω	ἀποκτενῶ	ἀπέκτεινα	—	—	—
be king, reign	βασιλεύω	βασιλεύσω	ἐβασίλευσα	—	—	—
rule	ἄρχω	ἄρξω	ἦρξα	ἦρχα	ἦργμαι	ἤρχθην
harm	βλάπτω	βλάψω	ἔβλαψα	βέβλαφα	βέβλαμμαι	ἐβλάβην / ἐβλάφθην
write	γράφω	γράψω	ἔγραψα	γέγραφα	γέγραμμαι	ἐγράφην
pursue	διώκω	διώξω / διώξομαι	ἐδίωξα	δεδίωχα	—	ἐδιώχθην
wish	ἐθέλω	ἐθελήσω	ἠθέλησα	ἠθέληκα	—	—
be	εἰμί	ἔσομαι	—	—	—	—
drive	ἐλαύνω	ἐλῶ	ἤλασα	-ελήλακα[2]	ἐλήλαμαι	ἠλάθην
hope	ἐλπίζω	—	ἤλπισα	—	—	ἠλπίσθην

	1 Present A/M	2 Future A/M	3 Aorist	4 Perfect A	5 Perfect M/P	6 Aorist P
find	εὑρίσκω	εὑρήσω	ηὗρον / εὗρον	ηὕρηκα / εὕρηκα	ηὕρημαι / εὕρημαι	ηὑρέθην / εὑρέθην
have	ἔχω	ἕξω / σχήσω	ἔσχον	ἔσχηκα	—	—
wonder	θαυμάζω	θαυμάσομαι	ἐθαύμασα	τεθαύμακα	τεθαύμασμαι	ἐθαυμάσθην
honor	θεραπεύω	θεραπεύσω	ἐθεράπευσα	τεθεράπευκα	τεθεράπευμαι	ἐθεραπεύθην
sacrifice	θύω	θύσω	ἔθυσα	τέθυκα	τέθυμαι	ἐτύθην
order	κελεύω	κελεύσω	ἐκέλευσα	κεκέλευκα	κεκέλευμαι	ἐκελεύθην
run risks	κινδυνεύω	κινδυνεύσω	ἐκινδύνευσα	κεκινδύνευκα	κεκινδύνευμαι	ἐκινδυνεύθην
cut	κόπτω	κόψω	ἔκοψα	-κέκοφα[2]	κέκομμαι	-εκόπην[2]
hinder	κωλύω	κωλύσω	ἐκώλυσα	κεκώλυκα	κεκώλυμαι	ἐκωλύθην
take	λαμβάνω	λήψομαι	ἔλαβον	εἴληφα	εἴλημμαι	ἐλήφθην
say	λέγω	λέξω	ἔλεξα	εἴρηκα	λέλεγμαι	ἐλέχθην
leave	λείπω	λείψω	ἔλιπον	λέλοιπα	λέλειμμαι	ἐλείφθην
loose	λύω	λύσω	ἔλυσα	λέλυκα	λέλυμαι	ἐλύθην
intend	μέλλω	μελλήσω	ἐμέλλησα	—	—	—
stay	μένω	μενῶ	ἔμεινα	μεμένηκα	—	—
think	νομίζω	νομιῶ	ἐνόμισα	νενόμικα	νενόμισμαι	ἐνομίσθην
teach	παιδεύω	παιδεύσω	ἐπαίδευσα	πεπαίδευκα	πεπαίδευμαι	ἐπαιδεύθην
prepare	(παρα)σκευάζω	παρασκευάσω	παρεσκεύασα	—	παρεσκεύασμαι	παρεσκευάσθην
stop	παύω	παύσω	ἔπαυσα	πέπαυκα	πέπαυμαι	ἐπαύθην
persuade	πείθω	πείσω	ἔπεισα	πέπεικα / πέποιθα[3]	πέπεισμαι	ἐπείσθην
send	πέμπω	πέμψω	ἔπεμψα	πέπομφα	πέπεμμαι	ἐπέμφθην
fall	πίπτω	πεσοῦμαι	ἔπεσον	πέπτωκα	—	—
trust	πιστεύω	πιστεύσω	ἐπίστευσα	πεπίστευκα	πεπίστευμαι	ἐπιστεύθην
do	πράττω	πράξω	ἔπραξα	πέπραχα / πέπραγα[3]	πέπραγμαι	ἐπράχθην
march	στρατεύω	στρατεύσω	ἐστράτευσα	ἐστράτευκα	ἐστράτευμαι	—
advise	(συμ)βουλεύω	συμβουλεύσω	συνεβούλευσα	συμβεβούλευκα	συμβεβούλευμαι	συνεβουλεύθην
save	σῴζω	σώσω	ἔσωσα	σέσωκα	σέσω(σ)μαι	ἐσώθην
draw up	τάττω	τάξω	ἔταξα	τέταχα	τέταγμαι	ἐτάχθην
carry	φέρω	οἴσω	ἤνεγκον	ἐνήνοχα	ἐνήνεγμαι	ἠνέχθην
flee	φεύγω	φεύξομαι	ἔφυγον	πέφευγα	—	—
say	φημί	φήσω	ἔφησα	—	—	—
guard	φυλάττω	φυλάξω	ἐφύλαξα	πεφύλαχα	πεφύλαγμαι	ἐφυλάχθην

1 The compound form is not used in the perfect active.

2 The simple form is not used in the perfect active or aorist passive.

3 The two perfect active forms have different meanings (Ch. 32.1).

CHAPTER 16

πολλὰ τὰ δεινὰ κοὐδὲν ἀν-
θρώπου δεινότερον πέλει·

— Sophocles, *Antigone* 332-333

σοφὸς Σοφοκλῆς, σοφώτερος δ' Εὐριπίδης·
ἀνδρῶν δ' ἁπάντων Σωκράτης σοφώτατος.

— Suda, *Lexicon*, sigma entry 820

1. μέγας, πολύς and adjectives of the τάλας type

Adjectives of the τάλας type have 3rd declension masculine and neuter forms and 1st declension feminine forms. μέγας and πολύς are variants of this type. Only the nom., acc. and voc. sing. of the masculine and neuter have 3rd declension endings; the other forms are 1st and 2nd declension.

wretched

		M	F	N
Sing.	Nom.	τάλας	τάλαινα	τάλαν
	Gen.	τάλανος	ταλαίνης	τάλανος
	Dat.	τάλανι	ταλαίνῃ	τάλανι
	Acc.	τάλανα	τάλαιναν	τάλαν
	Voc.	τάλαν	τάλαινα	τάλαν
Plur.	Nom.	τάλανες	τάλαιναι	τάλανα
	Gen.	ταλάνων	ταλαινῶν	ταλάνων
	Dat.	τάλασι(ν)	ταλαίναις	τάλασι(ν)
	Acc.	τάλανας	ταλαίνας	τάλανα
	Voc.	τάλανες	τάλαιναι	τάλανα

		big			much, many		
		M	F	N	M	F	N
Sing.	Nom.	μέγας	μεγάλη	μέγα	πολύς	πολλή	πολύ
	Gen.	μεγάλου	μεγάλης	μεγάλου	πολλοῦ	πολλῆς	πολλοῦ
	Dat.	μεγάλῳ	μεγάλῃ	μεγάλῳ	πολλῷ	πολλῇ	πολλῷ
	Acc.	μέγαν	μεγάλην	μέγα	πολύν	πολλήν	πολύ
Plur.	Nom.	μεγάλοι	μεγάλαι	μεγάλα	πολλοί	πολλαί	πολλά
	Gen.	μεγάλων	μεγάλων	μεγάλων	πολλῶν	πολλῶν	πολλῶν
	Dat.	μεγάλοις	μεγάλαις	μεγάλοις	πολλοῖς	πολλαῖς	πολλοῖς
	Acc.	μεγάλους	μεγάλας	μεγάλα	πολλούς	πολλάς	πολλά

2. Regular comparison of adjectives

The *comparative* and *superlative* in Greek share the English meanings; each also has further possible meanings.

Comparative	Superlative
wiser	wisest
more worthy	most worthy
fairly wise	very wise
somewhat wise	really wise
rather wise	

Some adjectives in English form the comparative by adding **-er** to the *positive* form, and the superlative by adding **-est**: 'wise, wiser, wisest'. These are the regular forms. Other adjectives are irregular in form: 'bad, worse, worst'. Greek also has both regular and irregular forms of comparison; this chapter deals with regular comparison.

The regular comparative and superlative in Greek are declined like 1st and 2nd declension adjectives (Ch. 7.1). The comparative ending is **-τερος, -τέρᾱ, -τερον**; the superlative ends in **-τατος**, **-τάτη**, **-τατον**. These endings are attached directly to the **ο** which ends the adjective stem. This **ο** will be either long or short, opposite to the length of the previous syllable.

- previous syllable long / short **ο**: μῶρος — μωρότερος, -ᾱ, -ον; ἀνδρεῖος — ἀνδρειότερος, -ᾱ, -ον
- previous syllable short / long **ο**: σοφός — σοφώτερος, -ᾱ, -ον; χαλεπός — χαλεπώτερος, -ᾱ, -ον

Sometimes the length of a syllable is clear. Short vowels make short syllables. Long syllables are made in several ways.

- long vowel
- diphthong, including **αι** and **οι** (Ch. 1.3)

- vowel followed by two or more consonants: ἐχθρός
- vowel followed by double consonant (**ζ**, **ξ**, **ψ**)

If the vowel in a syllable is **α**, **ι** or **υ**, the length is not obvious. The following is a list of such adjectives you have had so far, which form their comparatives and superlatives in the regular way. The long and short vowels are marked in the positive form.

Positive	Comparative	Superlative
ἄξῐος	ἀξιώτερος	ἀξιώτατος
ἰσχῡρός	ἰσχυρότερος	ἰσχυρότατος
μᾱκρός	μακρότερος	μακρότατος
μῑκρός	μικρότερος	μικρότατος
φίλῐος	φιλιώτερος	φιλιώτατος

3. Comparison with ἤ and the genitive of comparison

In Greek, there are two ways to express a comparison ('X is *bigger than* Y').

- with the word ἤ, 'than'; the two nouns compared are in the same case.

  ὁ Σωκράτης σοφώτερος ἦν ἢ οἱ ἄλλοι.
  Socrates was wiser *than the others.*

  οἱ Ἕλληνες ἔχουσι μικρότερον ναυτικὸν ἢ οἱ βάρβαροι.
  The Greeks have a smaller fleet *than the foreigners.*

- with *genitive of comparison* (no preposition); the second noun is in the genitive case.

  ὁ Σωκράτης σοφώτερος ἦν τῶν ἄλλων.
  Socrates was wiser *than the others.*

  οἱ Ἕλληνες ἔχουσι μικρότερον ναυτικὸν τῶν βαρβάρων.
  The Greeks have a smaller fleet *than the foreigners.*

In the construction with ἤ, the case agreement makes the meaning clear.

αἱ κάμηλοι δεινότεραι ἦσαν τοῖς στρατιώταις ἢ οἱ ναῦται.
The camels were more terrible to the soldiers *than the sailors (were).*

αἱ κάμηλοι δεινότεραι ἦσαν τοῖς στρατιώταις ἢ τοῖς ναύταις.
The camels were more terrible to the soldiers *than (to) the sailors.*

ἡ τοῦ ποιητοῦ γυνὴ σοφωτέρα ἐστὶν ἢ ὁ δοῦλος.
The poet's wife is wiser *than the slave.*

ἡ τοῦ ποιητοῦ γυνὴ σοφωτέρα ἐστὶν ἢ ἡ τοῦ δούλου.
The poet's wife is wiser *than the slave's (wife).*

4. Some uses of the genitive

- **The *partitive* genitive.** The genitive case may denote the whole (entity or group) of which a part is mentioned. We use the same construction in English: 'the biggest of the animals', 'many of the men', 'part of the city'.

  οἱ σοφώτατοι τῶν ἀνδρῶν
  the wisest of the men

  πολὺ τοῦ ἄστεως
  much of the town

  ἑκάστη τῶν νεῶν
  each of the ships

  ὁ Σωκράτης ἦν σοφώτατος τῶν τότε.
  Socrates was wisest of the people of that time.

  ὁ Σωκράτης ἦν ὁ σοφώτατος τῶν Ἀθηναίων.
  Socrates was the wisest of the Athenians.

- ***Subjective* and *objective* genitive.** As in English, a noun in the genitive may express either the subject or the object of an action or feeling. The subjective genitive is normally attributive; it is easy to confuse with the possessive genitive (Ch. 5.5), but this confusion rarely affects the translation. The objective genitive is normally predicate.

  ὁ τοῦ ζῴου φόβος
  the fear of the animal (subjective: the animal is afraid)

  ὁ φόβος τοῦ ζῴου
  the fear of the animal (objective: we fear the animal)

  ὁ τοῦ νεανίου ἔρως
  the young man's love (subjective: the young man is in love)

  ὁ ἔρως τοῦ νεανίου
  love of / for the young man (objective: she loves the young man)

5. Some uses of the dative

- **The dative of *manner*.** The dative case is used to express the manner of an action or the circumstances accompanying it.

  ὁ κριτὴς ἔλεξε πολλῇ σοφίᾳ.
  The judge spoke with much wisdom.

  ἀπέφυγον φόβῳ.
  They fled away in fear.

- **The dative of *degree of difference*.** The dative case is used with the comparative to express *by how much* something is bigger / stronger / etc.

  ὁ Σωκράτης πολλῷ σοφώτερος ἦν τῶν ἄλλων.

  Socrates was *much* wiser than the others.

  ὀλίγαις ἡμέραις ἡ ὁδὸς αὐτῶν ἦν μακροτέρα.

  Their journey was *a few* days longer.

- **The dative of *advantage* or *disadvantage*.** The dative case denotes the person for whose advantage or disadvantage something exists or is done.

  ἔγραψε νόμους τοῖς πολίταις.

  He wrote laws for the citizens.

  οἱ χειμῶνες κίνδυνός εἰσι τοῖς ναύταις.

  Storms are a danger for sailors.

EXERCISE 72.

1. οἱ Λακεδαιμόνιοι ὀλίγῳ ἀνδρειότεροί εἰσι τῶν Περσῶν.
2. οἱ πολέμιοι ἤλασαν ὀλίγας τῶν νεῶν ἐπὶ τὴν νῆσον.
3. ὁ Ἡρακλῆς ἦν ἰσχυρότατος ἢ τῶν νῦν ἢ τῶν τότε.
4. ἡ πόλις αὐτῶν οὐ πολλῷ μικροτέρα ἦν τῶν Ἀθηνῶν.
5. αἱ κάμηλοι δεινότεραι ἦσαν τοῖς στρατιώταις ἢ τὰ ὅπλα.
6. τὸ παῖδας παιδεύειν μέγα ἔργον ἐστὶ τοῖς πατράσιν.
7. ὁ χειμὼν ἦν χαλεπώτερος τοῖς Πέρσαις ἢ τοῖς Ἀθηναίοις.
8. ὁ τοῦ τάλανος βασιλέως φόβος μέγας ἦν· εὐθὺς οὖν ἀπήλασεν ἀπὸ τῆς μάχης.
9. ὁ τῆς Ἀλκήστιδος ἔρως μέγας ἦν, καί ἀξιωτάτη γυναικῶν νομίζεται εἶναι.
10. τότε δὲ οἱ Ἀθηναῖοι ἠναγκάσθησαν παρεσκευάσαι τεῖχος μέγα.

EXERCISE 73.

1. The Athenians sent many soldiers against each of their enemies.
2. The kings of that time always ran risks on behalf of their country.
3. The herald was a little more friendly than the other foreigners.
4. We think that we are not wiser than Socrates.
5. Those on the ship were hindered by the storm.
6. The children had a great fear of giants.
7. Many trees were being cut down by the Spartans.
8. The navy was very brave in the war.
9. The same exiles who remained on the island were wretched.
10. The city itself was more ancient than the walls by many years.

READING.

HOW THE EGYPTIANS AVOIDED GNATS

τοῖς δὲ Αἰγυπτίοις οἱ πολλοὶ κώνωπες ἄλγος εἰσίν. οἳ μὲν οὖν τὰς κώμας ἄνω τῶν λιμνῶν ἔχουσιν ἀναβαίνουσιν εἰς πύργους ὑψηλοὺς καὶ ἐκεῖ καθεύδουσιν· οἱ γὰρ κώνωπες διὰ τοὺς ἀνέμους οὐχ οἷοί τ' εἰσὶν ἀναβαίνειν· οἱ δὲ περὶ τὰς λίμνας Αἰγύπτιοι ἀντὶ τῶν πύργων τὰ σώματα ὧδε φυλάττουσιν· ἕκαστος ἀνὴρ αὐτῶν ἀμφίβληστρον ἔχει, ᾧ τῆς μὲν ἡμέρας [*by day*] ἰχθῦς θηρεύει, τῆς δὲ νυκτὸς [*by night*] περὶ κοίτην βάλλει τὸ ἀμφίβληστρον καὶ ὑπ' αὐτῷ καθεύδει. εἰ γὰρ μόνον ἐν ἱματίῳ καθεύδει, οἱ κώνωπες δι' αὐτοῦ δάκνουσιν, διὰ δὲ τοῦ ἀμφιβλήστρου οὔ.

Adapted from Herodotus II.95

Chapter 16 Vocabulary

Verb:

σπεύδω, σπεύσω, ἔσπευσα			hasten, hurry

Nouns:

Ἄλκηστις, -ιδος, ἡ	Alcestis	Ἡρακλῆς, -έους, ὁ	Heracles
ἔρως, -τος, ὁ	love, desire	φόβος, -ου, ὁ	fear
ἔτος, ἔτους, τό	year		

Adjectives:

ἄλλος, -η, -ο (endings as rel. pronoun)	other, another	**μέγας**, -άλη, μέγα	big, great, large
ἀρχαῖος, -α, -ον	ancient	**πολύς**, πολλή, πολύ	much, many
ἕκαστος, -η, -ον	each (of 3 or more), every[1]	τάλας, -αινα, -αν	wretched

Adverb:

τότε	then, at that time

Conjunction:

ἤ	than

1 Predicate if used with a noun with an article.

CHAPTER 17

τυφλὸς τά τ' ὦτα τόν τε νοῦν τά τ' ὄμματ' εἶ.
— Sophocles, *Oedipus Tyrannus* 371

1. The middle voice: meaning

So far you have learned the active and passive voices of the Greek verb. The subject of an active verb *performs* the verb action; the subject of a passive verb *receives* the action. Greek also has a third voice, appropriately called the *middle*. The middle voice adds an element of self-interest or self-involvement that the active voice does not: the subject of a middle verb does something *to* himself, or *for* himself.

Active	Middle	Passive
I stop (the train).	I stop (myself).	I am stopped (by the train).

The range of the middle voice really becomes clear in context, but the two basic meanings work as follows.

- what you do to yourself. The verb is reflexive: the subject both does and receives the action.

Active	Middle
παύω τὸν πόλεμον. I stop the war.	παύομαι τοῦ πολέμου. I cease from the war. (I stop fighting.)
τύπτει τὸ δένδρον. He hits the tree.	τύπτεται τὴν κεφαλήν. He hits his (own) head.

- what you do for yourself. When you see a middle instead of an active verb, you know that the subject is doing the action in his own interest. The verb may be transitive (with a direct object) or intransitive (without a direct object).

Active	Middle
λαμβάνω ἰχθύν. I catch a fish.	λαμβάνομαι ἰχθύν. I catch myself a fish.
πορεύει τοὺς γέροντας. He conveys the old men.	πορεύεται πρὸς τὴν νῆσον. He journeys to the island.

Some verbs take on a meaning in the middle that is different from the active meaning; the self-interest or involvement of the subject is usually clear.

ACTIVE		MIDDLE	
λύω	loose	λύομαι	ransom
μιμνῄσκω	remind	μιμνῄσκομαι	remember
πορεύω	carry, convey	πορεύομαι	march, journey
πείθω	persuade	πείθομαι	obey (+ *dat.*)

Note: πείθω is an interesting example. For the Greeks, obedience was evidently linked to persuasion, rather than to compulsion; 'I obey' implies 'I persuade myself / I am persuaded'.

Some verbs have *only* middle forms; the involvement of the subject is usually clear from the meaning. Such verbs are called *deponent* verbs.

δέχομαι τὰ δῶρα.
I receive the gifts.

μάχεται τοῖς Πέρσαις.
He is fighting the Persians.

Other verbs have an active present formation (1st principal part) but a middle future (2nd principal part): the future of ἀκούω is ἀκούσομαι. You will know if a principal part exists in the middle but not the active voice, because vocabulary lists and dictionaries list the middle form.

2. The middle voice: formation

Even though the translation of a middle form sounds active in meaning, the formation is different from the active. It resembles (and sometimes matches) the passive, which was originally developed from the reflexive sense of the middle.

- **1st principal part:** The indicative middle endings are identical to the passive in the present and imperfect (Ch. 15.2). Translation of these tenses thus depends on context and common sense. If you see a direct object, for example, the verb must be middle. If you see ὑπό + genitive, the verb must be passive.

MIDDLE	PASSIVE
λυόμεθα τοὺς ἄνδρας. We ransom the men.	λυόμεθα ὑπὸ τῶν στρατιωτῶν. We are set free by the soldiers.

Sometimes the construction really is ambiguous, especially in isolated sentences.

ἐπείθετο τοῖς νόμοις. He was obeying the laws.	ἐπείθετο τοῖς τοῦ ῥήτορος λόγοις. He was being persuaded by the orator's words.

- **2nd principal part:** The future middle is formed by adding the primary middle / passive endings to the future active stem.

Future:

		Stem λῡσ-	Translation	Endings
Sing.	1st	λύσ-ο-μαι	I will ransom	-ο-μαι
	2nd	λύσ-ῃ / -ει	you will ransom	-ῃ (-ε-σαι)
	3rd	λύσ-ε-ται	he / she / it will ransom	-ε-ται
Plur.	1st	λυσ-ό-μεθα	we will ransom	-ο-μεθα
	2nd	λύσ-ε-σθε	you will ransom	-ε-σθε
	3rd	λύσ-ο-νται	they will ransom	-ο-νται

- **3rd principal part:** The aorist middle is formed by adding the secondary middle / passive endings to the aorist active stem. Here are the paradigms for the 1st (weak) aorist of λύομαι, 'ransom', and the 2nd (strong) aorist of πείθομαι, 'obey'.

		Stem λῡσ-	Translation	Endings
Sing.	1st	ἐ-λυσ-ά-μην	I ransomed	-ᾰ-μην
	2nd	ἐ-λύσ-ω	you ransomed	-ω (-ᾰ-σο)
	3rd	ἐ-λύσ-α-το	he / she / it ransomed	-ᾰ-το
Plur.	1st	ἐ-λυσ-ά-μεθα	we ransomed	-ᾰ-μεθα
	2nd	ἐ-λύσ-α-σθε	you ransomed	-ᾰ-σθε
	3rd	ἐ-λύσ-α-ντο	they ransomed	-ᾰ-ντο

		Stem πῐθ-	Translation	Endings
Sing.	1st	ἐ-πιθ-ό-μην	I obeyed	-ο-μην
	2nd	ἐ-πίθ-ου	you obeyed	-ου (-ε-σο)
	3rd	ἐ-πίθ-ε-το	he / she / it obeyed	-ε-το
Plur.	1st	ἐ-πιθ-ό-μεθα	we obeyed	-ο-μεθα
	2nd	ἐ-πίθ-ε-σθε	you obeyed	-ε-σθε
	3rd	ἐ-πίθ-ο-ντο	they obeyed	-ο-ντο

3. Review of middle future forms

Look back at the Review of Principal Parts after Ch. 15. Some of those verbs have regular middle instead of active forms in the future tense (2nd principal part).

ἀκούω	ἀκούσομαι	λαμβάνω	λήψομαι
εἰμί	ἔσομαι	φεύγω	φεύξομαι
θαυμάζω	θαυμάσομαι		

EXERCISE 74. Translate the following verb forms:

1. λήψει
2. ἐμαχέσαντο
3. πείθεσθε
4. ἐπορεύετο
5. We obeyed
6. I stopped (myself)
7. She ransomed
8. They will hear

EXERCISE 75. Copy the following verb chart and fill in:

1. For ἀκούω in the 1st plural.
2. For λέγω in the 2nd singular.
3. For γράφω in the 3rd singular.
4. For θαυμάζω in the 3rd plural.

	Present	Imperfect	Future	Aorist
Active				
Middle				
Passive				

4. Some uses of the accusative

- **The accusative of *respect*.** The accusative case can denote the *respect* in which something is true. The appropriate English translation varies.

  ἀγαθός ἐστι <u>τὴν μάχην</u>.
  He is good *at battle.*

  ἐβλάβη <u>τὴν κεφαλήν</u>.
  He was injured *in the head.*

Note: The dative of means or instrument (Ch. 6.2, 15.3) and the infinitive used as verbal noun (Ch. 13.5) can be used in the same way.

  πείθεται <u>τοῖς χρήμασιν</u>.
  He is persuaded *by money.*

  ἀγαθὸς <u>μάχεσθαι</u>
  good *at fighting*

- **The accusative of *extent of space*.** The accusative case without a preposition can express the extent of space over which a motion occurs.

  ἐπορεύοντο μακρὰν ὁδόν.
  They journeyed (along) a long road.

- **The *double accusative*.** Sometimes one verb has two accusative objects, or an object and a predicate accusative.

  ◇ an *internal* object (the object done or effected) and an *external* object (the object done to or affected).

λέγει κακὰ τοὺς Λακεδαιμονίους.
He says bad things about the Spartans.

◇ some verbs, such as verbs of asking and reminding, take both a person and a thing as object.

μιμνῄσκει τὸν ἄνδρα τὰ χρήματα.
She reminds her husband about the money.

◇ some verbs, such as verbs of choosing, making, calling, considering, take both an object and a predicate noun or adjective in the accusative.

ὀνομάζουσι τοὺς ὁπλίτας ἀνδρείους.
They call the hoplites brave.

ἐποίησαν[1] τὸν ἄνδρα στρατηγόν.
They made the man general.

1 From ποιέω, Ch. 19.2.

EXERCISE 76.

1. οἱ νεανίαι ὠνόμαζον τὸν ἵππον Λαμπάδα.
2. ἀκούσεσθε τοῦ πρέσβεως, ὃς ἐθέλει λῦσαι τοὺς αἰχμαλώτους;
3. εἰ ἡ τῶν Ἑλλήνων στρατιὰ πρὸς τὴν θάλατταν ἐπορεύσατο, οἱ πολέμιοι οὐκ ἂν ἐστράτευον ἐπὶ τοὺς Ἀθηναίους.
4. οἱ ἵπποι ἐκωλύθησαν ὑπὸ τῶν καμήλων.
5. οἱ ἱππεῖς οὐχ οἷοί τ' ἦσαν παῦσαι τοὺς πολεμίους ἔξω τοῦ ἄστεως.
6. ὁ παῖς ἐπαύσατο τοῦ ἔργου· ἐβλάβη γὰρ τὸ σῶμα.
7. οὐκ ἐπιθόμεθα τοῖς τοῦ ῥήτορος λόγοις.
8. οἱ παῖδες παρὰ τῷ ποταμῷ ἦσαν καὶ ηὗρον πολλὰ χρήματα.
9. οἱ στρατιῶται ἤθελον μάχεσθαι ὑπὲρ τῆς πατρίδος.
10. οἱ Ἀθηναῖοι εἶχον τὸ στρατόπεδον ἐγγὺς τῆς κώμης.

EXERCISE 77.

1. We ransomed the general who was a prisoner of the Persians.
2. The hoplites were marching to the big town.
3. Wise men obey the laws that are written by the judges.
4. We are not able to send the army immediately.
5. The sailors ceased from the sea battle.
6. Many of the Athenians of that time educated themselves in wisdom.
7. Were you fighting the Persians or other foreigners?
8. We remained outside the walls of the city and drove away the cavalry of the enemy.
9. The general captured many of the weapons after the battle.
10. The judge said good things about the boys who were good at training horses.

5. Time expressions

The oblique cases in Greek (gen., dat., acc.) are used without preposition for different expressions of time.

- The accusative expresses *duration* or *length* of time, how long something lasts (similar to the extent of space, above, sec. 4).

  οἱ πολέμιοι ἔφευγον πέντε ἡμέρας

  The enemy were fleeing *for five days.*

- The dative expresses a *point in time*, the time at which something happens.

  ὁ στρατηγὸς ἔταξε τὴν στρατιὰν τῇ πέμπτῃ ἡμέρᾳ.

  The general drew up his army *on the fifth day.*

- The genitive expresses a range of time *within which* something happens.

  πέμψει τοὺς στρατιώτας πέντε ἡμερῶν.

  He will send the soldiers *within five days.*

  τῆς νυκτὸς ἐμένομεν ἐν τῇ οἰκίᾳ.

  At night we stayed in the house.

Some people find it helpful to visualize the accusative expression as a *line* along which an event continues; the dative as a *point* pinpointing the moment of an event; and the genitive as a *circle* or *window* representing the time within which an event occurs.

EXERCISE 78.

1. ἐμένομεν τὸν Ξενοφῶντα ἐν τῇ νήσῳ πέντε ἡμέρας.
2. ὁ ἔρως τῶν χρημάτων κίνδυνός ἐστι τοῖς κακοῖς.
3. ὀλίγων μηνῶν ἡ Ἑλλὰς ἐλευθέρα ἔσται.
4. οἱ δέκα στρατιῶται παρασκευάζουσι τὰ ὅπλα τῆς νυκτός.
5. πολλὰς ἡμέρας τὸ ναυτικὸν αὐτῶν ἐν τῷ λιμένι ἐμάχετο.
6. αἱ νῆες ἑτοῖμαι ἦσαν τῇ πέμπτῃ ἡμέρᾳ.
7. ὁ δοῦλος ἀπῆν ὀλίγας νύκτας ἀπὸ τῆς οἰκίας.
8. τῷ δεκάτῳ μηνὶ φαμὲν θύσειν τῇ μεγάλῃ θεᾷ.
9. ὀλίγοι τῶν νόμων ἀρχαιότατοι ἦσαν.
10. ἔταξα ἂν τοὺς ἱππέας, εἰ μὴ διὰ τὸν φόβον τῶν καμήλων ἔφυγον.

EXERCISE 79.

1. For five nights we were waiting for the allies.
2. Within ten days I shall bring back the soldiers who remain on the island.
3. On the same day we drove the enemy to the sea.
4. The war will stop within a few days, for the general drew up the hoplites for battle immediately.
5. If he were wiser, he would have taken the money for himself [*use middle*].

6. For ten years the city was ruled by a wise king.
7. For ten nights we were hindered by the cavalry.
8. Many of the laws were difficult for the citizens.
9. The herald said that the fleet had pursued the enemy for much time.
10. Some march by night, others by day.

READING.

VICTORY IN BAD WEATHER

Further episodes in the march of the Ten Thousand.

ἐν δὲ τῇ Ἀρμενίᾳ ἔπιπτε χιὼν πλείστη, ἣ ἀπέκρυψε καὶ τὰ ὅπλα καὶ τοὺς ἀνθρώπους· καὶ τὰ ὑποζύγια ἐκώλυσεν ἡ χιών· ἐν δὲ τῷ στρατοπέδῳ οἱ στρατιῶται ἐν ἀθυμίᾳ ἦσαν. ἐπεὶ δὲ Ξενοφῶν ἔσπευσε γυμνὸς κόψαι ξύλα, εὐθὺς καὶ ἄλλοι ἔκοπτον καὶ πῦρ ἔκαιον. ἔπειτα δὲ ὁ Ξενοφῶν ἐκέλευσε τοὺς στρατιώτας ἀπολιπεῖν τὸ χωρίον [*the place*], καὶ φυγεῖν εἰς τὰς κώμας εἰς οἰκίας.

ἀγγέλλει δ' αὐτοῖς αἰχμάλωτος ὅτι πολέμιοι ἐγγύς εἰσι καὶ ἐθέλουσι μάχεσθαι [-σθαι is infinitive ending] αὐτοῖς ἐν τῇ τοῦ ὄρους εἰσβολῇ. οἱ οὖν στρατηγοὶ συνήγαγον τὸν στρατὸν ἀπὸ τῶν κωμῶν καὶ ἐκέλευσαν τοὺς μὲν φυλάττειν τὸ στρατόπεδον, τοὺς δὲ πορεύεσθαι ἐπὶ τοὺς βαρβάρους· ὁ δὲ αἰχμάλωτος ἡγεμὼν ἦν αὐτοῖς. ἐπεὶ δὲ ὑπερέβαλλον τὸ ὄρος, οἱ πελτασταὶ οὐκ ἔμενον τοὺς ὁπλίτας, ἀλλὰ κραυγῇ ἔσπευδον ἐπὶ τὸ τῶν βαρβάρων στρατόπεδον. οἱ δὲ βάρβαροι, ὡς ἤκουσαν τὸν θόρυβον, οὐχ ὑπέμενον, ἀλλ' ἔφευγον. οἱ δὲ Ἕλληνες ὀλίγους τῶν βαρβάρων ἀποκτείνουσι καὶ λαμβάνουσιν εἴκοσιν ἵππους καὶ τὴν τοῦ ἄρχοντος σκηνὴν καὶ ἐν αὐτῇ κλίνας ἀργύρου καὶ ἐκπώματα. οἱ δὲ τῶν ὁπλιτῶν στρατηγοὶ ἐκέλευσαν τοὺς πελταστὰς παύσασθαι τῆς μάχης καὶ πορεύσασθαι πάλιν εἰς τὸ τῶν Ἑλλήνων στρατόπεδον.

Adapted from Xenophon, *Anabasis* IV.iv

Chapter 17 Vocabulary

From now on, the chapter vocabulary includes all principal parts of new verbs; dashes indicate that a principal part is not attested. The 4th and 5th principal parts will be presented later (Ch. 31.2-3, 32.1, 3). Appendix 1 is a complete list of principal parts.

Verbs:

δέχομαι, δέξομαι, ἐδεξάμην, —, δέδεγμαι, —	receive
λύομαι	ransom
μάχομαι, μαχοῦμαι, ἐμαχεσάμην, —, μεμάχημαι, — (+ *dat.*)	fight
μιμνῄσκω / μιμνήσκω, μνήσω, ἔμνησα, —, μέμνημαι, ἐμνήσθην	remind
μιμνῄσκομαι / μιμνήσκομαι	remember, mention
ὀνομάζω, ὀνομάσω, ὠνόμασα, ὠνόμακα, ὠνόμασμαι, ὠνομάσθην	name, call (by name)
παύομαι (+ *gen.*)	cease from
πείθομαι, πείσομαι, ἐπιθόμην, —, πέπεισμαι, ἐπείσθην (+ *dat.*)	obey
πορεύω, πορεύσω, ἐπόρευσα, —, πεπόρευμαι, ἐπορεύθην	carry, convey
πορεύομαι	march, journey

Nouns:

αἰχμάλωτος, -ου, ὁ	prisoner (of war)	μήν, μηνός, ὁ	month
		νόμος, -ου, ὁ	law
κεφαλή, -ῆς, ἡ	head	χρόνος, -ου, ὁ	time

Adjectives:

δέκατος, -η, -ον	tenth	πέμπτος, -η, -ον	fifth

Prepositions:

ἐγγύς (+ *gen.*)	near	παρά (+ *dat.*)	beside
ἔξω (+ *gen.*)	outside	πρό (+ *gen.*)	before, in front of

Adverb:

ἐγγύς	near

Numbers:

πέντε (*not declinable*)	five	**δέκα** (*not declinable*)	ten

CHAPTER 18

νίψον ἀνομήματα, μὴ μόναν ὄψιν.
— Greek palindrome (*Palatine Anthology* 16.387c line 5)

1. Active imperatives of thematic verbs

You learned the present 2nd person imperatives in Ch. 8.3. There are also 3rd person imperatives, corresponding to English 'Let him come!', 'They are to stay!'. These imperatives all exist in the aorist tense as well. The difference between the present and aorist imperatives is one of aspect, not time (Ch. 5.3, 13.4). When it refers to a continuing action, the imperative is present. When it refers to a single act, the imperative is aorist.

μενόντων οἱ ναῦται.
Let the sailors remain.

λῦσον τὸν ἵππον.
Loose the horse.

The present and aorist imperatives are formed as follows. (There is also a rare perfect imperative, which need not be learned now.)

Present		Active	Middle / Passive
Sing.	2nd	λῦ-ε	λύ-ου (-ε-σο)
	3rd	λυ-έ-τω	λυ-έ-σθω
Plur.	2nd	λύ-ε-τε	λύ-ε-σθε
	3rd	λυ-ό-ντων	λυ-έ-σθων

Weak Aorist		Active	Middle	Passive
Sing.	2nd	λῦ-σον	λῦ-σαι	λύ-θη-τι
	3rd	λυ-σά-τω	λυ-σά-σθω	λυ-θή-τω
Plur.	2nd	λύ-σα-τε	λύ-σα-σθε	λύ-θη-τε
	3rd	λυ-σά-ντων	λυ-σά-σθων	λυ-θέ-ντων

Strong Aorist (λείπω)		ACTIVE	MIDDLE	PASSIVE
Sing.	2nd	λίπ-ε	λιπ-οῦ (λιπ-ε-σο)	λείφ-θη-τι
	3rd	λιπ-έ-τω	λιπ-έ-σθω	λειφ-θή-τω
Plur.	2nd	λίπ-ε-τε	λίπ-ε-σθε	λείφ-θη-τε
	3rd	λιπ-ό-ντων	λιπ-έ-σθων	λειφ-θέ-ντων

Note: Five verbs have the 2nd singular active accent on the ultima (Position 1).

εἶπον (λέγω)	εἰπέ (Ch. 27)	λαμβάνω	λαβέ
ἔρχομαι	ἐλθέ (Ch. 26)	ὁράω	ἰδέ
εὑρίσκω	εὑρέ		

2. Imperatives of εἰμί, 'be'

The only tense of the imperative of εἰμί, 'be' is the present. You learned the 2nd person in Ch. 8.3; there is also a 3rd person.

Sing.	2nd	ἴσθι
	3rd	ἔστω
Plur.	2nd	ἔστε
	3rd	ὄντων

3. Future and aorist middle and passive infinitives of thematic verbs

The active infinitives were presented earlier (present, Ch. 6.3; future and aorist, Ch. 13.3). The middle and passive infinitives are formed and accented as follows; as in the indicative, the present forms are the same, but the future and aorist forms are different.

Form summary

- Present

  M/P: present stem + **ε** + -**σθαι** = -**εσθαι** λύεσθαι, πείθεσθαι
  accent on the stem

- Future

  M: future stem + **ε** + -**σθαι** = -**σεσθαι** λύσεσθαι, πείσεσθαι
  P: future stem + **ε** + -**σθαι** = -**θησεσθαι** λυθήσεσθαι, πεισθήσεσθαι
  accent on the stem (middle) or the **θη** (passive)

- Weak aorist

  M: aorist stem + **σα** + -**σθαι** = -**σασθαι** λύσασθαι
  P: aorist stem + -**ναι** = -**θηναι** λυθῆναι, πεισθῆναι
  accent on the stem (middle) or the **θη** (passive)

- Strong aorist

M:	aorist stem + **ε** + -**σθαι**	= -**εσθαι**	πιθέσθαι
P:	aorist stem + -**ναι**	= -**ηναι**	γραφῆναι

accent on the **ε** (middle) or the **η** (passive)

4. The future infinitive of εἰμί, 'be'

The future infinitive of εἰμί is ἔσεσθαι. The present infinitive, εἶναι, was introduced in Ch. 7.5. The only other tense of this verb is the imperfect, which has no infinitive form.

EXERCISE 80.

1. σώσατε τὴν πατρίδα, ὦ στρατιῶται.
2. πιστευόντων οἱ νεανίαι τοῖς τοῦ Σωκράτους λόγοις.
3. ὁ δοῦλος μέλλει λύσειν τὸν βοῦν.
4. εὐθὺς λυθέντων οἱ αἰχμάλωτοι.
5. εὗρε τὸν γέροντα, ὦ παῖ.
6. μενέτω ἡ εἰρήνη, ὦ πολῖται.
7. βουλευέσθων οἱ σύμμαχοι περὶ τοῦ πολέμου.
8. ἐλπίζεις δῶρον δέξεσθαι ἀπὸ τοῦ νεανίου;
9. οἱ μετὰ τοῦ Ξενοφῶντος ἔμελλον πορεύσεσθαι πρὸς τὴν θάλατταν.
10. καλὸν ἦν τοῖς Ἀθηναίοις σῶσαι τὴν πατρίδα.

EXERCISE 81.

1. Persuade the allies to remember those in the city.
2. Trust the ships, citizens.
3. The enemy intended to ransom their general.
4. Let there be peace in the country.
5. The herald said that the soldiers had destroyed the enemy.
6. The good slave hopes to find money.
7. Order him not to say foolish things.
8. The old men were about to be saved by the fleet.
9. Send the children to the village immediately, or they will be harmed.
10. You yourself will be free within a few months.

5. Personal pronouns, 1st and 2nd persons

The personal pronouns 'I / we' and 'you' are formed in Greek as follows.

		I / we		you	
Sing.	Nom.	ἐγώ		σύ	
	Gen.	ἐμοῦ	μου	σοῦ	σου
	Dat.	ἐμοί	μοι	σοί	σοι
	Acc.	ἐμέ	με	σέ	σε
Plur.	Nom.	ἡμεῖς		ὑμεῖς	
	Gen.	ἡμῶν		ὑμῶν	
	Dat.	ἡμῖν		ὑμῖν	
	Acc.	ἡμᾶς		ὑμᾶς	

The forms without accents are enclitic; therefore they can never begin a clause. Rarely are they used after a preposition. The accented forms are more emphatic. The nominative is *only* used for extra emphasis, since the verb ending already gives the same information.

Unemphatic	**Emphatic**
πείθεταί μοι. He obeys me.	πείθεται ἐμοί. He obeys *me* [and not you].
πείθομαι τοῖς νόμοις. I obey the laws.	ἐγὼ πείθομαι τοῖς νόμοις *I* obey the laws [but you don't].
ἔσωσας τὴν στρατιάν. You saved the army.	σὺ ἔσωσας τὴν στρατιάν. It was *you* who saved the army.

6. Possessive adjectives, 1st and 2nd persons

As you know (Ch. 4.4), an article can imply possession if the context is clear.

πειθομαι τῷ πατρί.
I obey my father.

Greek does have possessive adjectives, though, for the 1st and 2nd persons. They are formed from the personal pronouns and mean 'my', 'our', 'your'. They are declined like regular 1st and 2nd declension adjectives (Ch. 7.1).

ἐμός, ἐμή, ἐμόν	my	ἡμέτερος, -ᾱ, -ον	our
σός, σή, σόν	your (*sing.*)	ὑμέτερος, -ᾱ, -ον	your (*plur.*)

For the 1st and 2nd person, possession in Greek is conveyed either by a possessive adjective, or by the genitive of the personal pronoun. These phrases *always* include the article. The possessive adjective is always attributive (preceded by the article); the pronoun is always predicate.

ὁ ἐμὸς ἵππος
ὁ ἵππος μου
  my horse

Note: For the 3rd person, there is no possessive adjective; possession is expressed with the genitive pronoun αὐτοῦ, αὐτῆς, αὐτοῦ, αὐτῶν (Ch. 9.3).

ἔλυσα τὸν δοῦλον αὐτοῦ.
  I set free his slave.

EXERCISE 82. Write in Greek, with the noun in the case indicated:

1. Nom.: Your (s.) victory (*two ways*), their money
2. Gen.: His name, your (s.) prisoners (*two ways*)
3. Dat.: My house (*two ways*), our wives (*two ways*)
4. Acc.: Your (pl.) king (*two ways*), my city (*two ways*)

EXERCISE 83.

1. ὑμεῖς μὲν ἀνδρεῖοί ἐστε, ἐγὼ δὲ δειλός.
2. οἱ πολέμιοι οὐ καταλύσουσι τὴν ἡμετέραν πόλιν.
3. ἔμνησα τὸν ἐμὸν παῖδα τὰ ἔργα.
4. πολλοὶ ἵπποι ὑμῖν εἰσιν;
5. εἰ ὁ στρατηγὸς ἔλαβε τὰς ναῦς, ἐκέλευσεν ἂν ὑμᾶς πορεῦσαι αὐτὰς εἰς τὸν λιμένα.
6. ἡ Ἀρτεμισία παρῆν ἐν τῇ ναυμαχίᾳ· ὁ δὲ Ξέρξης ἐθαύμαζε τὴν ἀνδρείαν αὐτῆς.
7. οὔποτε πείσομεν ὑμᾶς μαχέσασθαι· ὁ γὰρ ὑμέτερος φόβος τοῦ πολέμου μεγάλη ἐστίν.
8. ἡ πόλις ἡμῶν ἀεὶ ἐλευθέρα ὠνομάζετο.
9. ὁ θεὸς ἡμᾶς κελεύει πιστεύειν ταῖς ναυσίν ἃς παρεσκευάσαμεν, εἰ ἐθέλομεν τοὺς Πέρσας ἀπελαύνειν.
10. ἐπιστεύσαμέν τε τῷ Δημοσθένει καὶ ἐπιθόμεθα τοῖς λόγοις αὐτοῦ.

EXERCISE 84.

1. The slave did not want to stay with me.
2. If you are wise, Socrates is wiser.
3. It is difficult for us to trust you or your father.
4. Is your fleet smaller than ours?
5. I ransomed my soldiers from the Spartans, and they marched away to our city.
6. The allies are not willing to die on our behalf.
7. We will obey you, Socrates.

8. We persuaded your father not to remain with us.
9. It was you who captured the city.
10. My slave is wiser than yours.

READING.

DOUBLE DEALINGS OF THEMISTOCLES

Although the Greeks had won a decisive naval victory at Salamis, the Persian army was not yet defeated, and this accounts for the attitude of the Spartans shown in this piece. When later in his life Themistocles lost his countrymen's trust and was exiled, he claimed credit from the Persians for having tried to help them.

μετὰ δὲ τὴν ἐν Σαλαμῖνι ναυμαχίαν, ὁ Θεμιστοκλῆς πρῶτον συνεβούλευε τοῖς Ἕλλησι διῶξαι τὸ τῶν Περσῶν ναυτικὸν καὶ λῦσαι τὰς ἐν τῷ Ἑλλησπόντῳ γεφύρας. ὁ δὲ Εὐρυβιάδης, ὁ τῶν Λακεδαιμονίων στρατηγός, τοὺς Ἕλληνας ἔπεισε μὴ καταλῦσαι τὰς γεφύρας. Ἄλλως γάρ, ἔλεξεν, ἀναγκαῖον ἔσται τῷ Πέρσῃ ἐν τῇ Ἑλλάδι μένειν· οὕτω δὲ οἷός τ' ἔσται καταστρέψασθαι τὴν ὅλην Εὐρώπην.

ὁ δὲ Θεμιστοκλῆς, οὐ γὰρ ἐνόμισε πείσειν τοὺς πολλοὺς στρατεύειν εἰς τὸν Ἑλλήσποντον, ἔλεγεν αὐτοῖς· Οὐχ ἡμεῖς ἐσώσαμεν ἡμᾶς αὐτούς τε καὶ τὴν Ἑλλάδα, ἀλλ' οἱ θεοὶ οἳ οὐκ ἤθελον τὸν αὐτὸν ἄνδρα τῆς τε Ἀσίας καὶ τῆς Εὐρώπης βασιλεῦσαι. νῦν οὖν ἀγαθόν ἐστι βασιλέα μὲν πορεύσασθαι εἰς τὴν Ἀσίαν, ἡμᾶς δὲ καταμένειν ἐν τῇ Ἑλλάδι. Θεμιστοκλῆς μὲν οὕτως ἔλεξεν, ὅτι ἀποθήκην ἔμελλε σχήσειν χάριτος πρὸς βασιλεῖ, οἱ δὲ Ἀθηναῖοι ἐπείθοντο· ἐνόμιζον γὰρ αὐτὸν σοφώτατον ἄνδρα εἶναι.

ἔπειτα δὲ ὁ Θεμιστοκλῆς ἔπεμψεν κήρυκας πρὸς βασιλέα, ἐν οἷς καὶ Σίκιννος ὁ οἰκέτης ἦν· καὶ ὁ Σίκιννος ἔλεγε τῷ Ξέρξῃ ὧδε· Ἔπεμψέ με ὁ Θεμιστοκλῆς, στρατηγὸς μὲν Ἀθηναίων, ἀνὴρ δὲ τῶν συμμάχων σοφώτατος· ὅτι βούλεται εὐεργέτης σοι εἶναι, ἔπεισε τοὺς Ἕλληνας μήτε διῶξαι τὰς σὰς ναῦς μήτε τὰς ἐν τῷ Ἑλλησπόντῳ γεφύρας καταλῦσαι. καὶ νῦν οἷός τ' ἔσει σῴζεσθαι εἰς τὴν σὴν χώραν.

Adapted from Herodotus VIII.108-110

Chapter 18 Vocabulary

Verbs:

βουλεύομαι	deliberate
βουλεύω, βουλεύσω, ἐβούλευσα, βεβούλευκα, βεβούλευμαι, ἐβουλεύθην	plan
πάρειμι, παρέσομαι	be present, be here, be there

Noun:

Ἀρτεμισία, -ας, ἡ	Artemisia

Adjectives:

δειλός, -ή, -όν	cowardly	**σός**, σή, σόν	your (*sing.*)
ἐμός, -ή, -όν	my	**ὑμέτερος**, -α, -ον	your (*pl.*)
ἡμέτερος, -α, -ον	our		

Pronouns:

ἐγώ, ἐμοῦ / μου	I	**σύ**, σοῦ / σου	you (*sing.*)
ἡμεῖς, ἡμῶν	we	**ὑμεῖς**, ὑμῶν	you (*pl.*)

Adverb:

οὔποτε	never

Preposition:

μετά (+ *gen.*)	with

CHAPTER 19

τάχιστον νοῦς· διὰ παντὸς γὰρ τρέχει.

— Thales (Diogenes Laertius, *vitae philosophorum* 1.35)

1. Contract verbs

Contract verbs are thematic verbs whose 1st principal part ends in a short vowel (**α**, **ε** or **ο**). This *contract vowel* must contract with the thematic vowel in the present and imperfect tenses. Dictionaries list the uncontracted form, but Attic Greek always uses the contracted forms. In the other principal parts, the contract vowel is lengthened, so no contractions occur.

The weakest vowel is **ε**, and the strongest is **ο/ω**. Contractions always result in a long form of the stronger vowel involved.

ε + ε = ει	α + ε = ᾱ	ο + ε = ου
ε + ει = ει	α + ει = ᾱͅ	ο + ει = οι
ε + ο = ου	α + ο = ω	ο + ο = ου
ε + ου = ου	α + ου = ω	ο + ου = ου
ε + ω = ω	α + ω = ω	ο + ω = ω

Note: The accent is already in place before the contraction occurs. If an accented syllable is contracted, the accent remains on the contracted syllable, and follows the accent rule for its new position.

2. Contract verbs in -εω

INDICATIVE Present		Active		Middle / Passive	
Sing.	1st	φιλῶ	(φιλέ-ω)	φιλοῦμαι	(φιλέ-ομαι)
	2nd	φιλεῖς	(φιλέ-εις)	φιλῇ / φιλεῖ	(φιλέ-εσαι)
	3rd	φιλεῖ	(φιλέ-ει)	φιλεῖται	(φιλέ-εται)
Plur.	1st	φιλοῦμεν	(φιλέ-ομεν)	φιλούμεθα	(φιλε-όμεθα)
	2nd	φιλεῖτε	(φιλέ-ετε)	φιλεῖσθε	(φιλέ-εσθε)
	3rd	φιλοῦσι(ν)	(φιλέ-ουσι)	φιλοῦνται	(φιλέ-ονται)

INDICATIVE Imperfect		ACTIVE		MIDDLE / PASSIVE	
Sing.	1st	ἐφίλουν	(ἐφίλε-ον)	ἐφιλούμην	(ἐφιλε-όμην)
	2nd	ἐφίλεις	(ἐφίλε-ες)	ἐφιλοῦ	(ἐφιλέ-εσο)
	3rd	ἐφίλει	(ἐφίλε-ε)	ἐφιλεῖτο	(ἐφιλέ-ετο)
Plur.	1st	ἐφιλοῦμεν	(ἐφιλέ-ομεν)	ἐφιλούμεθα	(ἐφιλε-όμεθα)
	2nd	ἐφιλεῖτε	(ἐφιλέ-ετε)	ἐφιλεῖσθε	(ἐφιλέ-εσθε)
	3rd	ἐφίλουν	(ἐφίλε-ον)	ἐφιλοῦντο	(ἐφιλέ-οντο)
IMPERATIVE					
Sing.	2nd	φίλει	(φίλε-ε)	φιλοῦ	(φιλέ-εσο)
	3rd	φιλείτω	(φιλε-έτω)	φιλείσθω	(φιλε-έσθω)
Plur.	2nd	φιλεῖτε	(φιλέ-ετε)	φιλεῖσθε	(φιλέ-εσθε)
	3rd	φιλούντων	(φιλε-όντων)	φιλείσθων	(φιλε-έσθων)
INFINITIVE					
		φιλεῖν	(φιλέ-ε-εν)	φιλεῖσθαι	(φιλέ-εσθαι)

EXERCISE 85. Identify and translate the following forms.

(*a*)

1. φιλοῦμεν
2. ἐφιλήθη
3. βοηθεῖτε
4. ἐποιεῖτο
5. ζητοῦσι
6. ἐβοηθοῦμεν
7. ἐφιλεῖσθε
8. ἐβοηθήσαμεν
9. βοηθεῖν
10. ποιηθήσεται
11. ἐβοηθοῦντο
12. ἐφίλησε
13. ζητεῖς
14. ποιηθῆναι
15. ἐζήτει

(*b*)

1. They made
2. You (pl.) make
3. We were seeking
4. He is loved
5. You (s.) help
6. To be loved
7. They loved
8. He was helped
9. I will make
10. He was helping
11. You (s.) were being helped
12. We helped
13. To keep seeking
14. Seek (s.)
15. She will be sought

3. Impersonal δεῖ

The contract verb δέω is used impersonally in the 3rd singular to mean 'it is necessary'. It is followed by the accusative and an infinitive (negative μή), but English translation can be flexible. The following examples show the present, future and imperfect; these are the only forms you need for now.

δεῖ ἡμᾶς μὴ φυγεῖν.
It is necessary for us not to flee.
We must not flee.

δεήσει τὸν παῖδα χρήματα εὑρεῖν.
It will be necessary for the child to find money.
The child will have to find money.

ἔδει τὸν στρατηγὸν διῶξαι τοὺς πολεμίους.
It was necessary for the general to pursue the enemy.
The general had to pursue the enemy.

EXERCISE 86.

1. εἰ οἱ φυγάδες φιλοῦσι τοὺς Πέρσας, μῶροί εἰσιν.
2. οἱ πολέμιοι οἷς ἐμαχεσάμεθα εὖ ἐποίουν τὰς γυναῖκάς τε καὶ τὰ τέκνα.
3. ἐν μὲν τῷ πολέμῳ οἱ Ἀθηναῖοι ἐποίησαν τὸν Θεμιστοκλῆ στρατηγόν, νῦν δὲ ἀπέφυγεν.
4. αἱ κάμηλοι ἐβοήθησαν τῷ Κύρῳ ἐν τῇ μάχῃ.
5. δεῖ τὴν ἡμετέραν πατρίδα ἀεὶ φιλεῖσθαι, ὡς ὁ δῆμος ἀγαθοὺς νόμους ἐποίει.

EXERCISE 87.

1. The king of the Persians never treated his soldiers well.
2. It was necessary for us to help the king with our weapons.
3. Some men treat slaves well, others badly.
4. Always help your country, citizens, and you will receive great honor.
5. If the cavalry had captured the general of the allies we would not be seeking him now.

4. Contract verbs in -αω

INDICATIVE Present		Active		Middle / Passive	
Sing.	1st	τιμῶ	(τιμά-ω)	τιμῶμαι	(τιμά-ομαι)
	2nd	τιμᾷς	(τιμά-εις)	τιμᾷ	(τιμά-εσαι)
	3rd	τιμᾷ	(τιμά-ει)	τιμᾶται	(τιμά-εται)
Plur.	1st	τιμῶμεν	(τιμά-ομεν)	τιμώμεθα	(τιμα-όμεθα)
	2nd	τιμᾶτε	(τιμά-ετε)	τιμᾶσθε	(τιμά-εσθε)
	3rd	τιμῶσι(ν)	(τιμά-ουσι)	τιμῶνται	(τιμά-ονται)
Imperfect					
Sing.	1st	ἐτίμων	(ἐτίμα-ον)	ἐτιμώμην	(ἐτιμα-όμην)
	2nd	ἐτίμας	(ἐτίμα-ες)	ἐτιμῶ	(ἐτιμά-εσο)
	3rd	ἐτίμα	(ἐτίμα-ε)	ἐτιμᾶτο	(ἐτιμά-ετο)
Plur.	1st	ἐτιμῶμεν	(ἐτιμά-ομεν)	ἐτιμώμεθα	(ἐτιμα-όμεθα)
	2nd	ἐτιμᾶτε	(ἐτιμά-ετε)	ἐτιμᾶσθε	(ἐτιμά-εσθε)
	3rd	ἐτίμων	(ἐτίμα-ον)	ἐτιμῶντο	(ἐτιμά-οντο)

IMPERATIVE		ACTIVE		MIDDLE / PASSIVE	
Sing.	2nd	τίμα	(τίμα-ε)	τιμῶ	(τιμά-εσο)
	3rd	τιμάτω	(τιμα-έτω)	τιμάσθω	(τιμα-έσθω)
Plur.	2nd	τιμᾶτε	(τιμά-ετε)	τιμᾶσθε	(τιμά-εσθε)
	3rd	τιμώντων	(τιμα-όντων)	τιμάσθων	(τιμα-έσθων)
INFINITIVE					
		τιμᾶν	(τιμά-ε-εν)	τιμᾶσθαι	(τιμά-εσθαι)

EXERCISE 88. Identify and translate the following forms.

(*a*)
1. νικῶσι
2. ἐτιμώμεθα
3. εἶδε
4. ἐνίκων
5. νικᾶτε
6. βοᾶν
7. ὤφθημεν
8. νικηθήσεται
9. ἐτίμησας
10. τίμα
11. ὄψεσθαι
12. ἐβόα
13. ὁρᾷς
14. βοήσονται
15. τιμᾶσθαι

(*b*)
1. We conquer
2. They are seen
3. You (s.) honor
4. They (pl.) see
5. We were shouting
6. I will see
7. He shouts
8. He was winning
9. Honor (pl.)
10. To honor (aor.)
11. They will shout
12. You (pl.) saw
13. You (s.) were conquered
14. She will be honored
15. Shout (s.)

EXERCISE 89.

1. χαλεπὸν ἦν τοῖς Ἕλλησι νικῆσαι τοὺς Πέρσας.
2. ὁ Ξέρξης ὁρᾷ τὴν ναυμαχίαν ἐν ᾗ ἡ Ἀρτεμισία κατέλυσε ναῦν φιλίαν.
3. ἐλπίζετε ὄψεσθαι τὴν θάλατταν ἀπὸ τοῦ ὄρους, ὦ σύμμαχοι;
4. ἀγαθόν ἐστι τιμηθῆναι ὑπὸ τοῦ δήμου.
5. τιμῶμεν ὑμᾶς, ὦ παῖδες, ὡς πείθεσθε τοῖς τε πατράσι καὶ ταῖς μητράσιν.

EXERCISE 90.

1. The young men saw the battle.
2. We conquered the army of the enemy.
3. Wise men were not always honored by the Athenians.
4. The Persians will be conquered in the sea battle.
5. Demosthenes wished to be honored by the citizens.

5. Contract verbs in -οω

INDICATIVE Present		ACTIVE		MIDDLE / PASSIVE	
Sing.	1st	δηλῶ	(δηλό-ω)	δηλοῦμαι	(δηλό-ομαι)
	2nd	δηλοῖς	(δηλό-εις)	δηλοῖ	(δηλό-εσαι)
	3rd	δηλοῖ	(δηλό-ει)	δηλοῦται	(δηλό-εται)
Plur.	1st	δηλοῦμεν	(δηλό-ομεν)	δηλούμεθα	(δηλο-όμεθα)
	2nd	δηλοῦτε	(δηλό-ετε)	δηλοῦσθε	(δηλό-εσθε)
	3rd	δηλοῦσι(ν)	(δηλό-ουσι)	δηλοῦνται	(δηλό-ονται)
Imperfect					
Sing.	1st	ἐδήλουν	(ἐδήλο-ον)	ἐδηλούμην	(ἐδηλο-όμην)
	2nd	ἐδήλους	(ἐδήλο-ες)	ἐδηλοῦ	(ἐδηλό-εσο)
	3rd	ἐδήλου	(ἐδήλο-ε)	ἐδηλοῦτο	(ἐδηλό-ετο)
Plur.	1st	ἐδηλοῦμεν	(ἐδηλό-ομεν)	ἐδηλούμεθα	(ἐδηλο-όμεθα)
	2nd	ἐδηλοῦτε	(ἐδηλό-ετε)	ἐδηλοῦσθε	(ἐδηλό-εσθε)
	3rd	ἐδήλουν	(ἐδήλο-ον)	ἐδηλοῦντο	(ἐδηλό-οντο)
IMPERATIVE					
Sing.	2nd	δήλου	(δήλο-ε)	δηλοῦ	(δηλό-εσο)
	3rd	δηλούτω	(δηλο-έτω)	δηλούσθω	(δηλο-έσθω)
Plur.	2nd	δηλοῦτε	(δηλό-ετε)	δηλοῦσθε	(δηλό-εσθε)
	3rd	δηλούντων	(δηλο-όντων)	δηλούσθων	(δηλο-έσθων)
INFINITIVE					
		δηλοῦν	(δηλό-ε-εν)	δηλοῦσθαι	(δηλό-εσθαι)

EXERCISE 91. Identify and translate the following forms.

(*a*)
1. δηλοῖ
2. ἐδήλους
3. ἐδουλώθη
4. ἠλευθεροῦμεν
5. ἐδήλωσας
6. ἐλευθερούμεθα
7. δήλου
8. δουλοῦσθαι
9. ἐδήλου
10. δουλωθήσονται
11. δουλώσετε
12. δηλοῦν
13. ἠλευθεροῦντο
14. δηλῶσαι
15. ἐλευθεροῖ

(*b*)
1. We show
2. He will free
3. They were freed
4. You (pl.) will show
5. He enslaves
6. To enslave (aor.)
7. To be shown
8. I was showing
9. He was freeing
10. Show (pl.)
11. You (s.) were shown
12. We shall be freed
13. They were enslaving
14. To be shown (pres.)
15. It was shown

EXERCISE 92.

1. ὁ ἡγεμὼν δηλοῖ τὴν ὁδὸν τοῖς Ἕλλησιν.
2. χαλεπὸν ἔσται ἐλευθεροῦσθαι ἀπὸ τῶν βαρβάρων.
3. οὐ μέλλομεν δουλώσειν ὑμᾶς, ὦ ἄνδρες.
4. ἡ Ἑλλὰς οὔποτε ἐδουλώθη, ὡς ἰσχυρὰ ἦν.
5. ἡ πόλις ἐλευθεροῦται ὑπὸ τοῦ στρατηγοῦ αὐτοῦ.

EXERCISE 93.

1. We do not show the way to bad men.
2. The soldiers are freeing the country from the enemy.
3. The city was enslaved by foreigners.
4. The citizen was showing to me the road to the harbor.
5. Free your city from the Persians, citizens.

6. Contract nouns and adjectives

Some nouns and adjectives also undergo contraction in Attic Greek (such as Ξενοφῶν, -ῶντος, ὁ, Ch. 10.1). The following examples show the contraction of stems in **-εα-** and **-οο-**. The contraction produces a long ultima, and the Position 1 accent is always circumflex. The noun γῆ, 'earth' has no plural.

		earth			mind		
Sing.	Nom.	ἡ	γῆ	(γέ-ᾱ)	ὁ	νοῦς	(νό-ος)
	Gen.		γῆς	(γέ-ᾱς)		νοῦ	(νό-ου)
	Dat.		γῇ	(γέ-ᾳ)		νῷ	(νό-ῳ)
	Acc.		γῆν	(γέ-ᾱν)		νοῦν	(νό-ον)
	Voc.		γῆ	(γέ-ᾱ)		νοῦ	(νό-ε)
Plur.	Nom.					νοῖ	(νό-οι)
	Gen.					νῶν	(νό-ων)
	Dat.					νοῖς	(νό-οις)
	Acc.					νοῦς	(νό-ους)
	Voc.					νοῖ	(νό-οι)

silver

		M		F		N	
Sing.	Nom.	ἀργυροῦς	(-έ-ος)	ἀργυρᾶ	(-έ-ᾱ)	ἀργυροῦν	(-έ-ον)
	Gen.	ἀργυροῦ	(-έ-ου)	ἀργυρᾶς	(-έ-ᾱς)	ἀργυροῦ	(-έ-ου)
	Dat.	ἀργυρῷ	(-έ-ῳ)	ἀργυρᾷ	(-έ-ᾳ)	ἀργυρῷ	(-έ-ῳ)
	Acc.	ἀργυροῦν	(-έ-ον)	ἀργυρᾶν	(-έ-ᾱν)	ἀργυροῦν	(-έ-ον)
Plur.	Nom.	ἀργυροῖ	(-έ-οι)	ἀργυραῖ	(-έ-αι)	ἀργυρᾶ	(-έ-α)
	Gen.	ἀργυρῶν	(-έ-ων)	ἀργυρῶν	(-έ-ων)	ἀργυρῶν	(-έ-ων)
	Dat.	ἀργυροῖς	(-έ-οις)	ἀργυραῖς	(-έ-αις)	ἀργυροῖς	(-έ-οις)
	Acc.	ἀργυροῦς	(-έ-ους)	ἀργυρᾶς	(-έ-ᾱς)	ἀργυρᾶ	(-έ-α)

Note: No distinct vocative forms of contract adjectives are known.

READING.

XERXES AND THE HELMSMAN

On his way back from Greece to Asia, says Herodotus, Xerxes actually returned by land to the Hellespont and was ferried across, as the bridges had been destroyed by a storm. He writes that the following alternative account "seems quite unworthy of belief."

ὁ δ' οὖν Ξέρξης ἐνικήθη καὶ ἀπὸ τῶν Ἀθηνῶν ἀπήλασεν· ἐπεὶ δὲ ἧκεν ἐπὶ τὸν Στρυμόνα,[1] οὐκέτι κατὰ γῆν τὴν ὁδὸν ἐποίει, ἀλλὰ τὴν μὲν στρατιὰν τῷ στρατηγῷ ἐπέτρεψε ἀπάγειν εἰς τὸν Ἑλλήσποντον, αὐτὸς δ' ἐπὶ νεὼς Φοινίσσης ἐπορεύετο εἰς τὴν Ἀσίαν. μέγας δὲ ἄνεμός τε καὶ χειμὼν κακῶς ἐποίουν τὴν ναῦν, ἣ ἔμελλε καταδύσεσθαι· πολλοὶ γὰρ Πέρσαι μετὰ βασιλέως ἐπορεύοντο καὶ ἐπὶ τοῦ καταστρώματος ἐπῆσαν. ὡς οὖν εἶδον τὸν κίνδυνον ἐβοῶντο, ὁ δὲ Ξέρξης καὶ ὁ κυβερνήτης ἐβουλεύοντο. καὶ ὁ κυβερνήτης λέγει· Δέσποτα, εἰ βούλει σῶσαι τὴν σὴν ψυχήν, ἀναγκαῖόν ἐστιν ἐλευθεροῦν τὴν ναῦν τῶν πολλῶν ἐπιβατῶν. ὁ δὲ Ξέρξης λέγει τοῖς Πέρσαις, Ἄνδρες Πέρσαι, νῦν καιρός[2] ἐστιν ὑμῖν δηλοῦν τὴν ὑμετέραν πρὸς ἐμὲ φιλίαν· ἐν ὑμῖν γὰρ δοκεῖ εἶναι ἐμοὶ ἡ σωτηρία. οἱ δὲ εὐθὺς ἐξάλλονται εἰς τὴν θάλατταν· καὶ οὕτως ἔσωσαν βασιλέα, ἐπεὶ ἐποίησαν τὴν ναῦν κουφοτέραν. ὁ δὲ Ξέρξης, ὡς ἐν γῇ ἐστίν, ὅτι μὲν ἔσωσε βασιλέως τὴν ψυχήν, παρέχει τῷ κυβερνήτῃ στέφανον χρυσοῦν, ὅτι δὲ πολλοὺς Πέρσας ἀπώλεσε [*destroyed*], ἀποτέμνει τὴν κεφαλὴν αὐτοῦ.

Adapted from Herodotus VIII.118

1 The Strymon river in Macedonia.

2 καιρός, 'precise moment', 'opportunity' as opposed to χρόνος, 'time'.

Chapter 19 Vocabulary

Verbs:

βοάω, βοήσομαι, ἐβόησα, —, —, —	shout
βοηθέω, βοηθήσω, ἐβοήθησα, βεβοήθηκα, βεβοήθημαι, — (+ *dat.*)	help
δεῖ, imperfect ἔδει (+ *dat.*), future δεήσει	it is necessary
δηλόω, δηλώσω, ἐδήλωσα, δεδήλωκα, δεδήλωμαι, ἐδηλώθην	show
δουλόω, δουλώσω, ἐδούλωσα, δεδούλωκα, δεδούλωμαι, ἐδουλώθην	enslave
ἐλευθερόω, ἐλευθερώσω, ἠλευθέρωσα, ἠλευθέρωκα, ἠλευθέρωμαι, ἠλευθερώθην	free
εὖ ποιέω	treat well
ζητέω, ζητήσω, ἐζήτησα, ἐζήτηκα, —, ἐζητήθην	seek
κακῶς ποιέω	treat badly
νικάω, νικήσω, ἐνίκησα, νενίκηκα, νενίκημαι, ἐνικήθην	win; conquer, defeat
ὁράω, ὄψομαι, εἶδον, ἑώρακα, ἑώραμαι, ὤφθην (*aor. stem* **ἰδ-**, *Attic impf.* ἑώρων)	see
ποιέω, ποιήσω, ἐποίησα, πεποίηκα, πεποίημαι, ἐποιήθην	make, do; treat
τιμάω, τιμήσω, ἐτίμησα, τετίμηκα, τετίμημαι, ἐτιμήθην	honor
φιλέω, φιλήσω, ἐφίλησα, πεφίληκα, πεφίλημαι, ἐφιλήθην	love

Nouns:

βίος, -ου, ὁ	life	**νοῦς**, νοῦ, ὁ	mind
γῆ, γῆς, ἡ	land, earth	**τύραννος**, -ου, ὁ	tyrant
δῆμος, -ου, ὁ	people		

Adjectives:

ἀργυροῦς, -ᾶ, -οῦν	of silver	χρυσοῦς, -ῆ, -οῦν	of gold

Conjunction:

ὡς	since, because; as

CHAPTER 20

ὁ βίος βραχύς, ἡ δὲ τέχνη μακρή.

— Hippocratic Aphorisms 1.1

σκηνὴ πᾶς ὁ βίος.

— Palatine Anthology X.72.1

1. Adjectives of the σώφρων and ἀληθής types

These types of adjective have 3rd declension endings, one set for the masculine and feminine and another for the neuter. For the M/F endings of σώφρων, compare ἡγεμών, -όνος, ὁ (Ch. 12.1); for ἀληθής, compare τριήρης, -ους, ἡ (Ch. 13.1).

		prudent		true	
		M/F	N	M/F	N
Sing.	Nom.	σώφρων	σῶφρον	ἀληθής	ἀληθές
	Gen.	σώφρονος	σώφρονος	ἀληθοῦς	ἀληθοῦς
	Dat.	σώφρονι	σώφρονι	ἀληθεῖ	ἀληθεῖ
	Acc.	σώφρονα	σῶφρον	ἀληθῆ	ἀληθές
	Voc.	σῶφρον	σῶφρον	ἀληθές	ἀληθές
Plur.	Nom.	σώφρονες	σώφρονα	ἀληθεῖς	ἀληθῆ
	Gen.	σωφρόνων	σωφρόνων	ἀληθῶν	ἀληθῶν
	Dat.	σώφροσι(ν)	σώφροσι(ν)	ἀληθέσι(ν)	ἀληθέσι(ν)
	Acc.	σώφρονας	σώφρονα	ἀληθεῖς	ἀληθῆ
	Voc.	σώφρονες	σώφρονα	ἀληθεῖς	ἀληθῆ

EXERCISE 94.

1. οἱ εὐγενεῖς οὐκ ἀεὶ εὐδαίμονές εἰσιν.
2. ὁ Ἄδμητος ἐφαίνετο μὲν εἶναι εὐτυχής, ἦν δ' οὔ.
3. ὁ πατὴρ ἔφη τοὺς παῖδας ἀσφαλεῖς ἔσεσθαι ἐν τῇ νήσῳ.
4. ἔδει τοὺς Ἀθηναίους ἀπελαύνειν τοὺς Πέρσας καὶ τοὺς μετ' αὐτῶν ἐκ τῆς Ἑλλάδος.

5. τῶν τυράννων οἱ μὲν τὰ χρήματα φιλοῦσιν, οἱ δὲ τὴν τιμήν.
6. τὰ ἀληθῆ ὑμᾶς ἐλευθέρους ποιήσει.
7. οὔποτε ὁ ἀνὴρ οὗ ὁ νοῦς χαλεπὸς ἦν οὐκ εὖ ἐποίει τοὺς δούλους.
8. πολλοὶ μέν εἰσιν οἱ τοῦ ῥήτορος λόγοι, ψευδεῖς δέ.
9. εὐτυχεῖς ἐσμεν· δῶρα γὰρ οὐκ ὀλίγα ἐδεξάμεθα ἀπὸ τῶν θεῶν.
10. οὐ σῶφρον ἐστὶ τοῖς πολίταις πιστεύειν τοῖς τείχεσιν.

EXERCISE 95.

1. If the orator's words were not clear we would not have obeyed him.
2. The Greeks were being led by a false guide.
3. The walls of the city were strong.
4. Few men are always fortunate.
5. The rule of the well-born was harsh.
6. Citizens, remember the truth and you will be safe.
7. The Athenians will be safe on account of their fleet.
8. Socrates was both wise and prudent.
9. The words of those with the army were false.
10. In five days you will receive the letter which I sent to you.

2. Adjectives of the ἡδύς type

Adjectives like ἡδύς, 'sweet' 'pleasant' have 3rd declension masculine and neuter forms, and 1st declension feminine forms. The masculine and neuter forms are similar to those of πρέσβυς and ἄστυ (Ch. 14.1), but the **ο** of the gen. sing. is short, and there is no contraction in the gen. sing., gen. pl. and neuter pl. nom. and acc. The gen. pl. of the feminine is always accented **-ῶν** (contracted from **-άων**), like 1st declension nouns (Ch. 3.5), rather than like 1st declension adjective forms (Ch. 7.1).

sweet

		M	F	N
Sing.	Nom.	ἡδύς	ἡδεῖα	ἡδύ
	Gen.	ἡδέος	ἡδείας	ἡδέος
	Dat.	ἡδεῖ	ἡδείᾳ	ἡδεῖ
	Acc.	ἡδύν	ἡδεῖαν	ἡδύ
	Voc.	ἡδύς	ἡδεῖα	ἡδύ
Plur.	Nom.	ἡδεῖς	ἡδεῖαι	ἡδέα
	Gen.	ἡδέων	ἡδειῶν	ἡδέων
	Dat.	ἡδέσι(ν)	ἡδείαις	ἡδέσι(ν)
	Acc.	ἡδεῖς	ἡδείας	ἡδέα
	Voc.	ἡδεῖς	ἡδεῖαι	ἡδέα

3. The adjective πᾶς

The adjective πᾶς, πᾶσα, πᾶν, 'all', 'every', has a masculine and neuter stem ending in **-ντ** (like γίγας, Ch. 10.1) and a feminine stem ending in **-σ** (type **c**, Ch. 3.3). The **α** is short in the masculine and neuter, long in the feminine. The stem was originally ***παντy-**; the circumflex accent in several masculine and neuter forms comes from *compensatory lengthening* when the extra consonants dropped out (Ch. 10.1).

all

		M	F	N
Sing.	Nom.	πᾶς	πᾶσα	πᾶν
	Gen.	παντός	πάσης	παντός
	Dat.	παντί	πάσῃ	παντί
	Acc.	πάντα	πᾶσαν	πᾶν
	Voc.	πᾶς	πᾶσα	πᾶν
Plur.	Nom.	πάντες	πᾶσαι	πάντα
	Gen.	πάντων	πασῶν	πάντων
	Dat.	πᾶσι(ν)	πάσαις	πᾶσι(ν)
	Acc.	πάντας	πάσας	πάντα
	Voc.	πάντες	πᾶσαι	πάντα

πᾶς has the following range of meanings; for each one, Greek and English word order are the same.

- 'whole' — ἡ πᾶσα χώρα — the whole country — (attributive)
  οἱ πάντες πολῖται — the whole (body of) citizens
- 'all' — πάντες οἱ πολῖται — all the citizens — (predicate)
- 'every' / 'all' — πᾶσα χώρα — every country — (no article)
  πάντες πολῖται — all citizens

4. The liquid future (2nd principal part)

Verbs whose stems end in a liquid (**λ**, **ρ**) or a nasal (**μ**, **ν**) have an **ε** contract vowel in the future instead of the usual marker **-σ**. They are conjugated just like the present tense of contract verbs in **-εω** (Ch. 19.2). For this reason, the *liquid future* is also called the *contract future*; also the *Attic future*, because it is a feature of this dialect. A few other verbs also have contract futures. μένω shows the active paradigm, and πίπτω shows the middle.

INDICATIVE		μένω		πίπτω	
Sing.	1st	μενῶ	(μενέ-ω)	πεσοῦμαι	(πεσέ-ομαι)
	2nd	μενεῖς	(μενέ-εις)	πεσῇ / πεσεῖ	(πεσέ-ῃ)
	3rd	μενεῖ	(μενέ-ει)	πεσεῖται	(πεσέ-εται)
Plur.	1st	μενοῦμεν	(μενέ-ομεν)	πεσούμεθα	(πεσε-όμεθα)
	2nd	μενεῖτε	(μενέ-ετε)	πεσεῖσθε	(πεσέ-εσθε)
	3rd	μενοῦσι(ν)	(μενέ-ουσι)	πεσοῦνται	(πεσέ-ονται)
INFINITIVE					
		μενεῖν	(μενέ-ειν)	πεσεῖσθαι	(πεσέ-εσθαι)

5. The liquid aorist (3rd principal part)

A few verbs whose stems end in a liquid (**λ, ρ**) or a nasal (**μ, ν**) have *liquid aorists* as well as liquid futures. These are weak aorist forms (Ch. 5.2), but the liquid followed by the tense marker **-σ** creates an unacceptable consonant cluster: ἔ-μενσ-α. The **σ** therefore drops out, and the stem vowel is lengthened to compensate, and to maintain the long syllable that liquid + **σ** had created (Ch. 16.1). This is an example of *compensatory lengthening* in verbs; you have already met it in nouns (Ch. 10.1) and adjectives (above, sec. 3). The aorist of μένω shows how the pattern works.

INDICATIVE		
Sing.	1st	ἔμεινα
	2nd	ἔμεινας
	3rd	ἔμεινε(ν)
Plur.	1st	ἐμείναμεν
	2nd	ἐμείνατε
	3rd	ἔμειναν
INFINITIVE		
		μεῖναι

6. Review of liquid future and aorist forms

Look back at the Review of Principal Parts after Ch. 15. Some of those verbs and some from Chapters 16-20 have liquid futures, and a few also have liquid aorists.

1 Present	2 Future	3 Aorist
ἀγγέλλω	ἀγγελῶ	ἤγγειλα
(ἀπο)θνῄσκω	ἀποθανοῦμαι	
(ἀπο)κτείνω	ἀποκτενῶ	ἀπέκτεινα
βάλλω	βαλῶ	
ἐλαύνω	ἐλῶ	
μάχομαι	μαχοῦμαι	
μένω	μενῶ	ἔμεινα
νομίζω	νομιῶ	
πίπτω	πεσοῦμαι	
τρέχω	δραμοῦμαι	
φαίνομαι	φανοῦμαι	

EXERCISE 96.

1. ἡδύ ἐστί μοι τοὺς τοῦ ποιητοῦ λόγους δέξασθαι.
2. εἰ ἡ πᾶσα στρατιὰ ὑμῶν εὐθὺς ἐμαχέσατο, οἱ πολέμιοι οὐκ ἂν ἔμειναν.
3. τὰ ἡμέτερα ὅπλα ἐβάλετε εἰς τὴν γῆν;
4. οἱ Ἀθηναῖοι λήψονται πάσας τὰς ταχείας τριήρεις τὰς τῶν βαρβάρων.
5. ἡ ὁδὸς ἡ διὰ τῆς εὐρείας ὕλης ἦν βραδεῖα.
6. σαφεῖς μὲν ἦσαν οἱ τοῦ ῥήτορος λόγοι, ἡδεῖς δέ.
7. εἰ ἐδιώξαμεν τοὺς θῆρας ὅπλοις βαρέσιν, ἐλαβόμεθα ἂν αὐτούς.
8. μέλλομεν μὲν ἀποκτενεῖν πάντας τοὺς Πέρσας, ὀλίγοι δὲ ἡμῶν πεσοῦνται ἐν τῇ μάχῃ.
9. συμβουλεύσω παντὶ παιδὶ μὴ ἀγγεῖλαι ψευδέα.
10. οἱ τότε οὐκ ἀπέκτειναν τοὺς φυγάδας οὓς εἶδον ἐν τῇ ὁδῷ.

EXERCISE 97.

1. The herald announced the victory to the Spartans, who did not help the Athenians.
2. We will send a swift ship to the island; for all the old men appear to be in danger.
3. It was not pleasant to be pelted with stones.
4. Will you wait for the young men who are hurrying to the mountain?
5. All the sailors were safe on the ship, and did not expect to die.
6. After the battle we ran by a short and quick road to the sea.
7. Every prisoner will be set free within five days.

8. The shields of the foreigners were not heavy for the hoplites.
9. The cavalry of the enemy are slow, and their horses will not obey them.
10. The slave said that he would not drive all the animals to the town.

READING.

POLYCRATES AND THE RING 1: ADVICE FROM AMASIS

Polycrates was tyrant of Samos, an island off the coast of Ionia, from 532 *to* 523 B.C. *He grew so prosperous that Amasis, king of Egypt, warned him that his success would provoke the jealousy of the gods. Amasis suggested that he should appease them by throwing away his most valuable possession.*

ὁ Πολυκράτης, ὃς ἦν ὁ τῆς Σάμου τύραννος, ἦν δυνατώτατος· φιλίαν δὲ ἐποιήσατο πρὸς Ἄμασιν τὸν Αἰγύπτου βασιλέα· ἔπεμψεν οὖν δῶρα αὐτῷ καὶ ἄλλα ἐδέξατο παρ' αὐτοῦ. ἐν χρόνῳ δὲ ὀλίγῳ ὁ Πολυκράτης ἐστράτευε πανταχοῦ καὶ εὖ ἔπραττε τῇ στρατιᾷ. πολλῶν μὲν δὴ τῶν τε νήσων ἐκράτησε καὶ τῶν ἐν τῇ ἠπείρῳ πόλεων.

τῷ δὲ Ἄμασι ἡ τοῦ Πολυκράτους εὐτυχία βαρὺ ἄλγος ἦν. ἔγραψεν οὖν βραχεῖαν ἐπιστολὴν καὶ ἔπεμψεν εἰς Σάμον· Ἄμασις Πολυκράτει ὧδε λέγει. ἡδὺ μέν ἐστιν, ὦ φίλε, νομίζειν ἄνδρα φίλον καὶ ξένον εὖ πράττειν, ἐμοὶ δὲ αἱ σαὶ μεγάλαι εὐτυχίαι οὐκ ἀρέσκουσιν· εἰ γάρ τις ἀεὶ εὐτυχής ἐστιν, οἱ θεοὶ φθονοῦσιν. πείθου οὖν ἐμοὶ καὶ ὧδε ποίησον· τῶν σῶν κτημάτων τὸ <u>πλείστου ἄξιον</u> [*worthy of most*, i.e. *most valuable*] ἀπόβαλε.

ὁ δὲ Πολυκράτης δέχεται τὴν ἐπιστολὴν καὶ ἀναγιγνώσκει· ἦν δ' αὐτῷ σφραγὶς σμαράγδου λίθου χρυσόδετος. ἐπεὶ οὖν ἐδόκει αὐτῷ ἀποβαλεῖν, ἐποίει ὧδε· ταχεῖαν ναῦν πληροῖ ἀνδρῶν καὶ αὐτὸς εἰσβαίνει εἰς αὐτήν, μετὰ δὲ ἀναγαγεῖν κελεύει τοὺς ναύτας εἰς τὸ εὐρὺ πέλαγος· ὡς δὲ ἀπὸ τῆς νήσου ἑκάς εἰσιν, βάλλει τὴν σφραγῖδα εἰς τὸ πέλαγος.

Adapted from Herodotus III.39-41

Chapter 20 Vocabulary

Verbs:

βάλλω, βαλῶ, ἔβαλον, βέβληκα, βέβλημαι, ἐβλήθην	throw, pelt
βούλομαι, βουλήσομαι, —, —, βεβούλημαι, ἐβουλήθην	want, wish, be willing
τρέχω, δραμοῦμαι, ἔδραμον, -δεδράμηκα, -δεδράμημαι, —	run
φαίνομαι, φανοῦμαι, —, —, πέφασμαι, ἐφάνθην / ἐφάνην	appear, seem

Adjectives:

ἀληθής, -ές	true	εὐρύς, -εῖα, -ύ	wide
τὰ ἀληθῆ	the truth	**εὐτυχής**, -ές	fortunate
ἀσφαλής, -ές	safe	**ἡδύς**, -εῖα, -ύ	sweet, pleasant
βαρύς, -εῖα, -ύ	heavy	**πᾶς**, πᾶσα, πᾶν	all, every, whole
βραδύς, -εῖα, -ύ	slow	σαφής, -ές	clear
βραχύς, -εῖα, -ύ	short	**σώφρων**, -ον	prudent
εὐγενής, -ές	well-born	**ταχύς**, -εῖα, -ύ	fast, swift, quick
εὐδαίμων, εὔδαιμον	happy	**ψευδής**, -ές	false

Preposition:

διά (+ *gen.*)	through, by

CHAPTER 21

φησὶ γάρ που πάντων χρημάτων μέτρον ἄνθρωπον εἶναι,
τῶν μὲν ὄντων ὡς ἔστι, τῶν δὲ μὴ ὄντων ὡς οὐκ ἔστιν.
— Protagoras (Plato, *Theaetetus* 152a3)

1. Participles

A participle is a verbal adjective (active: 'calling', 'having called'; passive: 'being called', 'having been called'). Because participles are verb forms, they occur in all tenses, except the imperfect and pluperfect. Because they are adjectives, they also have case, gender and number, so they can agree with whatever noun they modify.

2. The present active participle in -ων (1st principal part)

- **Thematic verbs:** The present participle of thematic verbs uses the thematic vowel **ο** throughout the paradigm. The endings are the same as the present participle of εἰμί, 'be'. The accent is on the last syllable of the stem, except that the feminine gen. pl. follows the 1st declension pattern with a circumflex on the ultima (Ch. 3.5).

		loosing			**being**		
		M	F	N	M	F	N
Sing.	Nom.	λύων	λύουσα	λῦον	ὤν	οὖσα	ὄν
	Gen.	λύοντος	λυούσης	λύοντος	ὄντος	οὔσης	ὄντος
	Dat.	λύοντι	λυούσῃ	λύοντι	ὄντι	οὔσῃ	ὄντι
	Acc.	λύοντα	λύουσαν	λῦον	ὄντα	οὖσαν	ὄν
	Voc.	λύων	λύουσα	λῦον	ὤν	οὖσα	ὄν
Plur.	Nom.	λύοντες	λύουσαι	λύοντα	ὄντες	οὖσαι	ὄντα
	Gen.	λυόντων	λυουσῶν	λυόντων	ὄντων	οὐσῶν	ὄντων
	Dat.	λύουσι(ν)	λυούσαις	λύουσι(ν)	οὖσι(ν)	οὔσαις	οὖσι(ν)
	Acc.	λύοντας	λυούσας	λύοντα	ὄντας	οὔσας	ὄντα
	Voc..	λύοντες	λύουσαι	λύοντα	ὄντες	οὖσαι	ὄντα

Note: The masculine and neuter dat. plural have the same ending as the 3rd plural present active indicative verb.

- **Contract verbs:** the vowel of the stem contracts as usual with the thematic vowel **ο** (Ch. 19).

M		F		N	
φιλῶν	(φιλέ-ων)	φιλοῦσα	(φιλέ-ουσα)	φιλοῦν	(φιλέ-ον)
τιμῶν	(τιμά-ων)	τιμῶσα	(τιμά-ουσα)	τιμῶν	(τιμά-ον)
δηλῶν	(δηλό-ων)	δηλοῦσα	(δηλό-ουσα)	δηλοῦν	(δηλό-ον)

The paradigms of φιλῶν, 'loving' and τιμῶν, 'honoring' are presented here. The endings of δηλῶν, 'showing' are the same as those of φιλῶν.

		loving			**honoring**		
		M	F	N	M	F	N
Sing.	Nom.	φιλῶν	φιλοῦσα	φιλοῦν	τιμῶν	τιμῶσα	τιμῶν
	Gen.	φιλοῦντος	φιλούσης	φιλοῦντος	τιμῶντος	τιμώσης	τιμῶντος
	Dat.	φιλοῦντι	φιλούσῃ	φιλοῦντι	τιμῶντι	τιμώσῃ	τιμῶντι
	Acc.	φιλοῦντα	φιλοῦσαν	φιλοῦν	τιμῶντα	τιμῶσαν	τιμῶν
	Voc.	φιλῶν	φιλοῦσα	φιλοῦν	τιμῶν	τιμῶσα	τιμῶν
Plur.	Nom.	φιλοῦντες	φιλοῦσαι	φιλοῦντα	τιμῶντες	τιμῶσαι	τιμῶντα
	Gen.	φιλούντων	φιλουσῶν	φιλούντων	τιμώντων	τιμωσῶν	τιμώντων
	Dat.	φιλοῦσι(ν)	φιλούσαις	φιλοῦσι(ν)	τιμῶσι(ν)	τιμώσαις	τιμῶσι(ν)
	Acc.	φιλοῦντας	φιλούσας	φιλοῦντα	τιμῶντας	τιμώσας	τιμῶντα
	Voc.	φιλῶν	φιλοῦσα	φιλοῦν	τιμῶντες	τιμῶσαι	τιμῶντα

3. The attributive participle

The *attributive participle* modifies a noun, and behaves like any attributive adjective (Ch. 7.2). When an attributive participle appears with a noun, it is in the attributive position.

οἱ φεύγοντες ἄνδρες
the fleeing men

Another way to translate the attributive participle is by a relative clause. Greek uses participial phrases much more frequently than English; a relative clause is often a better English translation.

οἱ φεύγοντες ἄνδρες
the men who are fleeing

Like any adjective, the attributive participle can also be used with an article to create a noun phrase (Ch. 7.2, 12.2). In this case too a relative clause is usually a good translation.

οἱ ἵππους διώκοντες στρατηγοί

οἱ στρατηγοὶ οἱ διώκοντες ἵππους
the generals *who are pursuing* horses

οὐ τιμῶμεν τοὺς ἐκ τῆς μάχης φεύγοντας.
We do not honor *those who are fleeing* from battle.

οἱ ἐν τῇ πόλει μένοντες ἀκούουσι τοῦ ῥήτορος.
Those who remain in the city are listening to the orator.

4. The circumstantial participle

Alone or in a phrase, the participle can also express a variety of *circumstances*, as is common in English.

I saw him *sitting by the fire.*

Running into the room, he tripped and fell.

This construction is even more common in Greek, which often uses a participle where English would use a subordinate clause. A clause beginning 'if', 'when', 'since' or 'although' is often a good translation of a Greek participial phrase. The least common of these types is the 'although' clause; the word καίπερ, 'although', is sometimes included to make the meaning clear.

φίλους ἔχοντες εὐδαίμονες ἐσόμεθα.
If / when / since we have friends we will be happy.

(καίπερ) φίλους ἔχοντες εὐδαίμονες οὔκ ἐσμεν.
Although we have friends, we are not happy.

The circumstantial participle stands in the predicate position. Comparison with the attributive participle makes the difference clear.

λαμβάνομεν τοὺς τρέχοντας ἵππους.
We catch the running horses. (attributive)

ὁρῶμεν τοὺς ἵππους τρέχοντας.
We see the horses running. (circumstantial)

τρέχοντες λαμβάνομεν τοὺς ἵππους.
While running, we catch the horses. (circumstantial)

ὁρῶμεν τοὺς ἄνδρας τοὺς ζῷα διώκοντας.
We see the men who are pursuing animals. (attributive)

ὁρῶμεν τοὺς ἄνδρας ζῷα διώκοντας.
We see the men pursuing animals. (circumstantial)

ηὕρομεν τοὺς ἄνδρας τοὺς ζῷα διώκοντας.
We found the men who were pursuing animals. (attributive)

ηὕρομεν τοὺς ἄνδρας ζῷα διώκοντας.
We found the men pursuing animals. (circumstantial)

5. Further notes on participles

Tense: The tense of a participle expresses time *relative* to that of the main verb. The present participle refers to an action in progress, or repeated (the usual aspect of this tense; Ch. 5.3, 13.4, 18.1), so normally at the *same* time as the main verb. In the following example, the seeing and the pursuing take place at the same time.

διώκων τὸν ἵππον παῖδα εἶδεν.
While pursuing the horse, he saw a child.

The future participle refers to a time *later* than the main verb (below, sec. 6). The aorist participle refers to a simple act (the usual aspect of this tense), usually *before* the time of the main verb (below, sec. 7).

μένομεν τοὺς σώσοντας ἡμᾶς.
We are waiting for those who will save us.

θαυμάζομεν τοὺς νικήσαντας.
We honor those who conquered.

Negatives: The negative with most participles is οὐ. μή is used in two particular cases:

- attributive participles referring to indefinite or generic people / things.

  οἱ μὴ ἔχοντες ἀγαθοὺς ἡγεμόνας οὐκ εὐτυχεῖς εἰσιν.
  Those who do not have good leaders are not fortunate.

  ὁ μὴ ἔχων ὅπλα οὐ μαχεῖται.
  Anyone who does not have weapons will not fight.

- circumstantial participles with conditional meaning (if).

  μὴ ἔχων ὅπλα οὐ μαχεῖται.
  If he does not have weapons he will not fight.

EXERCISE 98.

1. οἱ ἐν τῇ πόλει μένοντες μῶροί εἰσιν.
2. οἱ πολεμίους διώκοντες ἐκωλύθησαν τῷ χειμῶνι.
3. ἀκούεις τὰς τῶν θυόντων φωνάς;
4. τὸν ποταμὸν διαβαίνοντες ὁρώμεθα ὑπὸ τῶν φίλων.
5. ὁ Λεωνίδας ἔπεσεν ἐν τῇ μάχῃ ἄγων τοὺς Λακεδαιμονίους.
6. πολὺν χρόνον βουλευσάμενοι, οἱ στρατηγοὶ ἐκέλευσαν τὴν στρατιὰν πορεῦσαι τοὺς αἰχμαλώτους πρὸς τὸ στρατόπεδον.
7. πιστεύσομεν τοῖς τὴν πόλιν φυλάττουσιν.
8. ὁρῶσι τὰς καμήλους διωκούσας τοὺς ἵππους.
9. τιμῶμεν τοὺς ἐπὶ τοὺς Λακεδαιμονίους στρατεύοντας.
10. οἱ νεανίαι οἱ ἐν τοῖς ἀγῶσι νικῶντες τιμηθήσονται ὑπὸ τοῦ δήμου.

EXERCISE 99.

1. We see the enemy cutting down the trees.
2. Those who flee are not worthy of honor.
3. Remember the citizens who run risks on behalf of the fatherland.
4. While crossing the mountain we were hindered by the enemy.
5. I admire those who write beautiful things.
6. We can see the Persians marching away.
7. Those who were pursuing could not find the river.
8. While running from the city, our friends were hindered by the animals.
9. We do not always obey orators who speak well.
10. Since we do not have strong allies, we shall not be able to conquer.

6. The future active participle (2nd principal part)

Form: The *future active* participle has the same thematic vowel and endings as the present; they are attached to the future stem with the marker **-σ** (2nd principal part). The accent is always on the stem, except in the feminine gen. pl. (above, sec. 2).

λύσων λύσουσα λῦσον λύσοντος, etc.

Meaning: The future participle refers to a time later than the main verb. This relationship must be translated by a relative clause, since English does not have a future participle.

τιμῶ τοὺς σώσοντας τὴν πόλιν.
I honor those who will save the city.

7. The aorist active participle (3rd principal part)

Form:

- In the *weak* or *1st aorist active* participle, the tense stem ending **-σ**, with the stem vowel **α**, substitutes for the thematic vowel, just as in the indicative. The accent is on the stem, except in the feminine gen. pl. (above, sec. 2).

having loosed

		M	F	N
Sing.	Nom.	λύσας	λύσασα	λῦσαν
	Gen.	λύσαντος	λυσάσης	λύσαντος
	Dat.	λύσαντι	λυσάσῃ	λύσαντι
	Acc.	λύσαντα	λύσασαν	λῦσαν
	Voc.	λύσας	λύσασα	λῦσαν
Plur.	Nom.	λύσαντες	λύσασαι	λύσαντα
	Gen.	λυσάντων	λυσασῶν	λυσάντων
	Dat.	λύσασι(ν)	λυσάσαις	λύσασι(ν)
	Acc.	λύσαντας	λυσάσας	λύσαντα
	Voc.	λύσαντες	λύσασαι	λύσαντα

- The *strong* or *2nd aorist active* participle, uses the thematic vowel **ο**, just as in the indicative. Thus the endings are the same as in the present tense. However, the accent is on the thematic vowel, except in the feminine gen. pl. (above, sec. 2).

having left

		M	F	N
Sing.	Nom.	λιπών	λιποῦσα	λιπόν
	Gen.	λιπόντος	λιπούσης	λιπόντος
	Dat.	λιπόντι	λιπούσῃ	λιπόντι
	Acc.	λιπόντα	λιποῦσαν	λιπόν
	Voc.	λιπών	λιποῦσα	λιπόν
Plur.	Nom.	λιπόντες	λιποῦσαι	λιπόντα
	Gen.	λιπόντων	λιπουσῶν	λιπόντων
	Dat.	λιποῦσι(ν)	λιπούσαις	λιποῦσι(ν)
	Acc.	λιπόντας	λιπούσας	λιπόντα
	Voc.	λιπόντες	λιποῦσαι	λιπόντα

Meaning: The aorist participle refers to a simple act, generally before the time of the main verb. The participles in the following sentences could be translated in several ways, but the time relative to the main verb must be clear.

οἱ τοὺς πολεμίους διώξαντες νικήσουσιν.
Those having pursued the enemy will conquer.
Those who pursued the enemy will conquer.

διώξαντες τοὺς πολεμίους εἰς τὸν ποταμόν, ἐλίπομεν.
Having pursued the enemy to the river, we left.
After pursuing the enemy to the river, we left.
After / when we had pursued the enemy to the river, we left.

EXERCISE 100.

1. πείσας τὴν γυναῖκα ἀποθανεῖν, ὁ Ἄδμητος ἔτι ἐβασίλευεν.
2. ὁ πᾶς δῆμος τιμᾷ τοὺς τὴν πόλιν σώσοντας.
3. λύσας τοὺς βοῦς, ὁ γέρων οὐκ ἔμενεν ἐν τῷ λειμῶνι.
4. μαθὼν τὰ περὶ τοῦ Πολυκράτους, ὁ Ἄμασις οὐκ ἐνόμισε τὸν φίλον εἶναι σώφρονα.
5. ἐλάβομεν τοὺς παῖδας τοὺς τὰ δένδρα βλάψοντας.
6. οἱ πολέμιοι ἐλύσαντο πάντας τοὺς αἰχμαλώτους τοὺς ἔτι μένοντας ἐν τῇ νήσῳ.

7. φίλους ποιήσομεν τοὺς τὴν σφραγῖδα πέμψαντας.
8. χάριν ἔχομεν τοῖς φίλοις τοῖς τὴν πατρίδα σώσασιν.
9. πεισόμεθα πάντας τοὺς ἡμᾶς εὖ ποιοῦντας.
10. ἡδὺ ἦν πᾶσι τοῖς μετὰ τοῦ Ξενοφῶντος ὁρᾶν τὴν θάλατταν.

EXERCISE 101.

1. Having persuaded the allies to send help, the general was able to march.
2. Do you see those with the king?
3. Having captured the horses, the allies are advancing toward the city.
4. After sending away all the women and children to another land, the Athenians fought with their triremes.
5. It is wise to trust those who will make us safe.
6. All those who conquered in the sea battle are worthy of honor.
7. Socrates had the wisest mind of all the Greeks.
8. We shall guard the ships that remain in the harbor.
9. The king of Persia ordered all the cities to send earth and water.
10. Few are those who will send help, having learned the truth.

READING.

POLYCRATES AND THE RING 2: DESTINY IS DESTINY

μετὰ δὲ ἡμέρας ὀλίγας, ἀνὴρ ἁλιεὺς λαβὼν ἰχθὺν μέγαν τε καὶ καλόν, ἐνόμισεν αὐτὸν ἄξιον εἶναι δῶρον τῷ τυράννῳ. φέρων οὖν τὸν ἰχθὺν πρὸς τὴν τοῦ Πολυκράτους οἰκίαν, ἔφη ἐθέλειν λέγειν τῷ βασιλεῖ· τῷ δὲ Πολυκράτει ἐκβαίνοντι ἔλεγε παρέχων τὸν ἰχθύν· Ὦ βασιλεῦ, ἐγὼ μέγαν ἰχθὺν λαβὼν οὐκ ἤθελον φέρειν εἰς ἀγοράν, καίπερ ὀλίγα χρήματα ἔχων, ἀλλά μοι ἐδόκει σοῦ τε εἶναι ἄξιος καὶ τῆς σῆς ἀρχῆς· σοὶ δὴ αὐτὸν φέρων αἰτῶ σε δέξασθαι. ὁ δὲ ἡδόμενος τοῖς λόγοις λέγει· Εὖ τε ἐποίησας καί χάριν σοι ἔχομεν τῶν τε λόγων καὶ τοῦ δώρου· καί σε ἐπὶ δεῖπνον καλοῦμεν. ὁ μὲν οὖν ἁλιεὺς μάλιστα ἥδεται, ὡς οὕτω τιμᾶται· οἱ δὲ θεράποντες τὸν ἰχθὺν τέμνοντες εὑρίσκουσιν ἐν τῇ γαστρὶ τὴν Πολυκράτους σφραγῖδα ἣν ἀπέβαλεν. ὡς δὲ εἶδόν τε καὶ ἔλαβον αὐτήν, ἔφερον παρὰ τὸν Πολυκράτη καὶ τὸ πρᾶγμα ἐξηγοῦντο.

τῷ δὲ Ἄμασι, ἀκούσαντι τὰ περὶ τοῦ θαύματος, δῆλον ἦν ὅτι σῶσαί τε ἀδύνατόν ἐστι ἀνθρώπῳ ἄνθρωπον ἐκ τοῦ μέλλοντος γενήσεσθαι [*going to happen*] πράγματος, καὶ ὅτι οὐκ εὖ ἀποθανεῖται ὁ Πολυκράτης εὐτυχῶν τὰ πάντα, ὃς καὶ ἃ ἀποβάλλει εὑρίσκει. πέμψας δὲ κήρυκα αὐτῷ εἰς Σάμον διελύσατο τὴν φιλίαν· οὐ γὰρ ἤθελεν, ὅτε δεινὴ συμφορὰ τὸν Πολυκράτη καταλύσει, αὐτὸς ἄλγος πάσχειν ὡς περὶ ξένου ἀνδρός.

Adapted from Herodotus III.42-43

Chapter 21 Vocabulary

Verbs:

βαίνω, -βήσομαι, -ἔβην[1], βέβηκα, —, —	go, walk
διαβαίνω	cross
μανθάνω, μαθήσομαι, ἔμαθον, μεμάθηκα, —, —	learn

Nouns:

Ἄμασις, -ιος, ὁ	Amasis	**σφραγίς**, -ῖδος, ἡ	ring
Πολυκράτης, -ους, ὁ	Polycrates	**φίλος**, -ου, ὁ	friend

Conjunction:

καίπερ	although

1 For aorist conjugation see Ch. 27.5.

CHAPTER 22

τίς ποτ᾽ ὠνόμαζεν ὧδ᾽
ἐς τὸ πᾶν ἐτητύμως
....
Ἑλέναν; ἐπεὶ πρεπόντως
ἑλένας, ἕλανδρος, ἑλέπτολις...
— Aeschylus, *Agamemnon* 681-690

1. Present middle / passive participles (1st principal part)

Form:

- **Thematic verbs:** There is only one set of endings for middle and passive participles, except for the aorist passive (below, sec. 3). They are declined like normal 1st and 2nd declension adjectives (Ch. 7.1). In the present tense, the endings are attached to the present stem with the thematic vowel **ο**.

being loosed

		M	F	N
Sing.	Nom.	λυόμενος	λυομένη	λυόμενον
	Gen.	λυομένου	λυομένης	λυομένου
	Dat.	λυομένῳ	λυομένῃ	λυομένῳ
	Acc.	λυόμενον	λυομένην	λυόμενον
	Voc.	λυόμενε	λυομένη	λυόμενον
Plur.	Nom.	λυόμενοι	λυόμεναι	λυόμενα
	Gen.	λυομένων	λυομένων	λυομένων
	Dat.	λυομένοις	λυομέναις	λυομένοις
	Acc.	λυομένους	λυομένας	λυόμενα
	Voc.	λυόμενοι	λυόμεναι	λυόμενα

- **Contract verbs:** the vowel of the stem contracts as usual with the thematic vowel **o** (Ch. 19).

M		F		N	
φιλούμενος	(φιλε-όμενος)	φιλουμένη	(φιλε-ομένη)	φιλούμενον	(φιλε-όμενον)
τιμώμενος	(τιμα-όμενος)	τιμωμένη	(τιμά-ομένη)	τιμώμενον	(τιμα-όμενον)
δηλούμενος	(δηλο-όμενος)	δηλουμένη	(δηλό-ομένη)	δηλούμενον	(δηλο-όμενον)

The paradigms of φιλούμενος and τιμώμενος are presented here. The endings of δηλούμενος are the same as those of φιλούμενος.

being loved

		M	F	N
Sing.	Nom.	φιλούμενος	φιλουμένη	φιλούμενον
	Gen.	φιλουμένου	φιλουμένης	φιλουμένου
	Dat.	φιλουμένῳ	φιλουμένῃ	φιλουμένῳ
	Acc.	φιλούμενον	φιλουμένην	φιλούμενον
	Voc.	φιλούμενε	φιλουμένη	φιλούμενον
Plur.	Nom.	φιλούμενοι	φιλούμεναι	φιλούμενα
	Gen.	φιλουμένων	φιλουμένων	φιλουμένων
	Dat.	φιλουμένοις	φιλουμέναις	φιλουμένοις
	Acc.	φιλουμένους	φιλουμένας	φιλούμενα
	Voc.	φιλούμενοι	φιλούμεναι	φιλούμενα

being honored

		M	F	N
Sing.	Nom.	τιμώμενος	τιμωμένη	τιμώμενον
	Gen.	τιμωμένου	τιμωμένης	τιμωμένου
	Dat.	τιμωμένῳ	τιμωμένῃ	τιμωμένῳ
	Acc.	τιμώμενον	τιμωμένην	τιμώμενον
	Voc.	τιμώμενε	τιμωμένη	τιμώμενον
Plur.	Nom.	τιμώμενοι	τιμώμεναι	τιμώμενοι
	Gen.	τιμωμένων	τιμωμένων	τιμωμένων
	Dat.	τιμωμένοις	τιμωμέναις	τιμωμένοις
	Acc.	τιμωμένους	τιμωμένας	τιμώμενα
	Voc.	τιμώμενοι	τιμώμεναι	τιμώμενα

Meaning: The middle participle has the same range of active meanings as the middle indicative (Ch. 17.1): λυόμενος, 'ransoming', μαχόμενος, 'fighting', etc. The passive means 'being loosed', 'being sent', etc.

2. Future and aorist middle participles (2nd and 3rd principal parts)

Form:

- The *future middle* participle has the same endings as the present middle / passive, attached to the future stem (2nd principal part).

  λυσόμενος λυσομένη λυσόμενον

  λυσομένου, etc.

- The *weak* or *1st aorist middle* participle has the same endings as the present middle / passive, attached to the weak aorist stem (3rd principal part).

  λυσάμενος λυσαμένη λυσάμενον

  λυσαμένου, etc.

- The *strong* or *2nd aorist middle* participle has the same endings as the present middle / passive, attached to the strong aorist stem (3rd principal part).

  πιθόμενος πιθομένη πιθόμενον

  πιθομένου, etc.

Meaning:

- The *future middle* participle, like the future active (Ch. 21.6), must be translated by a clause.

  μένομεν τοὺς λυσομένους ἡμᾶς.
  We await those who will ransom us.

- The *aorist middle* participle, like the aorist active (Ch. 21.7), has a range of meanings, usually indicating time before the main verb.

  τιμῶμεν τοὺς λυσαμένους τοὺς συμμάχους.
  We honor those who ransomed the allies.

  λυσάμενοι τοὺς συμμάχους, τοῖς θεοῖς ἐθύσαμεν.
  Having ransomed our allies, we sacrificed to the gods.
  After ransoming our allies, we sacrificed to the gods.
  After / when we had ransomed our allies, we sacrificed to the gods.

3. Aorist and future passive participles (6th principal part)

Form:

- The *aorist passive* participle is formed from the 6th principal part. Like the aorist passive indicative (Ch. 15.5), it has active-looking endings. They are attached to the aorist passive stem, with a shortened tense vowel **-ε-** (**-ει-** in the masculine nom./voc. and the feminine). The accent is on this syllable.

having been loosed

		M	F	N
Sing.	Nom.	λυθείς	λυθεῖσα	λυθέν
	Gen.	λυθέντος	λυθείσης	λυθέντος
	Dat.	λυθέντι	λυθείσῃ	λυθέντι
	Acc.	λυθέντα	λυθεῖσαν	λυθέν
	Voc.	λυθείς	λυθεῖσα	λυθέν
Plur.	Nom.	λυθέντες	λυθεῖσαι	λυθέντα
	Gen.	λυθέντων	λυθεισῶν	λυθέντων
	Dat.	λυθεῖσι(ν)	λυθείσαις	λυθεῖσι(ν)
	Acc.	λυθέντας	λυθείσας	λυθέντα
	Voc.	λυθέντες	λυθεῖσαι	λυθέντα

- The *future passive* participle is also formed from the 6th principal part, + **-σ**. It has the same endings as the present middle / passive.

  λυθησόμενος λυθησομένη λυθησόμενον
  λυθησομένου, etc.

Meaning:

- The *aorist passive* participle can be translated 'having been -ed', 'those who were -ed' etc.

  οἱ νικηθέντες φεύγουσιν.
  Those who were conquered are fleeing.

- The *future passive* participle, like other future participles, must be translated by a clause.

  οἱ λυθησόμενοι ἵπποι εἰσὶν ἐν τῇ νήσῳ.
  The horses that will be freed are on the island.

4. The genitive absolute

When a circumstantial participle refers to a noun in the main clause, it agrees with that noun. When the participle refers to a noun not otherwise present in the sentence, it is said to be *absolute*. Both the participle and the noun it agrees with appear in the genitive case.

Like any other circumstantial participial phrase (Ch. 21.4), the genitive absolute is often best translated with a clause beginning 'if', 'when' / 'while', 'since' or 'although'.

τάξας τοὺς ἄνδρας ὁ στρατηγὸς ἀπεχώρησεν.
After he had drawn up his men, the general went away.

τοῦ στρατηγοῦ τοὺς ἄνδρας τάξαντος, ἀπεχωρήσαμεν.
After the general had drawn up his men, we went away.

ὁ ῥήτωρ εὖ λέγων πείθει ἡμᾶς.
The orator persuades us when he speaks well.

τοῦ ῥήτορος εὖ λέγοντος, πειθόμεθα.
Since the orator is speaking well, we are persuaded.

τοῦ ῥήτορος εὖ λέγοντος, πεισθησόμεθα.
If the orator speaks well, we will be persuaded.

Note: The genitive absolute construction is a good opportunity to practice your expectations of what will follow in a sentence (Ch. 6.5, 10.3, 12.6). If you see a genitive participle, you may be able to predict the construction.

5. Further comparison of adjectives in -τερος, -τατος

Many 3rd- (or 3rd- and 1st-) declension adjectives (Ch. 20.1-2) have the same comparative and superlative endings as the regular 1st- and 2nd-declension adjectives already presented (Ch. 16.2). These endings are usually added directly to the nom. sing. neuter form, as for ἀληθής and ταχύς; σώφρων, however, follow a different pattern.

Positive	Comparative	Superlative
ἀληθής	ἀληθέστερος	ἀληθέστατος
βαρύς	βαρύτερος	βαρύτατος
σώφρων	σωφρονέστερος	σωφρονέστατος

- Formed like βαρύς: βραδύς, εὐρύς
  βραχύς may follow this pattern or that of ἡδύς (Ch. 23.4)
- Formed like σώφρων: εὐδαίμων
- Formed like ἀληθής: ἀσφαλής, εὐγενής, εὐτυχής, σαφής, ψευδής

EXERCISE 102.

1. οἱ Ἀθηναῖοι λυσάμενοι τοὺς αἰχμαλώτους τὴν εἰρήνην ἐποιήσαντο.
2. ἀσφαλέστερόν ἐστι μὴ ἑλεῖν τοὺς λέοντας.
3. τῷ ποταμῷ κωλυθείς, ὁ στρατηγὸς ἐκέλευσεν ἡμᾶς τοὺς συμμάχους μένειν.
4. σωφρονεστάτου τυράννου ἄρχοντος, εἰρήνη ἦν τοῖς πολίταις.
5. ὁ Πολυκράτης ἦν πάντων ἀνθρώπων ὁ εὐτυχέστατος.
6. τοῦ τε ναυτικοῦ καὶ τοῦ στρατοῦ νικηθέντων, ὁ Ξέρξης ἀπεχώρησεν.
7. διωκόμενοί τε καὶ αἱρούμενοι ὑπὸ τῶν Ἀθηναίων, οἱ Πέρσαι φεύγουσιν εἰς τὴν θάλατταν.
8. κελεύσαντος τοῦ κριτοῦ, οἱ νεανίαι ἐβοήθησαν τοῖς γέρουσιν.

9. οἱ ὑμᾶς λυσόμενοι οὐ σπεύδουσιν.
10. ἡ ναῦς ἡ τῷ χειμῶνι κωλυθεῖσα ἔμενεν ἐγγὺς τῆς νήσου.

EXERCISE 103.

1. Having been hindered by the wide river, the enemy went away.
2. The king ordered those who had been freed to capture the walls.
3. It was necessary for the army to cross a very wide river while advancing.
4. We shall be safest in the islands.
5. Since the children were loved, their fathers were happy.
6. Leonidas fell while fighting the Persians.
7. The child was more fortunate than his father.
8. Obeying the god, the Athenians will trust not the walls themselves, but the ships.
9. Did you hear either truer or more useful words from other orators?
10. Are those who are taught wiser than those who teach?

READING.

THE INGENUITY OF CYRUS

Cyrus the Great, who ruled Persia from 549 *to* 529 B.C., *after conquering Lydia and Ionia, turned East and captured Babylon in* 538; *his campaigns had extended as far as India.*

οἱ δὲ Βαβυλώνιοι, νικηθέντες ὑπὸ τῶν Περσῶν μάχῃ ἔξω τῶν τειχῶν, εἰς τὴν πόλιν ἀπεχώρησαν. ὁ δὲ Κῦρος μάλιστα ἠπόρει· τοῖς γὰρ Βαβυλωνίοις ἦν σῖτος ἐτῶν δὴ πολλῶν. εἴτε δὴ οὖν ἄλλος αὐτῷ ἀποροῦντι συνεβούλευσεν, εἴτε καὶ αὐτὸς ἔμαθε καλὴν βουλήν, ἐποίει ὧδε· τάξας τὴν στρατιὰν πᾶσαν ἐξ ἐμβολῆς τοῦ Εὐφράτου καλουμένου ποταμοῦ, ᾗ εἰς τὴν πόλιν εἰσβάλλει, καὶ ὄπισθεν αὖθις τῆς πόλεως τάξας ἑτέρους, ᾗ ἐκβαίνει ἐκ τῆς πόλεως ὁ ποταμός, ἐκέλευσε τὸν στρατόν, ἐπεὶ ὄψονται τὸ ῥεῖθρον διαβατὸν ὄν, εἰσβαίνειν αὐτῷ εἰς τὴν πόλιν.

ἔπειτα δὲ ὁ Κῦρος ἤγαγε τοὺς λοιποὺς τῶν ἀνδρῶν πρὸς τὴν λίμνην, ἣν ἡ τῶν Βαβυλωνίων βασίλεια ἔπραξεν ἐν τῷ πρὶν χρόνῳ ἐγγὺς τοῦ ποταμοῦ. ὁ δὲ Κῦρος τὸν ποταμὸν διώρυχι εἰσαγαγὼν εἰς τὴν λίμνην οὖσαν ἕλος, τὸ ἀρχαῖον ῥεῖθρον διαβατὸν εἶναι ἐποίησεν. καὶ τοῦ ὕδατος ἀποφυγόντος, οἱ Πέρσαι οἱ ταχθέντες ἔξω τῆς πόλεως κατὰ τὸ ῥεῖθρον οἷοί τ᾽ ἦσαν εἰσβαίνειν εἰς τὴν πόλιν. εἰ μὲν ἔμαθον οἱ Βαβυλώνιοι τὸ ἐκ τοῦ Κύρου ποιούμενον, ὁρῶντες τοὺς Πέρσας εἰσβαίνοντας κατέλυσαν ἂν αὐτούς. νῦν δὲ οὐκ εἶδον· ὑπὸ γὰρ μεγέθους τῆς πόλεως, πολὺν χρόνον τὸν θάνατον τὸν τῶν περὶ τὰ ἔσχατα οἰκούντων οἱ ἐν τῷ μέσῳ οὐκ ἔμαθον, ἀλλὰ (τύχῃ γὰρ ἑορτὴ ἦν) ἐχόρευον καὶ ἐν εὐπαθείαις ἦσαν [*were making merry*]. καὶ Βαβυλὼν οὕτω τότε πρῶτον ᾑρέθη.

Adapted from Herodotus I.190-191

Chapter 22 Vocabulary

Verbs:

αἱρέω, αἱρήσω, εἷλον, ᾕρηκα, ᾕρημαι, ᾑρέθην (aor. stem **ἑλ-**)	take, capture
ἀποχωρέω, ἀποχωρήσω / ἀποχωρήσομαι, ἀπεχώρησα, ἀποκεχώρηκα, ἀποκεχώρημαι, ἀπεχωρήθην	go away, retreat
προχωρέω	go forward, advance

Noun:

στρατός, -οῦ, ὁ army

Adjective:

χρήσῐμος, -η, -ον useful

CHAPTER 23

Χρόνος δίκαιον ἄνδρα δείκνυσιν μόνος.
— Sophocles, *Oedipus Tyrannus* 614

1. Athematic (-μι) verbs

So far, almost all the verbs you have learned are *thematic* verbs; that is, many of their forms incorporate the thematic vowel (Ch. 2.2). **-μι** verbs, on the other hand, are *athematic* in the present and aorist active and middle systems (1st and 3rd principal parts). In place of the thematic vowel, each verb stem has its own vowel. The two **-μι** verbs you have encountered so far are εἰμί, 'be' (Ch. 7.5, 8.3, 10.2, 18.2, 4) and φημί, 'say' (Ch. 14.3).

The simplest type of **-μι** verb has a stem ending in **υ**, as in δείκνυμι, 'show'. The three common **-μι** verbs τίθημι, 'put', ἵστημι, 'stand', and δίδωμι, 'give' have more complicated present and aorist systems (below, sec. 2-3; see chapter vocabulary).

2. Athematic (-μι) verbs, 1st principal part

Stem: The stem of the 1st principal part is reduplicated, with the vowel **ι** standing between the repeated consonants.

δίδωμι: shows the pattern clearly.

τίθημι: reduplicated **θ** becomes **τ**; Greek never begins two syllables in a row with an aspirated consonant (Grassmann's law, Ch. 15.5).

ἵστημι: initial **σ** is weak and drops out, leaving a rough breathing.

Endings: The present active personal endings of **-μι** verbs are different from those of thematic verbs; the imperfect active, and the present middle and passive endings, are the same.

		Active		Middle / Passive	
		Present	Imperfect	Present	Imperfect
Sing.	1st	-μι	-ν	-μαι	-μην
	2nd	-ς	-ς	-σαι	-σο
	3rd	-σι(ν)	-	-ται	-το
Plur.	1st	-μεν	-μεν	-μεθα	-μεθα
	2nd	-τε	-τε	-σθε	-σθε
	3rd	-ᾱσι(ν)	-σαν	-νται	-ντο

The present system of δείκνυμι, τίθημι, ἵστημι and δίδωμι is shown below. Each uses its own stem vowel throughout, where thematic verbs would use the thematic vowel. In the indicative active this vowel is long in the singular, short in the plural forms.

PRESENT ACTIVE SYSTEM

		show	put	stand	give
INDICATIVE		**stem vowel υ**	**stem vowel ε**	**stem vowel α**	**stem vowel ο**
Present					
Sing.	1st	δείκνυμι	τίθημι	ἵστημι	δίδωμι
	2nd	δείκνυς	τίθης	ἵστης	δίδως
	3rd	δείκνυσι(ν)	τίθησι(ν)	ἵστησι(ν)	δίδωσι(ν)
Plur.	1st	δείκνυμεν	τίθεμεν	ἵσταμεν	δίδομεν
	2nd	δείκνυτε	τίθετε	ἵστατε	δίδοτε
	3rd	δεικνύασι(ν)	τιθέασι(ν)	ἱστᾶσι(ν)	διδόασι(ν)
Imperfect					
Sing.	1st	ἐδείκνυν	ἐτίθην	ἵστην	ἐδίδουν
	2nd	ἐδείκνυς	ἐτίθεις	ἵστης	ἐδίδους
	3rd	ἐδείκνυ	ἐτίθει	ἵστη	ἐδίδου
Plur.	1st	ἐδείκνυμεν	ἐτίθεμεν	ἵσταμεν	ἐδίδομεν
	2nd	ἐδείκνυτε	ἐτίθετε	ἵστατε	ἐδίδοτε
	3rd	ἐδείκνυσαν	ἐτίθεσαν	ἵστασαν	ἐδίδοσαν
IMPERATIVE					
Sing.	2nd	δείκνυ	τίθει	ἵστη	δίδου
	3rd	δεικνύτω	τιθέτω	ἱστάτω	διδότω
Plur.	2nd	δείκνυτε	τίθετε	ἵστατε	δίδοτε
	3rd	δεικνύντων	τιθέντων	ἱστάντων	διδόντων
INFINITIVE					
		δεικνύναι	τιθέναι	ἱστάναι	διδόναι
PARTICIPLE					
		δεικνύς, -ῦσα, -ύν δεικνύντος, etc.	τιθείς, -εῖσα, -έν τιθέντος, etc.	ἱστάς, -ᾶσα, -άν ἱστάντος, etc.	διδούς, -οῦσα, -όν διδόντος, etc.

PRESENT MIDDLE / PASSIVE SYSTEM

INDICATIVE		show	put	stand	give
Present					
Sing.	1st	δείκνυμαι	τίθεμαι	ἵσταμαι	δίδομαι
	2nd	δείκνυσαι	τίθεσαι	ἵστασαι	δίδοσαι
	3rd	δείκνυται	τίθεται	ἵσταται	δίδοται
Plur.	1st	δεικνύμεθα	τιθέμεθα	ἱστάμεθα	διδόμεθα
	2nd	δείκνυσθε	τίθεσθε	ἵστασθε	δίδοσθε
	3rd	δείκνυνται	τίθενται	ἵστανται	δίδονται
Imperfect					
Sing.	1st	ἐδεικνύμην	ἐτιθέμην	ἱστάμην	ἐδιδόμην
	2nd	ἐδείκνυσο	ἐτίθεσο	ἵστασο	ἐδίδοσο
	3rd	ἐδείκνυτο	ἐτίθετο	ἵστατο	ἐδίδοτο
Plur.	1st	ἐδεικνύμεθα	ἐτιθέμεθα	ἱστάμεθα	ἐδιδόμεθα
	2nd	ἐδείκνυσθε	ἐτίθεσθε	ἵστασθε	ἐδίδοσθε
	3rd	ἐδείκνυντο	ἐτίθεντο	ἵσταντο	ἐδίδοντο
IMPERATIVE					
Sing.	2nd	δείκνυσο	τίθεσο	ἵστασο	δίδοσο
	3rd	δεικνύσθω	τιθέσθω	ἱστάσθω	διδόσθω
Plur.	2nd	δείκνυσθε	τίθεσθε	ἵστασθε	δίδοσθε
	3rd	δεικνύσθων	τιθέσθων	ἱστάσθων	διδόσθων
INFINITIVE					
		δείκνυσθαι	τίθεσθαι	ἵστασθαι	δίδοσθαι
PARTICIPLE					
		δεικνύμενος, -η, -ον	τιθέμενος, -η, -ον	ἱστάμενος, -η, -ον	διδόμενος, -η, -ον
		δεικνυμένου, etc.	τιθεμένου, etc.	ἱσταμένου, etc.	διδομένου, etc.

3. Athematic (-μι) verbs, 3rd principal part

δείκνυμι has a regular thematic weak aorist, ἔδειξα, which is conjugated normally (Ch. 5.2, 11.4). δίδωμι and τίθημι have regular weak aorist personal endings, but the stem treatment is different from that in thematic verbs.

ἵστημι has both a weak and a strong aorist.

- The 1st (weak) aorist is transitive.

  ἔστησα τοὺς ἄνδρας ἐπὶ τοῦ τείχους.
  I made the men stand on the wall.
  I stood the men on the wall.

- The 2nd (strong) aorist is intransitive.

  ἔστην ἐπὶ τοῦ τείχους.
  I stood on the wall.

Note: In other tenses of ἵστημι, the middle voice expresses the intransitive meaning (Ch. 17.1).

The aorist forms of τίθημι and δίδωμι and the strong aorist of ἵστημι are presented here.

AORIST ACTIVE SYSTEM

INDICATIVE		put	stand	give
Sing.	1st	ἔθηκα	ἔστην	ἔδωκα
	2nd	ἔθηκας	ἔστης	ἔδωκας
	3rd	ἔθηκε	ἔστη	ἔδωκε
Plur.	1st	ἔθεμεν	ἔστημεν	ἔδομεν
	2nd	ἔθετε	ἔστητε	ἔδοτε
	3rd	ἔθεσαν	ἔστησαν	ἔδοσαν
IMPERATIVE				
Sing.	2nd	θές	στῆθι	δός
	3rd	θέτω	στήτω	δότω
Plur.	2nd	θέτε	στῆτε	δότε
	3rd	θέντων	στάντων	δόντων
INFINITIVE				
		θεῖναι	στῆναι	δοῦναι
PARTICIPLE				
		θείς, -εῖσα, -έν θέντος, etc.	στάς, -ᾶσα, -άν στάντος, etc.	δούς, -οῦσα, -όν δόντος, etc.

AORIST MIDDLE SYSTEM

INDICATIVE		put	give
Sing.	1st	ἐθέμην	ἐδόμην
	2nd	ἔθου	ἔδου
	3rd	ἔθετο	ἔδοτο
Plur.	1st	ἐθέμεθα	ἐδόμεθα
	2nd	ἔθεσθε	ἔδοσθε
	3rd	ἔθεντο	ἔδοντο
IMPERATIVE			
Sing.	2nd	θοῦ	δοῦ
	3rd	θέσθω	δόσθω
Plur.	2nd	θέσθε	δόσθε
	3rd	θέσθων	δόσθων
INFINITIVE			
		θέσθαι	δόσθαι
PARTICIPLE			
		θέμενος, -η, -ον θεμένου, etc.	δόμενος, -η, -ον δομένου, etc.

EXERCISE 104. Identify the following forms:

1. δοῦναι
2. ἔθετο
3. ἐδείκνυσο
4. στήσει
5. ἔδωκεν
6. ἵστασαν
7. διδόντα
8. ἵσταται
9. ἔθου
10. δομένων
11. δοῦ
12. τιθείσας
13. ἔστητε
14. ἐτιθέμεθα
15. ἔδειξαν

EXERCISE 105.

1. παιδεύων τὸν ἡμέτερον ἵππον ὁ παῖς ἔμαθε τὸν φόβον αὐτοῦ.
2. ὁ Σωκράτης δεινότερος λέγειν ἦν τῶν ἄλλων Ἀθηναίων.
3. τῶν στρατιωτῶν στάντων ἐπὶ τοῦ τείχους, οἱ πολέμιοι οὐχ οἷοί τ' ἦσαν προχωρεῖν.
4. ὁ γέρων ἐδείκνυ μοι τὴν πρὸς τὸν λιμένα ὁδόν.
5. οἱ στρατηγοὶ ἔστησαν τοὺς ἱππέας ἐγγὺς τοῦ στρατοπέδου.
6. οἱ σύμμαχοι χρήσιμα ξίφη δώσουσιν ἡμῖν.
7. μέγας ἐστὶν ὁ ἰχθὺς ὃς ἐδόθη τῷ βασιλεῖ.
8. τὸ μὲν ναυτικὸν οἱ Ἀθηναῖοι ἰσχυροὶ ἦσαν, τὸν δὲ στρατὸν οἱ Λακεδαιμόνιοι.

9. ἠθέλομεν τὰ χρήματα θεῖναι εἰς ἀσφαλῆ οἰκίαν.
10. αἱ κάμηλοι χρησιμώτεραι ἦσαν τῷ Κύρῳ ἢ τοῖς ἐν τῇ Βαβυλῶνι.

EXERCISE 106.

1. We were putting the prisoners into the ship.
2. He stood the sword in the earth.
3. The king was good at ruling but bad at war.
4. I set many soldiers on the wall.
5. The man to whom he gave the money is a sailor.
6. They were put in great danger by the lions.
7. The cities in Greece were given to the enemy.
8. He says that he will leave the slaves in the harbor.
9. The king of Persia captured Babylon, which is strong in respect to its walls.
10. All of the animals in the land were dangerous to humans.

4. Further comparison of adjectives in -(ῑ)ων, -(ι)στος

Some adjectives change to a different stem in the comparative and superlative. The comparative of these adjectives has 3rd-declension endings, one set for masculine and feminine forms and one for neuter. In some adjectives the **ῑ** is lost, and the suffix is simply **-ων**. The list below includes the neuter forms, to show the accentuation.

To make the superlative, the 1st- and 2nd-declension endings **-ιστος**, **-η**, **-ον** are added to the comparative stem.

Positive	Comparative	Superlative
ἀγαθός	ἀμείνων, ἄμεινον	ἄριστος
	βελτίων, βέλτιον	βέλτιστος
	κρείττων, κρεῖττον	κράτιστος
βραχύς	βραχίων, βράχιον	βράχιστος
	βραχύτερος, -α, -ον	βραχύτατος
ἕκαστος	ἑκάτερος, -α, -ον[1]	—
ἐχθρός	ἐχθίων, ἔχθιον	ἔχθιστος
ἡδύς	ἡδίων, ἥδιον	ἥδιστος
κακός	κακίων, κάκιον	κάκιστος
	ἥττων, ἧττον	
	χείρων, χεῖρον	χείριστος
καλός	καλλίων, κάλλιον	κάλλιστος
μέγας	μείζων, μεῖζον	μέγιστος

Positive	Comparative	Superlative
μικρός	ἐλάττων, ἔλαττον	ἐλάχιστος
	μικρότερος, -α, -ον	μικρότατος
ὀλίγος	μείων, μεῖον	ὀλίγιστος
	ἐλάττων, ἔλαττον	ἐλάχιστος
πολύς	πλείων, πλεῖον[2]	πλεῖστος[2]
	πλέων, πλέον	
ῥᾴδιος	ῥᾴων, ῥᾷον	ῥᾷστος
ταχύς	θάττων, θᾶττον	τάχιστος

1 The comparative means 'each (of two)'.

2 With the article, οἱ πλείονες and οἱ πλεῖστοι mean 'the majority', 'the greater / greatest number'; τὸ πλεῖον and τὸ πλεῖστον mean 'the greater / greatest part'.

5. Declension of comparatives in -(ῑ)ων

The 3rd-declension comparative forms in **-(ῑ)ων** all have short **-ο-** in the stem, like σώφρων, -ον, 'prudent' (Ch. 20.1). In Attic Greek, some cases have alternative, more colloquial, forms. The comparative of ἡδίων, -ον, 'sweeter' is shown here.

sweeter

		M/F		N	
Sing.	Nom.	ἡδίων		ἥδιον	
	Gen.	ἡδίονος		ἡδίονος	
	Dat.	ἡδίονι		ἡδίονι	
	Acc.	ἡδίονα	ἡδίω	ἥδιον	
	Voc.	ἥδιον		ἥδιον	
Plur.	Nom.	ἡδίονες	ἡδίους	ἡδίονα	ἡδίω
	Gen.	ἡδιόνων		ἡδιόνων	
	Dat.	ἡδίοσι(ν)		ἡδίοσι(ν)	
	Acc.	ἡδίονας	ἡδίους	ἡδίονα	ἡδίω
	Voc.	ἡδίονες	ἡδίους	ἡδίονα	ἡδίω

EXERCISE 107.

1. εἰ αἱ τῶν πολεμίων νῆες θάττονες ἦσαν τῶν ἡμετέρων, οὐκ ἂν ἐνικήσαμεν αὐτούς.
2. οἱ ἄρχοντες τῶν Περσῶν ἔχθιστοι ἦσαν τοῖς Ἕλλησιν.
3. οἱ δῶρα διδόντες εὐδαιμονέστεροί εἰσιν τῶν δεχομένων.
4. οἱ λόγοι οὓς ὁ θεὸς ἔλεξεν ἦσαν ἀληθέστατοι.

5. ἔδειξες τῷ πατρὶ τοὺς θάττονας ἵππους;
6. οἱ ἀποφεύγοντες ἐχθίονες ἡμῖν εἰσι ἢ οἱ πολέμιοι ἡμῶν.
7. τὸ τῶν Περσῶν ναυτικὸν ἦν μεῖζον ἢ τὸ τῶν Ἀθηναίων.
8. τῶν Περσῶν πολλῶν ὄντων, οἱ Λακεδαιμόνιοι ἔστησαν μὲν, ἐνικήθησαν δέ.
9. τὰ πλεῖστα ζῷα χρησιμώτερά ἐστιν.
10. ἐλάττονες ἱππεῖς ἡμῖν εἰσιν ἢ τοῖς συμμάχοις.

EXERCISE 108.

1. We are willing to wait for those who will ransom us.
2. The allies gave much money to the king of Persia.
3. The mind of the poet is very beautiful.
4. The swiftest ships are not always the safest.
5. We all think that the Athenians are greater than the majority of their enemies.
6. While marching through the land of the foreigners, the Greeks were in very great danger.
7. The men whom we found in the village were rather hostile to our army.
8. The same herald, being very fast, was present on the same day.
9. When the enemy had ransomed their prisoners, we went away.
10. It is worse to flee than to be conquered.

READING.

CROCODILES

Cambyses, son of Cyrus the Great, invaded Egypt, and Herodotus with his typical thoroughness devoted a whole book to an account of the country—including the crocodiles of the Nile.

ὁ δὲ κροκόδειλος τοῦ χειμῶνος ἐσθίει οὐδέν [*nothing*]. ἡ δὲ θήλεια τίκτει μὲν ᾠὰ ἐν γῇ καὶ ἐκλέπει καὶ ἐκεῖ διατρίβει τὸ πλεῖστον τῆς ἡμέρας, τὴν δὲ νύκτα πᾶσαν ἐν τῷ ποταμῷ· θερμότερον γὰρ δή ἐστι τὸ ὕδωρ τῆς δρόσου. πάντων δὲ ὧν ἡμεῖς γιγνώσκομεν ζῴων ὁ κροκόδειλος ἐξ ἐλαχίστου μέγιστος γίγνεται [*becomes*]· τὰ μὲν γὰρ ᾠὰ χηνῶν οὐ πολλῷ μείζον' ἐστίν, αὐξανόμενος δὲ ὁ κροκόδειλος γίγνεται ἑπτακαίδεκα πήχεις καὶ μείζων ἔτι. ἔχει δὲ ὀφθαλμοὺς μὲν ὑός, ὀδόντας δὲ μεγάλους· γλῶτταν δὲ μόνον θηρίων οὐκ ἔχει. οὐδὲ κινεῖ τὴν κάτω γνάθον, ἀλλὰ τὴν ἄνω γνάθον προσάγει τῇ κάτω. τυφλὸς δὲ ἐν ὕδατί ἐστιν, ἐν δὲ τῇ γῇ εὖ ὁρᾷ.

τοῖς μὲν δὴ τῶν Αἰγυπτίων ἱεροί εἰσι οἱ κροκόδειλοι, τοῖς δὲ οὔ. οἱ δὲ περὶ Θήβας[1] οἰκοῦντες νομίζουσιν αὐτοὺς εἶναι ἱερωτάτους. ἐκ πάντων δὲ ἕνα θεραπεύουσι κροκόδειλον, χρυσὸν θέντες εἴς τε τὰ ὦτα καὶ περὶ τοὺς πόδας. οἱ δὲ περὶ Ἐλεφαντίνην[1] πόλιν οἰκοῦντες καὶ ἐσθίουσιν αὐτούς, οὐ νομίζοντες ἱεροὺς εἶναι. ὁ δὲ βουλόμενος κροκόδειλον αἱρεῖν, νῶτον ὑὸς τίθησι περὶ ἄγκιστρον καὶ εἰσβάλλει εἰς τὸν ποταμόν· αὐτὸς δὲ ἐν τῇ γῇ ἔχων ὗν ζωόν, αὐτὸν τύπτει. ἀκούσας δὲ ὁ κροκόδειλος σπεύδει πρὸς τὴν φωνήν, εὑρὼν δὲ τὸ νῶτον καταπίνει· οἱ δὲ ἐν τῇ γῇ λαμβάνουσιν αὐτόν. πρῶτον δὲ πάντων πηλῷ καλύπτουσι τοὺς ὀφθαλμοὺς αὐτοῦ· ἔπειτα δὲ ῥᾴδιόν ἐστιν αὐτὸν ἀποκτεῖναι.

Adapted from Herodotus II.68-70

1 Egyptian Thebes (modern Luxor) with its hundred gates was destroyed by Cambyses. It lay some 550 miles upstream from the Nile delta; Elephantine was about 120 miles beyond it.

Chapter 23 Vocabulary

Verbs:

δείκνυμι, δείξω, ἔδειξα, δέδειχα, δέδειγμαι, ἐδείχθην	show
δίδωμι, δώσω, ἔδωκα, δέδωκα, δέδομαι, ἐδόθην	give
ἵστημι, στήσω, ἔστησα / ἔστην, ἕστηκα, ἕσταμαι, ἐστάθην	make stand, set; stand
τίθημι, θήσω, ἔθηκα, τέθηκα, τέθειμαι, ἐτέθην	put, place

Nouns:

Βαβυλών, -ῶνος, ἡ	Babylon	**ξίφος**, -ους, τό	sword

CHAPTER 24

οὐκ ἔστ᾽ ἔτυμος λόγος οὗτος,
οὐδ᾽ ἔβας ἐν νηυσὶν εὐσέλμοις,
οὐδ᾽ ἵκεο πέργαμα Τροίας.
— Stesichorus *PMG* 192

1. Reflexive pronouns

The reflexive pronoun in English is 'myself', 'ourselves', etc. The Greek reflexive is formed by combining a personal pronoun (the 3rd person uses an old personal pronoun ἑ) with the correct form of αὐτός, '-self' (Ch. 9.2): σῴζω ἐμαυτόν, 'I save myself'. In the singular the pronoun and -αυτός are combined and written as one word. In the plural, the 1st and 2nd person forms are written as two words; each is fully declinable. The 2nd and 3rd person singular have alternate contracted forms.

		myself / ourselves		yourself / yourselves			
		M	F	M		F	
Sing.	Gen.	ἐμαυτοῦ	ἐμαυτῆς	σεαυτοῦ	σαυτοῦ	σεαυτῆς	σαυτῆς
	Dat.	ἐμαυτῷ	ἐμαυτῇ	σεαυτῷ	σαυτῷ	σεαυτῇ	σαυτῇ
	Acc.	ἐμαυτόν	ἐμαυτήν	σεαυτόν	σαυτόν	σεαυτήν	σαυτήν
Plur.	Gen.	ἡμῶν αὐτῶν	ἡμῶν αὐτῶν	ὑμῶν αὐτῶν		ὑμῶν αὐτῶν	
	Dat.	ἡμῖν αὐτοῖς	ἡμῖν αὐταῖς	ὑμῖν αὐτοῖς		ὑμῖν αὐταῖς	
	Acc.	ἡμᾶς αὐτούς	ἡμᾶς αὐτάς	ὑμᾶς αὐτούς		ὑμᾶς αὐτάς	

For the 3rd person, one-word and two-word versions both exist, but the one-word version given here is far more common. Only a rough breathing distinguishes the alternate contracted form from the personal pronoun αὐτοῦ, αὐτῆς, αὐτοῦ.

		himself / herself / itself / themselves					
		M		F		N	
Sing.	Gen.	ἑαυτοῦ	αὑτοῦ	ἑαυτῆς	αὑτῆς	ἑαυτοῦ	αὑτοῦ
	Dat.	ἑαυτῷ	αὑτῷ	ἑαυτῇ	αὑτῇ	ἑαυτῷ	αὑτῷ
	Acc.	ἑαυτόν	αὑτόν	ἑαυτήν	αὑτήν	ἑαυτό	αὑτό
Plur.	Gen.	ἑαυτῶν	αὑτῶν	ἑαυτῶν	αὑτῶν	ἑαυτῶν	αὑτῶν
	Dat.	ἑαυτοῖς	αὑτοῖς	ἑαυταῖς	αὑταῖς	ἑαυτοῖς	αὑτοῖς
	Acc.	ἑαυτούς	αὑτούς	ἑαυτάς	αὑτάς	ἑαυτά	αὑτά

Note: Reflexive pronouns exist only in the oblique cases. In the nominative case αὐτός, αὐτή, αὐτό means 'himself', 'herself', etc. (Ch. 9.2).

2. Direct and indirect reflexives

The genitive of the reflexive pronoun is used to express the reflexive possessive 'his own', 'our own' etc. Unlike other personal pronouns, it stands in the attributive position.

- **Direct reflexive:** A *direct reflexive* pronoun refers to the subject of its own clause.

  ἡ Ἀθήνη σώζει τοὺς ἑαυτῆς πολίτας.
  Athena protects her own citizens.

  In this example ἑαυτῆς is feminine sing. because it refers to Athena, the subject of the clause (and the sentence).

- **Indirect reflexive:** An *indirect reflexive* pronoun stands in a subordinate clause, but refers to the subject of the main clause instead of its own.

  ὁ στρατηγὸς ἐκέλευσεν ἡμᾶς ἐλθεῖν εἰς τὴν ἑαυτοῦ χώραν.
  The general ordered us to come into his own country.

Note: Remember that when a 3rd person possessive is not reflexive, but refers to a different person or group, the genitive of αὐτός, -ή, -ό is used (Ch. 9.3).

οἱ Πέρσαι προυχώρησαν εἰς τὴν ἑαυτῶν χώραν.
The Persians advanced into their own country. (reflexive)

οἱ Πέρσαι προυχώρησαν εἰς τὴν χώραν αὐτῶν.
The Persians advanced into their country. (not reflexive)

3. The reciprocal pronoun

The reciprocal pronoun 'each other' is formed from the stem of ἄλλος, 'other': ἀλλήλων. There is no singular, since this pronoun must always refer to more than one person. Like reflexive pronouns, ἀλλήλων exists only in the oblique cases: φιλοῦμεν ἀλλήλους, 'we love each other'.

each other

		M	F	N
Plur.	Gen.	ἀλλήλων	ἀλλήλων	ἀλλήλων
	Dat.	ἀλλήλοις	ἀλλήλαις	ἀλλήλοις
	Acc.	ἀλλήλους	ἀλλήλας	ἄλληλα

Note: The neuter acc. ends in a short vowel, allowing the accent to stand in its true position, on the antepenult (Position 3). In all other forms the long last syllable moves the accent to the penult (Position 2; Ch. 1.4).

4. Questions

Simple questions ('does he...'?) are sometimes introduced with ἆρα; the word is just a marker, and is not translated. Two more specialized markers also exist.

- ἆρα οὐ expects the answer 'yes' ('you do..., don't you?, 'don't you...'?).

  ἆρα οὐ λέγεις τὰ ἀληθῆ;

  You are telling the truth, aren't you?

- ἆρα μή expects, or hopes for, the answer 'no' ('he doesn't..., does he'?, 'surely...not'?).

  ἆρα μὴ φιλεῖ τοὺς κακούς;

  Surely he doesn't love bad men?

EXERCISE 109.

1. ἔγραψα πολλὰς ἐπιστολὰς τῇ αὐτῇ ἡμέρᾳ.
2. ἆρα ἡ Ἄλκηστις αὐτὴ ἐθέλει ἀποθνῄσκειν ὑπὲρ τοῦ ἀνδρός;
3. ὁ βασιλεὺς ἐνόμισε τοὺς πολίτας φιλήσειν τοὺς ἑαυτοῦ νόμους.
4. ἆρα μὴ ὁ στρατηγὸς αὐτὸς ἔπεσεν ἐν τῇ μάχῃ;
5. ἡ αὐτὴ λίμνη χρησιμωτάτη ἦν τῷ Κύρῳ.
6. καταλύσασα ναῦν φιλίαν, ἡ Ἀρτεμισία ἔσωσεν ἑαυτὴν ἐν τῇ ναυμαχίᾳ καὶ ἀπέπλευσεν.
7. ὁ Θεμιστοκλῆς οὐκ ἐδίωξε βασιλέα, ἀλλ' ἄνδρα ὡς αὐτὸν ἔπεμψεν.
8. τῶν ναυτῶν ἀποβαλόντων ἑαυτοὺς ἐκ τῆς νεώς, οἷός τ' εἶ σῶσαι σεαυτόν.
9. ἆρα οὐ οἱ Πέρσαι ἀπέφυγον εἰς τὴν ἑαυτῶν χώραν;
10. οἱ τύραννοι οὐ πολλὰ χρήματα ἐδίδουν τοῖς ἑαυτῶν.

EXERCISE 110.

1. The king of Persia did not trust his own soldiers.
2. The lucky man found a ring in the big fish and gave it to the king.
3. Most men are willing to fight for their own country and for each other.

4. It is not easy for friends to learn each other's minds, is it?
5. We sailed to many of the islands, but we found more animals than money.
6. Is it necessary for you yourselves to drive them away?
7. In the same year the Greeks conquered both by land and by sea.
8. I do not intend to stand with you near that lake.
9. Many of the Athenians admired Socrates and his wisdom, didn't they?
10. It is difficult for me to save myself.

5. Demonstrative pronouns / adjectives

The demonstratives οὗτος, ἐκεῖνος and ὅδε correspond to English 'this' and 'that'. ὅδε is just the definite article with the suffix **-δε** added to it. The neuter nom. and acc. sing. of ἐκεῖνος and οὗτος end in **-ο**, like the definite article.

		this			that		
		M	F	N	M	F	N
Sing.	Nom.	οὗτος	αὕτη	τοῦτο	ἐκεῖνος	ἐκείνη	ἐκεῖνο
	Gen.	τούτου	ταύτης	τούτου	ἐκείνου	ἐκείνης	ἐκείνου
	Dat.	τούτῳ	ταύτῃ	τούτῳ	ἐκείνῳ	ἐκείνῃ	ἐκείνῳ
	Acc.	τοῦτον	ταύτην	τοῦτο	ἐκεῖνον	ἐκείνην	ἐκεῖνο
Plur.	Nom.	οὗτοι	αὗται	ταῦτα	ἐκεῖνοι	ἐκεῖναι	ἐκεῖνα
	Gen.	τούτων	τούτων	τούτων	ἐκείνων	ἐκείνων	ἐκείνων
	Dat.	τούτοις	ταύταις	τούτοις	ἐκείνοις	ἐκείναις	ἐκείνοις
	Acc.	τούτους	ταύτας	ταῦτα	ἐκείνους	ἐκείνας	ἐκεῖνα

Note: The stem vowel of οὗτος alternates between **-ο-** and **-α-**, to match the vowel of the ending.

		this		
		M	F	N
Sing.	Nom.	ὅδε	ἥδε	τόδε
	Gen.	τοῦδε	τῆσδε	τοῦδε
	Dat.	τῷδε	τῇδε	τῷδε
	Acc.	τόνδε	τήνδε	τόδε
Plur.	Nom.	οἵδε	αἵδε	τάδε
	Gen.	τῶνδε	τῶνδε	τῶνδε
	Dat.	τοῖσδε	ταῖσδε	τοῖσδε
	Acc.	τούσδε	τάσδε	τάδε

ἐκεῖνος means 'that', while ὅδε and οὗτος both mean 'this'. ἐκεῖνος may also mean 'the former', and οὗτος 'the latter'. ὅδε, as opposed to οὗτος, often specifically refers to something actually present, that you can point at: ὅδε ὁ ἀνήρ, 'this man here'. A further distinction is that in historical narrative, though not necessarily elsewhere, οὗτος may look back to a preceding speech, while ὅδε looks forward to a following speech.

Used by themselves, these demonstratives are pronouns: οὗτοι, 'these men'; ἐκείνη, 'that woman', etc. They may also be used as adjectives, modifying a noun. The definite article is always present, and the demonstrative is always in the predicate position: ἥδε ἡ γυνή, 'this woman'; τὰ δένδρα ταῦτα, 'these trees'; etc.

6. τοιοῦτος, τοσοῦτος

These demonstratives are compounds of οὗτος, and are declined just like it. τοιοῦτος, τοιαύτη, τοιοῦτο refers to the *quality* of a person or thing: τοιοῦτος ἀνήρ, 'this kind of man', 'such a man as this'. τοσοῦτος, τοσαύτη, τοσοῦτο refers to *quantity*: τοσαύτη στρατιά, 'such a large army as this'; τοσαῦτα δένδρα, 'so many trees', 'this many trees'.

Here is the paradigm of τοιοῦτος; τοσοῦτος works in just the same way.

this kind

		M	F	N
Sing.	Nom.	τοιοῦτος	τοιαύτη	τοιοῦτο
	Gen.	τοιούτου	τοιαύτης	τοιούτου
	Dat.	τοιούτῳ	τοιαύτῃ	τοιούτῳ
	Acc.	τοιοῦτον	τοιαύτην	τοιοῦτο
Plur.	Nom.	τοιοῦτοι	τοιαῦται	τοιαῦτα
	Gen.	τοιούτων	τοιούτων	τοιούτων
	Dat.	τοιούτοις	τοιαύταις	τοιούτοις
	Acc.	τοιούτους	τοιαύτας	τοιαῦτα

Note: These demonstratives may be used without the article, or in the attributive position with the article: ὁ τοιοῦτος ἀνήρ. The meaning is the same.

EXERCISE 111.

1. οὗτοι οἱ στρατιῶται ἐγγὺς τοῦ εὐρέος ποταμοῦ ἐστάθησαν.
2. ἡ σφραγὶς ἡ εἰς τόνδε τὸν ἰχθὺν τεθεῖσα χρυσῆ ἦν.
3. μετὰ τοῦτο ὁ Ξέρξης ἐκ τῆς Ἑλλάδος ἀπεχώρησεν.
4. ἐκείνη ἡ ναῦς κατελύθη ὑπὸ τῆς Ἀρτεμισίας.
5. οὗτοί εἰσιν ἀξιώτεροι τῆς τιμῆς ἢ ἐκεῖνοι.

6. ὁ Θεμιστοκλῆς πέμπει τὴν τοιαύτην ἐπιστολὴν ὡς βασιλέα.
7. ἐθήκαμεν τὰ ἡμῶν αὐτῶν χρήματα εἰς ἐκείνην τὴν τριήρη.
8. μακραί εἰσιν αὗται αἱ ἐπιστολαὶ ἃς οἱ πρέσβεις ἔδοσαν ἀλλήλοις.
9. τοῦτο μαθών, οὐκ ἐθέλω πιστεῦσαι ὑμῖν.
10. τοσαῦτα δῶρα ἐπέμφθη τῷ θεῷ ὑπὸ τῶν Ἀθηναίων.

EXERCISE 112.

1. The same king made their town more beautiful.
2. That tyrant is always fortunate and his city is doing well.
3. Those very big trees were harmed by the Spartans.
4. On account of this we do not cross the river at night.
5. She will be saved by the friend of Admetus.
6. Surely you do not think that you will capture the city?
7. Having been persuaded by Demosthenes, those men will attack the Persians with their swords.
8. This many soldiers were standing in the forest.
9. We cannot conquer this kind of army.
10. Each of your allies thought that they were the best at fighting.

READING.

A STRANGE RESCUE

This interesting story is a mere digression of Herodotus. Periander was tyrant of Corinth about 600 B.C.; *he promoted both commerce and the arts. Arion is said to have invented a new form of poetry.*

ἦν δέ ποτε ἐν Κορίνθῳ κιθαρῳδός, ὀνόματι Ἀρίων, οὐδενὸς δεύτερος [*second to nobody*] τῶν τότε ὄντων· καὶ οὗτος ὁ Ἀρίων, ὡς λέγουσι, τὸν πολὺν τοῦ χρόνου μείνας παρὰ Περιάνδρῳ, τῷ Κορίνθου τυράννῳ, ἔπλευσεν εἰς Ἰταλίαν τε καὶ Σικελίαν. τέλος δὲ χρήματα μεγάλα ἐκεῖ δεξάμενος διὰ τὴν τέχνην, ἐβούλετο πάλιν εἰς Κόρινθον πλεῖν. πιστεύων δὲ μάλιστα τοῖς Κορινθίοις ἐμισθώσατο πλοῖον ἀνδρῶν Κορινθίων. ἀπέπλευσαν μὲν οὖν ἀπὸ Τάραντος,[1] ἐν δὲ τῷ πελάγει οἱ ναῦται ἐπεβούλευσαν τὸν Ἀρίονα ἐκβαλόντες ἔχειν τὰ χρήματα αὐτοῦ· ὁ δέ τοῦτο μαθὼν ᾔτησεν αὐτοὺς χρήματα μὲν λαβεῖν, τὴν δ᾽ ἑαυτοῦ ψυχὴν σῶσαι. ἀλλ᾽ οὐ πεισθέντες οἱ ναῦται ἐκέλευσαν αὐτὸν ἢ ἑαυτὸν ἀποκτείνειν, εἰ τάφον βούλεται ἐν γῇ, ἢ εὐθὺς ἐκπηδᾶν εἰς τὴν θάλατταν. ὁ δὲ Ἀρίων εἶπεν αὐτοῖς· Ἐᾶτέ με πρῶτον ἐν τῇ σκευῇ πάσῃ ἀείδειν. οἱ δὲ ἀπεχώρησαν ἐκ τῆς πρύμνης εἰς μέσην τὴν ναῦν. ἔπειτα δὲ ὁ μὲν Ἀρίων, λαβὼν τὴν κιθάραν καὶ ἀείσας, ἔβαλεν ἑαυτὸν εἰς τὴν θάλατταν, τὴν σκευὴν πᾶσαν φορῶν. οἱ δὲ ναῦται ἀπέπλευσαν εἰς Κόρινθον.

καὶ τότε δὴ μέγιστον θαῦμα ἐγένετο· δελφὶς γὰρ αὐτὸν ὑπολαβὼν ἐπόρευσεν εἰς γῆν. ὁ μὲν οὖν Ἀρίων ἐπορεύσατο εἰς Κόρινθον καὶ ἥκων πᾶν τὸ πρᾶγμα ἐξηγεῖτο τῷ Περιάνδρῳ· ὁ δὲ οὐκ ἐπίστευσεν ἐκείνῳ. τῶν δὲ ναυτῶν τέλος εἰς Κόρινθον πορευσαμένων, ἠρώτησεν ὁ τύραννος περὶ τοῦ Ἀρίονος· λιπεῖν αὐτὸν ἔφασαν εὖ πράττοντα ἐν Τάραντι. τοῦτο λεγόντων, ἐπεφαίνετο αὐτοῖς ὁ Ἀρίων αὐτός, φορῶν τὴν αὐτὴν σκευήν· οἱ δὲ ναῦται τῷδε τῷ τρόπῳ ψευδεῖς ἐδηλώθησαν.

Adapted from Herodotus I.23-24

1 Taras or Tarentum, in Southern Italy, was the only colony founded by Sparta.

Chapter 24 Vocabulary

Verb:

ἀποβάλλω	throw away
ἀποπλέω	sail away
πλέω, πλεύσομαι, ἔπλευσα, πέπλευκα, πέπλευσμαι, —	sail

Noun:

λίμνη, -ης, ἡ	lake, marsh

Pronouns:

ἀλλήλων, -ων, -ων	each other	ἐμαυτοῦ, -ῆς, -οῦ	myself
		ἡμῶν αὐτῶν	ourselves
ἑαυτοῦ, -ῆς, -οῦ etc.	himself, herself,	σεαυτοῦ, -ῆς, -οῦ	yourself
		ὑμῶν αὐτῶν	yourselves

Pronouns / Adjectives:

ἐκεῖνος, -η, -ο	that	**τοιοῦτος**, -αύτη, -οῦτο	this kind, such
ὅδε, ἥδε, τόδε	this		
οὗτος, αὕτη, τοῦτο	this	**τοσοῦτος**, -αύτη, -οῦτο	this much / great many; so much / great / many

Preposition:

ὡς (+ *acc.*)	to (a person)

Particle:

ἆρα	(introduces a question; not translated)
ἆρα μή	surely...not (introduces a question; expects the answer 'no')
ἆρα οὐ	surely (introduces a question; expects the answer 'yes')

CHAPTER 25

πίνωμεν, παίζωμεν, ἴτω διὰ νυκτὸς ἀοιδή.
— Ion of Chios fr. 27.7 (Athenaeus, *Deipnosophistae* 11.463a-c)

1. The subjunctive mood

The subjunctive mood in Greek is used in a variety of situations, usually in subordinate clauses, to express a possibility or an assumption. It has aspect (Ch. 5.3, 13.4, 18.1), but no time value; the present subjunctive describes a continuing action, the aorist a single, simple act. All three tenses of the subjunctive (present, aorist and perfect) have primary endings and are associated with primary tenses of the main verb. The perfect subjunctive will be presented later (Ch. 33.1).

Note: The negative used with subjunctives is always μή.

2. The subjunctive of thematic and athematic (-μι) verbs

The marker for the subjunctive is a long thematic vowel. The personal endings for present and aorist are the regular primary endings of thematic verbs; the same endings are used for both thematic and athematic (**-μι**) verbs. In the athematic verbs, the stem vowel (**α**, **ε** or **ο**) must contract with the ending, as happens in the contract verbs.

REGULAR THEMATIC VERBS

Present		ACTIVE	MIDDLE / PASSIVE
Sing.	1st	λύ-ω	λύ-ω-μαι
	2nd	λύ-ῃς	λύ-ῃ
	3rd	λύ-ῃ	λύ-η-ται
Plur.	1st	λύ-ω-μεν	λυ-ώ-μεθα
	2nd	λύ-η-τε	λύ-η-σθε
	3rd	λύ-ω-σι(ν)	λύ-ω-νται

Aorist		ACTIVE weak	ACTIVE strong	MIDDLE weak	MIDDLE strong	PASSIVE
Sing.	1st	λύσ-ω	λάβ-ω	λύσ-ω-μαι	λά-βω-μαι	λυθ-ῶ
	2nd	λύσ-ῃς	λάβ-ῃς	λύσ-ῃ	λά-βῃ	λυθ-ῇς
	3rd	λύσ-ῃ	λάβ-ῃ	λύσ-η-ται	λά-βη-ται	λυθ-ῇ
Plur.	1st	λύσ-ω-μεν	λάβ-ω-μεν	λυσ-ώ-μεθα	λαβ-ώ-μεθα	λυθ-ῶ-μεν
	2nd	λύσ-η-τε	λάβ-η-τε	λύσ-η-σθε	λάβ-η-σθε	λυθ-ῆ-τε
	3rd	λύσ-ω-σι(ν)	λάβ-ω-σι(ν)	λύσ-ω-νται	λάβ-ω-νται	λυθ-ῶ-σι(ν)

CONTRACT VERBS

Present		ACTIVE			MIDDLE / PASSIVE		
Sing.	1st	φιλῶ	τιμῶ	δηλῶ	φιλῶμαι	τιμῶμαι	δηλῶμαι
	2nd	φιλῇς	τιμᾷς	δηλοῖς	φιλῇ	τιμᾷ	δηλοῖ
	3rd	φιλῇ	τιμᾷ	δηλοῖ	φιλῆται	τιμᾶται	δηλῶται
Plur.	1st	φιλῶμεν	τιμῶμεν	δηλῶμεν	φιλώμεθα	τιμώμεθα	δηλώμεθα
	2nd	φιλῆτε	τιμᾶτε	δηλῶτε	φιλῆσθε	τιμᾶσθε	δηλῶσθε
	3rd	φιλῶσι(ν)	τιμῶσι(ν)	δηλῶσι(ν)	φιλῶνται	τιμῶνται	δηλῶνται

ATHEMATIC VERBS, PRESENT AND AORIST SYSTEMS

Present		ACTIVE			MIDDLE / PASSIVE		
Sing.	1st	τιθῶ	ἱστῶ	διδῶ	τιθῶμαι	ἱστῶμαι	διδῶμαι
	2nd	τιθῇς	ἱστῇς	διδῷς	τιθῇ	ἱστῇ	διδῷ
	3rd	τιθῇ	ἱστῇ	διδῷς	τιθῆται	ἱστῆται	διδῶται
Plur.	1st	τιθῶμεν	ἱστῶμεν	διδῶμεν	τιθώμεθα	ἱστώμεθα	διδώμεθα
	2nd	τιθῆτε	ἱστῆτε	διδῶτε	τιθῆσθε	ἱστῆσθε	διδῶσθε
	3rd	τιθῶσι(ν)	ἱστῶσι(ν)	διδῶσι(ν)	τιθῶνται	ἱστῶνται	διδῶνται

Strong Aorist		ACTIVE			MIDDLE		
Sing.	1st	θῶ	στῶ	δῶ	θῶμαι		δῶμαι
	2nd	θῇς	στῇς	δῷς	θῇ		δῷ
	3rd	θῇ	στῇ	δῷς	θῆται		δῶται
Plur.	1st	θῶμεν	στῶμεν	δῶμεν	θώμεθα		δώμεθα
	2nd	θῆτε	στῆτε	δῶτε	θῆσθε		δῶσθε
	3rd	θῶσι(ν)	στῶσι(ν)	δῶσι(ν)	θῶνται		δῶνται

EXERCISE 113. Fill in the blanks in the subjunctive mood:

	form	tense	voice	person + number	verb
1.	______	aorist	active	3rd singular	νομίζω
2.	παυσθῶσι	______	______	______	______
3.	φεύγητε	______	______	______	______
4.	______	present	middle	3rd plural	λέγω
5.	______	present	active	1st plural	γράφω
6.	τιμήσω	______	______	______	______
7.	διδῶσι	______	______	______	______
8.	______	aorist	active	3rd singular	λαμβάνω
9.	φιλῇ	______	______	______	______
10.	______	aorist	middle	2nd plural	τίθημι

3. Exhortations

The 1st plural of the subjunctive is used to express an exhortation, such as English 'Let's do it!'. The negative is μή. The difference in meaning between the present and aorist subjunctive is one of aspect only; the aorist subjunctive is preferred for single acts, the present for ongoing actions.

θαυμάζωμεν τοὺς ἀγαθούς.
Let us admire the good (people).

λύσωμεν τὸν ἵππον.
Let's loose the horse.

μὴ παυσώμεθα τούτου τοῦ πολέμου.
Let us not cease from this war.

4. The deliberative subjunctive

The subjunctive is used in questions about what is to happen or what one should do. As usual the choice of present or aorist subjunctive is one of aspect.

πειθώμεθα τοῖς νόμοις;
Shall we obey the laws?

οἱ Πέρσαι νικηθῶσιν;
Are the Persians to be defeated?

5. Prohibitions

μή (and μηδείς, Ch. 33.4) are used with the aorist subjunctive to express a *specific prohibition*, one that refers to a specific occasion. A *general prohibition* is expressed by μή (or μηδείς) with the present imperative (Ch. 8.3, 18.1).

μὴ ἀποπέμψῃς τοὺς συμμάχους.
Don't send away the allies (right now). (specific)

μὴ βλάπτε τοὺς φίλους.
Don't (ever) harm your friends. (general)

μὴ πιστεύσῃ τῷ ῥήτορι.
Let him not believe the orator (right now). (specific)

μὴ οἱ γέροντες βλαπτέσθων.
Let the old men not be harmed (ever). (general)

Note: A 3rd person specific prohibition may occasionally use the aorist imperative instead of the aorist subjunctive.

6. γίγνομαι

γίγνομαι is a deponent verb with several possible meanings: 'become', 'come into being', 'happen'. The strong aorist ἐγενόμην supplies the missing aorist tense of εἰμί, 'be' in constructions where that tense is needed. Like εἰμί, γίγνομαι takes a predicate nominative instead of a direct object.

τοῦτο ἐγένετο τῆς νυκτός.
This happened at night.

οἱ νεανίαι στρατιῶται γενήσονται.
The young men will become soldiers.

εἰ ὁ παῖς σοφώτερος ἦν, κριτὴς ἂν ἐγένετο.
If the boy were wiser, he would have become a judge.

EXERCISE 114.

1. ἀεὶ τὰ ἀληθῆ λέγωμεν;
2. μὴ βλάπτετε ἀλλήλους, ὦ παῖδες, ἢ κακοὶ γενήσεσθε.
3. φύγωμεν εἰς τὰ ὄρη, τῶν πολεμίων προσβαλλόντων τῇ πόλει.
4. τύραννος γενόμενος ὁ Πολυκράτης εὖ ἐποίησε τὸν δῆμον.
5. μὴ ὁ αἰχμάλωτος οὗτος λυθῇ.
6. μεγίστη ναυμαχία ἐγένετο ἐν τῷ λιμένι.
7. μὴ παύεσθε τοῦ παιδεύεσθαι, ὦ νεανίαι.
8. ὁ στρατηγὸς ἐκεῖνος μὴ βοηθείτω τοῖς πολεμίοις.
9. μήτε διώξητε τοὺς Πέρσας, ὦ ἄνδρες, μήτε αὐτοὺς κωλύσητε.
10. καίπερ κακῶς πράττοντες μὴ πέμψωμεν ἀγγέλους ὡς βασιλέα.

EXERCISE 115.

1. Let us send our children away to Athens and educate them.
2. Do not put the horses among these trees.
3. Let them not be persuaded by money.
4. Let us not become more fortunate than the gods.
5. Do not make the army stand beside the walls.
6. Hinder neither the ambassadors nor each other.
7. Let us always fight for our country.
8. Do not treat those prisoners badly.
9. Let the soldiers not attack the city before night.
10. Are the gifts to be given immediately?

READING.

ARISTAGORAS AND HIS MAP

The Greeks in Ionia, as has already been said, had been subjected in turn to Lydia and Persia. In 499 B.C. Aristagoras resigned his position as tyrant in Miletus (a city in Ionia, southeast of Samos) and headed the Ionian revolt against Persia. He attempted to get help from Sparta before going to Athens and Eretria. Sparta's traditional opponents up to this time were her neighbors in the Peloponnese, Messenians to the west and Argives to the northeast.

ὁ δὲ Ἀρισταγόρας, ὁ τῆς Μιλήτου τύραννος, ἐβούλετο ἐλευθεροῦν τοὺς Ἴωνας ἀπὸ τῆς τῶν Περσῶν ἀρχῆς. ἔπλευσεν οὖν εἰς τὴν Σπάρτην καὶ διελέγετο τῷ Κλεομένει, τῷ τὴν ἀρχὴν ἔχοντι· καὶ ἔφερεν, ὡς οἱ Λακεδαιμόνιοι λέγουσιν, χαλκοῦν πίνακα, ἐν ᾧ γῆς πάσης περίοδος ἐγέγραπτο [*had been inscribed*] καὶ θάλαττά τε πᾶσα καὶ ποταμοὶ πάντες. Ὦ Κλεόμενες, ἔφη, μὴ θαυμάσῃς ὅτι δεῦρο ἥκω· ὅτι οἱ τῶν Ἰώνων παῖδές εἰσι δοῦλοι ἀντ᾽ ἐλευθέρων μέγιστον μὲν γὰρ ἄλγος ἐστὶν ἡμῖν αὐτοῖς, ἔτι δὲ ὑμῖν, οἳ ἀριστεύετε ἐν τῇ Ἑλλάδι. νῦν οὖν πρὸς θεῶν [*by the gods*] σώσατε τοὺς Ἴωνας ἐκ δουλοσύνης, ἄνδρας ὁμαίμονας. ῥᾴδιον δὲ ὑμῖν ἐστι ταῦτα ποιεῖν· οὔτε γὰρ οἱ βάρβαροι ἀνδρεῖοί εἰσιν, ὑμεῖς τε ἄριστοί ἐστε τὸν πόλεμον. ἥ τε μάχη αὐτῶν τοιαύτη ἐστίν, τόξα καὶ αἰχμὴ βραχεῖα· ἀναξυρίδας δὲ ἔχοντες μάχονται καὶ κυρβασίας ἐπὶ ταῖς κεφαλαῖς. οὕτω ῥᾴδιοι νικηθῆναί εἰσιν. ἔστι δὲ καὶ ἀγαθὰ τοῖς τὴν ἤπειρον ἐκείνην οἰκοῦσιν, χρυσός τε καὶ ἄργυρος, καὶ ὑποζύγιά τε καὶ δοῦλοι· ἃ βουλόμενοι αὐτοὶ οἷοί τ᾽ ἐστὲ σχεῖν.

ἔλεγε δὲ ταῦτα δεικνὺς τὴν τῆς γῆς περίοδον, ἣν ἔφερε ἐν τῷ πίνακι γραφεῖσαν· ἐξηγεῖτο δὲ τὰς χώρας πάντων τῶν βαρβάρων, ἐξηγούμενος τὸν πλοῦτον ἑκάστης, καὶ τὰ Σοῦσα[1] αὐτά, ἐν οἷς οἱ βασιλέως μεγάλου θησαυροὶ ἐνῆσαν. Λαβόντες ταύτην τὴν πόλιν, ἔφη, χρήματα πολλὰ σχήσετε. ἀλλὰ περὶ χώρας οὐ πολλῆς οὐδὲ χρησίμης δεῖ ὑμᾶς μάχας παῦσαι, πρός τε Μεσσηνίους καὶ Ἀργείους, οἷς οὔτε χρυσός ἐστιν οὔτε ἄργυρος. Ἀρισταγόρας μὲν ταῦτα ἔλεξε, Κλεομένης δὲ εἶπε τάδε· Ὦ ξένε Μιλήσιε, τριῶν [*three*] ἡμερῶν ἀποκρινοῦμαι. ἐπεὶ δὲ ἡ κυρία ἡμέρα ἐγένετο, ὁ Κλεομένης ἠρώτησε, Πόσων ἡμερῶν ἐστιν ἡ ὁδὸς ἀπὸ τῆς τῶν Ἰώνων θαλάττης παρὰ βασιλέα; ὁ δὲ Ἀρισταγόρας εἶπεν, Τριῶν μηνῶν. ὁ δὲ Κλεομένης εὐθὺς ἀπεκρίνατο· Ὦ ξένε Μιλήσιε, ἀποχώρησον ἐκ Σπάρτης πρὸ νυκτός· οὐ γὰρ εὖ συμβουλεύεις τοῖς Λακεδαιμονίοις, ἐθέλων αὐτοὺς ἀπὸ θαλάττης τριῶν μηνῶν ὁδὸν ἀγαγεῖν.

Adapted from Herodotus V.49-50

1 Susa, the capital of the Persian empire, lay north of the Persian Gulf; the Royal Road ran all the way there from Ephesus in Ionia.

Chapter 25 Vocabulary

Verbs:

ἀποπέμπω	send away
γίγνομαι, γενήσομαι, ἐγενόμην, γέγονα, γεγένημαι, —	become, happen
προσβάλλω (+ *dat.*)	attack

Noun:

ἄγγελος, -ου, ὁ   messenger

CHAPTER 26

Servant: τί δῆτα φήσω χρόνιος οὖσ' ἐκ δωμάτων;
Andromache: πολλὰς ἂν εὕροις μηχανάς· γυνὴ γὰρ εἶ.

— Euripides, *Andromache* 84-85

1. The optative mood

The optative mood in Greek is used in a variety of situations, usually in subordinate clauses, to express a possibility or a wish. The present, aorist and perfect tenses of the optative have aspect (Ch. 5.3, 13.4, 18.1, 25.3), but no time value; the present optative describes a continuing action, the aorist a single, simple act. The perfect optative will be presented later (Ch. 33.1). These tenses have secondary endings and are associated with secondary tenses of the main verb. The future optative is rare, and occurs only in indirect discourse.

Note: The negative used with optatives is often μή, but **οὐ** appears in some constructions, e.g. the potential optative (below, sec. 5) and the apodosis of certain conditional sentences (Ch. 28.3).

2. The optative of regular thematic verbs

The marker for the optative is **ι**, accompanied by the thematic vowel **ο** or its usual substitute tense vowel (1st aorist active **-α-**, 1st aorist passive **-ε-**, 2nd aorist passive **-ε-**). The weak aorist forms in **-ειας**, **-ειε(ν)** and **-ειαν** are more common in Attic than the short forms in **-αι-**.

Present		Active	Middle / Passive
Sing.	1st	λύ-οι-μι	λυ-οί-μην
	2nd	λύ-οι-ς	λύ-οι-ο (-οι-σο)
	3rd	λύ-οι	λύ-οι-το
Plur.	1st	λύ-οι-μεν	λυ-οί-μεθα
	2nd	λύ-οι-τε	λύ-οι-σθε
	3rd	λύ-οι-εν	λύ-οι-ντο

Future		Active	Middle	Passive
Sing.	1st	λύσ-οι-μι	λυσ-οί-μην	λυθησ-οί-μην
	2nd	λύσ-οι-ς	λύσ-οι-ο (οι-σο)	λυθήσ-οι-ο (οι-σο)
	3rd	λύσ-οι	λύσ-οι-το	λυθήσ-οι-το
Plur.	1st	λύσ-οι-μεν	λυσ-οί-μεθα	λυθησ-οί-μεθα
	2nd	λύσ-οι-τε	λύσ-οι-σθε	λυθήσ-οι-σθε
	3rd	λύσ-οι-εν	λύσ-οι-ντο	λυθήσ-οι-ντο

Weak Aorist		Active		Middle	Passive	
Sing.	1st	λύσ-αι-μι		λυσ-αί-μην	λυθ-εί-ην	
	2nd	λύσ-ει-ας	[λύσ-αι-ς]	λύσ-αι-ο	λυθ-εί-ης	
	3rd	λύσ-ει-ε(ν)	[λύσ-αι]	λύσ-αι-το	λυθ-εί-η	
Plur.	1st	λύσ-αι-μεν		λυσ-αί-μεθα	λυθ-εῖ-μεν	[λυθ-εῖ-μεν]
	2nd	λύσ-αι-τε		λύσ-αι-σθε	λυθ-εῖ-τε	[λυθ-εῖ-τε]
	3rd	λύσ-ει-αν	[λύσ-αι-εν]	λύσ-αι-ντο	λυθ-εῖ-εν	[λυθ-εῖ-εν]

Note: Diphthongs in the 3rd singular active endings of the optative count as long for accent purposes. Thus in the aorist active, the optative of λύω is λύσαι, while the infinitive is λῦσαι.

		Active	Middle	Passive
Strong Aorist		take		write
Sing.	1st	λάβ-οι-μι	λαβ-οί-μην	γραφ-εί-ην
	2nd	λάβ-οι-ς	λάβ-οι-ο	γραφ-εί-ης
	3rd	λάβ-οι	λάβ-οι-το	γραφ-εί-η
Plur.	1st	λάβ-οι-μεν	λαβ-οί-μεθα	γραφ-εῖ-μεν
	2nd	λάβ-οι-τε	λάβ-οι-σθε	γραφ-εῖ-τε
	3rd	λάβ-οι-εν	λάβ-οι-ντο	γραφ-εῖ-εν

3. The optative of contract verbs

In the present tense of contract verbs, the usual contractions take place between the stem and thematic vowels.

-εω: ε + οι = οι
-αω: α + οι = ῳ
-οω: ο + οι = οι

Contract verbs have two alternate sets of endings in the present active. The longer forms in -οιην, etc. are more common in the singular; in the plural, the shorter forms in -οιμεν, etc. are more common. The paradigms of φιλέω and τιμάω are presented here. δηλόω has the same endings as φιλέω.

		ACTIVE				MIDDLE / PASSIVE	
Present		love		honor		love	honor
Sing.	1st	φιλοίην	[φιλοῖμι]	τιμῴην	[τιμῷμι]	φιλοίμην	τιμῴμην
	2nd	φιλοίης	[φιλοῖς]	τιμῴης	[τιμῷς]	φιλοῖο	τιμῷο
	3rd	φιλοίη	[φιλοῖ]	τιμῴη	[τιμῷ]	φιλοῖτο	τιμῷτο
Plur.	1st	φιλοῖμεν	[φιλοίημεν]	τιμῷμεν	[τιμῴημεν]	φιλοίμεθα	τιμῴμεθα
	2nd	φιλοῖτε	[φιλοίητε]	τιμῷτε	[τιμῴητε]	φιλοῖσθε	τιμῷσθε
	3rd	φιλοῖεν	[φιλοίησαν]	τιμῷεν	[τιμῴησαν]	φιλοῖντο	τιμῷντο

4. The optative of athematic (-μι) verbs

In the present optative of **-μι** verbs, the marker **-ι-** is added to the stem vowel: **-ει-**, **-αι-**, **-οι-**. In the present and aorist active plural there are two alternate sets of endings; the shorter forms are more common.

		ACTIVE				M/P	M
		Present		Aorist		Present	Aorist
Sing.	1st	τιθείην		θείην		τιθείμην	θείμην
	2nd	τιθείης		θείης		τιθεῖο	θεῖο
	3rd	τιθείη		θείη		τιθεῖτο	θεῖτο
Plur.	1st	τιθεῖμεν	[τιθείημεν]	θεῖμεν	[θείημεν]	τιθείμεθα	θείμεθα
	2nd	τιθεῖτε	[τιθείητε]	θεῖτε	[θείητε]	τιθεῖσθε	θεῖσθε
	3rd	τιθεῖεν	[τιθείησαν]	θεῖεν	[θείησαν]	τιθεῖντο	θεῖντο
Sing.	1st	ἱσταίην		σταίην	ἱσταίμην	σταίμην	
	2nd	ἱσταίης		σταίης	ἱσταῖο	σταῖο	
	3rd	ἱσταίη		σταίη	ἱσταῖτο	σταῖτο	
Plur.	1st	ἱσταῖμεν	[ἱσταίημεν]	σταῖμεν	[σταίημεν]	ἱσταίμεθα	σταίμεθα
	2nd	ἱσταῖτε	[ἱσταίητε]	σταῖτε	[σταίητε]	ἱσταῖσθε	σταῖσθε
	3rd	ἱσταῖεν	[ἱσταίησαν]	σταῖεν	[σταίησαν]	ἱσταῖντο	σταῖντο
Sing.	1st	διδοίην		δοίην	διδοίμην	δοίμην	
	2nd	διδοίης		δοίης	διδοῖο	δοῖο	
	3rd	διδοίη		δοίη	διδοῖτο	δοῖτο	
Plur.	1st	διδοῖμεν	[διδοίημεν]	δοῖμεν	[δοίημεν]	διδοίμεθα	δοίμεθα
	2nd	διδοῖτε	[διδοίητε]	δοῖτε	[δοίητε]	διδοῖσθε	δοῖσθε
	3rd	διδοῖεν	[διδοίησαν]	δοῖεν	[δοίησαν]	διδοῖντο	δοῖντο

EXERCISE 116. Fill in the blanks in the optative mood:

	form	tense	voice	person + number	verb
1.	______	aorist	passive	3rd singular	ἄγω
2.	δηλοῖο	______	______	______	______
3.	πέμψαιμι	______	______	______	______
4.	δοῖντο	______	______	______	______
5.	______	aorist	middle	1st plural	τίθημι
6.	ἕξοιτε	______	______	______	______
7.	γραφείης	______	______	______	______
8.	______	aorist	active	3rd singular	λαμβάνω
9.	______	future	middle	2nd singular	ποιέω
10.	______	present	active	2nd plural	ἵστημι

5. The potential optative

The optative with the particle ἄν expresses a possibility or probability. The particle usually stands after the verb, or second in the verb phrase after a negative or an adverb. The words 'would', 'may', 'might' are good ways of translating the potential optative.

The verb tense conveys aspect: present optative for a continuous action, aorist for a single act. The negative is οὐ.

οἱ βάρβαροι οὐκ ἂν προσβάλοιεν ταύτῃ τῇ πόλει.
The foreigners would not attack this city.

ἡδέως ἂν δοίην αὐτοῖς τὰ χρήματα.
I would gladly give them the money.

ἀεὶ τιμῴη ἂν τὴν τῆς πόλεως θεάν;
Might he always honor the goddess of the city?

6. Wishes

Wishes can express regret that something did not happen in the past, or is not happening now: 'would that he had come sooner'; 'if only they were wiser'. Wishes about the future express hope that the wish will come true: 'may the gods bring victory'; 'if only you would meet me tomorrow'. In Greek the two kinds are handled differently.

- **Wishes referring to the present or past:** Since these wishes cannot be fulfilled they are contrary to fact, and their construction recalls that of contrary-to-fact conditions (Ch. 12.6). The verb is in the indicative mood; the imperfect tense refers to the present, while the aorist refers to the past. The negative is μή. The wish is introduced by εἴθε or εἰ γάρ; both mean something like 'if only…', 'would that…'.

εἴθε οἱ σύμμαχοι μὴ ἐνικήθησαν.
If only the allies had not been defeated [but they were].

εἰ γὰρ εἴχομεν σώφρονας κριτάς.
If only we had prudent judges [but we don't].

- **Wishes referring to the future:** Wishes about the future may be fulfilled, and they are expressed in Greek in the optative mood, reflecting this potential. They are often, but not always, introduced by εἴθε or εἰ γάρ. As usual, the tense of the optative conveys aspect: present for a continuous action, aorist for a single act. The negative is μή.

  εἰ γὰρ ἡ θεὰ ἀεὶ ἡμᾶς σῴζοι.
  If only the goddess would always protect us.

  ἡ θεὰ μὴ βλάψειεν ἡμᾶς.
  Would that the goddess might not harm us.

  εἴθε οἱ πολέμιοι μὴ νικήσειαν ἡμᾶς.
  May the enemy not conquer us.

Reading expectations

	↗ optative	= future wish
εἴθε / εἰ γάρ	→ imperfect indicative	= present wish
(neg. μή)	↘ aorist indicative	= past wish

EXERCISE 117.

1. εἴθε ὁ στρατηγὸς πλεύσαι πρὸς τὴν Ἑλλάδα.
2. κρείττονες νόμοι ἀγαθοὶ ἂν εἶεν τῇ πόλει.
3. εἰ γὰρ μὴ τοῦτο ἐγίγνετο.
4. εἴθε ὁ Δημοσθένης ἔπεισε τοὺς πολίτας.
5. οὐκ ἂν μαχοίμεθα ὑπὲρ κακῶν ἀνδρῶν.
6. εἰ γὰρ ἀφικοίμεθα εἰς τὴν πόλιν πρὸ τῆς νυκτός.
7. εἴθε οἱ στρατιῶται εὖ ἐφύλαττον τὰ τείχη.
8. μὴ νικηθείη ὁ στρατὸς ὃς ἔρχεται ἀπὸ τῶν συμμάχων ἡμῶν.
9. οὐκ ἂν βλάψαιτε τὰ δένδρα.
10. μὴ γράψῃς ἐπιστολὴν τοῖς συμμάχοις οἳ ἀπῆλθον.

EXERCISE 118.

1. We might come to the island in five days.
2. If only he had become wiser than his father.
3. Would the orator always speak the truth?
4. If only the enemy were not attacking those beside the river.
5. Polycrates, who was a tyrant, became most fortunate.
6. Would that some guide might show us the way.

7. Do not order the allies to go away.
8. The judge would give very many gifts to his children.
9. If only I had become a sailor.
10. May the women and children not be harmed.

READING 1.

MARATHON 1: VAIN APPEAL TO SPARTA

The expedition sent by Darius in 490 B.C. *to punish Athens and Eretria for their role in the Ionian revolt (Ch. 25 reading note) sailed up the west coast of Euboea and sacked Eretria. The Persians then landed in Attica in the bay of Marathon.*

οἱ δὲ Ἀθηναῖοι ἦσαν ἐν μεγάλῳ κινδύνῳ· Φιλιππίδης οὖν ἐπέμφθη κῆρυξ ὑπὸ τῶν στρατηγῶν καὶ δευτεραῖος ἐκ τοῦ Ἀθηναίων ἄστεως ἦν ἐν Σπάρτῃ,[1] ἥκων δὲ ἐπὶ τοὺς ἄρχοντας ἔλεγε· Ὦ Λακεδαιμόνιοι, εἴθε ἐθέλοιτε τοῖς Ἀθηναίοις βοηθῆσαι, μηδὲ πόλις ἀρχαιοτάτη ἐν τοῖς Ἕλλησι δουλοῖτο ὑπὸ βαρβάρων ἀνδρῶν· καὶ γὰρ Ἐρετρία ἐδουλώθη, ἡμῖν σύμμαχος ἀγαθὸς οὖσα. οἱ δὲ Λακεδαιμόνιοι ἤθελον μὲν βοηθεῖν τοῖς Ἀθηναίοις, ἀδύνατον δὲ ἦν αὐτοῖς τὸ εὐθὺς ποιεῖν ταῦτα, οὐ βουλομένοις λῦσαι τὸν νόμον· ἔδει γὰρ αὐτοὺς τὴν πανσέληνον μένειν.

Adapted from Herodotus VI.105-106

1 The distance was 140 miles.

READING 2.

MARATHON 2: THE BATTLE

ἐν δὲ τῷ μεταξὺ [*meanwhile*] οἱ μὲν βάρβαροι ἤχθησαν εἰς τὸν Μαραθῶνα ὑπὸ Ἱππίου τοῦ Πεισιστράτου παιδός,[1] καὶ ἀφικόμενοι εἰς γῆν ἔστησαν· τῶν δὲ Ἀθηναίων ἐκεῖ ταχθέντων, τοῖς ἑαυτῶν στρατηγοῖς δύο ἐγένοντο αἱ γνῶμαι, τῶν μὲν οὐκ ἐθελόντων εὐθὺς μάχεσθαι (οἱ μὲν γὰρ Ἀθηναῖοι ὀλίγοι ἦσαν, οἱ δὲ Πέρσαι πολλοί), τῶν δὲ κελευόντων, ἐν οἷς καὶ Μιλτιάδης ἦν. ὡς δὲ ἐνίκα ἡ χείρων τῶν γνωμῶν, πρὸς τὸν πολέμαρχον,[2] ὀνόματι Καλλίμαχον, ἐλθὼν ὁ Μιλτιάδης ἔλεξε τάδε· Ἐν σοὶ νῦν, ὦ Καλλίμαχε, ἔστιν ἢ δουλῶσαι τὰς Ἀθήνας ἢ ἐλευθέρας ποιήσαντα μνημόσυνον λιπέσθαι εἰς τὸν πάντα ἀνθρώπων βίον. ἡμῶν γὰρ τῶν στρατηγῶν δύο γίγνονται αἱ γνῶμαι, τῶν μὲν κελευόντων μάχεσθαι, τῶν δὲ οὔ. πάντα οὖν ἐκ σοῦ ἄρτηται [*depends on you*]. ὁ δὲ Καλλίμαχος ἐπείσθη ὑπὸ τοῦ Μιλτιάδου μάχην ψηφίζεσθαι.

ἐν δὲ τῇ μάχῃ οἱ Ἀθηναῖοι δρόμῳ προυχώρησαν ἐπὶ τοὺς βαρβάρους καὶ προσέβαλον αὐτοῖς. καὶ τὸ μὲν μέσον ἐνικῶντο οἱ Ἀθηναῖοι καὶ ἐδιώκοντο εἰς τὴν μεσογείαν· τὸ δὲ κέρας ἑκάτερον οἱ Ἀθηναῖοι ἐνίκων. ἔπειτα δὲ οἱ Ἀθηναῖοι συναγαγόντες ἀμφότερα τὰ κέρατα προσέβαλον τοῖς τὸ μέσον τρέψασιν, καὶ ἐνίκων. καὶ οὕτως οἱ Πέρσαι ἐδιώχθησαν εἰς τὴν θάλατταν.

Adapted from Herodotus VI.107-113

1 Both Pisistratus and his son Hippias had been tyrants of Athens in the 6th century B.C. Hippias, having fled to Persia after his expulsion from Athens in 510 B.C., served as advisor to king Darius.

2 The polemarch, as commander-in-chief, had a vote.

Chapter 26 Vocabulary

Verbs:

ἀπέρχομαι	go away, depart
ἀφικνέομαι, ἀφίξομαι, ἀφικόμην, —, ἀφῖγμαι, — (+ εἰς)	arrive, reach
ἔρχομαι, ἐλεύσομαι, ἦλθον, ἐλήλυθα, —, —	come, go

Particles:

εἰ γάρ	if only, would that, may	**εἴθε**	if only, would that, may

CHAPTER 27

Οὕτως γὰρ ἠγάπησεν ὁ θεὸς τὸν κόσμον, ὥστε τὸν υἱὸν τὸν μονογενῆ ἔδωκεν, ἵνα πᾶς ὁ πιστεύων εἰς αὐτὸν μὴ ἀπόληται ἀλλ' ἔχῃ ζωὴν αἰώνιον.

— John 3:16

1. Sequence of moods

The subjunctive and optative are used in similar ways in several kinds of subordinate clauses. When the main verb in a sentence is in a primary tense (present, future, perfect), you usually find the subjunctive in the subordinate clause. When the main verb is in a secondary tense (imperfect, aorist, pluperfect), the subordinate clause usually has the optative. This variation is called a *sequence of moods.*

> **Note:** Some authors occasionally use the subjunctive in place of the optative after a secondary tense main verb; the construction is then more vivid and immediate, since it effectively treats the past as present.

English instead has a *sequence of tenses*; that is, the tense of the verb in a subordinate clause is affected by the tense of the main verb. This pattern is visible in a variety of sentence types.

Primary Sequence	Secondary Sequence
I *am* afraid that he *will* not come.	I *was* afraid that he *would* not come.
I *come* so that I *may* see you.	I *came* so that I *might* see you.

2. Purpose (final) clauses

The second example above illustrates the *purpose clause*, which expresses the reason why something is done. In English, a purpose can be expressed in various ways.

Primary Sequence	Secondary Sequence
I *come* so that I *may* see you.	I *came* so that I *might* see you.
I *come* in order to see you.	I *came* in order to see you.
I *come* to see you.	I *came* to see you.

In Greek, the infinitive is not used to express purpose. Rather, a Greek purpose clause uses the subjunctive (after a primary tense main verb) or the optative (after a secondary tense main verb). A purpose clause is introduced by any of three conjunctions: ἵνα, ὡς or ὅπως. The tense of the subjunctive or optative verb shows aspect: the present for an ongoing or repeated action, the aorist for a single, simple act. The negative in a purpose clause is μή, but most purposes are positive, not negative.

τρέχομεν ἵνα τὴν μάχην παύσωμεν.
We are running in order to stop the battle. (primary)

ἐδράμομεν ἵνα τὴν μάχην παύσαιμεν.
We ran in order to stop the battle. (secondary)

νόμοις πειθόμεθα ὅπως εἰρήνην ἔχωμεν.
We obey laws to have peace / so that we may have peace. (primary)

νόμοις ἐπειθόμεθα ὅπως εἰρήνην ἔχοιμεν.
We obeyed laws to have peace / so that we might have peace. (secondary)

ἐλευσόμεθα ἵνα οἱ παῖδες μὴ βλάψωσι τὰ δένδρα.
We will come so that the children may not harm the trees. (primary)

ἤλθομεν ἵνα οἱ παῖδες μὴ βλάψειαν τὰ δένδρα.
We came so that the children might not harm the trees. (secondary)

3. The future participle to express purpose

Purpose in Greek is also expressed by the future participle, especially after verbs of motion ('go', 'send' etc.). It may, but need not, be introduced by ὡς (never by ἵνα or ὅπως). The participle agrees with the doer of the action, which might not be in the nominative case. The negative is οὐ, but most purposes are positive, not negative.

ἔπεμψα τὸν παῖδα λύσοντα τοὺς ἵππους.
I sent the boy to loose the horses.

ἐλευσόμεθα τοῦ ῥήτορος ἀκουσόμενοι.
We will come in order to listen to the orator.

Reading expectations

primary verb ↗ ἵνα + subjunctive / ↘ future participle = He goes *in order to do x.*

secondary verb ↗ ἵνα → optative / ↘ future participle = He went *in order to do x.*

EXERCISE 119.

1. οὗτοι ἐπέμφθησαν ἵνα τὰ δένδρα κόψειαν.
2. ἐρχόμεθα τῷ θεῷ θύσοντες.
3. ὁ Ξέρξης ἄξει στρατιάν, ὅπως οἱ Ἀθηναῖοι νικηθῶσιν.
4. οἱ πολέμιοι παρῆσαν ἐπὶ τοῦ ὄρους, ὡς προσβάλοιεν τοῖς Ἕλλησιν.
5. ἵνα μὴ ληφθεῖεν, οἱ Πέρσαι εἰς τὴν θάλατταν ἔφυγον.

6. ὁ Πολυκράτης ἀποπλεῖ, ὅπως ἀποβάλῃ τὴν σφραγῖδα.
7. οἱ Ἀθηναῖοι ἀπέπεμψαν τὰς γυναῖκας, ὡς ἀσφαλεῖς ἐσομένας.
8. ἡ Ἀρτεμισία κατέλυσε τὴν ναῦν ὅπως ἑαυτὴν σώσειεν.
9. αὐτοὶ ἀφικνούμεθα ὡς εὕρωμεν τὰ ζῷα ταῦτα.
10. δώσομεν πολλὰ δῶρα τοῖς θεοῖς, ἵνα μὴ ἀποθάνωμεν ἐν τῇ μάχῃ ταύτῃ.

EXERCISE 120.

1. The general is sending cavalry in order that he may hinder the enemy.
2. The Greeks and Persians fought each other for many years.
3. I became a sailor in order to see many countries.
4. We sent many soldiers to guard that village.
5. The Athenians gave very fine gifts to the general in order to honor him.
6. A guide arrived to lead the Greeks to the sea.
7. The generals waited for the king, in order to deliberate with him.
8. So that they might not be defeated, the Athenians asked us to help them.
9. We are crossing the river in order to escape from the lions.
10. Themistocles persuaded this many citizens to prepare ships in order to save their city.

4. οἶδα

The verb οἶδα ('know') is related to the aorist εἶδον, 'saw'; in form it is an irregular perfect tense (Ch. 32.1), but it has the present meaning 'I know' (i.e., because I have seen). The past tense is pluperfect in form (Ch. 32.1), but has the imperfect meaning 'I knew'. The future is a regular middle form, εἴσομαι (Ch. 17.2). The conjugation is as follows (for the participle, see Ch. 32.4).

Note: The alternate singular pluperfect forms do not occur in Attic until the 4th cy. BCE.)

INDICATIVE		Perfect	Pluperfect	
Sing.	1st	οἶδα	ᾔδη	[ᾔδειν]
	2nd	οἶσθα	ᾔδησθα	[ᾔδεις]
	3rd	οἶδε(ν)	ᾔδει(ν)	
Plur.	1st	ἴσμεν	ᾖσμεν	[ᾔδεμεν]
	2nd	ἴστε	ᾖστε	[ᾔδετε]
	3rd	ἴσασι(ν)	ᾖσαν	[ᾔδεσαν]

SUBJUNCTIVE		Perfect	
Sing.	1st	εἰδῶ	
	2nd	εἰδῇς	
	3rd	εἰδῇ	
Plur.	1st	εἰδῶμεν	
	2nd	εἰδῆτε	
	3rd	εἰδῶσι(ν)	
OPTATIVE			
Sing.	1st	εἰδείην	
	2nd	εἰδείης	
	3rd	εἰδείη	
Plur.	1st	εἰδεῖμεν	[εἰδείημεν]
	2nd	εἰδεῖτε	[εἰδείητε]
	3rd	εἰδεῖεν	[εἰδείησαν]
IMPERATIVE			
Sing.	2nd	ἴσθι	
	3rd	ἴστω	
Plur.	2nd	ἴστε	
	3rd	ἴστων	
INFINITIVE			
		εἰδέναι	
PARTICIPLE			
		εἰδώς, εἰδυῖα, εἰδός εἰδότος, etc.	

5. Irregular strong aorists

A few verbs have irregular strong aorists, without the thematic vowel. Here are the full aorist active paradigms of βαίνω, 'go' and γιγνώσκω, 'know'. The forms of βαίνω are the same as those of the strong aorist of ἵστημι (Ch. 23.3).

INDICATIVE		go	know
Sing.	1st	ἔ-βη-ν	ἔ-γνω-ν
	2nd	ἔ-βη-ς	ἔ-γνω-ς
	3rd	ἔ-βη	ἔ-γνω
Plur.	1st	ἔ-βη-μεν	ἔ-γνω-μεν
	2nd	ἔ-βη-τε	ἔ-γνω-τε
	3rd	ἔ-βη-σαν	ἔ-γνω-σαν
SUBJUNCTIVE			
Sing.	1st	βῶ	γνῶ
	2nd	βῇς	γνῷς
	3rd	βῇ	γνῷ
Plur.	1st	βῶμεν	γνῶμεν
	2nd	βῆτε	γνῶτε
	3rd	βῶσι(ν)	γνῶσι(ν)
OPTATIVE			
Sing.	1st	βαίην	γνοίην
	2nd	βαίης	γνοίης
	3rd	βαίη	γνοίη
Plur.	1st	βαῖμεν	γνοῖμεν
	2nd	βαῖτε	γνοῖτε
	3rd	βαῖεν	γνοῖεν
IMPERATIVE			
Sing.	2nd	βῆθι	γνῶθι
	3rd	βήτω	γνώτω
Plur.	2nd	βῆτε	γνῶτε
	3rd	βάντων	γνόντων
INFINITIVE			
		βῆναι	γνῶναι
PARTICIPLE			
		βάς, βᾶσα, βάν, βάντος, etc.	γνούς, γνοῦσα, γνόν, γνόντος, etc.

6. Supplementary participles in indirect statement

In indirect statement, many Greek verbs of knowing and perceiving often take a construction very similar to the one presented in Ch. 14.5, except that a supplementary participle is used instead of an infinitive. This construction is used to show physical perception (sense perception). Verbs that introduce it include the following:

αἰσθάνομαι, 'perceive'

γιγνώσκω, 'know', 'perceive' (above, sec. 5)

μανθάνω, 'learn'

οἶδα, 'know' (above, sec. 4)

ὁράω, 'see', ἀκούω, 'hear', and other verbs of sense perception

πυνθάνομαι, 'learn'

Note: γιγνώσκω and οἶδα with the infinitive mean 'know how to'; μανθάνω with the infinitive means 'learn how to'.

In this construction, the participle agrees in gender, number and case with its subject, which is nominative if it is the subject of the main verb, and accusative if it is not. As in the infinitive construction, the tense of the participle expresses time relative to the main verb: present for same time, future for later time, aorist for earlier time.

αἰσθάνομαι οὐ σοφὸς ὤν.
I perceive that I am not wise.

εἶδον τὴν ἐμὴν γυναῖκα σοφὴν οὖσαν.
I saw that my wife was wise.

οἶδεν αὐτὸς ποιήσας τοῦτο.
He knows that he himself did this.

ἠκούσαμεν τοὺς ἵππους εὐθὺς ἐλευσομένους.
We heard that the horses would come immediately.

Note: As in the infinitive construction, the negative with participles in indirect statement is οὐ.

7. Indirect statement with ὅτι or ὡς

The third type of indirect statement in Greek is closest to English wording. It is used after most verbs of saying (except φημί, Ch. 14.5), and after some of the same verbs that also take the participle construction (above, sec. 6). The ὅτι or ὡς construction, however, shows intellectual as opposed to physical perception. Verbs that commonly introduce this construction include the following:

ἀγγέλλω, 'announce'

αἰσθάνομαι, 'perceive'

ἀκούω, 'hear'

ἀποκρίνομαι, 'answer'

λέγω, 'say'

εἶπον, 'said'

ὁράω, 'see'

πυνθάνομαι, 'learn'

The indirect statement itself is introduced by ὅτι or ὡς, 'that'. ὅτι usually indicates an objective fact, ὡς a personal opinion. As in the infinitive and participle constructions, the tense of the verb in the indirect statement expresses time relative to the main verb: present for same time, future for later time, aorist for earlier time. The negative is οὐ.

After a primary tense main verb, the verb in the indirect statement is indicative. After a secondary tense main verb, the verb in the indirect statement may be indicative or optative. The tense is the same in either case.

εἶπον ὡς ὁ Σωκράτης σοφός ἐστιν / εἴη.
They said that Socrates was wise.

ἤγγειλαν ὅτι οἱ πολέμιοι ἔφυγον / φυγοῖεν.
They announced that the enemy had fled.

ἀπεκρίνατο ὅτι οἱ πολέμιοι ἔφευγον / φεύγοιεν τῶν ἱππέων ἀφικνουμένων.
He answered that the enemy were fleeing when the cavalry arrived.

Note: As in the third example, an imperfect indicative would become a present optative (and a pluperfect would become a perfect optative, Ch. 33.1), but in fact these tenses usually stay in the indicative mood.

EXERCISE 121.

1. ὁ Ἀρισταγόρας ἤγγειλεν ὡς οἱ βάρβαροι οὐκ ἀνδρεῖοι εἶεν.
2. ὁ βασιλεὺς εἶδε τὸν ἰχθὺν μέγαν ὄντα.
3. ὁ Πολυκράτης ᾔσθετο τὴν σφραγῖδα σωθεῖσαν.
4. ἐπυθόμεθα ὅτι οἱ πολέμιοι προχωροῦσι πρὸς τὸν ποταμόν.
5. οἱ Λακεδαιμόνιοι ἀπεκρίναντο ὡς πέμψοιεν πρέσβεις.
6. ἠγγέλθη ὅτι ὁ Λεωνίδας ἀπέθανεν.
7. ἡ Ἀρτεμισία ὁρᾷ αὐτὴ οὖσα ἐν μεγίστῳ κινδύνῳ.
8. ἀκούομεν τοὺς Πέρσας εἰς τὴν πόλιν ἐλθόντας.
9. ὁ Θεμιστοκλῆς εἶπεν ὡς δεῖ τοὺς Ἀθηναίους πιστεύειν τῷ ναυτικῷ.
10. ὁ ἄγγελος λέγει ὅτι οἱ πολέμιοι πάρεισιν.

EXERCISE 122.

1. We know that we are not safe.
2. I replied that I had not heard this.
3. We saw that the enemy were waiting on the mountain.
4. Some say that this is true, others that it is false.
5. The ambassadors say that the enemy will easily capture the city.

6. The Athenians heard that the Spartans would not come at once.
7. We perceived that we were being pursued by the enemy.
8. The tyrant says that it is easy to conquer the Persians.
9. The sailors learned that the ships were ready.
10. Who does not know that the Greeks were saved by their fleet?

READING.

AN ARGUMENT ABOUT COMMAND 1: GELON'S OFFER

In the autumn of 481 B.C. *a congress of Greeks was held at the Isthmus of Corinth to decide upon measures for resisting the threatened invasion by Xerxes. Ambassadors were sent to ask for help from various states, including Syracuse in Sicily. Syracuse had been founded by Corinth, and was ruled at this time by the tyrant Gelon.*

Ὡς δὲ οἱ τῶν Ἑλλήνων ἄγγελοι ἀφίκοντο εἰς τὰς Συρακούσας, τῷ Γέλωνι ἔλεγον τάδε· Ἔπεμψαν ἡμᾶς οἵ τε Λακεδαιμόνιοι καὶ οἱ Ἀθηναῖοι καὶ οἱ τούτων σύμμαχοι, παραληψομένους σε πρὸς τὸν βάρβαρον· οἶσθα γὰρ ὅτι ὁ Πέρσης ἀνὴρ μέλλει, διαβὰς τὸν Ἑλλήσποντον καὶ ἐπαγαγὼν πάντα τὸν ἑαυτοῦ στρατὸν ἐκ τῆς Ἀσίας, στρατεύσειν ἐπὶ τὴν Ἑλλάδα. ὡς δέ σοι, τῷ τῆς Σικελίας ἄρχοντι, μοῖρά ἐστιν οὐκ ἐλαχίστη τῆς Ἑλλάδος, βοήθει τοῖς τὴν Ἑλλάδα ἐλευθεροῦσι καὶ ἅμα ἐλευθέρου σεαυτόν· νικηθέντων γὰρ ἡμῶν, καὶ σὺ νικηθήσει.

ὁ δὲ Γέλων ἀπεκρίνατο· Ἄνδρες Ἕλληνες, ἐτολμήσατε μὲν δεῦρο ἐλθεῖν, ὅπως ἐμὲ σύμμαχον ἐπὶ τὸν βάρβαρον παρακαλέσαιτε· αὐτοὶ δέ, πολέμου γιγνομένου ἐμοὶ πρὸς τοὺς Καρχηδονίους[1], οὐκ ἤλθετε ὡς βοηθήσοντες. νῦν δέ, ἐπεὶ ὁ πόλεμος ἀφικνεῖται εἰς ὑμᾶς, πρὸς τὸν Γέλωνα ἔρχεσθε. ἀτιμηθεὶς δὲ ὑφ᾽ ὑμῶν, οὐχ ὑμᾶς ἀτιμήσω, ἀλλ᾽ ἑτοῖμός εἰμι βοηθεῖν, παρέχων διακοσίας τριήρεις καὶ δισμυρίους ὁπλίτας καὶ δισχιλίους ἱππέας, αὐτὸς ὢν στρατηγός τε καὶ ἡγεμὼν τῶν Ἑλλήνων πρὸς τὸν βάρβαρον· ἐπὶ λόγῳ τούτῳ [*on this condition*] τάδε ὑφίσταμαι. ἐπ᾽ ἄλλῳ δὲ λόγῳ οὔτ᾽ ἂν αὐτὸς ἔλθοιμι οὔτ᾽ ἂν ἄλλους πέμψαιμι.

Adapted from Herodotus VII.157-158

1 No details are known of this war, but in 480 the Carthaginians invaded Sicily and were decisively defeated at the battle of Himera, said to have been fought on the same day as the battle of Salamis.

Chapter 27 Vocabulary

Verbs:

αἰσθάνομαι, αἰσθήσομαι, ᾐσθόμην, —, ᾔσθημαι, —	perceive
ἀποκρίνομαι, ἀποκρινοῦμαι, ἀπεκρινάμην, —, ἀποκέκριμαι, ἀπεκρίθην	answer, reply
γιγνώσκω, γνώσομαι, ἔγνων, ἔγνωκα, ἔγνωσμαι, ἐγνώσθην	know, perceive
εἶπον (*aorist; stem* **εἰπ-**)	said
οἶδα (*perfect*), fut. εἴσομαι	know
πυνθάνομαι, πεύσομαι, ἐπυθόμην, —, πέπυσμαι, —	learn

Noun:

Ἀρισταγόρας, -ου, ὁ	Aristagoras

Conjunctions:

ἵνα	in order (to, that), so that
ὅπως	in order (to, that), so that
ὅτι	that (*objective fact*)
ὡς	in order (to, that), so that; that (*personal opinion*)

CHAPTER 28

ἐὰν ᾖς φιλομαθής, ἔσει πολυμαθής.

— Isocrates 1.18

ἀρετὴ δὲ κἂν θάνῃ τις οὐκ ἀπόλλυται.

— Euripides fr. 734.1 Nauck

1. Future and general conditions

Ch. 12.4-6 covered simple and contrary-to-fact conditions, which use the indicative mood. Other types of conditions require the subjunctive or optative. As usual, the tense of the subjunctive or optative conveys aspect: present for an ongoing action, aorist for a single, simple act.

Note: In all types of conditions, the negative is μή in the protasis and οὐ in the apodosis.

Future conditions: In Greek two kinds of conditions refer to the future. The following English sentences illustrate the two types.

If it rains, we will stay home.

If it should rain, we would stay home.

The first is called a *future more vivid* condition, and the second a *future less vivid* condition. A future more vivid condition sounds more likely to happen, and the verb in the protasis (if-clause) is subjunctive; the indicative (or equivalent) appears in the apodosis (then-clause). A future less vivid condition sounds more doubtful, and the use of the optative in both clauses reflects this lack of probability.

General conditions: Also presented below are *present general* and *past general* conditions. These state an outcome that is (was) always true every time the condition is (was) fulfilled.

If Socrates speaks, we (always) listen.

If the general (ever) gave an order, the soldiers (always) obeyed him.

Since the subjunctive is associated with primary tenses, it is used in present general conditions. Since the optative is associated with secondary tenses, it is used in past general conditions.

2. Conditions with the subjunctive

Future more vivid: Expresses a strong probability that the condition will be fulfilled. The protasis has a subjunctive verb, and is introduced by the word ἐάν, a combination of εἰ, 'if' and the conditional particle ἄν, which you encountered in the apodosis of contrary-to-fact conditions (Ch. 12.6) and in the potential optative construction (Ch. 26.5). The verb in the apodosis is usually a future indicative, but occasionally another verb looking to the future, like an imperative, or δεῖ + infinitive (negative μή with the infinitive).

Protasis	**Apodosis**
ἐάν + subjunctive (neg. μή)	future indicative (or equivalent) (neg. οὐ)
If he comes	we will persuade him.

ἐὰν χρήματα ἔχῃς, φίλους ἕξεις.
If you have money, you will have friends.

ἐὰν ἔλθῃ, πείσομεν αὐτόν.
If he comes, we will persuade him.

ἐὰν ἔλθῃ, πεῖθε αὐτόν.
If he comes, persuade him.

ἐὰν ἔλθῃ, δεῖ πεῖσαι αὐτόν.
If he comes, it is necessary to persuade him.

Present general: Expresses an outcome that is always true, if the condition is fulfilled. As in future more vivid conditions, the protasis has a subjunctive verb, and is introduced by the word ἐάν. The verb in the apodosis is a present indicative.

Protasis	**Apodosis**
ἐάν + subjunctive (neg. μή)	present indicative (neg. οὐ)
If you have money	you always have friends.

ἐὰν χρήματα ἔχῃς, φίλους ἔχεις.
If you have money, you have friends.

ἐὰν πέμψωμεν δῶρον αὐτῷ, ἀεὶ εὐδαίμων ἐστίν.
If we send him a gift, he is always happy.

EXERCISE 123. Identify the type of condition; then translate:

1. ἐὰν διώκῃς τὴν ἀρετήν, σοφὸς εἶ.
2. ἐὰν οἱ πολέμιοι ἔλθωσιν οὐ μενοῦμεν ἐν τῇ κώμῃ.
3. οἱ πολῖται πείσονται τῷ ῥήτορι ἐὰν πιστεύωσι τοῖς λόγοις αὐτοῦ.
4. If the children honor their father, he treats them well.
5. You will arrive before night if you don't journey by sea.

3. Conditions with the optative

Future less vivid: Expresses a more remote probability that the condition will be fulfilled, so the optative mood is used in both clauses. εἰ introduces the protasis; ἄν appears in the apodosis. The apodosis is equivalent in form and meaning to a potential optative (Ch. 26.5). The protasis can be translated in various ways.

Protasis	**Apodosis**
εἰ + optative (neg. μή)	optative + ἄν (neg. οὐ)
If he should come If he were to come, If he came,	we would persuade him.

εἰ χρήματα ἔχοις, φίλους ἂν ἔχοις.
If you should have money, you would have friends.

εἰ ἀκούσαι, πείσαιμεν ἂν αὐτόν.
If he should listen, we would persuade him.

Past general: Expresses an outcome that was always true, if the condition was fulfilled. The optative occurs in the protasis only; the imperfect indicative in the apodosis reflects the general nature of the outcome. The particle ἄν does not appear at all.

Protasis	**Apodosis**
εἰ + optative (neg. μή)	imperfect indicative (neg. οὐ)
If he had money,	he always had friends.

εἰ χρήματα ἔχοις, φίλους εἶχες.
If you had money, you had friends.

εἰ πέμψαιμεν δῶρον αὐτῷ, ἀεὶ εὐδαίμων ἦν.
If we sent him a gift, he was always happy.

EXERCISE 124. Identify the type of condition; then translate:

1. ἆρα μάχοισθε ἂν ὑπὲρ τῆς πατρίδος, εἰ οἱ Πέρσαι προσβάλοιεν ὑμῖν;
2. εἰ ἡ μήτηρ κελεύσαι, οἱ παῖδες ἀεὶ ἐπείθοντο αὐτῇ.
3. εἰ ναύτης γενοίμην, πορευοίμην ἂν πρὸς πολλὰς χώρας.
4. If the king wanted a fish, he always had it.
5. The men would not leave the island if the enemy should come.

Reading expectations

Protasis (neg. μή)	**Apodosis** (neg. οὐ)	
ἐάν → subjunctive	↗ future indicative (or equivalent)	= future more vivid
	↘ present indicative	= present general
εἰ → optative	↗ optative + ἄν	= future less vivid
	↘ imperfect indicative	= past general
εἰ → indicative	↗ indicative	= simple condition
	↘ indicative + ἄν	= contrary-to-fact

imperfect = present time
aorist = past time

4. Directional suffixes

-δε, 'toward', and -θεν, 'from' can be attached to place names and a few other words. Common examples include:

οἴκαδε	homeward
οἴκοθεν	from home
Ἀθήναζε	to Athens (Ἀθήνας + δε: ζ = σδ)
Ἀθήνηθεν	from Athens
ὅθεν	from which (place, person, cause)

EXERCISE 125. Identify all conditional types, and translate:

1. κακὸν ἂν εἴη εἰ θεῖμεν τὰ ὅπλα ἐν τῇ ὕλῃ.
2. ἐὰν ἀδικήσῃς, δεῖ σε οἴκοθεν ἀποφυγεῖν.
3. ἐὰν ὁ τύραννος εὖ ἄρχῃ τῆς πόλεως, οἱ πολῖται εὐδαίμονές τε καὶ ἀσφαλεῖς εἰσιν.
4. ἀεὶ ἠκούομεν τοῦ ῥήτορος εἰ τὰ ἀληθῆ λέγοι.
5. ὁ Ἄδμητος εὐτυχὴς ἂν εἴη εἰ ἡ γυνὴ ἐθέλοι ἀποθανεῖν ὑπὲρ ἑαυτοῦ.
6. Ἀθήναζε πέμψωμεν τοὺς νεανίας ἵνα εὖ παιδεύωνται.
7. εἰ οἱ παῖδες λάβοιεν τὸν ἵππον μου, οἱ ἑαυτῶν πατέρες ἀποδοῖεν ἂν αὐτόν.
8. ἐὰν ὁ βασιλεὺς κατὰ γῆν πορεύσηται, κινδυνεύσει.
9. εἰ ἔμαθες τὸ καλὸν οὐκ ἂν νῦν ἠδίκεις.
10. ὁ ἡγεμὼν ἤγαγε τοὺς Ἕλληνας πρὸς τὸ ὄρος ὅθεν εἶδον τὴν θάλατταν.

EXERCISE 126. Identify all conditional types, and translate:

1. If you send her these things she will love you.
2. Nobody would honor him if he attacked his own country.
3. If a lion pursues you, flee away!
4. Everyone believes us if we speak the truth.
5. If we were able to do that, we would be doing it.
6. Would you do this if the enemy retreated homeward by land?
7. If the king were better at speaking, he would still be ruling the citizens.
8. If the child sent a gift, his father always wrote a letter to him.
9. If the sailors reach the harbor, they will stop the war.
10. If you give money to foreigners, they never give it back.

READING.

AN ARGUMENT ABOUT COMMAND 2: THE GREEK RESPONSE

ἄγγελος δέ τις Λακεδαιμόνιος, ταῦτα ἀκούσας, εἶπε τάδε· Οὔ σοι ἐπιτρέψομεν τὴν ἡγεμονίαν· ἀλλ' ἐὰν μὲν βούλῃ βοηθεῖν τῇ Ἑλλάδι, ἀρχθήσει ὑπὸ Λακεδαιμονίων· εἰ δὲ μὴ ἐθέλεις ἄρχεσθαι, σὺ δὲ μηδὲ ἔθελε βοηθεῖν. πρὸς δὲ ταῦτα ὁ Γέλων ἀπεκρίνατο· Ὦ ξένε Λακεδαιμόνιε, ἐμὲ ὑβρίσας, οὔ με ἔπεισας ὑβρίζειν σε. πολλῷ μὲν μείζων ἐστὶν ἡ ἐμὴ στρατιά, πολλῷ δὲ πλείονες αἱ νῆες, ἀλλὰ ὑπείξομεν σοί. ἐὰν τοῦ μὲν πεζοῦ ὑμεῖς ἡγεμονεύητε, τοῦ δὲ ναυτικοῦ ἐγὼ ἄρξω· εἰ δὲ ὑμῖν ἡδύ ἐστι κατὰ θάλατταν ἡγεμονεύειν, τοῦ πεζοῦ ἐγὼ ἐθέλω. ἐὰν δὲ μὴ ὑπείξητε τοῦτο, ἄνευ συμμάχων ἀπελεύσεσθε.

ὁ δὲ τῶν Ἀθηναίων ἄγγελος εὐθὺς εἶπε τάδε· Ὦ βασιλεῦ Συρακοσίων, ἡ Ἑλλὰς ἀπέπεμψεν ἡμᾶς πρός σε οὐχ ἵνα ἡγεμόνα αἰτήσαιμεν, ἀλλὰ στρατιάν· οὐδ' ἐὰν ὁ Λακεδαιμόνιος βούληταί σοι ἐπιτρέπειν τὴν τοῦ ναυτικοῦ ἀρχήν, ἡμεῖς ταῦτα οὐκ ἐάσομεν· ἡμετέρα γάρ ἐστιν αὕτη, μὴ αὐτῶν βουλομένων τῶν Λακεδαιμονίων. ἀπεκρίνατο δὲ Γέλων· Ξένε Ἀθηναῖε, ὑμεῖς δοκεῖτε τοὺς μὲν ἄρχοντας ἔχειν, τοὺς δὲ ἀρχομένους οὐχ ἕξειν. ἐπεὶ τοίνυν, οὐδὲν [*in nothing*] ὑπείκοντες, ἔχειν τὸ πᾶν ἐθέλετε, εὐθὺς ἀποχωρήσατε εἰς τὴν Ἑλλάδα.

Adapted from Herodotus VII.159-162

Chapter 28 Vocabulary

Verbs:

ἀδικέω, ἀδικήσω, ἠδίκησα, ἠδίκηκα, ἠδίκημαι, ἠδικήθην	do wrong, be unjust, wrong (someone)
ἀποδίδωμι	give back

Conjunction:

ἐάν εἰ + *conditional particle* ἄν

Preposition:

κατά (+ *acc.*) by way of
- κατὰ γῆν by land
- κατὰ θάλατταν by sea

Other:

Ἀθήναζε	to Athens	**οἴκαδε**	homeward
Ἀθήνηθεν	from Athens	οἴκοθεν	from home
ὅθεν	from where, from which (place, person, cause)		

CHAPTER 29

ἐπάμεροι· τί δέ τις; τί δ' οὔ τις; σκιᾶς ὄναρ ἄνθρωπος.

— Pindar, *Pythian* 8.95-96

1. Adverbs

Adverbs ('happily', 'swiftly', etc.) as a rule look like the masculine genitive plural of any adjective, with final **-ς** instead of **-ν**.

Adjective	Gen. Pl.	Adverb	
ἀνδρεῖος	ἀνδρείων	ἀνδρείως	bravely
εὐτυχής	εὐτυχῶν	εὐτυχῶς	fortunately
ἡδύς	ἡδέων	ἡδέως	sweetly, gladly
σοφός	σοφῶν	σοφῶς	wisely
σώφρων	σωφρόνων	σωφρόνως	prudently
ταχύς	ταχέων	ταχέως	quickly

A comparative adverb ('more —ly') is the nom./acc. neuter *singular* of the comparative adjective. A superlative adverb ('most —ly') is the nom./acc. neuter *plural* of the superlative adjective. There is no rigid rule about the placement of adverbs, but they often precede the verb or adjective they modify.

Note: ὡς + superlative (adjective or adverb) means 'as...as possible':

ὡς σοφώτατος ἦν ὁ Σωκράτης.
Socrates was as wise as possible.

ὡς τάχιστα ἔσπευδον.
They were hurrying as quickly as possible.

2. ἔχω + adverb

ἔχω can be used with an adverb to describe a state of being. The phrase is equivalent to the verb εἰμί, 'be' with an adjective.

ἔχω καλῶς.
I am (doing) well.

κακῶς ἔχει.
It is going badly.

ἔμενε ὡς εἶχε.
He stayed as he was.

3. μάλα, μᾶλλον, μάλιστα

The adverb μάλα is quite common, as are its comparative and superlative:

μάλα much, very   μᾶλλον more   μάλιστα very much

As adverbs, these words can modify verbs and adjectives, but not nouns. A phrase like 'more soldiers' requires not μᾶλλον, but the adjective πλείων / πλέων, the comparative of πολύς. μᾶλλον + positive adjective is equivalent to a comparative adjective, but not as common.

μᾶλλον φιλοῦμεν τὸ καλόν.
We love the good more. (μᾶλλον modifies verb)

μᾶλλον σώφρων ἐστίν.
He is more prudent. (μᾶλλον modifies adjective)

ἔχομεν πλείονας ναῦς.
We have more ships. (πλείονας modifies noun)

EXERCISE 127.

1. ἡδέως ἠκούσαμεν ἐκείνου τοῦ ῥήτορος.
2. ἄμεινόν ἐστιν ἀποχωρῆσαι ἢ τὰ χρήματα ἀποδοῦναι.
3. οἱ Ἀθηναῖοι ἀγαθῶς ἐποίησαν τοὺς ἐν τῇ πόλει.
4. κατελύσαμεν πλείονας τριήρεις ἢ οἱ πολέμιοι.
5. ῥᾷόν ἐστι λέγειν ἢ πείθειν.
6. μάλιστα ἐπάθομεν ἐν τῷ πολέμῳ ἐκείνῳ.
7. τῶν τῆς πόλεως κακῶς ἐχόντων, οἱ πολῖται ὡς τάχιστα ἄλλους ἡγεμόνας ηὗρον.
8. οἱ ἀνδρείως μαχόμενοι ἔστησαν πρὸ τοῦ στρατοπέδου, ἵνα τοὺς πολεμίους ἀπελαύνοιεν.
9. οἱ Ἀθηναῖοι μᾶλλον ἐπίστευον τῷ ναυτικῷ ἢ τῇ στρατιᾷ.
10. οὐ ταχέως νικηθησόμεθα ὑπὸ τῶν ἱππέων τῶν προσβαλλόντων ἡμῖν.

EXERCISE 128.

1. The army of the Spartans was very small.
2. Do not hinder the soldiers who are guarding the town.
3. If the enemy were to go away as quickly as possible, they would not be conquered.
4. When doing well, even the worst men have friends.
5. Few cities are more beautiful than Athens.
6. That leader managed the city's affairs wisely, didn't he?
7. The father knew that his children were staying safely in the house.

8. Since the Persians were very many, Leonidas was easily defeated.
9. I see that those women will not be taught easily.
10. The horses were running more quickly to the sea.

4. The interrogative pronoun / adjective

The interrogative pronoun τίς, τί, 'who?' 'what?' is used as in English, to introduce questions. Its accent is always acute, never grave. The alternate forms of the gen. and dat. sing. are also found in Attic Greek.

who? what?

		M/F		N	
Sing.	Nom.	τίς		τί	
	Gen.	τίνος	τοῦ	τίνος	τοῦ
	Dat.	τίνι	τῷ	τίνι	τῷ
	Acc.	τίνα		τί	
Plur.	Nom.	τίνες		τίνα	
	Gen.	τίνων		τίνων	
	Dat.	τίσι		τίσι	
	Acc.	τίνας		τίνα	

Besides standing alone as a pronoun, τίς, τί is also used as an adjective ('what', 'which'), with an accompanying noun. It usually precedes the noun.

τίς λέγει;
Who is speaking?

τί βούλεσθε;
What do you want?

τίς στρατηγὸς ἄξει αὐτούς;
What general will lead them?

Note: τί is also an adverb meaning 'why':

τί φεύγεις;
Why are you fleeing?

5. The indefinite pronoun / adjective

The indefinite pronoun τις, τι ('someone', 'something', 'anyone', 'anything') is identical in formation to the interrogative pronoun, except that like many indefinite words it is enclitic (Ch. 7.4).

Besides standing alone as a pronoun, τις, τι is also used as an adjective ('some', 'any', 'a certain'), to make an accompanying noun (or adjective functioning as a substantive) indefinite. As an enclitic, it always follows the noun or adjective it modifies.

κόπτει τις τὰ δένδρα.
Someone is cutting down the trees.

πέμψω δῶρά τινα ὡς βασιλέα.
I will send some gifts to the king of Persia.

ζῷά τινα εἴδετε ἐν τῇ νήσῳ;
Did you see any animals on the island?

ἔλαβέ τις ἰχθὺν μέγιστον.
Someone caught a very large fish.

πέμψω αὐτὸ ἄλλῳ τινί.
I will send it to someone else.

δεῖ με εὑρεῖν σοφόν τινα.
It is necessary for me to find some wise person.

6. Interrogative and indefinite adverbs

Greek has a number of interrogative adverbs. Those relating to place and manner are covered here; for other types, see Ch. 30.3. Each of these is made indefinite by removing its accent and making it enclitic. These forms can carry an acute accent before punctuation, or before a following enclitic.

ποῦ	where?	που	somewhere
πόθεν	from where?	ποθέν	from somewhere
ποῖ	to where?	ποι	to somewhere
πῶς	how?	πως	somehow

EXERCISE 129.

1. τῶν Ἀθηναίων τινὲς οὐκ ἐφίλουν τὸν Δημοσθένη.
2. ἦν Ἀθηναῖός τις, ὀνόματι Θεμιστοκλῆς, ὅς ἄγγελον ἔπεμψεν ὡς βασιλέα.
3. τίς κωλύσει τοὺς πολεμίους ἐὰν ὁ στρατηγὸς ἀποθάνῃ;
4. βάρβαρός τις ἔβη ποθὲν εἰς τὴν πόλιν ἐκείνην.
5. τί οἱ ἄγγελοι λέξουσι τοῖς πολίταις;
6. ἆρ᾽ οὐ μάλιστα τὸν Ἄδμητον ἐφίλησέ πως ἡ Ἄλκηστις;
7. ποῖ καὶ τί ἐπορεύοντο οἱ Πέρσαι;
8. ἆρα μὴ τοὺς ὑμετέρους συμμάχους καταλείψετε;
9. τίνες πεμφθήσονται ἀπὸ τῆς Ἑλλάδος εἰς τὴν τῶν βαρβάρων χώραν;
10. ἐκείνη ἡ παῖς ἐπαίδευσέ πως τὸν ἵππον.

EXERCISE 130.

1. Someone was announcing the victory of the Athenians.
2. Where did you leave the money?
3. A certain messenger was sent to their city.
4. From where were the enemy marching?
5. Some of the allies were not willing to help the Athenians.
6. You admire this good leader, don't you?
7. Why are you marching through our country?
8. What are we to do in this danger, citizens?
9. How did the orator persuade them to do this?
10. The Greeks were journeying quickly to somewhere.

READING.

BORN TO BE KING 1: A HIGH-HANDED CHILD

Astyages, the last king of the Medes, dreamt that he would be overthrown by his grandson Cyrus, whose father Cambyses was a Persian. As soon as Cyrus was born, Astyages ordered him to be put to death, but a herdsman to whom the deed was entrusted substituted his own dead baby, and brought up Cyrus as his own son. Years later, Cyrus organized a rebellion and became king of the Medes and Persians in 549 B.C. The empire of Media, founded in about 700 B.C., had stretched from the Caspian Sea to the Persian Gulf and included Assyria and Persia.

ὁ δὲ Κῦρος, ὅτε ἦν δεκαετὴς καὶ ἔτι ἐνομίζετο εἶναι παῖς τοῦ βουκόλου, ἔπαιζεν ἐν τῇ κώμῃ μετ' ἄλλων τινῶν παίδων. καὶ οὗτοι παίζοντες εἵλοντο ἑαυτῶν βασιλέα εἶναι αὐτόν. τοῦ δὲ Κύρου κελεύσαντος, οἱ μὲν αὐτῶν οἰκίας παρεσκεύαζον, οἱ δὲ δορυφόροι ἦσαν, οἱ δὲ ἄλλα ἔργα ἐποίουν. τούτων δὴ τῶν παίδων τις, παῖς ὢν Ἀρτεμβάρους, ἀνδρὸς δοκίμου ἐν Μήδοις, οὐ γὰρ δὴ ἐποίησεν ἃ ὁ Κῦρος προσέταξεν, ἐκέλευε ὁ Κῦρος τοὺς ἄλλους παῖδας αὐτὸν λαβεῖν. πειθομένων δὲ τῶν παίδων, ὁ Κῦρος τὸν παῖδα μάστιγι ἐκόλασεν· ὁ δέ, ἐπεὶ ἀπέφυγεν, μάλιστα ὀργιζόμενος ἤγγειλε τὸ γενόμενον τῷ πατρί. ὁ δ' Ἀρτεμβάρης, ὀργῇ ὡς εἶχε ἐλθὼν παρὰ τὸν Ἀστυάγη καὶ ἅμα ἄγων τὸν παῖδα, εἶπεν, Ὦ βασιλεῦ, ὑπὸ τοῦ σοῦ δούλου, βουκόλου δὲ παιδὸς ὧδε ὑβριζόμεθα, δεικνὺς τοὺς τοῦ παιδὸς ὤμους. ἀκούσας δὲ καὶ ἰδών, ὁ Ἀστυάγης ἐθέλων κολάσαι τὸν παῖδα τιμῆς τῆς Ἀρτεμβάρους ἕνεκα, μετεπέμπετο τόν τε βουκόλον καὶ τὸν παῖδα.

Adapted from Herodotus I.114

Chapter 29 Vocabulary

Verb:

πάσχω, πείσομαι, ἔπαθον, πέπονθα, —, —			suffer

Pronouns / Adjectives:

τίς, τί	who?, what?	**τις**, τι	someone, something; anyone, anything; some; any

Adverbs:

μάλα	very	μᾶλλον	more
μάλιστα	very much, most, especially	**ὡς** + *sup.*	as...as possible

Interrogative adverbs:

πόθεν	from where?	πῶς	how?
ποῖ	to where?	τί	why?
ποῦ	where?		

Indefinite adverbs:

ποθέν	from somewhere	που	somewhere
ποι	to somewhere	πως	somehow

CHAPTER 30

ὃν οἱ θεοὶ φιλοῦσιν ἀποθνῄσκει νέος.

— Menander, *The Double Deceiver* fragment 4
(Stobaeus, Eclogae 4.52b 27)

νέος δ' ἀπόλλυθ' ὅντιν' ἂν φιλῇ θεός.

— Stobaeus, *Florilegium* 120.13

1. The indefinite relative pronoun / adjective

The indefinite relative pronoun ὅστις, 'whoever / whatever', 'anyone who / anything which / that', is simply the indefinite version of the relative pronoun ὅς, ἥ, ὅ (Ch. 10.3). It consists of the relative pronoun with indefinite τις (Ch. 29.5) added. Both components of the word are fully declinable. The alternate forms in the following paradigm are common in poetry but not in prose.

Like τις alone, ὅστις can also be used as an adjective, to make another noun indefinite: στρατηγὸς ὅστις, 'any general who...'.

		M		F	N	
Sing.	Nom.	ὅστις		ἥτις	ὅ τι	
	Gen.	οὗτινος	ὅτου	ἧστινος	οὗτινος	ὅτου
	Dat.	ᾧτινι	ὅτῳ	ᾗτινι	ᾧτινι	ὅτῳ
	Acc.	ὅντινα		ἥντινα	ὅ τι	
Plur.	Nom.	οἵτινες	αἵτινες	ἅτινα	ἅττα	
	Gen.	ὧντινων	ὅτων	ὧντινων	ὧντινων	ὅτων
	Dat.	οἷστισι(ν)	ὅτοις	αἷστισι(ν)	οἷστισι(ν)	ὅτοις
	Acc.	οὕστινας	ἅστινας	ἅτινα	ἅττα	

Note: The neuter singular ὅ τι is written as two words, which helps to distinguish it from ὅτι, 'that'. In the other forms, the accented and enclitic components are written as one word, but accented as if they were two words.

2. Correlative pronouns / adjectives

Some Greek pronouns / adjectives are related in form and meaning. They are called *correlatives*, and may be correlated in a sentence, as they may be in English.

Whatever you sow, that you will reap.

The following table summarizes the relationship in form and meaning among the various types of Greek pronouns / adjectives. They share some patterns of formation. An initial **π** is characteristic of most interrogative forms,[1] indefinites are enclitic, an initial rough breathing marks the relatives, etc.

Interrogative	Indefinite	Demonstrative	Relative	Indefinite Relative *or* Indirect Interrogative
τίς[1], who?	τις, someone	οὗτος, this	ὅς, who	ὅστις, whoever
πόσος, how much?	ποσός, some amount	τοσοῦτος, this much	ὅσος, as much as	ὁπόσος, however much
ποῖος, what kind	ποιός, some kind	τοιοῦτος, this kind	οἷος, the kind which	ὁποῖος, whatever kind

1 An older labio-velar consonant **k**^{w} became **π** in Classical Greek before vowels formed in the back of the mouth, like **ο**. Before front vowels like the **ι** in **τίς**, the labio-velar became **τ**.

3. Correlative adverbs

The same relationships in form and meaning observed among correlative pronouns / adjectives also hold for correlative adverbs:

Interrogative	Indefinite	Demonstrative	Relative	Indefinite Relative *or* Indirect Interrogative
ποῦ, where?	που, somewhere	ἐνταῦθα, here, there	οὗ, where	ὅπου, where, wherever
πόθεν, from where?	ποθέν, from somewhere	ἐντεῦθεν, from here	ὅθεν, from where	ὁπόθεν, from where, from wherever
ποῖ, to where?	ποι, to somewhere	ἐνταῦθα, to here, to there	οἷ, to where	ὅποι, to where, to wherever
πότε, when?	ποτέ, once, sometime, ever	τότε, then	ὅτε, when, whenever	ὁπότε, when, whenever
πῶς, how?	πως, somehow	οὕτως, thus	ὡς, as, how	ὅπως, how, however

4. Conditional relative and temporal clauses

Some subordinate clauses closely resemble the protasis of a condition (Ch. 28), except they are introduced by a relative pronoun or adverb instead of 'if'. Here are English examples of the most common types. Some are *temporal*, referring to time ('when', 'whenever'); others express other types of circumstances ('wherever', whoever', etc.). The antecedent is always indefinite.

Whenever he comes we will begin.	(future more vivid)
Whoever obeys the laws is a good man.	(present general)
I would do *whatever you wanted.*	(future less vivid)
They always went *wherever he led.*	(past general)
I would have liked *whatever he had brought.*	(contrary-to-fact)

A *conditional relative* sentence in Greek uses the same construction as the type of condition it resembles, except that the protasis is introduced by a relative pronoun or adverb instead of εἰ or ἐάν.

These clauses can be introduced either by a simple relative pronoun or adverb, or by an indefinite one (above, sec. 2-3). Two particular rules apply to future more vivid and present general constructions.

- When ὅστις introduces the protasis, the verb may be indicative, instead of subjunctive (ἄν omitted), because ὅστις already has an indefinite meaning.
- When ἄν appears in the protasis, it is combined into one word with the relative adverbs ὅτε and ὁπότε: ὅταν, ὁπόταν. With other relative adverbs and with pronouns it is usually written as a separate word (though ἐπειδάν from ἐπειδή is common).

ὅς ἄν μὴ πείθηται τοῖς νόμοις κακός ἐστιν.
ὅστις μὴ πείθεται τοῖς νόμοις κακός ἐστιν.
ὅστις ἄν μὴ πείθηται τοῖς νόμοις κακός ἐστιν.
Whoever does not obey the laws is bad. (present general)

ὅστις πείθοιτο τοῖς νόμοις ἀγαθὸς ἦν.
Whoever obeyed the laws was good. (past general)

ὅταν ἔλθῃ στρατεύσομεν.
Whenever he comes, we will march. (future more vivid)

ὅτε ἔλθοι στρατεύσαιμεν ἄν.
Whenever he should come, we would march. (future less vivid)

πιστεύσομεν ὅς ἄν πείθηται τοῖς νόμοις.
We will trust whoever obeys the laws. (future more vivid)

πιστεύοιμεν ἄν ὅστις πείθοιτο τοῖς νόμοις.
We would trust whoever obeyed the laws. (future less vivid)

ἐπιστεύσαμεν ἄν ὅστις σοφὸς ἦν.
We would have trusted anyone who was wise. (contrary-to-fact)

Note: In the last set of examples, the relative pronoun is nominative because its function as subject of the relative clause is more important than its function as the object of πιστεύω.

EXERCISE 131. Identify the following constructions, and translate:

1. ὅπου ἂν ξίφη εὕρωμεν, ληψόμεθα αὐτά.
2. δοῖεν ἂν τὰ χρήματα ᾧτινι πιστεύσειαν.
3. ὁπότε πόλεμος γένοιτο, ἀνδρείως ἐμάχοντο.
4. ὅστις βούλεται ἄρχειν μάλα κινδυνεύει.

EXERCISE 132.

1. ὅ τι ἂν λέγῃ ὁ ῥήτωρ, ἀκουσόμεθα αὐτοῦ.
2. ἐποίμεθα ἂν ὅποι κελεύσαι ὁ ἡγεμών.
3. οἵτινες μὴ θύσειαν τοῖς θεοῖς οὐκ ἐλάμβανον δῶρα ἀπ᾽ αὐτῶν.
4. σχήσεις ἵππον ὁποῖον ἂν βούλῃ.
5. ὅστις μὴ πείθοιτο τοῖς νόμοις, οὐκ ἂν ποιοῖμεν στρατηγόν.
6. ὁπόσα ἂν χρήματα ἔχητε, οὐκ ἀσφαλεῖς ἐστε.
7. ἐπειδὰν εὖ παιδεύωνται οἱ παῖδες, καλῶς ἔχουσιν.
8. δεῖ στῆσαι τοὺς ὁπλίτας ὅπου ἂν χρησιμώτατοι ἔσονται.
9. ἐλαύνοιμι ἂν ταῦτα τὰ ζῷα ὅποι οἷά τε εἴη ὕδωρ εὑρεῖν.
10. τιμῶμεν τοὺς κριτὰς ὅταν εὖ πράττωσι τὰ τῆς πόλεως.

EXERCISE 133.

1. Whenever the children left the city, their fathers advised them to hurry homeward.
2. Whoever had money always had friends.
3. The animals always followed that boy to wherever he led them.
4. It is necessary for the gods to have as many gifts as they want.
5. Anyone who waits for those men will not arrive before night.
6. We hope to persuade anyone who will listen to us.
7. Whenever we see that a storm is coming, we hasten into the house.
8. I will not listen to you, however many words you speak.
9. Anyone whom the general saw was ordered to fight.
10. The king of Persia would send soldiers to wherever he should wish.

READING.

BORN TO BE KING 2: KING HEREAFTER

τούτων δὲ παρόντων, βλέψας πρὸς τὸν Κῦρον ὁ Ἀστυάγης ἔφη· Σὺ δὴ ὢν παῖς τοιούτου ἀνδρὸς ἐτόλμησας τὸν τοῦδε παῖδα ὄντος πρώτου παρ' ἐμοὶ ὧδε ὑβρίζειν; ὁ δὲ ἀπεκρίνατο· Ὦ δέσποτα, ἐγὼ ταῦτα δικαίως ἐποίησα. οἱ γὰρ ἐκ τῆς κώμης παῖδες, ὧν καὶ ὅδε ἦν, παίζοντες ἐμὲ ἐστήσαντο ἑαυτῶν βασιλέα. ἐδόκουν γὰρ αὐτοῖς εἶναι ἐπιτηδειότατος. οἱ μὲν οὖν ἄλλοι παῖδες ἃ ἐκέλευσα ἔπραξαν, οὗτος δὲ οὐκ ἐπείθετο· ἐκολάσθη οὖν. εἰ οὖν δὴ τούτου ἕνεκα ἄξιος κακοῦ τινός εἰμι, ὅδε πάρειμι. ταῦτα λέγοντος τοῦ παιδός, ὁ Ἀστυάγης ἐδόκει ἀναγνωρίζειν τὸ πρόσωπον αὐτοῦ καὶ πολὺν χρόνον ἄφθογγος ἦν. τοῦ δὲ Ἀρτεμβάρους ἀποπεμφθέντος, ἐκέλευσε τοὺς θεράποντας ἔσω ἄγειν τὸν Κῦρον. ἐπεὶ δὲ παρῆν ὁ βουκόλος μόνος, ὁ Ἀστυάγης τάδε ἠρώτησεν· Πόθεν ἔλαβες τὸν παῖδα καὶ τίς σοι ἔδωκεν αὐτόν; ὁ δὲ ἀπεκρίνατο ὅτι ἐστὶν ὁ ἑαυτοῦ παῖς. ὁ δὲ Ἀστυάγης ἐσήμαινε τοῖς δορυφόροις συλλαμβάνειν καὶ τύπτειν αὐτόν. ὁ δὲ ἐν μεγίστῃ ἀπορίᾳ ὢν πάντα ἐξηγεῖτο καὶ ᾔτησε τὸν βασιλέα ἑαυτῷ συγγιγνώσκειν.

Adapted from Herodotus I.115-116

Chapter 30 Vocabulary

Verb:

ἕπομαι, ἕψομαι, ἑσπόμην, —, —, — (+ *dat.*) follow
impf. εἱπόμην

Pronouns / Adjectives: above, sec. 2

ὅστις, ὅ τι anyone who, anything which / that, whoever, whatever

Adverbs: above, sec. 3

CHAPTER 31

ἦ που ἔτι ζώει καὶ ὁρᾷ φάος ἠελίοιο,
ἦ ἤδη τέθνηκε καὶ εἰν Ἀΐδαο δόμοισιν.
— Homer, *Odyssey* 4.833-834

1. The perfect system

Like the present and future, the perfect is a *primary* tense in Greek. It emphasizes the present *result* of a past action, not the action itself.

Perfect	Aorist
I have climbed the tree. (and here I am at the top)	I climbed the tree. (yesterday)
He has arrived.	He arrived.

Because of this specialized and restricted meaning, the perfect is much less common in Greek than in English.

The pluperfect tense is the past tense version of the perfect tense. It presents the result of a previous action, all within past time.

I had climbed the tree (when the bull reached it).

He had arrived (by the time I came).

Both the perfect and the pluperfect occur in all three voices.

	Active	Middle	Passive
Perfect	I have loosed	I have ransomed	I have been loosed
Pluperfect	I had loosed	I had ransomed	I had been loosed

2. The perfect and pluperfect active indicative of regular verbs (4th principal part)

perfect: The perfect active tense is formed from the 4th principal part, and has two regular markers.

- *reduplication* at the beginning of the word. Most verbs beginning with consonants reduplicate the first letter with **ε**, as in λέλυκα (other types of reduplication are covered in Ch. 32.2).

- the stem ending **-κ** for the 1st or weak perfect, or the verb's own consonant for the 2nd or strong perfect (Ch. 32.1), with the stem vowel **-α-**. This sequence replaces the thematic vowel, as **-σ-α** does in the aorist active / middle (Ch. 5.2, 17.2).

The personal endings of the perfect active are very similar to the weak aorist active endings (Ch. 5.2), except that the 3rd plural has the primary ending **-ασι(ν)**.

		Stem **λελῠκ-**	Translation	Endings
Sing.	1st	λέ-λυκ-α	I have loosed	-ᾰ-
	2nd	λέ-λυκ-α-ς	you have loosed	-ᾰ-ς
	3rd	λέ-λυκ-ε(ν)	he / she / it has loosed	-ε-(ν)
Plur.	1st	λε-λύκ-α-μεν	we have loosed	-ᾰ-μεν
	2nd	λε-λύκ-α-τε	you have loosed	-ᾰ-τε
	3rd	λε-λύκ-α-σι(ν)	they have loosed	-ᾱ-σῐ(ν)

pluperfect: The pluperfect active uses the same reduplicated stem as the perfect, with stem vowel **η/ε**. Because it is a past tense, it also has an augment and secondary endings (Ch. 4.3, 5.2, 11.2).

		Stem **λελῠκ -**	Translation	Endings
Sing.	1st	ἐ-λε-λύκ-η	I had loosed	-η-
	2nd	ἐ-λε-λύκ-η-ς	you had loosed	-η-ς
	3rd	ἐ-λε-λύκ-ει(ν)	he / she / it had loosed	-ει-(ν)
Plur.	1st	ἐ-λε-λύκ-ε-μεν	we had loosed	-ε-μεν
	2nd	ἐ-λε-λύκ-ε-τε	you had loosed	-ε-τε
	3rd	ἐ-λε-λύκ-ε-σαν	they had loosed	-ε-σαν

Note: The long ᾱ in the 3rd plural of the perfect tense is due to compensatory lengthening (Ch. 10.1, 20.3,5); the original ending was ***-ᾰντι**.

3. The perfect and pluperfect middle / passive indicative of regular verbs (5th principal part)

perfect: The perfect middle and passive have identical forms, and come from the 5th principal part. As a primary tense, it uses the regular primary middle / passive personal endings (Ch. 15.2). These are attached directly to the verb stem. The only marker is the reduplication at the beginning of the word. The following paradigm gives a translation for the passive only.

		Stem λελῠ-	Translation	Endings
Sing.	1st	λέ-λυ-μαι	I have been loosed	-μαι
	2nd	λέ-λυ-σαι	you have been loosed	-σαι
	3rd	λέ-λυ-ται	he / she / it / has been loosed	-ται
Plur.	1st	λε-λύ-μεθα	we have been loosed	-μεθα
	2nd	λέ-λυ-σθε	you have been loosed	-σθε
	3rd	λέ-λυ-νται	they have been loosed	-νται

pluperfect: The pluperfect middle / passive have identical forms, and use the same reduplicated stem as the perfect. Because they are past tenses, they also have an augment and secondary endings (Ch. 4.3, 11.2, 15.2). The following paradigm gives a translation for the passive only.

		Stem λελῠ-	Translation	Endings
Sing.	1st	ἐ-λε-λύ-μην	I had been loosed	-μην
	2nd	ἐ-λέ-λυ-σο	you had been loosed	-σο
	3rd	ἐ-λέ-λυ-το	he / she / it / had been loosed	-το
Plur.	1st	ἐ-λε-λύ-μεθα	we had been loosed	-μεθα
	2nd	ἐ-λέ-λυ-σθε	you had been loosed	-σθε
	3rd	ἐ-λέ-λυ-ντο	they had been loosed	-ντο

4. The dative of personal agent

With perfect and pluperfect passive verbs, the personal agent is in the dative with no preposition (*dative of personal agent*), rather than in the genitive with ὑπό (Ch. 15.3).

ἡ πόλις τετίμηται τοῖς ποιηταῖς.
The city has been honored by the poets.

ἡ πόλις τιμᾶται ὑπὸ τῶν ποιητῶν.
The city is honored by the poets.

EXERCISE 134.

1. οἱ παῖδες λελύκασι τοὺς βαρβάρους τοὺς δουλωθέντας.
2. ὁ ῥήτωρ ἐκεῖνος πεπαίδευκε πολλοὺς τῶν Ἀθηναίων.
3. οἱ ἐν ταῖς Ἀθήναις εὖ συμβεβούλευνται τῷ Δημοσθένει.
4. ἐκείνῳ τῷ ἡγεμόνι οὐκ ἀεὶ πεπιστεύκαμεν.
5. οἱ δοῦλοι οὔπω πέπαυνται τῶν ἔργων.
6. οἵτινες τεθεράπευνται τῷ δήμῳ τὰ τῆς πόλεως πράξουσιν.
7. διὰ τὸν χειμῶνα οὐκ ἐλελύκεμεν τοὺς ἵππους.

8. οἱ ἱππεῖς θᾶττον διώκοντες ἐκεκωλύκεσαν τοὺς πολεμίους.
9. ὁ στρατηγὸς πάντας τοὺς αἰχμαλώτους λέλυται.
10. οἱ ὁπλῖται αὐτοὶ οὔπω ἐπεπαίδευντο στρατεῦσαι.

EXERCISE 135.

1. We have kept the horses from the river so that they will not cross it.
2. Those who are ready have been ordered to march immediately.
3. That tyrant had enslaved all the women in the village.
4. Who has sacrificed to the god of this river?
5. The walls have been destroyed by some giants.
6. The wise old man had been king [*use* βασιλεύω] for many years.
7. Many young men had been honored by the people whom they saved.
8. What soldiers had been trained better by their generals?
9. The very lucky king has not yet run risks in battle.
10. You have ransomed all the men on that island, haven't you?

5. The perfect infinitive (4th and 5th principal parts)

The perfect infinitive is far less common than the aorist infinitive. Like the perfect indicative it always emphasizes the result of a completed action.

Perfect	**Aorist**
ἀγαθόν ἐστι πεπαῦσθαι τῶν ἔργων. It is good to have ceased from work.	ἀγαθόν ἐστι παύσασθαι τῶν ἔργων. It is good to cease from work.
νομίζει σεσωκέναι τὴν πατρίδα. He thinks he has saved the fatherland.	νομίζει σῶσαι τὴν πατρίδα. He thinks he saved the fatherland.

The perfect infinitives are formed as follows.

A:	perfect stem + **ε** + **-ναι** accent on the **-ε-**	= **-εναι**	λελυκέναι, πεποιθέναι
M/P:	perfect stem + **-σθαι** accent on the last syllable of the verb stem	= **-σθαι**	λελύσθαι, πεπεῖσθαι

EXERCISE 136. Translate:

1. ἐπεπαύκει
2. κεκωλῦσθαι
3. τεθαυμάκατε
4. δεδωκέναι
5. καταλέλυται
6. They have hindered
7. We had been ordered
8. You (pl.) have been educated
9. I had ransomed
10. To have stopped

6. Result (consecutive) clauses

A result clause expresses either an actual result (something that did happen) or a natural, probable result (something that would naturally happen).

I was so hungry that I ate the whole thing. (actual result)

I was hungry enough to eat an ox. (natural result)

I was so foolish as to believe them. (natural result)

In Greek, both types of result clause are introduced by ὥστε, '(so) that', '(so) as to', which is often, but not always, anticipated by a phrase with οὕτω(ς), 'so', τοσοῦτος, 'so much', etc.

- **Actual result:** The result clause uses a verb in the indicative mood (negative οὐ). The subject is in the nominative case.

  ἀγαθὸς στρατηγὸς ἦν ὥστε ἔπαυσε τὴν μάχην.
  He was a good general and so he stopped the battle.

  οὕτω μῶρός ἐστιν ὥστε οὐ πιστεύομεν αὐτῷ.
  He is so foolish that we do not trust him (now).

- **Natural or probable result:** The result clause uses an infinitive (negative μή). The subject of the infinitive is in the nominative case, if it is the subject of the main verb; if different, it is accusative. The infinitive is usually either present or aorist, depending on aspect.

  οὕτω μῶρός ἐστιν ὥστε ἡμᾶς μὴ πιστεύειν αὐτῷ.
  He is so foolish that we do not believe him (ever).

  οὕτω κακός ἐστι ὥστε λαβεῖν τὰ σὰ χρήματα.
  He is so bad as to take your money.

  After a comparative, ἢ ὥστε is used with the infinitive.

  ὁ Σωκράτης σοφώτερός ἐστιν ἢ ὥστε τοῦτο λέξαι.
  Socrates is too wise (lit., wiser than) to say this.

Reading expectations

οὕτω(ς) → ὥστε ↗ indicative (neg. οὐ) = actual result He is so wise that he did x.
οὕτω(ς) → ὥστε ↘ infinitive (neg. μή) = natural result He is so wise as to do x.
comparative → ἢ ὥστε → infinitive (neg. μή) = natural result He is too wise to do x.

EXERCISE 137.

1. οὕτω ταχεῖα ἦν ἡ ναῦς ἐκείνη ὥστε μὴ ληφθῆναι ὑπὸ τῶν Περσῶν.
2. ἡ Ἄλκηστις οὕτως ἐφίλησε τὸν ἄνδρα ὥστε ἠθέλησεν ἀποθανεῖν ὑπὲρ αὐτοῦ.
3. τοσοῦτοι ἦσαν οἱ Πέρσαι ὥστε οἱ Ἀθηναῖοι οὐκέτι ἔμειναν ἐν τῇ πόλει.
4. οἱ βάρβαροι δειλότεροι ἦσαν ἢ ὥστε μάχεσθαι.

5. οἱ Λακεδαιμόνιοι οὕτως ἀνδρείως ἐμαχέσαντο, ὥστε ἀεὶ ἐτιμῶντο ὑπὸ τῶν Ἑλλήνων.
6. ὁ Δημοσθένης οὕτως εὖ ἔλεξεν ὥστε τοὺς Ἀθηναίους αὐτῷ πιθέσθαι.
7. αἱ γυναῖκες σοφώτεραι ἦσαν ἢ ὥστε πιστεῦσαι τούτῳ τῷ γέροντι.
8. ὁ νεανίας ᾧ ἔδωκα τὸ δῶρον οὕτω χάριν εἶχεν ὥστε ἕσπετό μοι τὴν πᾶσαν ἡμέραν.
9. ὁ ποταμός ἐστιν οὕτω χαλεπός, ὥστε μηδένα αὐτὸν διαβαίνειν.
10. τοσαῦτα τὰ τῶν πολεμίων ὅπλα ἐστὶν ὥστε οὐκέτι μενοῦμεν, ἀλλ' ὡς τάχιστα ἀποφευξόμεθα.

EXERCISE 138.

1. The orator speaks so sweetly that he always persuades us.
2. Were you too few to attack the enemy?
3. The Persians were so many that nobody hindered them.
4. Those who won were so brave that even the enemy honored them.
5. The children were so bad that we no longer trusted them.
6. The enemy are so few that we have quickly defeated them.
7. The general was too prudent to cross the mountain by night.
8. The fish is so big that I have given it to the king.
9. Few men are so foolish as not to honor their country.
10. The ship sailed away so quickly that we did not catch it.

READING.

PYLOS AND SPHACTERIA 1: AN ILL WIND

In the year 425 B.C., during the Peloponnesian War, when Athens had to face both Sparta and Corinth, an Athenian fleet on its way to Sicily was overtaken by a storm off the coast of Messenia in the Peloponnese.

Τοσοῦτος δὲ ἦν ὁ χειμών, ὥστε κατήνεγκε τὰς τῶν Ἀθηναίων ναῦς εἰς τὴν Πύλον. ἔδοξε δὲ τῷ Δημοσθένει, ὃς ἦν στρατηγός, εὐθὺς τειχίζειν τὸ χωρίον· εὐπορία γὰρ ἦν ξύλων τε καὶ λίθων. οἱ δὲ στρατιῶται οὕτω ταχέως εἰργάζοντο, ὥστε ἓξ ἡμερῶν τὸ χωρίον ἐτείχισαν· οἱ δὲ ἄλλοι στρατηγοὶ τὸν μὲν Δημοσθένη μετὰ νεῶν πέντε ἐνταῦθα φύλακα κατέλιπον, ταῖς δὲ πλείοσι ναυσὶ πρὸς Σικελίαν ἀπέπλευσαν. οἱ δὲ Λακεδαιμόνιοι εὐθὺς ἐπορεύοντο ἐπὶ τὴν Πύλον, καὶ ἐκέλευσαν τοὺς συμμάχους βοηθεῖν ὡς τάχιστα καὶ πέμψαι ἑξήκοντα ναῦς· παρῆν δὲ ἤδη καὶ ὁ πεζὸς στρατός. ἐν δὲ τούτῳ καὶ ὁ Δημοσθένης μετεπέμψατο ἄλλας ναῦς. οἱ δὲ Λακεδαιμόνιοι παρεσκευάζοντο ὡς τῷ τειχίσματι προσβαλοῦντες κατά τε γῆν καὶ κατὰ θάλατταν, ἐλπίζοντες ῥᾳδίως αἱρήσειν τὸ χωρίον, ἀνθρώπων ὀλίγων ἐνόντων. διεβίβασαν δὲ ὁπλίτας εἰς τὴν νῆσον Σφακτηρίαν, ἣ ἐπικεῖται τῇ Πύλῳ, καὶ ἐν τῇ ἠπείρῳ ἄλλους ἔταξαν, ὥστε τοῖς Ἀθηναίοις τήν τε νῆσον πολεμίαν εἶναι τήν τε ἤπειρον. μετὰ δὲ τοῦτο προσέβαλον μὲν τῷ τειχίσματι ναυσί τε ἅμα καὶ πεζῷ, μάτην δέ.

ἐπεὶ δὲ πεντήκοντα ἄλλαι νῆες ἀφίκοντο, οἱ Ἀθηναῖοι προσέβαλον τῷ τῶν Λακεδαιμονίων ναυτικῷ, ὥστε ἔκοψαν μὲν πολλὰς ναῦς, πέντε δὲ ἔλαβον, καὶ ἀπέλαβον πολλοὺς ἄνδρας ἐν τῇ νήσῳ. μετὰ δὲ τὴν ναυμαχίαν ἔδοξε τοῖς Ἀθηναίοις εὐθὺς τὴν νῆσον περιπλεῖν καὶ φυλάττειν. εἰς δὲ τὴν Σπάρτην ὡς ἠγγέλθη τὰ γενόμενα περὶ Πύλον, ἔδοξε τοῖς Λακεδαιμονίοις σπονδὰς ποιήσασθαι καὶ πρέσβεις πέμψαι εἰς τὰς Ἀθήνας, ὅπως τοὺς ἄνδρας ὡς τάχιστα σώσειαν.

Adapted from Thucydides IV.3-15

Chapter 31 Vocabulary

Adverbs:

οὐκέτι	no longer	**οὕτω(ς)**	so

Conjunction:

ὥστε	(so) that, (so) as to

CHAPTER 32

τὰ δ᾽ ἄλλα σιγῶ· βοῦς ἐπὶ γλώσσῃ μέγας
βέβηκεν·

— Aeschylus, *Agamemnon* 36-37

λάθε βιώσας.

— Epicurean saying (Plutarch, *De latenter vivendo* 1128A1)

1. The 2nd (strong) perfect active

The 2nd (strong) perfect active closely resembles the regular 1st perfect (Ch. 31.2), except that the stem has its own consonant, and uses the tense vowel **-α-** without **-κ**. In some verbs the original stem consonant appears, in others the aspirated version of it: δεδίωχα from διώκω. In some verbs the stem itself is altered, as happens with strong aorists (Ch. 11.5, 27.5).

ἀκούω	ἀκήκοα
βαίνω	βέβηκα
λαμβάνω	εἴληφα
λείπω	λέλοιπα

PERFECT		**Stem λελοιπ-**	**Translation**	**Endings**
Sing.	1st	λέ-λοιπ-α	I have loosed	-ᾰ-
	2nd	λέ-λοιπ-α-ς	you have loosed	-ᾰ-ς
	3rd	λέ-λοιπ-ε(ν)	he / she / it has loosed	-ε-(ν)
Plur.	1st	λε-λοίπ-α-μεν	we have loosed	-ᾰ-μεν
	2nd	λε-λοίπ-α-τε	you have loosed	-ᾰ-τε
	3rd	λε-λοίπ-α-σι(ν)	they have loosed	-ᾱ-σι(ν)

PLUPERFECT		Stem λελοιπ -	Translation	Endings
Sing.	1st	ἐ-λε-λοίπ-η	I had loosed	-η-
	2nd	ἐ-λε-λοίπ-η-ς	you had loosed	-η-ς
	3rd	ἐ-λε-λοίπ-ει(ν)	he / she / it had loosed	-ει-(ν)
Plur.	1st	ἐ-λε-λοίπ-ε-μεν	we had loosed	-ε-μεν
	2nd	ἐ-λε-λοίπ-ε-τε	you had loosed	-ε-τε
	3rd	ἐ-λε-λοίπ-ε-σαν	they had loosed	-ε-σαν

A few verbs have two perfect active forms, with different meanings.

πράττω: πέπραχα, 'I have done'
    πέπραγα, 'I have fared'

πείθω: πέπεικα, 'I have persuaded'
    πέποιθα, 'I trust'

2. Reduplication

In this section, the perfect active is used here to illustrate the various types of reduplication. The same rules apply to the perfect middle / passive.

Reduplication for most verbs consists of repeating the initial consonant, with **ε** (Ch. 31.2). This pattern applies to verbs that begin with a single consonant, or with a stop followed by a liquid (**λ**, **μ**, **ν**, **ρ**).

παύω	πέπαυκα
βλάπτω	βέβλαφα
πράττω	πέπραχα / πέπραγα

Note: Grassmann's law applies to the perfect tense as it does to the aorist passive (Ch. 15.5): τέθυκα from θύω.

In other verbs, reduplication is formed like the augment.

- in verb stems beginning with a vowel or diphthong, short vowels are lengthened (a long vowel would remain unchanged).

ἄγω	ἦχα
αἱρέω	ᾕρηκα
ἐθέλω	ἠθέληκα

- to verb stems beginning with a double consonant (**ζ**, **ξ**, **ψ**) or two consonants (except stop followed by liquid), the prefix **ε-** is added.

ζητέω	ἐζήτηκα
στρατεύω	ἐστράτευκα
ἵστημι	ἕστηκα

Note: Though it resembles the augment, this reduplication occurs in all perfect tense moods, and in the perfect infinitive and participle. Augments are restricted to the indicative mood (Ch. 4.3, 5.2, 11.2).

3. The perfect middle / passive of consonant stem verbs

Since the perfect middle / passive endings are added directly to the stem of the 5th principal part, some consonant clusters will result between stops at the end of verb stems and the consonants of the personal endings. You have already seen how stops combine with **σ** (Ch. 1.2, 8.1, 11.4, 13.2, 14.2). The complete list follows.

$$\left.\begin{matrix}\pi\\ \beta\\ \varphi\end{matrix}\right\} + \mu = \mu\mu \qquad \left.\begin{matrix}\pi\\ \beta\\ \varphi\end{matrix}\right\} + \sigma = \psi \qquad \left.\begin{matrix}\pi\\ \beta\\ \varphi\end{matrix}\right\} + \tau = \pi\tau \qquad \left.\begin{matrix}\pi\\ \beta\\ \varphi\end{matrix}\right\} + \sigma\theta = \varphi\theta$$

$$\left.\begin{matrix}\tau\\ \delta\\ \theta\end{matrix}\right\} + \mu = \sigma\mu \qquad \left.\begin{matrix}\tau\\ \delta\\ \theta\end{matrix}\right\} + \sigma = \sigma \qquad \left.\begin{matrix}\tau\\ \delta\\ \theta\end{matrix}\right\} + \tau = \sigma\tau \qquad \left.\begin{matrix}\tau\\ \delta\\ \theta\end{matrix}\right\} + \sigma\theta = \sigma\theta$$

$$\left.\begin{matrix}\kappa\\ \gamma\\ \chi\end{matrix}\right\} + \mu = \gamma\mu \qquad \left.\begin{matrix}\kappa\\ \gamma\\ \chi\end{matrix}\right\} + \sigma = \xi \qquad \left.\begin{matrix}\kappa\\ \gamma\\ \chi\end{matrix}\right\} + \tau = \kappa\tau \qquad \left.\begin{matrix}\kappa\\ \gamma\\ \chi\end{matrix}\right\} + \sigma\theta = \chi\theta$$

Note: A stop becomes voiced, unvoiced, or aspirated to match the following consonant. Similar adjustments are made in English: we say 'practical' but 'pragmatic'.

The following paradigms show the perfect and pluperfect of a labial stem (γράφω), a dental stem (πείθω) and a palatal stem (ἄγω).

Note: The 3rd plural consists of the nom. pl. participle (below, sec. 4) and a 3rd plural form of the verb εἰμί, 'be'. This solution avoids a complicated consonant cluster (consonant + **-νται**).

γεγραμμένοι εἰσί	they have been written	(part. + present)
γεγραμμένοι ἦσαν	they had been written	(part. + imperfect)

INDICATIVE		write	persuade	lead
Perfect				
Sing.	1st	γέγραμμαι	πέπεισμαι	ἦγμαι
	2nd	γέγραψαι	πέπεισαι	ἦξαι
	3rd	γέγραπται	πέπεισται	ἦκται
Plur.	1st	γεγράμμεθα	πεπείσμεθα	ἤγμεθα
	2nd	γέγραφθε	πέπεισθε	ἦχθε
	3rd	γεγραμμένοι εἰσί(ν)	πεπεισμένοι εἰσί(ν)	ἠγμένοι εἰσί(ν)

INDICATIVE		write	persuade	lead
Pluperfect				
Sing.	1st	ἐγεγράμμην	ἐπεπείσμην	ἤγμην
	2nd	ἐγέγραψο	ἐπέπεισο	ἦξο
	3rd	ἐγέγραπτο	ἐπέπειστο	ἦκτο
Plur.	1st	ἐγεγράμμεθα	ἐπεπείσμεθα	ἤγμεθα
	2nd	ἐγέγραφθε	ἐπέπεισθε	ἦχθε
	3rd	γεγραμμένοι ἦσαν	πεπεισμένοι ἦσαν	ἠγμένοι ἦσαν
INFINITIVE				
		γεγράφθαι	πεπεῖσθαι	ἦχθαι
PARTICIPLE				
		γεγραμμένος, -η, -ον γεγραμμένου, etc.	πεπεισμένος, -η, -ον πεπεισμένου, etc.	ἠγμένος, -η, -ον ἠγμένου, etc

4. The perfect active participle

Form: The *perfect active* participle has 3rd declension masculine and neuter endings, and 1st declension feminine endings, added to the perfect active stem (4th principal part).

		M	F	N
Sing.	Nom.	λελυκώς	λελυκυῖα	λελυκός
	Gen.	λελυκότος	λελυκυίας	λελυκότος
	Dat.	λελυκότι	λελυκυίᾳ	λελυκότι
	Acc.	λελυκότα	λελυκυῖαν	λελυκός
	Voc.	λελυκός	λελυκυία	λελυκός
Plur.	Nom.	λελυκότες	λελυκυῖαι	λελυκότα
	Gen.	λελυκότων	λελυκυιῶν	λελυκότων
	Dat.	λελυκόσι(ν)	λελυκυίαις	λελυκόσι(ν)
	Acc.	λελυκότας	λελυκυίας	λελυκότα
	Voc.	λελυκότες	λελυκυῖαι	λελυκότα

Meaning: Like the perfect indicative, the perfect participle is only used to express the result of a completed action; οἱ τεθνηκότες, 'the dead', 'those who have died'. The simple translation is 'having —ed'. An aorist participle may be translated the same way, for example 'having pursued'. But in the perfect tense, the verb itself may carry the idea of completion: 'having arrived', 'having finished'. The difference is clear when the participle is translated as a relative clause: οἱ ἀποθανόντες, 'those who died'; οἱ τεθνηκότες, 'those who have died'.

Note: The form τέθνηκα, from the simple verb θνῄσκω, 'die', is used in the perfect tense instead of the compound ἀποθνῄσκω.

5. The perfect middle / passive participle

Form: The *perfect middle / passive* participle is formed from the 5th principal part, with the same set of endings as the present middle / passive participle (Ch. 22.1). The accent is on the **ε** of the ending throughout.

		M	F	N
Sing.	Nom.	λελυμένος	λελυμένη	λελυμένον
	Gen.	λελυμένου	λελυμένης	λελυμένου
	Dat.	λελυμένῳ	λελυμένῃ	λελυμένῳ
	Acc.	λελυμένον	λελυμένην	λελυμένον
	Voc.	λελυμένος	λελυμένη	λελυμένον
Plur.	Nom.	λελυμένοι	λελυμέναι	λελυμένα
	Gen.	λελυμένων	λελυμένων	λελυμένων
	Dat.	λελυμένοις	λελυμέναις	λελυμένοις
	Acc.	λελυμένους	λελυμένας	λελυμένα
	Voc.	λελυμένοι	λελυμέναι	λελυμένα

Meaning: The perfect middle participle can be translated like the active, 'having —ed', 'those who have —ed', etc. The passive is translated 'having been —ed', 'those who have been —ed', etc. As in the active, the difference between aorist and perfect is clear when you translate the participle as a clause.

EXERCISE 139. Review principal parts, with reference to the list in Appendix 1. Identify and translate:

1. πέπεισθε
2. ἐκεκώλυσο
3. τετιμήκασιν
4. λελειμμένος
5. ἠργμένοι εἰσί
6. βεβλάφθαι
7. τέθεινται
8. πεφύλακται
9. ηὑρήμεθα
10. ἕστηκε
11. τεθύσθαι
12. σεσωκέναι

EXERCISE 140. Review principal parts, with reference to the list in Appendix 1. Translate (for participles give nom. masc. sing.):

1. We have written
2. To have loved
3. He had been led
4. Having given
5. You (s.) have spoken
6. They have been pursued
7. I have shown
8. To have been carried
9. She had seen
10. Having been taken
11. We had gone
12. It has been found

6. Supplementary participles not in indirect statement

Some verbs occur with a *supplementary* participle in Greek, as in English, to complete their meaning. Verbs using this construction include those meaning 'start', 'stop' or 'continue' (doing), and verbs of emotion. The participle agrees with whoever is doing the action of the participle.

ἥδομαι ἀκούων τῶν ποιητῶν.
I enjoy listening to poets.

ἔπαυσα αὐτὸν λέγοντα.
I made him stop speaking.

ἐπαυσάμην λέγων.
I stopped speaking.

The tense of the participle generally indicates aspect: present for an ongoing action, aorist for a single, simple act.

The verb τυγχάνω, 'happen (upon)' can take an object in the genitive case. In the meaning 'happen (to)' it takes a supplementary participle in Greek. In English an infinitive completes the meaning of this verb, so a smooth English translation of τυγχάνω + participle will change the participle to an infinitive.

ὁ στρατηγὸς τυγχάνει τάττων τοὺς στρατιώτας.
The general happens to be drawing up his soldiers.

ὁ παῖς ἔτυχε γράφων ἐπιστολήν.
The child happened to be writing a letter.

οἱ παῖδες ἔτυχον ἵππον εὑρόντες.
The children happened to find a horse.

Note: After a present or imperfect main verb, the aorist participle may express previous time.

ὁ παῖς τυγχάνει γράψας ἐπιστολήν.
The child happens to have written a letter.

οἱ παῖδες τυγχάνουσιν ἰδόντες τὸν Σωκράτη.
The children happen to have seen Socrates.

λανθάνω and φθάνω are likewise used with a supplementary participle to complete their meanings. These verbs have no really good English equivalent, so translation should not be literal. In both cases, the participle describes the action taking place, so it is best expressed in English by a main verb. The main verb describes *how* the action took place, and can be translated with an adverbial phrase.

- λανθάνω literally means something like 'escape the notice (of)'. It signifies that the action of the participle is not noticed by someone: "I λανθάνω you, doing something." It can also appear without a direct object. There are several ways to express this construction in good English.

  οἱ πολέμιοι λανθάνουσι τοὺς φύλακας φεύγοντες.
  The enemy flees without the guards seeing them.
  The enemy is fleeing unbeknownst to the guards.

οἱ πολέμιοι ἔλαθον φυγόντες.
The enemy fled unnoticed.
The enemy fled without being seen.

- φθάνω works in a very similar way. It literally means something like 'be / do before', 'anticipate'. It signifies that the action of the participle occurs before something else happens: "I φθάνω you, doing something." Like λανθάνω, it can appear without a direct object.

ἡ γυνὴ φθάνει τοὺς παῖδας ὁρῶσα τὸν ἵππον.
The woman sees the horse before the children do.

ἡ γυνὴ ἔφθασεν ἰδοῦσα τὸν ἵππον.
The woman saw the horse first.

Note: These two verbs are usually in the same tense (present or aorist) as the accompanying participle. Occasionally a present participle may occur with an aorist verb, to mark continuing aspect.

EXERCISE 141.

1. λήσεις τὴν μητέρα ἐκβαίνων ἐκ τῆς οἰκίας;
2. πότε ὁ τύραννος ἦρξεν εὖ πράττων;
3. ὁ κῆρυξ φθάνει τοὺς πρέσβεις ἀφικνούμενος εἰς τὴν ἑαυτοῦ πόλιν.
4. εἰ ὁ ῥήτωρ τυγχάνοι λέγων τοῖς πολίταις, ἡδέως ἂν μένοιμεν.
5. οἱ ναῦται οὐκ ἔλαθον τοὺς πολεμίους πορευσάμενοι εἰς τὸν λιμένα.
6. ἐτύχομεν γίγαντός τινος ἐν τῇ ὕλῃ.
7. ὁ ποιητὴς ἔφθασε βὰς εἰς τὴν κώμην.
8. οὐ πολλοὶ τυγχάνουσιν ἀεὶ εὐτυχεῖς ὄντες.
9. λάθοιμεν ἂν ῥᾳδίως τοὺς φύλακας προσβαλόντες τῇ πόλει.
10. ἄγγελός τις ἐτύγχανε ἔχων παῖδας μὲν πολλούς, φίλους δ' ὀλίγους.

EXERCISE 142.

1. You don't enjoy fighting, do you?
2. I happen to think that he does not manage his affairs prudently.
3. How many horses escaped without the cavalry noticing?
4. The enemy will not attack before our soldiers do.
5. We happened to find big trees on the island.
6. Unbeknownst to those in Babylon, Cyrus' soldiers were invading.
7. Are you willing to stop throwing stones at last?
8. If he happens upon some weapons he will be very happy.
9. Did those exiles leave the country before the army?
10. Without Polycrates knowing it, the ring was saved.

READING.

PYLOS AND SPHACTERIA 2: STALEMATE

οἱ δὲ πρέσβεις ἀφικόμενοι εἰς τὰς Ἀθήνας εἶπον ὅτι οἱ Λακεδαιμόνιοι προκαλοῦνται μὲν τοὺς Ἀθηναίους εἰς εἰρήνην καὶ συμμαχίαν, ἀνταιτοῦσι δὲ τοὺς ἐκ τῆς νήσου ἄνδρας. οἱ μὲν οὖν Λακεδαιμόνιοι τοσαῦτα εἶπον, νομίζοντες τοὺς Ἀθηναίους, ἤδη πολλάκις νικηθέντας, εἰρήνην ἡδέως δέξεσθαι. οἱ δέ, ἔχοντες τοὺς ἄνδρας τοὺς ἐν τῇ νήσῳ, ἔτι πλείονα σχήσειν ἤλπιζον. μάλιστα δὲ αὐτοὺς ἐνῆγε Κλέων, ἀνὴρ δεινότατος· οἱ δὲ πρέσβεις ἀπεχώρησαν ἐκ τῶν Ἀθηνῶν ἄπρακτοι.

ἀφικομένων δὲ αὐτῶν εἰς τὴν Πύλον, αἱ σπονδαὶ εὐθὺς διελύθησαν. οἱ δὲ Ἀθηναῖοι ἔτι ἐπολιόρκουν τοὺς ἐν τῇ νήσῳ Λακεδαιμονίους, καὶ ἡ τῶν Λακεδαιμονίων στρατιὰ ἔμενεν ἐν τῇ ἠπείρῳ. χαλεπὸν δ' ἦν τοῖς Ἀθηναίοις τὸ φυλάττειν δι' ἀπορίαν σίτου τε καὶ ὕδατος. πρὸς δὲ τούτῳ μάλιστα ἠθύμουν, ὡς ἐνόμιζον ἐκπολιορκήσειν τοὺς πολεμίους ἡμερῶν ὀλίγων. οἱ δὲ Λακεδαιμόνιοι παρέσχον πολὺ ἀργύριον τοῖς βουλομένοις εἰς τὴν νῆσον εἰσάγειν σῖτόν τε καὶ οἶνον· μάλιστα δὲ εἰσῆγον οἱ Εἵλωτες[1], λαβόντες ὁπόθεν τύχοιεν καὶ εἰσφέροντες τῆς νυκτός· οὕτω γὰρ ῥᾷον τοὺς Ἀθηναίους ἐλάνθανον.

ἐν δὲ ταῖς Ἀθήναις, ὅτε ἠγγέλθη ὅτι σῖτος τοῖς ἐν τῇ νήσῳ εἰσάγεται, οἱ πολῖται μάλιστα ἠπόρουν· οὐ γὰρ ἔλαθεν αὐτοὺς ἡ στρατιὰ οὐκ εὖ πράττουσα. Κλέων δὲ πρῶτον μὲν οὐκ ἔφη τοὺς ἀγγέλλοντας τὰ ἀληθῆ λέγειν, ὕστερον δὲ τῷ Νικίᾳ, στρατηγῷ ὄντι, εἶπεν ὡς ῥᾴδιον ἂν εἴη, εἰ ἄνδρες εἶεν οἱ στρατηγοί, λαβεῖν τοὺς ἐν τῇ νήσῳ, καὶ αὐτὸς ἄν, εἰ ἦρχεν, ἐποίησε τοῦτο. ὁ δὲ Νικίας ἐκέλευε τὸν Κλέωνα ἥντινα στρατιὰν βούλεται λαβόντα ἐπιχειρεῖν ἀντὶ τῶν στρατηγῶν. ὁ δὲ ἀνεχώρει καὶ οὐκ ἔφη αὐτὸς ἀλλ' ἐκεῖνον στρατηγὸν εἶναι. οἱ δὲ Ἀθηναῖοι, οἷον ὄχλος φιλεῖ ποιεῖν, ὅσῳ μᾶλλον ὁ Κλέων ἀνεχώρει, τόσῳ ἐνῆγον τὸν Νικίαν παραδιδόναι τὴν ἀρχὴν καὶ ἐκείνῳ ἐπεβόων πλεῖν. τέλος δὲ ἔφη ὁ Κλέων τοῦτο ποιήσειν καὶ ἡμερῶν εἴκοσιν ἢ ἄξειν τοὺς Λακεδαιμονίους ζῶντας ἢ ἐκεῖ ἀποκτενεῖν.

Adapted from Thucydides IV.16-28

1 The Helots were the original inhabitants of territory taken over by Sparta; they were reduced to the position of serfs, and in wartime served as light-armed troops.

Chapter 32 Vocabulary

Verbs:

ἄρχω	begin
ἐκβαίνω	go out, come out
ἥδομαι, ἡσθήσομαι, —, —, —, ἥσθην (+ *dat. or part.*)	enjoy
λανθάνω, λήσω, ἔλαθον, λέληθα, -λέλησμαι, — (+ *part.*)	(escape the notice of)
τυγχάνω, τεύξομαι, ἔτυχον, τετύχηκα, —, — (+ *gen. or part.*)	happen to, happen upon
φθάνω, φθήσομαι, ἔφθασα / ἔφθην, —, —, — (+ *part.*)	(be / do before, anticipate)

Adverb:

τέλος	at last

CHAPTER 33

τὸ μὲν γὰρ ἓν στιγμή, τὰ δὲ δύο γραμμή, τὰ δὲ τρία τρίγωνον, τὰ δὲ τέσσερα πυραμίς....τὰ αὐτὰ δὲ καὶ ἐν τῇ γενέσι· πρώτη μὲν γὰρ ἀρχὴ εἰς μέγεθος στιγμή, δευτέρα γραμμή, τρίτη ἐπιφάνεια, τέταρτον στερεόν.

— Pythagorean belief (Speusippos, *ap. Theologumena Arithemeticae* p. 84.10 de Falco)

1. The perfect subjunctive and optative

The subjunctive and optative of perfect tenses are rarely needed, since the perfect tense is restricted and specialized in meaning (Ch. 31.1).

The forms consist of the perfect participle with a (present) subjunctive or optative form of εἰμί, 'be'. The participle must agree with the subject, so it is masculine, feminine or neuter and singular or plural, as appropriate. The paradigm of λύω is shown here with the masculine participle; all types of verbs work the same way, each using its own perfect active and middle / passive participles.

SUBJUNCTIVE		ACTIVE		MIDDLE / PASSIVE	
Sing.	1st	λελυκὼς ὦ		λελυμένος ὦ	
	2nd	λελυκὼς ᾖς		λελυμένος ᾖς	
	3rd	λελυκὼς ᾖ		λελυμένος ᾖ	
Plur.	1st	λελυκότες ὦμεν		λελυμένοι ὦμεν	
	2nd	λελυκότες ἦτε		λελυμένοι ἦτε	
	3rd	λελυκότες ὦσι(ν)		λελυμένοι ὦσι(ν)	
OPTATIVE					
Sing.	1st	λελυκὼς εἴην		λελυμένος εἴην	
	2nd	λελυκὼς εἴης		λελυμένος εἴης	
	3rd	λελυκὼς εἴη		λελυμένος εἴη	
Plur.	1st	λελυκότες εἶμεν	[εἴημεν]	λελυμένοι εἶμεν	[εἴημεν]
	2nd	λελυκότες εἶτε	[εἴητε]	λελυμένοι εἶτε	[εἴητε]
	3rd	λελυκότες εἶεν	[εἴησαν]	λελυμένοι εἶεν	[εἴησαν]

A rare alternative in the active is the perfect stem with regular subjunctive or optative endings: λελύκω, -ῃς, -ῃ; γεγράφω, -ῃς, -ῃ, etc. In the middle / passive this alternative is restricted to a few verbs. Among these are μιμνῄσκω (or μιμνήσκω), 'remind', middle / passive 'remember', and κτάομαι, 'acquire', perfect 'possess'.

	Perfect	**Perf. Subj.**	**Perf. Opt.**
μιμνῄσκω	μέμνημαι	μεμνῶμαι	μεμνῄμην
κτάομαι	κέκτημαι	κεκτῶμαι	κεκτῄμην / κεκτῴμην

2. Numbers

Here are the Greek cardinal (one, two, three...) and ordinal (first, second, third...) numbers from 1 to 100.

- All the ordinals are fully declinable adjectives, with 1st and 2nd declension endings (Ch. 7.1). Nearly all have a feminine ending **-η**; the **-ρ** in δεύτερος means that **-ᾱ** appears throughout the singular.
- Of the cardinals, only 1-4 are declinable; the rest always appear in the same form, whatever the case, gender and number of the noun they modify.

	Cardinal	**Ordinal**
1.	εἷς, μία, ἕν	πρῶτος, -η, -ον
2.	δύο	δεύτερος, -α, -ον
3.	τρεῖς, τρία	τρίτος, -η, -ον
4.	τέτταρες, τέτταρα	τέταρτος, -η, -ον
5.	πέντε	πέμπτος, -η, -ον
6.	ἕξ	ἕκτος, -η, -ον
7.	ἑπτά	ἕβδομος, -η, -ον
8.	ὀκτώ	ὄγδοος, -η, -ον
9.	ἐννέα	ἔνατος, -η, -ον
10.	δέκα	δέκατος, -η, -ον
11.	ἕνδεκα	ἑνδέκατος, -η, -ον
12.	δώδεκα	δωδέκατος, -η, -ον
13.	τρεῖς καὶ δέκα	τρίτος καὶ δέκατος
14.	τέτταρες καὶ δέκα	τέταρτος καὶ δέκατος
15.	πεντεκαίδεκα	πέμπτος καὶ δέκατος
16.	ἑκκαίδεκα	ἕκτος καὶ δέκατος
17.	ἑπτακαίδεκα	ἕβδομος καὶ δέκατος
18.	ὀκτωκαίδεκα	ὄγδοος καὶ δέκατος
19.	ἐννεακαίδεκα	ἔνατος καὶ δέκατος
20.	εἴκοσι(ν)	εἰκοστός, -ή, -όν

21.	εἷς καὶ εἴκοσι(ν) / εἴκοσι καὶ εἷς, etc.	πρῶτος καὶ εἰκοστός, etc.
30.	τριάκοντα	τριακοστός, -ή, -όν
40.	τετταράκοντα	τετταρακοστός, -ή, -όν
50.	πεντήκοντα	πεντηκοστός, -ή, -όν
60.	ἑξήκοντα	ἑξηκοστός, -ή, -όν
70.	ἑβδομήκοντα	ἑβδομηκοστός, -ή, -όν
80.	ὀγδοήκοντα	ὀγδοηκοστός, -ή, -όν
90.	ἐνενήκοντα	ἐνενηκοστός, -ή, -όν
100.	ἑκατόν	ἑκατοστός, -ή, -όν

3. Declension of numbers

The numbers 1 to 4 are declined as follows.

	one			two	three		four	
	M	F	N	M/F/N	M/F	N	M/F	N
Nom.	εἷς	μία	ἕν	δύο	τρεῖς	τρία	τέτταρες	τέτταρα
Gen.	ἑνός	μιᾶς	ἑνός	δυοῖν	τριῶν	τριῶν	τεττάρων	τεττάρων
Dat.	ἑνί	μιᾷ	ἑνί	δυοῖν	τρισί(ν)	τρισί(ν)	τέτταρσι(ν)	τέτταρσι(ν)
Acc.	ἕνα	μίαν	ἕν	δύο	τρεῖς	τρία	τέτταρας	τέτταρα

4. The negative pronouns / adjectives οὐδείς and μηδείς

The Greek word for 'no one', 'nothing' consists of the negative οὐδέ, 'not even', combined with the number one: οὐδείς. The word is not normally used in the plural.

	M	F	N
Nom.	οὐδείς	οὐδεμία	οὐδέν
Gen.	οὐδενός	οὐδεμιᾶς	οὐδενός
Dat.	οὐδενί	οὐδεμιᾷ	οὐδενί
Acc.	οὐδένα	οὐδεμίαν	οὐδέν
Voc.	οὐδείς	οὐδεμία	οὐδέν

οὐδείς can appear both alone as a pronoun, and as an adjective modifying a noun:

οὐδέν ἐστι ῥᾴδιον.
Nothing is easy.

οὐδεὶς στρατηγὸς ἀποφεύγει.
No general flees away.

οὐδεὶς τῶν στρατηγῶν ἀποφεύγει.
None of the generals flees away.

Note: Wherever μή is used instead of οὐ, μηδείς replaces οὐδείς.

μηδεὶς πιστεύσῃ τῷ ῥήτορι.
Let no one believe the orator.

βούλομαι μηδένα βλάψαι τὰ δένδρα.
I want nobody to harm the trees.

5. Clauses of fearing

Greek uses verbs that express fear or concern in several ways. The most common such verb is φοβέομαι, 'fear', 'be afraid of'. This verb can have a direct object, or a complementary infinitive:

φοβοῦμαι τὸν λέοντα.
I fear the lion.

οὐ φοβοῦμαι προσβαλεῖν τῇ πόλει.
I am not afraid to attack the city.

Another construction is the *clause of fearing*, which is introduced by the verb of fearing + μή (positive), or + μὴ οὐ (negative). Fear may be expressed about the past or present, or more commonly about the future.

- A fear referring to the present or past has an indicative verb; the tense is the same as it would be in a main clause.

  φοβοῦμαι μὴ προσβάλλουσιν.
  I am afraid they are attacking.

  φοβοῦμαι μὴ οὐκ ἦλθεν.
  I am afraid he did not come.

- When a fear concerns the future, the regular sequence of moods applies (Ch. 27.1): the subjunctive is used after a primary tense main verb, the optative after a secondary tense. As usual, aspect determines whether the subjunctive or optative is present or aorist.

Primary Sequence	**Secondary Sequence**
φοβοῦμαι μὴ ἔλθῃ. I am afraid he may come.	ἐφοβούμην μὴ οἱ πολέμιοι ἔλθοιεν. I was afraid that the enemy would come.
φοβοῦμαι μὴ οὐ μένῃ. I am afraid he may not stay.	ἐφοβούμην μὴ οὐ μένοι ὁ στρατηγός. I was afraid the general might not stay.

Note: Occasionally the subjunctive is used after a secondary tense main verb, for extra vividness.

Reading expectations

φοβοῦμαι μή →	present indicative	= present fear	I fear he does / is doing x.
φοβοῦμαι μή ↘	past indicative	= past fear	I fear he did / was doing x.
ἐφοβούμην μή ↗	past indicative	= past fear	I feared he had done x.
φοβοῦμαι μή →	subjunctive	= future fear	I fear he will do x.
ἐφοβούμην μή ↗	subjunctive	= vivid future fear	I feared he would do x.
ἐφοβούμην μή ↘	optative	= future fear	I feared he would do x.

EXERCISE 143.

1. οὐδεὶς οὕτω ἀνδρεῖος ἦν ὥστε μὴ τοὺς γίγαντας φοβεῖσθαι.
2. ἐφοβούμην μὴ ὁ τῶν πολεμίων στρατηγὸς τέλος νικήσαι τὴν στρατιὰν ἡμῶν.
3. τὸ ὄρος οὕτως ὑψηλόν ἐστιν ὥστε μηδένα οἷόν τε εἶναι μένειν ἐκεῖ τὴν πᾶσαν νύκτα.
4. τοσοῦτός ἐστιν ὁ κίνδυνος ὥστε φοβοῦμαι μὴ οὐκ ἀποφύγω.
5. οὐδένα φίλον μιμνῃσκόμεθα ἀμείνονα ἢ τὸν Σωκράτη.
6. τοσαῦτα χρήματα δέδωκα τῷ πατρὶ ὥστε οὐδὲν νῦν ἔχω.
7. τρία ἔτη ἐφοβούμεθα μὴ οἱ Πέρσαι κτήσαιντο τὴν πατρίδα ἡμῶν.
8. φοβεῖ μὴ οὐκ εἶχε πολλὰ χρήματα;
9. τεττάρων ἡμερῶν ἐλευσόμεθα ἵνα λάβωμεν τοὺς ἵππους.
10. εἰ τὸν βασιλέα ἀποκτείνοις, εὐθὺς ἂν τεθνηκὼς εἴης.

EXERCISE 144.

1. Were you afraid that the orator would not persuade you?
2. This war is so difficult that I fear it will never cease.
3. We know that nobody is wiser than Socrates.
4. Let no citizen fear the king, for he is too prudent to harm his own people.
5. I am afraid that man will not be happy, however many gifts you give him.
6. The sailors feared that the storm was very great.
7. On the fourth day let us remember those who have died.
8. I am afraid he will not acquire money easily.
9. The enemy have attacked without the soldiers knowing it.
10. Is anyone afraid that he has few friends?

6. Indirect questions

Sometimes questions, like statements, are reported indirectly. These *indirect questions* are expressed just like indirect statements with ὅτι or ὡς (Ch. 27.7). The subject of the indirect question is therefore nominative, and the verb is normally indicative. The optative may be substituted after a secondary tense main verb. As in indirect statement, the tense of the verb is relative to the main verb: present for same time, future for later time, aorist for earlier time.

Indirect questions can be introduced by a conjunction like εἰ, 'whether' or πότερον... ἤ, 'whether...or' (two alternatives). Any *interrogative* pronoun or adverb may also introduce an indirect question. Alternatively, the equivalent *indefinite relative* pronoun or adverb may be used instead of the interrogative.

ἐρωτᾷ τὸν ἄγγελον τίνες οἱ πολέμιοί εἰσιν.
ἐρωτᾷ τὸν ἄγγελον οἵτινες οἱ πολέμιοί εἰσιν
He asks the messenger who the enemy are.

ἤρετο ὅπου οἱ πολέμιοί εἰσιν / πολέμιοι εἶεν.
He asked where the enemy were.

ἐπυθόμεθα τί οὐ προσέβαλον / προσβάλοιεν.
We learned why they had not attacked.

ἠρόμεθα αὐτοὺς τί ποιήσουσιν / or ποιήσοιεν.
We asked them what they would do.

οὐκ ᾖσμεν πότερον ἐνίκησαν ἢ οὔ.
We did not know if they had won or not.

Note: After εἰ, the negative can be either οὐ or μή. οὐ is usually used after interrogative pronouns, adjectives and adverbs, but μή appears when it would have been used in the direct question.

The main verb that introduces an indirect question is often not a verb of asking at all. Verbs of saying, warning, seeing, hearing, finding out, knowing, etc. can also introduce an indirect question. Since these verbs can also introduce indirect statements, it is important to distinguish between the two.

οἶδα αὐτὸν φεύγοντα.
I know that he is fleeing.

οἶδα τί οὐ φεύγει.
I know why he is not fleeing.

EXERCISE 145.

1. ἐρωτήσω τοὺς ἄνδρας εἰ ἐβλάβησαν τὴν κεφαλήν.
2. οὐκ ἴσμεν ὅποι οἱ πολέμιοι φεύγουσιν.
3. ὁ τύραννος ἤρετο τὸν ἄνδρα ὅπου τὸν ἰχθὺν εὗρεν.
4. ἐβουλόμεθα μαθεῖν πότερον οἱ Πέρσαι μενοῦσιν ἢ ἀποχωρήσουσιν.
5. ἆρ' οἶσθα εἰ ὁ στρατηγὸς νενίκηκε τοὺς Πέρσας ἢ οὔ;

6. ἠρωτήσαμεν εἰ οἱ πολέμιοι προσβαλοῦσιν ἡμῖν ἐκείνῃ τῇ ἡμέρᾳ.
7. ἐβουλόμεθα εὑρεῖν ποῦ τέλος παύσαιντο οἱ πολέμιοι.
8. οἱ Ἀθηναῖοι ἠρώτων εἰ ἡ οἰκία καταλυθήσεται τῷ χειμῶνι.
9. οὐκ ᾔσμεν εἰ οἱ σύμμαχοι ἀγαθοὶ εἶεν μάχεσθαι.
10. οἱ πολῖται ἤροντο τίνες ἐσμὲν καὶ πόθεν ἤλθομεν.

EXERCISE 146.

1. We are asking who the old man is.
2. The enemy wanted to know where the road was.
3. We wanted to discover where the allies had gone.
4. I asked that sailor whether the ship had arrived at last.
5. Have you heard where the ships are being sent?
6. The Greeks did not know whether the Persians had freed the prisoners or killed them.
7. We were not able to find out what the enemy would do.
8. The general asked the messenger where the enemy's camp was.
9. Demosthenes asked the Athenians whether they wanted to save their country.
10. The citizens were good at speaking but bad at fighting.

READING.

PYLOS AND SPHACTERIA 3: A BOAST FULFILLED?

Ἐν δὲ τούτῳ, ἐπεὶ ἡ ἐν τῇ νήσῳ ὕλη ὑπὸ στρατιώτου τινὸς ὡς ἐπὶ τὸ πολὺ [*for the most part*] κατεκαύθη [*was burned down*, from κατακαίω], ῥᾶον ἦν τῷ Δημοσθένει εὑρίσκειν ὁπόσοι εἰσὶν οἱ Λακεδαιμόνιοι καὶ ὅπου ἔξεστιν ἀποβαίνειν. Κλέων δὲ στρατιὰν ἔχων ἀφικνεῖται εἰς Πύλον. οἱ δὲ στρατηγοί, πάντας τοὺς ὁπλίτας νυκτὸς ἐπιβιβάσαντες ἐπ' ὀλίγας ναῦς, ὀλίγον τῆς νήσου ἀπέβαινον ἑκατέρωθεν, καὶ ἐχώρουν δρόμῳ ἐπὶ τὸ πρῶτον φυλακτήριον τῆς νήσου· τοὺς δὲ φύλακας λανθάνουσιν ἀποβαίνοντες εἰς γῆν καὶ εὐθὺς διαφθείρουσιν ἔτι ἀναλαμβάνοντας τὰ ὅπλα. ὕστερον δὲ πᾶς ὁ ἄλλος στρατὸς ἀπέβη πλὴν τῶν ἐν τῇ Πύλῳ φυλάκων. οἱ δὲ Λακεδαιμόνιοι, ὡς εἶδον τὸ φυλακτήριον διεφθαρμένον καὶ στρατὸν προχωροῦντα, τοῖς ὁπλίταις τῶν Ἀθηναίων προσέβαλλον, βουλόμενοι εἰς χεῖρας ἐλθεῖν [*come to grips*]. οἱ δὲ Ἀθηναῖοι, αἰσθόμενοι αὐτοὶ πολλῷ πλείονες ὄντες τῶν πολεμίων, ἔβαλλον λίθοις τε καὶ τοξεύμασιν. τέλος δὲ οἱ Λακεδαιμόνιοι ἐχώρησαν εἰς τὸ ἔσχατον φυλακτήριον τῆς νήσου.

χρόνον μὲν οὖν πολὺν ἀμφότεροι ἐμάχοντο, πιεζόμενοι τῇ μάχῃ καὶ τῇ δίψῃ καὶ τῷ ἡλίῳ· προσελθὼν δὲ ὁ τῶν Μεσσηνίων[1] στρατηγὸς Κλέωνι καὶ Δημοσθένει ἔφη ἐκείνους μὲν μάτην πονεῖν, αὐτὸς δέ, εἰ βούλονται ἑαυτῷ παρέχειν τοξότας καὶ ψιλούς, περιελεύσεσθαι κατὰ νώτου. λαβὼν δὲ τούτους ἔλαθε τοὺς πολεμίους περιελθών, καὶ αὐτοὺς ἐξέπληξεν. καὶ οἱ Λακεδαιμόνιοι βαλλόμενοι ἑκατέρωθεν οὐκέτι ἀντεῖχον. ὁ δὲ Κλέων καὶ ὁ Δημοσθένης, βουλόμενοι λαβεῖν αὐτοὺς ζῶντας, ἔπαυσαν τὴν μάχην. καὶ οὕτως ὁ Κλέων εἴκοσιν ἡμερῶν ἤγαγε τοὺς ἄνδρας Ἀθήναζε, ὥσπερ ὑπέστη.

Adapted from Thucydides IV.29-39

1 Helots in Messenia had revolted in 464 B.C.; when Sparta suppressed the rebellion, the helots were given a settlement by the Athenians at Naupactus on the Corinthian Gulf.

Chapter 33 Vocabulary

Verbs:

ἐρωτάω, ἐρωτήσω, ἠρόμην / ἠρώτησα, ἠρώτηκα, ἠρώτημαι, ἠρωτήθην	ask
κτάομαι, κτήσομαι, ἐκτησάμην, —, κέκτημαι, ἐκτήθην	acquire
φοβέω, φοβήσω, ἐφόβησα, —, πεφόβημαι, ἐφοβήθην	frighten, terrify
φοβέομαι	fear, be afraid

Pronouns / Adjectives:

μηδείς, μηδεμία, μηδέν	no one, nothing	**οὐδείς**, οὐδεμία, οὐδέν	no one, nothing
πότερος, -α, -ον	which of two		

Conjunctions:

εἰ	whether	πότερον...ἤ	whether...or

Numbers: above, sec. 2

CHAPTER 34

οἱ δὲ ἀκούσαντες τοῦ βασιλέως ἐπορεύθησαν, καὶ ἰδοὺ ὁ ἀστὴρ ὃν εἶδον ἐν τῇ ἀνατολῇ προῆγεν αὐτοὺς ἕως ἐλθὼν ἐστάθη ἐπάνω οὗ ἦν τὸ παιδίον.

— Matthew 2.9

1. εἶμι, 'go'

Though it is present in form, the indicative of εἶμι, 'go' often has the future meaning 'I shall go'. (The subjunctive always has this future meaning. The infinitive, participle and optative can have either a present or a future sense.) It has no other principal part. εἶμι is more common than ἔρχομαι in the imperfect and future tenses.

1 Present	2 Future	3 Aorist
ἔρχομαι impf. ᾖα	εἶμι	ἦλθον

The forms of εἶμι are distinguished from those of εἰμί, 'be' both by the accent and by the presence of **ι** in all forms. Here are the two paradigms for comparison.

PRESENT SYSTEM

		εἶμι, 'go'			εἰμί, 'be'	
INDICATIVE		Present	Imperfect		Present	Imperfect	
Sing.	1st	εἶμι	ᾖα	ᾔειν[2]	εἰμί	ἦ	ἦν
	2nd	εἶ(ς)[1]	ᾔεισθα	ᾔεις	εἶ	ἦσθα	
	3rd	εἶσι(ν)	ᾔειν	ᾔει	ἐστί(ν)	ἦν	
Plur.	1st	ἴμεν	ᾖμεν		ἐσμέν	ἦμεν	
	2nd	ἴτε	ᾖτε		ἐστέ	ἦτε	
	3rd	ἴᾱσι(ν)	ᾖσαν	ᾔεσαν	εἰσί(ν)	ἦσαν	

1 εἶ is the Attic form, while εἶς is more common elsewhere.

2 The alternate forms are found in later authors.

SUBJUNCTIVE

Sing.	1st	ἴω	ὦ
	2nd	ἴῃς	ᾖς
	3rd	ἴῃ	ᾖ
Plur.	1st	ἴωμεν	ὦμεν
	2nd	ἴητε	ἦτε
	3rd	ἴωσι(ν)	ὦσι(ν)

OPTATIVE

Sing.	1st	ἴοιμι ἰοίην	εἴην
	2nd	ἴοις	εἴης
	3rd	ἴοι	εἴη
Plur.	1st	ἴοιμεν	εἶμεν [εἴημεν]
	2nd	ἴοιτε	εἶτε [εἴητε]
	3rd	ἴοιεν	εἶεν [εἴησαν]

IMPERATIVE

Sing.	2nd	ἴθι	ἴσθι
	3rd	ἴτω	ἔστω
Plur.	2nd	ἴτε	ἔστε
	3rd	ἰόντων	ἔστων ὄντων

INFINITIVE

	ἰέναι	εἶναι

PARTICIPLE

	ἰών, ἰοῦσα, ἰόν ἰόντος, etc.	ὤν, οὖσα, ὄν ὄντος, etc.

2. ἵημι

This athematic verb ἵημι, 'throw' has an **ε**-stem like τίθημι. It is not irregular, but contraction of vowels sometimes obscure the regular pattern. The rough breathing helps to distinguish its forms from those of εἰμί, 'be' and εἶμι, 'go'. The aorist and (plu)perfect tenses are normally found only in compounds.

PRESENT SYSTEM

		Active		Middle / Passive	
INDICATIVE		**Present**	**Imperfect**	**Present**	**Imperfect**
Sing.	1st	ἵημι	ἵην	ἵεμαι	ἱέμην
	2nd	ἵης	ἵεις	ἵεσαι	ἵεσο
	3rd	ἵησι(ν)	ἵει	ἵεται	ἵετο
Plur.	1st	ἵεμεν	ἵεμεν	ἱέμεθα	ἱέμεθα
	2nd	ἵετε	ἵετε	ἵεσθε	ἵεσθε
	3rd	ἱᾶσι(ν)	ἵεσαν	ἵενται	ἵεντο
SUBJUNCTIVE					
Sing.	1st	ἱῶ	ἱῶμαι		
	2nd	ἱῇς	ἱῇ		
	3rd	ἱῇ	ἱῆται		
Plur.	1st	ἱῶμεν	ἱώμεθα		
	2nd	ἱῆτε	ἱῆσθε		
	3rd	ἱῶσι(ν)	ἱῶνται		
OPTATIVE					
Sing.	1st	ἱείην	ἱείμην		
	2nd	ἱείης	ἱεῖο		
	3rd	ἱείη	ἱεῖτο		
Plur.	1st	ἱεῖμεν	ἱείημεν	ἱείμεθα	
	2nd	ἱεῖτε	ἱείητε	ἱεῖσθε	
	3rd	ἱεῖεν	ἱείησαν	ἱεῖντο	
IMPERATIVE					
Sing.	2nd	ἵει	ἵεσο		
	3rd	ἱέτω	ἱέσθω		
Plur.	2nd	ἵετε	ἵεσθε		
	3rd	ἱέντων	ἱέσθων		
INFINITIVE					
		ἱέναι		ἵεσθαι	
PARTICIPLE					
		ἱείς, ἱεῖσα, ἱέν ἱέντος, etc.		ἱέμενος, -μένη, -μενον ἱεμένου, etc.	

AORIST SYSTEM

INDICATIVE		Active		Middle
Sing.	1st	ἀφῆκα		ἀφείμην
	2nd	ἀφῆκας		ἀφεῖσο
	3rd	ἀφῆκε(ν)		ἀφεῖτο
Plur.	1st	ἀφεῖμεν		ἀφείμεθα
	2nd	ἀφεῖτε		ἀφεῖσθε
	3rd	ἀφεῖσαν		ἀφεῖντο
SUBJUNCTIVE				
Sing.	1st	ἀφῶ		ἀφῶμαι
	2nd	ἀφῇς		ἀφῇ
	3rd	ἀφῇ		ἀφῆται
Plur.	1st	ἀφῶμεν		ἀφώμεθα
	2nd	ἀφῆτε		ἀφῆσθε
	3rd	ἀφῶσι(ν)		ἀφῶνται
OPTATIVE				
Sing.	1st	ἀφείην		ἀφείμην
	2nd	ἀφείης		ἀφεῖο
	3rd	ἀφείη		ἀφεῖτο
Plur.	1st	ἀφεῖμεν	ἀφείημεν	ἀφείμεθα
	2nd	ἀφεῖτε	ἀφείητε	ἀφεῖσθε
	3rd	ἀφεῖεν	ἀφείησαν	ἀφεῖντο
IMPERATIVE				
Sing.	2nd	ἄφες		ἀφοῦ
	3rd	ἀφέτω		ἀφέσθω
Plur.	2nd	ἄφετε		ἄφεσθε
	3rd	ἀφέντων		ἀφέσθων
INFINITIVE				
		ἀφεῖναι		ἀφέσθαι
PARTICIPLE				
		ἀφείς, ἀφεῖσα, ἀφέν ἀφέντος, etc.		ἀφέμενος, -η, -ον ἀφεμένου, etc.

3. Temporal clauses with ἕως, μέχρι and ἔστε

Temporal clauses describe the time frame of an action. They are introduced by the conjunctions ἕως, μέχρι, ἔστε, 'as long as', 'while', 'until'. The time referred to may be definite or indefinite. The construction varies accordingly, and resembles a parallel type of condition. The most common types are the following.

- Definite time in the past (occasionally the present): This construction follows the pattern of simple conditions (Ch. 12.5), with ἕως, etc. + indicative (negative οὐ) after a secondary tense main verb.

  ἐμένομεν ἕως ἦλθον.
  We waited until they came.

  μένομεν μέχρι οἱ βάρβαροι πάρεισιν.
  We are remaining as long as / while the foreigners are present.

  ἔδραμον ἔστε οὐκέτι ἐν κινδύνῳ ἦσαν.
  They ran until they were no longer in danger.

- Indefinite time in the present or past: The time is indefinite because the action is / was regularly repeated. The construction resembles present and past general conditions (Ch. 28.2-3), with ἕως, etc. + subjunctive or optative (negative μή).

  ἕως ἂν εὖ πράττωσιν, εὐδαίμονές εἰσιν.
  As long as they fare well, they are happy. (present general)

  ἀεὶ ἔμενον μέχρι ὁ ῥήτωρ παύσαιτο λέγων.
  We always waited until the orator finished speaking. (past general)

- Indefinite time in the future: This construction commonly resembles future more vivid conditions (Ch. 28.2), with ἕως, etc. + ἄν + subjunctive (negative μή). The main verb is normally future (or equivalent), but may be present if it anticipates a future action.

  μαχούμεθα ἕως ἂν ἐν κινδύνῳ ὦμεν.
  We will fight as long as we are in danger. (future more vivid)

  μαχούμεθα ἕως ἂν μὴ ἐν κινδύνῳ ὦμεν.
  We will fight until we are no longer in danger. (future more vivid)

  μένε ἕως ἂν ἔλθω.
  Wait until I come. (future more vivid)

  μένομεν ἔστε ἂν ἔλθωσιν οἱ πρέσβεις.
  We are waiting until the ambassadors come.
  We are waiting in expectation that the ambassadors may come.

  When the reference to an anticipated action follows a past tense, the optative (without ἄν) replaces the subjunctive, following the regular sequence of moods.

  ἐμένομεν ἔστε ἔλθοιεν οἱ πρέσβεις.
  We were waiting until the ambassadors came.
  We were waiting in expectation that the ambassadors might come.

Reading expectations

secondary tense → ἕως, etc.	↗ indicative (neg. οὐ)	= definite past time
	↘ optative (neg. μή)	= indefinite past time OR time anticipated in the past
present tense → ἕως, etc.	↗ indicative (neg. οὐ)	= definite present time
	↘ ἄν + subjunctive (neg. μή)	= indefinite present time OR time anticipated in the present
future tense → ἕως, etc.	→ ἄν + subjunctive (neg. μή)	= indefinite future time

4. Temporal clauses with πρίν

The conjunction πρίν has two possible senses: with a finite verb it means 'until', and with an infinitive it means 'before'.

- πρίν with a finite verb: the main clause is usually negative (otherwise ἕως, etc. would appear), and often contains an adverb meaning 'before', 'sooner'. The range of constructions is like that for ἕως, etc. (above, sec. 3).

  οὐ πρότερον ἀπέβημεν πρὶν ἦλθον.
  We did not go away until they came. (definite past)

  οὔποτε παύεται πρὶν ἂν εἰς κώμην τινὰ ἀφίκηται.
  He never stops until he reaches a village. (indefinite present)

  οὐ πρόσθεν παύσεται πρὶν ἂν εἰς τὴν πόλιν ἀφίκηται.
  He will not stop until he reaches the city. (indefinite future)

- πρίν with an infinitive: the main clause is usually affirmative, and may contain an adverb meaning 'before', 'sooner'. If the subject of the infinitive is different from the main subject, it appears in the accusative. The tense of the infinitive conveys aspect: the aorist is normal, but a present infinitive is occasionally used for an ongoing, repeated or attempted action. When πρίν is used with an infinitive, it must mean 'before' and not 'until'.

  ἦλθον πρὶν ἡμᾶς ἀποβῆναι.
  They came before we went away.

  ἴμεν οἴκαδε πρὶν ὑμᾶς ἀφικέσθαι.
  We will go home before you arrive.

  ἀεὶ ἔμενον τρεῖς ἡμέρας πρὶν ἀποβαίνειν.
  They always stayed three days before going away.

  οἶσθα τὰ ἀληθῆ καὶ πρὶν ἐμὲ λέγειν τι.
  You know the truth even before I try to say anything.

Reading expectations

negative main clause → πρίν → finite verb (constr. as ἕως, etc.)	= 'until'
affirmative main clause → πρίν → infinitive	= 'before'

EXERCISE 147.

1. ὁρᾷς τὸν παῖδα λίθους ἱέντα εἰς τὸν ποταμόν;
2. ἐμαχόμεθα ἕως οἱ τῶν πολεμίων σύμμαχοι ἀφίκοντο.
3. πρὶν προσβάλλειν οἱ Λακεδαιμόνιοι ἀεὶ ἔθυον τοῖς θεοῖς.
4. οὐ πρόσθεν πιστεύσω αὐτῷ πρὶν ἂν εἰδῶ τί βούλεται.
5. οὕτω ἐφίλησε τὸν ναύτην ὥστε ἔμενεν αὐτὸν τέτταρα ἔτη ἕως ἀπῆν.
6. ζητήσομεν τὴν χώραν αὐτῶν μέχρι ἂν εὕρωμεν αὐτήν.
7. ἐξῆλθεν ὁ πρέσβυς πρὶν τὸν Σωκράτη λέξαι.
8. ἕως πείθοιντο τοῖς κακοῖς πολίταις, ὀλίγους φίλους εἶχον.
9. ἑκάστη ἡμέρᾳ οἱ παῖδες παιδεύονται ἔστε ἂν ὁ πατὴρ τέλος εἰσέλθῃ.
10. μὴ ἀφῆτε τὰ ὅπλα πρὶν ἂν κελεύσῃ ὁ στρατηγός.

EXERCISE 148.

1. It will be difficult to ransom the men until we acquire money.
2. It is wiser to learn the the truth before answering.
3. As long as the storm is dangerous we will not go out of the harbor.
4. We will not have peace until the Persians are defeated.
5. That young man did not find his horse until he remembered where it was.
6. The general arrived before the cavalry attacked.
7. We were in danger until the triremes were sent.
8. The prisoners did not answer until the king freed them.
9. Why did you cease from your work before I ordered you to?
10. We did not stop until at last we learned the truth.

READING.

SOCRATES' DEFENSE SPEECH

In 399 B.C. Socrates went on trial in Athens. The charges were that he (1) introduced strange new gods; (2) corrupted the youth; (3) made the weaker argument appear the stronger. The first charge in particular is without apparent foundation; nevertheless Socrates was found guilty. After proposing an insufficient lesser penalty, he was sentenced to death. This section of his defense speech comes after his conviction is announced, while the penalty is under debate.

ἴσως οὖν ἄν τις εἴποι· Σιγῶν δὲ καὶ ἡσυχίαν ἄγων, ὦ Σώκρατες, οὐχ οἷός τ' ἔσει ἀπιέναι καὶ ζῆν ἐν ἄλλῃ τινὶ χώρᾳ; τοῦτο δή ἐστι πάντων χαλεπώτατον πεῖσαί τινας ὑμῶν. ἐὰν μὲν γὰρ λέγω ὅτι τῷ θεῷ ἀπειθεῖν τοῦτ' ἔστι, καὶ διὰ τοῦτο ἀδύνατον ἡσυχίαν ἄγειν, οὐ πείσεσθέ μοι· ἐὰν δὲ λέγω ὅτι τοῦτο τυγχάνει μέγιστον ἀγαθὸν ὂν ἀνθρώπῳ, ἑκάστης ἡμέρας περὶ ἀρετῆς διαλέγεσθαι καὶ τῶν ἄλλων περὶ ὧν ὑμεῖς ἐμοῦ ἀκούετε διαλεγομένου, ὁ δ' ἀνεξέταστος βίος οὐ βιωτὸς ἀνθρώπῳ, ταῦτα δ' ἔτι ἧττον πείσεσθέ μοι λέγοντι. εἰ μὲν γὰρ ἦν μοι χρήματα, ἐτιμησάμην [*propose a penalty*] ἂν χρημάτων ὅσα ἔμελλον ἐκτείσειν· οὐδὲν γὰρ ἂν ἐβλάβην. νῦν δέ, οὐ γὰρ ἔστι μοι χρήματα πολλά, ἴσως ἂν δυναίμην ἐκτεῖσαι ὑμῖν μνᾶν ἀργυρίου· τοσούτου οὖν τιμῶμαι.

Adapted from Plato, *Apology* 37e-38b

Chapter 34 Vocabulary

Verbs:

ἀφίημι	throw away
εἶμι, —, —, —, —, —	go (*future sense*)
εἰσέρχομαι	enter, come in
ἵημι, ἥσω, -ἧκα, -εἷκα, -εἷμαι, -εἵθην	throw

Adverbs:

πρότερον	before, formerly	πρόσθεν	before, sooner

Conjunctions:

ἔστε	as long as, while, until	μέχρι	as long as, while, until
ἕως	as long as, while, until	πρίν	before, until

GREEK–ENGLISH GLOSSARY

The first appearance of a word in a lesson vocabulary is given in parentheses. Words that appear only in reading exercises have no chapter designation.

ἀγαθός, -ή, -όν, good (7)
ἀγγεῖον, -ου, τό, vessel
ἀγγέλλω, announce (7)
ἄγγελος, -ου, ὁ, messenger (25)
ἄγκιστρον, -ου, τό, hook
ἀγορά, -ᾶς, ἡ, market-place (3)
ἄγω, lead, bring (2)
ἀγών, -ῶνος, ὁ, contest, game (12)
ἀδικέω, do wrong, be unjust, wrong (someone) (28)
ἀδικία, -ας, ἡ, injustice, wrongdoing
Ἄδμητος, -ου, ὁ, Admetus (13)
ἀδύνατος, -ον, impossible
ἀεί, always (4)
ἀείδω (*aor. part.* ἀείσας), sing
Ἀθήναζε, to Athens (28)
Ἀθῆναι, -ῶν, αἱ, Athens (4)
Ἀθηναῖος, -ου, ὁ, an Athenian (5)
Ἀθήνη, -ης, ἡ, Athena (4)
Ἀθήνηθεν, from Athens (28)
ἀθροίζω, collect
ἀθυμέω, be disheartened
ἀθυμία, -ας, ἡ, despondency
Αἴγινα, -ης, ἡ, Aegina
Αἰγινήτης, -ου, ὁ, an Aeginetan
Αἰγύπτιος, -ου, ὁ, an Egyptian
Αἴγυπτος, -ου, ἡ, Egypt
αἴθω, burn
αἶξ, αἰγός, ὁ/ἡ, goat
αἱρέω, take, capture (22); αἱρέομαι, choose, elect
αἰσθάνομαι, perceive (27)
αἰτέω, ask, ask for, demand
αἰχμάλωτος, -ου, ὁ, prisoner (of war) (17)
αἰχμή, -ῆς, ἡ, spear, spear point
ἀκούω, hear, listen to, (+ *acc.* thing, + *gen.* person) (11)
ἄκρον, -ου, τό, peak
ἀκρόπολις, -εως, ἡ, acropolis, citadel
ἀκτή, -ῆς, ἡ, shore
ἄλγος, -ους, τό, pain, grief
ἀληθής, -ές, true (20); **ἀληθῆ, τά**, the truth (20)
ἁλιεύς, -έως, ὁ, fisherman
Ἁλικαρνασσεύς, -εως, ὁ, a Halicarnassian
Ἄλκηστις, -ιδος, ἡ, Alcestis (16)
ἀλλά, but (2)
ἀλλήλων, -ων, -ων (*oblique cases*), each other (24)
ἄλλος, -η, -ο, other, another (16); *plur.*, more (additional); ὁ ἄλλος, remaining (rest of)
ἄλλως, otherwise
Ἅλυς, -υος, ὁ, Halys river
ἅμα, at the same time
Ἄμασις, -ιος, ὁ, Amasis (21)
ἀμείνων, ἄμεινον, better, *comp. of* ἀγαθός (23)
ἀμφίβληστρον, -ου, τό, net
ἀμφότερος, -α, -ον, both
ἄν, *conditional particle* (12)
ἀναβαίνω, mount, climb (up)
ἀναγιγνώσκω, read
ἀναγκάζω, force, compel (11)
ἀναγκαῖος, -α, -ον, necessary
ἀνάγκη, -ης, ἡ, necessity
ἀναγνωρίζω, recognize
ἀνάγω, put out (to sea)
ἀναλαμβάνω, take up
ἀναξυρίδες, -ων, αἱ, trousers
ἀναχωρέω, retreat
ἀνδρεία, -ας, ἡ, courage, bravery (14)
ἀνδρεῖος, -α, -ον, brave (7)
ἀνδρείως, bravely (29)
ἄνεμος, -ου, ὁ, wind
ἀνεξέταστος, -ον, unexamined
ἄνευ, without (+ *gen.*)
ἀνήρ, ἀνδρός, ὁ, man, husband (11)
ἄνθρωπος, -ου, ὁ, man, human (7)
ἀνταιτέω, ask for in return
ἀντέχω, hold out, resist
ἀντί, instead of (+ *gen.*)
ἄνω, upper (*adv.*); above (+ *gen.*)
ἄξιος, -α, -ον, worthy (9)
ἀπάγω, lead away, bring back (13)
ἀπέθανον, *aor. of* ἀποθνῄσκω (16)
ἀπειθέω, disobey (+ *dat.*)
ἄπειμι (εἰμί, 'be'), be absent (12)
ἄπειμι (εἶμι, 'go'), go away
ἀπελαύνω, drive away, march away (15)
ἀπέρχομαι, go away, depart (26)
ἀπό, from, away from (+ *gen.*) (4)

ἀποβαίνω, go away, disembark
ἀποβάλλω, throw away (24)
ἀποδίδωμι, give back (28)
ἀποθανεῖν, *aor. inf. of* ἀποθνήσκω (16)
ἀποθήκη, -ης, ἡ, storehouse, store
ἀποθνήσκω, die, be killed (10)
ἀποκρίνομαι, answer, reply (27)
ἀποκρύπτω, hide away
ἀποκτείνω, kill (10)
ἀπολαμβάνω, cut off
ἀπολείπω, leave, abandon
Ἀπόλλων, -ωνος, ὁ, Apollo
ἀποπέμπω, send away (25)
ἀποπλέω, sail away (24)
ἀπορέω, be at a loss, be in difficulty
ἀπορία, -ας, ἡ, difficulty, want (of something)
ἀποτέμνω, cut off
ἀποφεύγω, flee away, escape (11)
ἀποχωρέω, go away, retreat (22)
ἄπρακτος, -ον, unsuccessful
ἆρα, *interrogative particle* (24); **ἆρα μή**, surely... not (24); **ἆρα οὐ**, surely (24)
Ἀργεῖοι, -ων, οἱ, Argives
ἀργύριον, -ου, τό, money
ἄργυρος, -ου, ὁ, silver
ἀργυροῦς, -ᾶ, -οῦν, of silver (19)
ἀρέσκω, please
ἀρετή, -ῆς, ἡ, excellence (28)
ἀριθμός, -οῦ, ὁ, number
Ἀρισταγόρας, -ου, ὁ, Aristagoras (27)
ἀριστεύω, be best, be superior
ἄριστος, -η, -ον, best, *sup. of* ἀγαθός (23)
Ἀρίων, -ονος, ὁ, Arion
Ἀρμενία, -ας, ἡ, Armenia
Ἀρμένιος, -ου, ὁ, an Armenian
Ἀρτεμβάρης, -ους, ὁ, Artembares
Ἀρτεμισία, -ας, ἡ, Artemisia (18)
ἀρχαῖος, -α, -ον, ancient (16)
ἀρχή, -ῆς, ἡ, rule, empire, command
ἄρχω, rule, command (+ *gen.*) (11); begin (+ *gen.*) (32)
ἄρχων, -οντος, ὁ, ruler, chief, magistrate
Ἀσία, -ας, ἡ, Asia
ἀσπίς, -ίδος, ἡ, shield (9)
ἄστυ, -εως, τό, town (14)
Ἀστυάγης, -ους, ὁ, Astyages
ἀσφαλής, -ές, safe (20)
ἀτιμάω, slight, dishonor
Ἀττική, -ῆς, ἡ, Attica
Ἀττικός, -ή, -όν, Attic
αὖθις, again
αὐξάνω, grow
αὐτόμολος, -ου, ὁ, deserter
αὐτός, -ή, -ό, self (*intensive*) (9); *in oblique cases*, him, her, it, them (9); *attributive*, same (9)

ἄφθογγος, -ον, speechless
ἀφίημι, throw away (34)
ἀφικνέομαι, arrive, reach (+ εἰς) (26)

Βαβυλών, -ῶνος, ἡ, Babylon (23)
Βαβυλώνιοι, -ων, οἱ, Babylonians
βαίνω, go, walk (21)
βάλλω, throw, pelt (20)
βάρβαρος, -ου, ὁ, foreigner (non-Greek) (7)
βαρύς, -εῖα, -ύ, heavy (20)
βασίλεια, -ας, ἡ, queen
βασιλεύς, -έως, ὁ, king; *without article*, the king of Persia (15)
βασιλεύω, be king, reign (+ *gen.*) (4)
βέλτιστος, -η, -ον, best, *sup. of* ἀγαθός (23)
βελτίων, βέλτιον, better, *comp. of* ἀγαθός (23)
βία, -ας, ἡ, force; πρὸς βίαν, by force
βίος, -ου, ὁ, life (19)
βιωτός, -ή, -όν, worth living
βλάπτω, harm, injure, damage (6)
βλέπω (*aor. part.* βλέψας), look
βοάω, shout (19)
βοή, -ῆς, ἡ, shout
βοηθέω, help (+ *dat.*) (19)
βουκόλος, -ου, ὁ, herdsman
βουλεύω, plan (18); βουλεύομαι, deliberate (18)
βουλή, -ῆς, ἡ, plan
βούλομαι, want, wish, be willing (20)
βοῦς, βοός, ὁ/ἡ, ox (15)
βραδύς, -εῖα, -ύ, slow (20)
βράχιστος, -η, -ον, shortest, *sup. of* βραχύς (23)
βραχίων, βράχιον, shorter, *comp. of* βραχύς (23)
βραχύς, -εῖα, -ύ, short (20)

γάρ, for, because (*postpos.*) (8)
γαστήρ, γαστρός, ἡ, belly
Γέλων, -ωνος, ὁ, Gelon
γέρων, -οντος, ὁ, old man (10)
γέφυρα, -ας, ἡ, bridge (3)
γῆ, γῆς, ἡ, earth, land (19)
γίγας, -αντος, ὁ, giant (10)
γίγνομαι, become, happen (25)
γιγνώσκω, know, perceive (27)
γλῶττα, -ης, ἡ, tongue
γνάθος, -ου, ἡ, jaw
γνώμη, -ης, ἡ, opinion
γραῦς, γραός, ἡ, old woman (15)
γράφω, write (2)
γυμνός, -ή, -όν, naked, lightly clad
γυνή, γυναικός, ἡ, woman, wife (15)

δάκνω, bite
δακρύω, weep
δαρεικός, -οῦ, ὁ, daric (Persian coin)
Δαρεῖος, -ου, ὁ, Darius (11)

δέ, but, and (*postpos.*) (8)
δεῖ, it is necessary (19)
δείκνυμι, show (23)
δειλός, -ή, -όν, cowardly (18)
δεινός, -ή, -όν, strange, terrible, clever (7)
δεῖπνον, -ου, τό, dinner
δέκα, ten (17)
δεκαετής, -ές, ten years old
δέκατος, -η, -ον, tenth (17)
δελφίς, -ῖνος, ὁ, dolphin
Δελφοί, -ῶν, οἱ, Delphi
δένδρον, -ου, τό, tree (6)
δεσπότης, -ου, ὁ, master (of a household) (7)
δεῦρο, hither
δευτεραῖος, -α, -ον, on the second day
δέχομαι, receive (17)
δή, indeed (*postpos.*)
δηλόω, show (19)
δῆμος, -ου, ὁ, people (19)
Δημοσθένης, -ους, ὁ, Demosthenes (13)
διά, on account of (+ *acc.*) (10); through, by (+ *gen.*) (20)
διαβαίνω, cross (21)
διαβατός, -ή, -όν, crossable
διαβιβάζω, take across
διακόσιοι, -αι, -α, two hundred
διαλέγομαι, converse with (+ *dat.*)
διαλύομαι, put an end to, break off
διατρίβω, spend (time)
διαφεύγω, escape
διαφθείρω (*perf. M/P* διέφθαρμαι), destroy, kill
δίδωμι, give (23)
Διηνέκης, -ους, ὁ, Dieneces
δικαιοσύνη, -ης, ἡ, justice (4)
δικαίως, justly
δισμύριοι, -αι, -α, twenty thousand
δισχίλιοι, -αι, -α, two thousand
δίψα, -ης, ἡ, thirst
διώκω, pursue (2)
διῶρυξ, -υχος, ἡ, trench
δοκέω (*aor.* ἔδοξα), seem, seem good; think
δόκιμος, -η, -ον, notable
δόξα, -ης, ἡ, glory (3)
δορυφόρος, -ου, ὁ, bodyguard
δοῦλος, -ου, ὁ, slave (5)
δουλοσύνη, -ης, ἡ, slavery
δουλόω, enslave (19)
δραχμή, ῆς, ἡ, drachma (coin worth a day's wage for a skilled craftsman)
δρόμος, -ου, ὁ, running, course; δρόμῳ, at the double
δρόσος, -ου, ἡ, dew
δύναμαι, be able
δυνατώτατος, -η, -ον, very powerful
δύο, two (33)
δῶρον, -ου, τό, gift (6)

ἐάν, εἰ + *conditional particle* ἄν (28)
ἑαυτοῦ, -ῆς, -οῦ (*oblique cases*), himself, herself, itself, themselves; *possessive gen.* his own, etc. (24)
ἐάω, allow
ἐγγύς, near (*adv.*) (17); near (+ *gen.*) (17)
ἐγενόμην, *aor. of* γίγνομαι (25)
ἐγώ, ἐμοῦ / μου, I (18)
ἐθέλω, be willing, wish (6)
εἰ, if (12); whether (33); **εἰ γάρ**, if only, would that, may (26)
εἰδέναι, *inf. of* οἶδα (27)
εἶδον, *aor. of* ὁράω (19)
εἴθε, if only, would that, may (26)
εἴκοσι(ν), twenty (33)
εἷλον, *aor. of* αἱρέω (22)
Εἵλως, -ωτος, ὁ, Helot (a serf of the Spartans)
εἰμί, be (*present indic. encl. except 2 sing.*) (7)
εἶμι, go (*fut. sense*) (34)
εἶναι, *inf. of* εἰμί, 'be' (7)
εἶπον, said (*used as aor. of* λέγω) (27)
εἰρήνη, -ης, ἡ, peace (4)
εἰς, into, onto, to (+ *acc.*) (3); for (a purpose) (+ *acc.*) (11)
εἷς, μία, ἕν, one (33)
εἰσάγω, bring in, lead in
εἰσβαίνω, enter, go in, go on board
εἰσβάλλω (+ εἰς), throw into, invade (11); flow into
εἰσβολή, -ῆς, ἡ, (mountain) pass
εἰσέρχομαι, enter, come in (34)
εἴσοδος, -ου, ἡ, entrance
εἰσφέρω, bring in
εἴτε...εἴτε (εἰ + τε), either...or, whether...or
ἐκ, ἐξ, out of, from (+ *gen.*) (3)
ἑκάς, far
ἕκαστος, -η, -ον, each (of 3 or more), every (16)
ἑκάτερος, -α, -ον, each of two (23)
ἑκατέρωθεν, on both sides
ἐκβαίνω, go out, come out (32)
ἐκβάλλω, throw out
ἐκεῖ, there (12)
ἐκεῖνος, -η, -ο, that (24)
ἐκλέπω, hatch
ἐκπηδάω, leap out
ἐκπλήττω (*aor.* ἐξέπληξα), scare, startle
ἐκπολιορκέω, capture by siege
ἔκπωμα, -ατος, τό, drinking-cup
ἐκτίνω (*fut.* ἐκτείσω, *aor.* ἐξέτεισα), pay in full
ἕκτος, -η, -ον, sixth (33)
ἔλαθον, *aor. of* λανθάνω (32)0
ἐλάττων, ἔλαττον, less, smaller, fewer, *comp. of* μικρός, ὀλίγος (23)
ἐλαύνω, drive, march (15)

ἐλάχιστος, -η, -ον, least, smallest, fewest, *sup. of* μικρός, ὀλίγος (23)
ἐλεύθερος, -α, -ον, free (10)
ἐλευθερόω, free (19)
Ἐλεφαντίνη, -ης, ἡ, Elephantine (city in Egypt)
ἐλθεῖν, *aor. inf. of* ἔρχομαι (26)
Ἑλλάς, -άδος, ἡ, Greece (9)
Ἕλλην, -ηνος, ὁ, a Greek (12)
Ἑλληνικός, -ή, -όν, Greek
Ἑλλήσποντος, -ου, ὁ, Hellespont
ἕλος, -ους, τό, marsh
ἐλπίζω, hope, expect (+ *fut. inf.*) (13)
ἐλπίς, -ίδος, ἡ, hope, expectation (9)
ἔμαθον, *aor. of* μανθάνω (21)
ἐμαυτοῦ, -ῆς (*oblique cases*), myself; *possessive gen.* my own (24)
ἐμβάλλω, ram (+ *dat.*)
ἐμβολή, -ῆς, ἡ, invasion, entrance
ἐμός, -ή, -όν, my (18)
ἔμπροσθε(ν), in front of (+ *gen.*)
ἐν, in, on, (+ *dat.*) (3); among (+ *dat. pl.*) (6); ἐν δὲ τούτῳ, meanwhile
ἐνάγω, lead on, urge
ἔνδον, inside
ἔνειμι (εἰμί, 'be'), be in, be among
ἕνεκα, for the sake of (+ *gen*; *postpos.*)
ἐνταῦθα, here, there, to here, to there (30)
ἐντεῦθεν, from here, from there (30)
ἐξ, ἐκ, out of, from (+ *gen.*) (3)
ἕξ, six (33)
ἐξάγω, lead out, bring out
ἐξάλλομαι, leap out
ἔξεστι, it is possible (from ἔξειμι)
ἐξηγέομαι, explain, recount
ἑξήκοντα, sixty (33)
ἔξω, outside (+ *gen.*) (17)
ἑορτή, -ῆς, ἡ, feast, festival
ἐπάγω, lead against
ἐπεί, when, since, as
ἐπειδάν, ἐπειδή + *conditional particle* ἄν (30)
ἐπειδή, since, after (30)
ἔπειμι (εἰμί, 'be'), be upon (+ *gen.*)
ἔπειτα, then, next
ἔπεσον, *aor. of* πίπτω (12)
ἐπί, against, on to (+ *acc.*) (8); on, upon (+ *gen.*) (15); on (+ *dat.*)
ἐπιβάτης, -ου, ὁ, marine (fighting man on a ship)
ἐπιβιβάζω, put on board
ἐπιβοάω, call upon, cry out (to)
ἐπιβουλεύω, plot
ἐπικεῖμαι, lie opposite (+ *dat.*)
ἐπιστάτης, -ου, ὁ, overseer
ἐπιστολή, -ῆς, ἡ, letter (3)
ἐπιτηδειότατος, -η, -ον, most fit, most suitable
ἐπιτρέπω, entrust
ἐπιφαίνομαι, appear
ἐπιχειρέω, make an attempt
ἕπομαι, follow (+ *dat.*) (30)
ἐποτρύνω, urge on
ἑπτακαίδεκα, seventeen (33)
ἐργάζομαι (*impf.* εἰργαζόμην), work
ἔργον, -ου, τό, work, deed (6)
ἔρχομαι, come, go (26)
ἔρως, -τος, ὁ, love, desire (16)
ἐρωτάω, ask (33)
ἐσθίω, eat
ἔστε, as long as, while, until (34)
ἔσχατος, -η, -ον, furthest; ἔσχατα, -ων, τά, outskirts
ἔσω, inside
ἕτερος, -α, -ον, other
ἔτι, still, yet (12); ἔτι δέ, still more
ἑτοῖμος, -η, -ον, ready (13)
ἔτος, -ους, τό, year (16)
ἔτυχον, *aor. of* τυγχάνω (32)
εὖ, well (12)
εὖ ποιέω, treat well (19)
εὖ πράττω, fare well (12)
εὐγενής, -ές, well-born (20)
εὐδαίμων, εὔδαιμον, happy (20)
εὐεργέτης, -ου, ὁ, benefactor
εὐθύς, immediately, at once (13)
εὔνοια, -ας, ἡ, kindness
εὐπορία, -ας, ἡ, plenty
εὑρίσκω, find, find out (8)
Εὐρυβιάδης, -ου, ὁ, Eurybiades
εὐρύς, -εῖα, -ύ, wide (20)
Εὐρώπη, -ης, ἡ, Europe
εὐτυχέω, prosper
εὐτυχής, -ές, fortunate (20)
εὐτυχία, -ας, ἡ, good fortune, prosperity
Εὐφράτης, -ου, ὁ, Euphrates
ἔφην, *aor. of* φημί (14)
ἐχθίων, ἔχθιον, more hostile, *comp. of* ἐχθρός (23)
ἔχθιστος, -η, -ον, most hostile, *sup. of* ἐχθρός (23)
ἐχθρός, -ά, -όν, hostile (7)
ἔχω, have (2); hold, keep
ἑώρων, *Attic impf. of* ὁράω (19)
ἕως, as long as, while, until (34)

ζάω (*pres. inf.* ζῆν), live
Ζεύς, Διός, ὁ, Zeus (15)
ζητέω, seek (19)
ζυγόν, -οῦ, τό, yoke (6)
ζῷον, -ου, τό, animal (6)
ζωός, -ή, -όν, living

ἤ, or (8); than (16); **ἤ...ἤ**, either...or (8)
ᾗ, where
ἡγεμονεύω, command (+ *gen.*)

ἡγεμονία, -ας, ἡ, leadership
ἡγεμών, -όνος, ὁ, leader, guide (12)
ἤδη, already (7)
ᾔδη, *pluperf. of* οἶδα (27)
ἥδιστος, -η, ον, sweetest, *sup. of* ἡδύς (23)
ἡδίων, ἥδιον, sweeter, *comp. of* ἡδύς (23)
ἥδομαι, enjoy (+ *dat. or part.*); be pleased with (+ *dat.*) (32)
ἡδύς, -εῖα, -ύ, sweet, pleasant (20)
ἥκω, have come (11)
ἤλασα, *aor. of* ἐλαύνω (15)
ἦλθον, *aor. of* ἔρχομαι (26)
ἥλιος, -ου, ὁ, sun
ἡμεῖς, ἡμῶν, we (18)
ἡμέρα, -ας, ἡ, day (3)
ἡμέτερος, -α, -ον, our (18)
ἡμῶν αὐτῶν (*oblique cases*), ourselves; *possessive gen.* your own (24)
ἤνεγκον, *aor. of* φέρω (11)
ἤπειρος, -ου, ἡ, mainland, continent
Ἡρακλῆς, -έους, ὁ, Heracles (16)
ἠρόμην, *aor. of* ἐρωτάω (33)
ᾐσθόμην, *aor. of* αἰσθάνομαι (27)
ἥττων, ἧττον, less, weak, inferior, *comp. of* κακός (23)
ἡσυχίαν ἄγω, keep quiet

θάλαττα, -ης, ἡ, sea (3)
θάνατος, -ου, ὁ, death (15)
θάττων, θᾶττον, faster, swifter, quicker, *comp. of* ταχύς (23)
θαῦμα, -ατος, τό, wonder
θαυμάζω, wonder at, admire (9)
θεά, -ᾶς, ἡ, goddess (3)
Θεμιστοκλῆς, -έους, ὁ, Themistocles (14)
θεός, -οῦ, ὁ, god (10)
θεράπαινα, -ης, ἡ, (female) servant
θεραπεύω, honor, worship (3); heal, cure, tend (5)
θεράπων, -οντος, ὁ, (male) servant
Θερμοπύλαι, -ῶν, αἱ, Thermopylae
θερμότερος, -α, -ον, warmer
Θῆβαι, -ῶν, αἱ, Thebes
θῆλυς, -εια, -υ, female
θήρ, θηρός, ὁ, wild beast (11)
θηρίον, -ου, τό, beast, wild animal
θησαυρός, -οῦ, ὁ, treasure, treasure-house
Θήχης, -ου, ὁ Theches (*mountain in Armenia*)
-θνήσκω, die (32)
θόρυβος, -ου, ὁ, uproar
θρόνος, -ου, ὁ, throne
θύω, sacrifice (2)
θώραξ, -ακος, ὁ, breastplate (8)

ἰατρός, -οῦ, ὁ, doctor (5)
ἰδέα, -ας, ἡ, appearance
ἰδών, *aor. part. of* ὁράω
ἱερεύς, -έως, ὁ, priest (15)
ἱερός, -ά, -όν, sacred
ἵημι, throw (34)
ἱμάτιον, -ου, τό, cloak
ἵνα, in order (to, that), so that (27)
ἱππεύς, -έως, ὁ, cavalryman; *plur.*, cavalry (15)
Ἱππίας, -ου, ὁ, Hippias
ἵππος, -ου, ὁ, horse (5)
Ἰσθμός, -οῦ, ὁ, Isthmus (of Corinth)
ἵστημι, make stand, set; ἵσταμαι *with* ἔστην, stand (23)
ἰσχῡρός, -ά, -όν, strong (7)
ἴσως, perhaps
Ἰταλία, -ας, ἡ, Italy
ἰχθύς, -ύος, ὁ, fish (14)
Ἴωνες, -ων, οἱ, Ionians

καθεύδω, sleep
καθίζω, sit
καί, and, also, even (2); **καί...καί**, both...and... (8)
καίπερ, although (21)
καιρός, -οῦ, ὁ, precise moment, opportunity
καίω, burn, kindle
κάκιστος, -η, -ον, worst, *sup. of* κακός (23)
κακίων, κάκιον, worse, *comp. of* κακός (23)
κακός, -ή, -όν, bad (7)
κακῶς, badly (12)
κακῶς ποιέω, treat badly (19)
κακῶς πράττω, fare badly (12)
κάλαμος, -ου, ὁ, reed
καλέω, call, summon
Καλλίμαχος, -ου, ὁ, Callimachus
κάλλιστος, -η, -ον, most beautiful, finest, *sup. of* καλός (23)
καλλίων, κάλλιον, more beautiful, finer, *comp. of* καλός (23)
καλός, -ή, -όν, beautiful, fine (7)
καλύπτω, cover
κάμηλος, -ου, ὁ/ἡ, camel (11)
καρπός, -οῦ, ὁ, fruit (6)
Καρχηδόνιος, -ου, ὁ, a Carthaginian
κατά, by way of (+ *acc.*) (28); κατὰ γῆν, by land (28), κατὰ θάλατταν, by sea (28); under (+ *gen.*)
καταβαίνω, go down
καταδύω, sink
καταλαμβάνω, capture
καταλείπω, leave behind (14)
καταλύω, destroy (11)
καταμένω, stay behind
καταπίνω, swallow down
κατασκευάζω, build
καταστρέφω, subdue
κατάστρωμα, -ατος, τό, deck

καταφέρω, bring down, bring to land
κάτω, underneath (*adv.*)
κελεύω, order (6); κελεύω χαίρειν, bid farewell
κέρας, -ατος, τό, wing (*of army*)
κεφαλή, -ῆς, ἡ, head (17)
κῆρυξ, -υκος, ὁ, herald (8)
κιθάρα, -ας, ἡ, harp
κιθαρῳδός, -οῦ, ὁ, harpist
κινδυνεύω, run risks (5)
κίνδυνος, -ου, ὁ, danger (12)
κινέω, move
Κλεομένης, -ου, ὁ, Cleomenes
Κλέων, -ωνος, ὁ, Cleon
κλῖμαξ, -ακος, ἡ, ladder
κλίνη, -ης, ἡ, couch
κοινόν, -οῦ, τό, public treasury
κοίτη, -ης, ἡ, bed
κολάζω (*aor. pass.* ἐκολάσθην), punish
κολωνός, -οῦ, ὁ, cairn
κόπτω, cut, cut down (6)
Κορίνθιος, -ου, ὁ, a Corinthian
Κόρινθος, -ου, ἡ, Corinth
κόρυς, -υθος, ἡ, helmet (9)
κουφότερος, -α, -ον, lighter (in weight)
κρατέω, conquer, become master of (+ *gen.*)
κράτιστος, -η, -ον, best, *sup. of* ἀγαθός (23)
κραυγή, -ῆς, ἡ, shout
κρείττων, κρεῖττον, better, *comp. of* ἀγαθός (23)
κριτής, -οῦ, ὁ, judge (4)
Κροῖσος, -ου, ὁ, Croesus
κροκόδειλος, -ου, ὁ, crocodile
κρύπτω, hide (14)
κτάομαι, acquire (33)
κτῆμα, -ατος, τό, possession
κυβερνήτης, -ου, ὁ, helmsman
κυρβασία, -ας, ἡ, turban
κύριος, -α, -ον, appointed
Κῦρος, -ου, ὁ, Cyrus (11)
κωλύω, hinder, prevent (2); κωλύω ἀπό, keep (someone) from (+ *gen.*) (4)
κώμη, -ης, ἡ, village (3)
κώνωψ, -ωπος, ὁ, gnat

Λακεδαιμόνιος, -ου, ὁ, a Spartan (8)
λαμβάνω, take, capture, catch (8); arrest
λαμπάς, -άδος, ἡ, torch (9)
λανθάνω, (escape the notice of) (+ *part.*) (32)
λέγω, say, speak, tell (7)
λειμών, -ῶνος, ὁ, meadow (12)
λείπω, leave (14)
λέων, -οντος, ὁ, lion (10)
Λεωνίδας, -ου, ὁ, Leonidas (11)
λήψομαι, *fut. of* λαμβάνω (11)
λίθινος, -η, -ον, of stone
λίθος, -ου, ὁ, stone (14)
λιμήν, -ένος, ὁ, harbor (12)
λίμνη, -ης, ἡ, marsh, lake (24)
λόγος, -ου, ὁ, word (5)
λοιπός, -ή, -όν, rest, remaining
λοχαγός, -οῦ, ὁ, captain
Λυδός, -οῦ, ὁ, a Lydian
λύω, loose, set free (2); break (the law); **λύομαι**, ransom (17)

μᾱκρός, -ά, -όν, long (7)
μάλα, very, much (29)
μάλιστα, very much, most, especially, *sup. of* μάλα (29)
μᾶλλον, more, *comp. of* μάλα (29)
μανθάνω, learn (21)
μαντεῖον, -ου, τό, oracle
Μαραθών, -ῶνος, ὁ, Marathon
μάστιξ, -ιγος, ὁ, whip
μάτην, in vain
μάχη, -ης, ἡ, battle (3)
μάχομαι, fight (+ *dat.*) (17)
μέγας, μεγάλη, μέγα, big, great, large (16)
μέγεθος, -ους, τό, size
μέγιστος, -η, -ον, biggest, *sup. of* μέγας (23)
μείζων, μεῖζον, bigger, *comp. of* μέγας (23)
μείων, μεῖον, less, fewer, *comp. of* ὀλίγος (23)
μέλλω, be about to, intend (+ *fut. inf.*) (13)
μέμνημαι, *perf. mid. of* μιμνῄσκω (17)
μέν, *sets up contrast with* δέ (*postpos.*) (8)
μέντοι, however (*postpos.*)
μένω, stay, remain (5); await, wait for (13)
μεσογεία, -ας, ἡ, interior
μέσος, -η, -ον, middle
Μεσσήνιος, -ου, ὁ, a Messenian
μετά, after (+ *acc.*) (9); with (+ *gen.*) (18)
μεταπέμπομαι, send for
μέχρι, as long as, while, until (34)
μή, not (6)
μηδέ, and not
μηδείς, μηδεμία, μηδέν, no, not one (*adj.*) (33); no one, nothing (*pronoun*) (33)
Μῆδος, -ου, ὁ, a Mede
μήν, μηνός, ὁ, month (17)
μήτε...μήτε, neither...nor (8)
μήτηρ, μητρός, ἡ, mother (11)
μία, *fem. of* εἷς (33)
μῑκρός, -ά, -όν, small (8)
Μιλήσιος, -α, -ον, Milesian, of Miletus
Μίλητος, -ου, ἡ, Miletus
Μιλτιάδης, -ου, ὁ, Miltiades
μιμνήσκω / μιμνῄσκω, remind (17); **μιμνῄσκομαι**, remember (17)
μισθόομαι, hire
μνᾶ, μνᾶς, ἡ, mina (*coin worth 100 drachmas*)
μνημόσυνον, -ου, τό, memorial, reminder

μοῖρα, -ας, ἡ, part, share
μόνον, only (*adv.*)
μόνος, -η, -ον, alone, only (*adj.*)
Μοῦσα, -ης, ἡ, Muse (3)
μύζω, μύξω, suck
μῶρος, -α, -ον, foolish (11)

ναυμαχία, -ας, ἡ, sea battle (15)
ναῦς, νεώς, ἡ, ship (15)
ναύτης, -ου, ὁ, sailor (4)
ναυτικόν, -οῦ, τό, fleet, navy (14)
νεανίας, -ου, ὁ, young man (4)
νῆσος, -ου, ἡ, island (5)
νικάω, win; conquer, defeat (19)
νίκη, -ης, ἡ, victory (7)
Νικίας, -ου, ὁ, Nicias
νομίζω, think (14)
νόμος, -ου, ὁ, law (17)
νοῦς, νοῦ, ὁ, mind (19)
νόσος, -ου, ἡ, illness, plague (5)
νῦν, now (10)
νύξ, νυκτός, ἡ, night (10)
νῶτον, -ου, τό, back

ξενίζω, entertain
ξένος, -ου, ὁ, friend, stranger, guest
Ξενοφῶν, -ῶντος, ὁ, Xenophon (10)
Ξέρξης, -ου, ὁ, Xerxes (4)
ξίφος, -ους, τό, sword (23)
ξύλινος, -η, -ον, of wood, wooden
ξύλον, -ου, τό, wood, firewood

ὁ, ἡ, τό, the (4); **οἱ μέν...οἱ δέ**, some...others (8)
ὅδε, ἥδε, τόδε, this (24)
ὀδμή, -ῆς, ἡ, smell
ὁδός, -οῦ, ἡ, road, way, journey (5)
ὀδούς, ὀδόντος, ὁ, tooth
ὅθεν, from where, from which (place, person, cause) (28)
οἷ, to where (30)
οἶδα, know (27)
οἴκαδε, homeward (28)
οἰκεῖος, -α, -ον, related
οἰκέτης, -ου, ὁ, member of the household, slave
οἰκέω, live; inhabit
οἰκία, -ας, ἡ, house (3)
οἴκοθεν, from home (28)
οἶνος, -ου, ὁ, wine
οἷος, -α, -ον, the kind which, of such a kind (30); **οἷός τέ εἰμι**, be able, can (9)
οἴσω, *fut. of* φέρω (11)
ὀλίγιστος, -η, -ον, least, fewest, *sup. of* ὀλίγος (23)
ὀλίγος, -η, -ον, little, few (13)
ὅλος, -η, -ον, whole
ὁμαίμων, -ον, related by blood

ὄνομα, -ατος, τό, name (8)
ὀνομάζω, name, call (by name) (17)
ὄπισθε(ν), behind (+ *gen.*) (11)
ὅπλα, -ων, τά, arms, weapons (6)
ὁπλίζω, arm (8)
ὁπλίτης, -ου, ὁ, hoplite (*heavy-armed soldier*) (10)
ὁπόθεν, from wherever (30)
ὅποι, to where, to wherever (30)
ὁποῖος, -α, -ον, whatever kind (30)
ὁπόσος, -η, -ον, however much / many (30)
ὁπόταν, ὁπότε + *conditional particle* ἄν (30)
ὁπότε, when, whenever (30)
ὅπου, where, wherever (30)
ὅπως, in order (to, that), so that (27); how, however (30)
ὁράω, see (19)
ὀργή, -ῆς, ἡ, anger
ὀργίζομαι, grow angry
ὄρνις, -ιθος, ὁ/ἡ, bird (9)
ὄρος, -ους, τό, mountain (13)
ὀρυκτός, -ή, -όν, dug out
ὅς, ἥ, ὅ, who, which, that (10)
ὅσος, -η, -ον, as much / many as (30)
ὅστις, ἥτις, ὅ τι, anyone who, anything which / that, whoever, whatever (30)
ὅταν, ὅτε + *conditional particle* ἄν (30)
ὅτε, when (30)
ὅτι, because (10); that (*objective fact*) (27)
οὐ, οὐκ (*before smooth breathing*), οὐχ (*before rough breathing*), not (2)
οὗ, where (30)
οὐδέ, and not, nor
οὐδείς, οὐδεμία, οὐδέν, no, not one (*adj.*) (33); no one, nothing (*pronoun*) (33)
οὐκέτι, no longer (31)
οὖν, therefore (*postpos.*) (8)
οὔποτε, never (18)
οὔπω, not yet (31)
οὖς, ὠτός, τό, ear
οὔτε...οὔτε, neither...nor (8)
οὗτος, αὕτη, τοῦτο, this (24)
οὕτω(ς), thus, in this way, *adv. of* οὗτος (30); so (31)
ὀφθαλμός, -οῦ, ὁ, eye
ὄχλος, -ου, ὁ, mob, crowd
ὄψομαι, *aor. of* ὁράω (19)

παιδεύω, educate, teach, train (4)
παίζω, play
παῖς, παιδός, ὁ/ἡ, child, boy, girl (9)
πάλαι, of old, long ago (12)
πάλιν, back
πανσέληνος, -ου, ἡ, full moon
πανταχοῦ, everywhere
παρά, from (+ *gen.*); beside (+ *dat.*) (17); to, to the presence of (+ *acc.*)

παραδίδωμι, give over, hand over
παρακαλέω, summon
παραλαμβάνω, invite
παρασκευάζω, prepare (13)
πάρειμι (εἰμί, 'be'), be present, be here, be there (18)
παρέχω, provide, cause, produce (6)
πᾶς, πᾶσα, πᾶν, all, every, whole (20)
πάσχω, suffer (29)
πατήρ, πατρός, ὁ, father (11)
πατρίς, -ίδος, ἡ, fatherland, own country (9)
παύω, stop (3); **παύομαι**, cease from (+ *gen.*) (17)
πέδη, -ης, ἡ, fetter
πεζός, -οῦ, ὁ, footsoldier; *sing. and plur.*, infantry
πείθω, persuade (*with perf.* πέπεικα) (3); trust (*with perf.* πέποιθα) (32); **πείθομαι**, obey (+ *dat.*) (17)
Πεισίστρατος, -ου, ὁ, Pisistratus
πέλαγος, -ους, τό, sea
Πελοποννήσιος, -ου, ὁ, a Peloponnesian
πελταστής, -οῦ, ὁ, targeteer (*soldier with light shield*)
πέμπτος, -η, -ον, fifth (17)
πέμπω, send (2)
πέντε, five (17)
πεντήκοντα, fifty (33)
περί, about, concerning (+ *gen.*) (14); around (+ *acc.*)
Περίανδρος, -ου, ὁ, Periander
περιβάλλω, embrace
περιέρχομαι, *with inf.* περιιέναι (εἶμι, 'go'), go around
περίοδος, -ου, ἡ, map
περιπλέω, sail around
Πέρσης, -ου, ὁ, a Persian (4)
Περσικός, -ή, -όν, Persian
πεσοῦμαι, *fut. of* πίπτω (20)
πηλός, -οῦ, ὁ, mud, clay
πῆχυς, -εως, ὁ, cubit (*about* 18 *inches*)
πιέζω, weigh down
πιθέσθαι, *aor. inf. of* πείθομαι (17)
πίναξ, -ακος, ὁ, tablet
πίπτω, fall (12)
πιστεύω, trust, believe (+ *dat.*) (4)
πλεῖστος, -η, -ον, very much / many, most, *sup. of* πολύς (23)
πλείων, πλεῖον, more, *comp. of* πολύς (23)
πλέω, sail (24)
πλέων, πλέον, more, *comp. of* πολύς (23)
πληγή, -ῆς, ἡ, blow
πλήν, except (+ *gen.*)
πληρόω, fill, man
πλοῖον, -ου, τό, boat
πλοῦτος, -ου, ὁ, wealth
πόθεν (*interrogative*), from where? (29)
ποθέν, from somewhere (*encl.*) (29)
ποῖ (*interrogative*), to where? (29)
ποι, to somewhere (*encl.*) (29)
ποιέω, make, do; treat (19); **εὖ ποιέω**, treat well (19); **κακῶς ποιέω**, treat badly (129)
ποιητής, -οῦ, ὁ, poet (4)
ποιμήν, -ένος, ὁ, shepherd (12)
ποῖος, -α, -ον (*interrogative*), what kind? (30)
ποιός, -ά, -όν, some kind (*encl.*) (30)
πολέμαρχος, -ου, ὁ, commander-in-chief
πολέμιοι, -ων, οἱ, enemy (*group*) (6)
πόλεμος, -ου, ὁ, war (5)
πολιορκέω, besiege
πόλις, -εως, ἡ, city (14)
πολίτης, -ου, ὁ, citizen (4)
πολλάκις, often
πολλῷ, by much, far (16)
Πολυκράτης, -ους, ὁ, Polycrates (21)
πολύς, πολλή, πολύ, much, many (16)
πονέω, toil
πορεύω, carry, convey (17); **πορεύομαι**, march, journey (17)
πόσος, -η, -ον (*interrogative*), how much / many? (30)
ποσός, -ή, -όν, some amount (*encl.*) (30)
ποταμός, -οῦ, ὁ, river (5)
πότε (*interrogative*), when? (30)
ποτέ, once, sometime, ever (*encl.*) (30)
πότερον, whether (33)
πότερος, -α, -ον (*interrogative*), which of two (33)
ποῦ (*interrogative*), where? (29)
που, somewhere (*encl.*) (29)
πούς, ποδός, ὁ, foot
πρᾶγμα, -ατος, τό, matter, affair
πράττω, do, manage; fare (*with perf. act.* πέπραγα) (11); **εὖ πράττω**, fare well (12); **κακῶς πράττω**, fare badly (12)
πρέσβυς, -εως, ὁ, elder; *plur.*, ambassadors (14)
πρίν, before (*adv.*); before, until (34)
πρό, before, in front of (+ *gen.*) (17)
προκαλέομαι, invite
προπέμπω, send forth (11)
πρός, to, toward, (+ *acc.*) (4); against; near, in the presence of (+ *dat.*); in addition to (+ *dat.*); πρὸς βίαν, by force
προσάγω, move (something) toward
προσβάλλω, attack (+ *dat.*) (25)
προσέρχομαι, approach
πρόσθεν, before, sooner (34)
προστάττω, order, assign
πρόσωπον, -ου, τό, face
πρότερον, before, formerly (34)
προχωρέω, advance (22)
πρύμνα, -ης, ἡ, stern
πρῶτον, first, at first
πρῶτος, -η, -ον, first (33)

Πυθία, -ας, ἡ, Pythia, priestess of Apollo
πύλη, -ης, ἡ, gate (3)
Πύλος, -ου, ἡ, Pylos
πυνθάνομαι, learn (27)
πῦρ, πυρός, τό, fire
πύργος, -ου, ὁ, tower
πῶς (*interrogative*), how? (29)
πως, somehow (*encl.*) (29)

ῥᾴδιος, -α, -ον, easy (8)
ῥᾷστος, -η, -ον, easiest, *sup. of* ῥᾴδιος (23)
ῥᾴων, ῥᾷον, easier, *comp. of* ῥᾴδιος (23)
ῥεῖθρον, -ου, τό, river, river bed
ῥήτωρ, -ορος, ὁ, orator (11)

Σαλαμίς, -ῖνος, ἡ, Salamis
Σάμος, -ου, ἡ, Samos
σαφής, -ές, clear (20)
σεαυτοῦ, -ῆς, -οῦ (*oblique cases*), yourself; *possessive gen.* your own (24)
σημαίνω, signify, mean, signal
σιγάω, keep silent
Σικελία, -ας, ἡ, Sicily
Σίκιννος, -ου, ὁ, Sicinnus
σῖτος, -ου, ὁ, food (6)
σκευή, -ῆς, ἡ, dress, attire
σκηνή, -ῆς, ἡ, tent
σκιά, -ᾶς, ἡ, shade
σμάραγδος, -ου, ὁ, smaragdus, a precious stone of green color
σός, σή, σόν, your (*sing.*) (18)
Σοῦσα, -ων, τά, Susa
σοφία, -ας, ἡ, wisdom (3)
σοφός, -ή, -όν, wise (7)
Σπάρτη, -ης, ἡ, Sparta (4)
σπεύδω, hasten, hurry (16)
σπονδαί, -ῶν αἱ, truce
στέφανος, -ου, ὁ, crown
στόμα, -ατος, τό, mouth, entrance
στρατεύω, march (3)
στρατηγός, -οῦ, ὁ, general (5)
στρατιά, -ᾶς, ἡ, army (3)
στρατιώτης, -ου, ὁ, soldier (4)
στρατόπεδον, -ου, τό, (army) camp (6)
στρατός, -οῦ, ὁ, army (22)
Στρυμών, -όνος, ὁ, Strymon
σύ, σοῦ / σου, you (*sing.*) (18)
συγγιγνώσκω, pardon (+ *dat.*)
συλλαμβάνω, arrest
συμβουλεύω, advise (+ *dat.*) (11)
συμμαχία, -ας, ἡ, alliance
σύμμαχος, -ου, ὁ, ally (8)
συμφορά, -ᾶς, ἡ, misfortune, disaster
σύν, with (+ *dat.*) (11)
συνάγω, lead together, assemble
Συρακόσιος, -ου, ὁ, a Syracusan
Συράκουσαι, -ῶν, αἱ, Syracuse
Σφακτηρία, -ας, ἡ, Sphacteria
σφραγίς, -ῖδος, ἡ, ring (21)
σχήσω, *fut. of* ἔχω (11)
σῴζω, save, protect (10)
Σωκράτης, -ους, ὁ, Socrates (13)
σῶμα, -ατος, τό, body (8)
σωτηρία, -ας, ἡ, safety
σώφρων, -ον, prudent (20)

τάλας, τάλαινα, τάλαν, wretched (16)
ταμίας, -ου, ὁ, steward (4)
Τάρας, -αντος, ὁ, Tarentum
ταράττω, throw into confusion (11)
τάττω, draw up (11)
τάφος, -ου, ὁ, tomb
ταχέως, quickly (29)
ταχθείς, -εῖσα, -έν, *aor. part. of* τάττω (22)
τάχιστος, -η, -ον, fastest, swiftest, quickest, *sup. of* ταχύς (23)
ταχύς, -εῖα, -ύ, fast, swift, quick (20)
τε, and (*encl.*); **τε...καί, τε... τε**, both...and (8)
τειχίζω, fortify
τείχισμα, -ατος, τό, fortification
τεῖχος, -ους, τό, wall (13)
τέκνον, -ου, τό, child (6)
τέλος, at last (32)
τέμνω, cut, cut up
τέτταρες, -α, four (33)
τέταρτος, -η, -ον, fourth (33)
τέχνη, -ης, ἡ, skill, art
τί (*interrogative*), why? (29)
τίθημι, put, place (23)
τίκτω, breed, lay (eggs), give birth
τιμάω, honor (19)
τιμή, -ῆς, ἡ, honor (3)
τίς, τί (*interrogative*), who, what? (29)
τις, τι, someone, something, anyone, anything (*encl.*) (29)
τοίνυν, therefore, moreover (*postpos.*)
τοιοῦτος, τοιαύτη, τοιοῦτο, this kind, such (24)
τολμάω, dare
τόξευμα, -ατος, τό, arrow
τόξα, -ων, τά, bow
τοξότης, -ου, ὁ, archer
τόσος, -η, -ον, this much, so much
τοσοῦτος, τοσαύτη, τοσοῦτο, this much / great / many; so much / great / many (24)
τότε, then (16)
τρεῖς, τρία, three (33)
τρέπω, turn, rout
τρέχω, run (20)
τριακόσιοι, -αι, -α, three hundred
τριήραρχος, -ου, ὁ, captain of a trireme

τριήρης, -ους, ἡ, trireme (13)
Τροιζήν, -ῆνος, ἡ, Troezen
τρόπος, -ου, ὁ, way
τυγχάνω, happen to (+ *part.*), happen upon (32)
τύπτω, strike, hit (14)
τύραννος, -ου, ὁ, tyrant (19)
τυφλός, -ή, -όν, blind
τύχῃ, by chance

ὑβρίζω, insult
ὕδωρ, ὕδατος, τό, water (15)
ὕλη, -ης, ἡ, wood, forest (10)
ὑμεῖς, ὑμῶν, you (*plur.*) (18)
ὑμέτερος, -α, -ον, your (*plur.*) (18)
ὑμῶν αὐτῶν (*oblique cases*), yourselves; *possessive gen.* your own (24)
ὑπείκω, yield, give in
ὑπέρ, on behalf of, for (+ *gen.*) (10)
ὑπερβάλλω, cross
ὑπό, by (+ *gen.* of personal agent) (15); *of cause*, from, by reason of (+ *gen.*); under (+ *dat.*)
ὑποζύγιον, -ου, τό, beast of burden
ὑπολαμβάνω, take on one's back
ὑπομένω, stand firm
ὗς, ὑός, ὁ/ἡ, pig
ὕστερον, later
ὑφίσταμαι (*aor.* ὑπέστην), engage or promise (to do)
ὑψηλός, -ή, -όν, high (13)

φαίνομαι, seem, appear (20)
φανερός, -ά, -όν, visible
Φεραί, -ῶν, αἱ, Pherae
φέρω, carry, bear (2)
φεύγω, flee (2)
φημί, say (*present indic. encl. except 2 sing.*) (14)
φθάνω, (be / do before, anticipate) (+ *part.*) (32)
φθείρω, lay waste
φθονέω, be jealous
φιάλη, -ης, ἡ, drinking bowl
φιλέω, love (19)
φιλία, -ας, ἡ, friendship (6)
φίλῐος, -α, -ον, friendly (7)
Φιλιππίδης, -ου, ὁ, Philippides
φίλος, -ου, ὁ, friend (21)
φοβέω, frighten, terrify (33); **φοβέομαι**, fear, be afraid (33)

φόβος, -ου, ὁ, fear (16)
Φοῖνιξ, -ικος, ὁ, a Phoenician
Φοίνισσα (*fem. adj.*), Phoenician
φορέω, wear
φυγάς, -άδος, ὁ/ἡ, exile (*a person*) (9)
φυλακτήριον, -ου, τό, fort, guardpost
φύλαξ, -ακος, ὁ, guard (8)
φυλάττω, guard (2)
φωνή, -ῆς, ἡ, voice (11)

χαλεπαίνω, grow annoyed
χαλεπός, -ή, -όν, difficult, dangerous, harsh (7)
χαλκοῦς, -ῆ, -οῦν, of bronze
χάρις, -ιτος, ἡ, grace, thanks (9); χάριν ἔχω, be grateful (9)
χειμών, -ῶνος, ὁ, storm, winter (12)
χείριστος, -η, -ον, worst, *sup. of* κακός (23)
χείρων, χεῖρον, worse, *comp. of* κακός (23)
χήν, χηνός, ἡ, goose
χιών, -όνος, ἡ, snow
χορεύω, dance
χρῆμα, -ατος, τό, thing; *plur.*, money (8)
χρήσῐμος, -η, -ον, useful (22)
χρόνος, -ου, ὁ, time (17)
χρυσόδετος, -ον, bound with gold, set in gold
χρυσός, -οῦ, ὁ, gold
χρυσοῦς, -ῆ, -οῦν, of gold (19)
χώρα, -ας, ἡ, country (3)
χωρέω, advance, withdraw

ψευδής, -ές, false (20)
ψηφίζομαι, vote (for)
ψιλοί, -ῶν, οἱ, light-armed troops
ψυχή, -ῆς, ἡ, soul, life

ὦ, (*used with voc.*) (3)
ὧδε, thus, in this way, as follows
ὦμος, -ου, ὁ, shoulder
ᾠόν, -οῦ, τό, egg
ὥρα, -ας, ἡ, right time, season, hour
ὡς, since, because (19); as (19); to (a person) (+ *acc.*) (24); in order (to, that), so that (27); that (*personal opinion*) (27); how (30); when
ὡς + *sup.*, as...as possible (29)
ὥσπερ, just as
ὥστε, (so) that, (so) as to (31)
ὦτα, *acc. of* οὖς

ENGLISH-GREEK GLOSSARY

able, be, οἷός τέ εἰμι (9)
about to, be, μέλλω (+ *fut. inf.*) (13)
about (concerning), περί (+ *gen.*) (14)
absent, be, ἄπειμι (εἰμί, 'be') (12)
account of, on, διά (+ *acc.*) (10)
acquire, κτάομαι (33)
Admetus, Ἄδμητος, -ου, ὁ (13)
admire, θαυμάζω (9)
advance, προχωρέω (22)
advise, συμβουλεύω (+ *dat.*) (11)
affairs of, the τά (+ *gen.*) (12)
afraid, be, φοβέομαι (33)
after, μετά (+ *acc.*) (9); ἐπειδή (30)
against, ἐπί (+ *acc.*) (8)
ago, long, πάλαι (12)
Alcestis, Ἄλκηστις, -ιδος, ἡ (16)
all, πᾶς, πᾶσα, πᾶν (20)
ally, σύμμαχος, -ου, ὁ (8)
already, ἤδη (7)
also, καί (2)
although, καίπερ (21)
always, ἀεί (4)
Amasis, Ἄμασις, -ιος, ὁ (21)
ambassadors, *plur. of* πρέσβυς, -εως, ὁ (14)
among, ἐν (+ *dat. pl.*) (6)
amount, some, ποσός, -ή, -όν (30)
ancient, ἀρχαῖος, -α, -ον (16)
and, καί (2); δέ (8); τε (8)
animal, ζῷον, -ου, τό (6)
announce, ἀγγέλλω (7)
another, ἄλλος, -η, -ο (16)
answer, ἀποκρίνομαι (27)
(anticipate), φθάνω (+ *part.*) (32)
anyone, anything, τις, τι (*encl.*) (29)
anyone who, anything which / that, ὅστις, ὅ τι (30)
appear, φαίνομαι (20)
Aristagoras, Ἀρισταγόρας, -ου, ὁ (27)
arm, ὁπλίζω (8)
arms, ὅπλα, -ων, τά (6)
army, στρατιά, -ᾶς, ἡ (3); στρατός, -οῦ, ὁ (22)
(army) camp, στρατόπεδον, -ου, τό (6)
arrive, ἀφικνέομαι (+ εἰς) (26)
Artemisia, Ἀρτεμισία, -ας, ἡ (18)
as (since), ὡς (19)
as...as possible, ὡς + *sup.* (29)
as to, so, ὥστε (31)
ask, ἐρωτάω (33)
at (*within, time expressions*), *gen. without preposition* (17)
at (*a point, time expressions*), *dat. without preposition* (17)
Athena, Ἀθήνη, -ης, ἡ (4)
Athenian, an, Ἀθηναῖος, -ου, ὁ (5)
Athens, Ἀθῆναι, -ῶν, αἱ (4)
Athens, to, Ἀθήναζε (28)
Athens, from, Ἀθήνηθεν (28)
attack, προσβάλλω (+ *dat.*) (25)
await, μένω (13)
away from, ἀπό (+ *gen.*) (4)

Babylon, Βαβυλών, -ῶνος, ἡ (23)
bad, κακός, -ή, -όν (7)
badly, κακῶς (12)
battle, μάχη, -ης, ἡ (3)
be, εἰμί (7)
be grateful, χάριν ἔχω (9)
bear, φέρω (2)
beast, θήρ, θηρός (11)
beautiful, καλός, -ή, -όν (7)
beautiful, more, καλλίων, κάλλιον (23)
beautiful, most, κάλλιστος, -η, -ον (23)
because, γάρ (*postpos.*) (8); ὅτι (10); ὡς (19)
become, γίγνομαι (25)
before, πρό (+ *gen.*) (17)
before (*adv.*) πρότερον (34); πρόσθεν (34); (*conj.*) πρίν (34)
before, be, φθάνω (32)
before, do, φθάνω (32)
begin, ἄρχω (32)
behalf of, on, ὑπέρ (+ *gen.*) (10)
behind, ὄπισθε(ν) (+ *gen.*) (11)
behind, leave, καταλείπω (14)
believe, πιστεύω (+ *dat.*) (4)
beside, παρά (+ *dat.*) (17)
best, ἄριστος, -η, -ον (23); βέλτιστος, -η, -ον (23); κράτιστος, -η, -ον (23)
better, ἀμείνων, ἄμεινον (23); βελτίων, βέλτιον (23); κρείττων, κρεῖττον (23)
big, μέγας, μεγάλη, μέγα (16)
bigger, μείζων, μεῖζον (23)
biggest, μέγιστος, -η, -ον (23)
bird, ὄρνις, -ιθος, ὁ/ἡ (9)
body, σῶμα, -ατος, τό (8)

both...and, τε...καί (8); τε... τε (*encl.*) (8); καί...καί (8)
boy, παῖς, παιδός, ὁ (9)
brave, ἀνδρεῖος, -α, -ον (7)
bravery, ἀνδρεία, -ας, ἡ (14)
breastplate, θώραξ, -ακος, ὁ (8)
bridge, γέφυρα, -ας, ἡ (3)
bring (*of living creatures*), ἄγω (2)
bring back, ἀπάγω (13)
but, ἀλλά (2); δέ (*postpos.*) (8)
by (*agent*), ὑπό (+ *gen.*) (15); (*with perfect / pluperfect*), dat. *without preposition* (31)
by (means of), *dat. without preposition* (6)
by way of, κατά (+ *acc.*) (28)

call by name, ὀνομάζω (17)
camel, κάμηλος, -ου, ὁ/ἡ (11)
camp (army), στρατόπεδον, -ου, τό (6)
can (be able), οἷός τέ εἰμι (9)
capture, λαμβάνω (8); αἱρέω (22)
carry, φέρω (2); πορεύω (17)
catch, λαμβάνω (8)
cause, παρέχω (6)
cavalry, *plur. of* ἱππεύς, -έως, ὁ (15)
cavalryman, ἱππεύς, -έως, ὁ (15)
cease from, παύομαι (+ *gen.*) (17)
child, τέκνον, -ου, τό (6); παῖς, παιδός, ὁ/ἡ (9)
citizen, πολίτης, -ου, ὁ (4)
city, πόλις, -εως, ἡ (14)
clear, σαφής, -ές (20)
clever, δεινός, -ή, -όν (7)
come, ἔρχομαι (26)
come, have, ἥκω (11)
come in, εἰσέρχομαι (34)
come out, ἐκβαίνω (32)
command, ἄρχω (+ *gen.*) (11)
compel, ἀναγκάζω (11)
concerning, περί (+ *gen.*) (14)
confusion, throw into, ταράττω (11)
conquer, νικάω (19)
contest, ἀγών, -ῶνος, ὁ (12)
convey, πορεύω (17)
country, χώρα, -ας, ἡ (3)
country, own, πατρίς, -ίδος, ἡ (9)
courage, ἀνδρεία, -ας, ἡ (14)
cowardly, δειλός, -ή, -όν (18)
cross, διαβαίνω (21)
cure, θεραπεύω (5)
cut, cut down, κόπτω (6)
Cyrus, Κῦρος, -ου, ὁ (11)

damage, βλάπτω (6)
danger, κίνδυνος, -ου, ὁ (12)
dangerous, χαλεπός, -ή, -όν (7)
Darius, Δαρεῖος, -ου, ὁ (11)
day, ἡμέρα, -ας, ἡ (3)
death, θάνατος, -ου, ὁ (15)
deed, ἔργον, -ου, τό (6)
defeat, νικάω (19)
deliberate, βουλεύομαι (18)
Demosthenes, Δημοσθένης, -ους, ὁ (13)
depart, ἀπέρχομαι (26)
desire, ἔρως, -τος, ὁ (16)
destroy, καταλύω (11)
die, ἀποθνήσκω (10), θνήσκω (32)
difficult, χαλεπός, -ή, -όν (7)
discover, εὑρίσκω (8), μανθάνω (21)
do, πράττω (10); ποιέω (18)
do wrong, ἀδικέω (28)
doctor, ἰατρός, -οῦ, ὁ (5)
draw up, τάττω (11)
drive, ἐλαύνω (15)
drive away, ἀπελαύνω (15)
during (*time expressions*), *gen. without preposition* (17)

each (of 3 or more), ἕκαστος, -η, -ον (16)
each other, ἀλλήλων, -ων, -ων (24)
earth, γῆ, γῆς, ἡ (19)
easier, ῥᾴων, ῥᾷον (23)
easiest, ῥᾷστος, -η, -ον (23)
easy, ῥᾴδιος, -α, -ον (8)
educate, παιδεύω (4)
either...or, ἤ...ἤ (8)
elder, πρέσβυς, -εως, ὁ (14)
enemy (*group*), πολέμιοι, -ων, οἱ (6)
enjoy, ἥδομαι (32)
enslave, δουλόω (19)
enter, εἰσέρχομαι (34)
escape, ἀποφεύγω (11)
(escape the notice of), λανθάνω (+ *part.*) (32)
especially, μάλιστα (29)
even, καί (2)
ever, ποτέ (*encl.*) (30)
every, ἕκαστος, -η, -ον (16); πᾶς, πᾶσα, πᾶν (20)
excellence, ἀρετή, -ῆς, ἡ (28)
exile (*a person*), φυγάς, -άδος, ὁ/ἡ (9)
expect, ἐλπίζω (+ *fut. inf.*) (13)
expectation, ἐλπίς, -ίδος, ἡ (9)

fall, πίπτω (12)
false, ψευδής, -ές (20)
fare, πράττω (*with perf. act.* πέπραγα) (11)
fare badly, κακῶς πράττω (12)
fare well, εὖ πράττω (12)
fast, ταχύς, -εῖα, -ύ (20)
faster, θάττων, θᾶττον (23)
fastest, τάχιστος, -η, -ον (23)
father, πατήρ, πατρός, ὁ (11)
fatherland, πατρίς, -ίδος, ἡ (9)

fear, φόβος, -ου, ὁ (16)
fear, φοβέομαι (33)
few, *plur. of* ὀλίγος, -η, -ον (13)
fewer, *plur. of* ἐλάττων, ἔλαττον (23); *plur. of* μείων, μεῖον (23)
fewest, *plur. of* ἐλάχιστος, -η, -ον (23); *plur. of* ὀλίγιστος, -η, -ον (23)
fifth, πέμπτος, -η, -ον (17)
fight, μάχομαι (+ *dat.*) (17)
find, find out, εὑρίσκω (8)
fine, καλός, -ή, -όν (7)
finer, καλλίων, κάλλιον (23)
finest, κάλλιστος, -η, -ον (23)
fish, ἰχθύς, -ύος, ὁ (14)
five, πέντε (17)
flee, φεύγω (2)
flee away, ἀποφεύγω (11)
fleet, ναυτικόν, -οῦ, τό (14)
follow, ἕπομαι (+ *dat.*) (30)
food, σῖτος, -ου, ὁ (6)
foolish, μῶρος, -α, -ον (11)
for (*because*), γάρ (8)
for (*indirect obj., etc.*), *dat. without preposition* (3)
for (*time expressions*), *acc. without preposition* (17)
for (*on behalf of*), ὑπέρ (+ *gen.*) (10)
for (a purpose), εἰς (+ *acc.*) (11)
force, ἀναγκάζω (11)
foreigner (*non-Greek*), βάρβαρος, -ου, ὁ (7)
forest, ὕλη, -ης, ἡ (10)
formerly, πρότερον (34)
fortunate, εὐτυχής, -ές (20)
four, τέτταρες, -ων (33)
fourth, τέταρτος, -η, -ον (33)
free, ἐλευθερόω (19)
free, ἐλεύθερος, -α, -ον (10)
friend, φίλος, -ου, ὁ (21)
friendly, φίλιος, -α, -ον (7)
friendship, φιλία, -ας, ἡ (6)
frighten, φοβέω (33)
from, ἀπό (+ *gen.*) (4); ἐκ, ἐξ (+ *gen.*) (3)
front of, in, πρό (+ *gen.*) (17)
fruit, καρπός, -οῦ, ὁ (6)

game, ἀγών, -ῶνος, ὁ (12)
gate, πύλη, -ης, ἡ (3)
general, στρατηγός, -οῦ, ὁ (5)
giant, γίγας, -αντος, ὁ (10)
gift, δῶρον, -ου, τό (6)
girl, παῖς, παιδός, ἡ (9)
give, δίδωμι (23)
give back, ἀποδίδωμι (28)
gladly, ἡδέως (29)
glory, δόξα, -ης, ἡ (3)
go, βαίνω (21), ἔρχομαι (26), εἶμι (*fut. sense*) (34)
go away, ἀποχωρέω (22); ἀπέρχομαι (26)
go out, ἐκβαίνω (32)
god, θεός, -οῦ, ὁ (10)
goddess, θεά, -ᾶς, ἡ (3)
gold, of, χρυσοῦς, -ῆ, -οῦν (19)
good, ἀγαθός, -ή, -όν (7)
grace, χάρις, -ιτος, ἡ (9)
grateful, be, χάριν ἔχω (9)
great, μέγας, μεγάλη, μέγα (16)
great, so, τοσοῦτος, τοσαύτη, τοσοῦτο (24)
greater, μείζων, μεῖζον (23)
greater number / part, οἱ πλεῖονες (23)
greatest, μέγιστος, -η, -ον (23)
greatest number / part, οἱ πλεῖστοι (23)
Greece, Ἑλλάς, -άδος, ἡ (9)
Greek, a, Ἕλλην, -ηνος, ὁ (12)
guard, φυλάττω (2)
guard, φύλαξ, -ακος, ὁ (8)
guide, ἡγεμών, -όνος, ὁ (12)

happen, γίγνομαι (25)
happen to, τυγχάνω (+ *part.*) (32)
happen upon, τυγχάνω (32)
happy, εὐδαίμων, εὔδαιμον (20)
harbor, λιμήν, -ένος, ὁ (12)
harm, βλάπτω (6)
harsh, χαλεπός, -ή, -όν (7)
hasten, σπεύδω (16)
have, ἔχω (2)
have come, ἥκω (11)
head, κεφαλή, -ῆς, ἡ (17)
heal, θεραπεύω (5)
hear, ἀκούω (+ *acc.* thing, + *gen.* person) (11)
heavy, βαρύς, -εῖα, -ύ (20)
helmet, κόρυς, -υθος, ἡ (9)
help, βοηθέω (+ *dat.*) (19)
her, *oblique cases of* αὐτή (9)
her (*possessive*), αὐτῆς (9)
her own, ἑαυτῆς (24)
Heracles, Ἡρακλῆς, -έους, ὁ (16)
herald, κῆρυξ, -υκος, ὁ (8)
here, ἐνταῦθα (30)
here, be, πάρειμι (18)
here, from, ἐντεῦθεν (30)
here, to, ἐνταῦθα (30)
herself (*intensive*), αὐτή (9)
herself (*reflexive*), *oblique cases of* ἑαυτῆς (24)
hide, κρύπτω (14)
high, ὑψηλός, -ή, -όν (13)
him, *oblique cases of* αὐτός (9)
himself, herself, itself, themselves (*intensive*), αὐτός, -ή, -ό (9)
himself, herself, itself, themselves (*reflexive*), *oblique cases of* ἑαυτοῦ, -ῆς, -οῦ (24)
hinder, κωλύω (2)
his, αὐτοῦ (9)

his own, ἑαυτοῦ (24)
hit, τύπτω (14)
home, from, οἴκοθεν (28)
homeward, οἴκαδε (28)
honor, θεραπεύω (3); τιμάω (19)
honor, τιμή, -ῆς, ἡ (3)
hope, ἐλπίζω (+ *fut. inf.*) (13)
hope, ἐλπίς, -ίδος, ἡ (9)
hoplite, ὁπλίτης, -ου, ὁ (10)
horse, ἵππος, -ου, ὁ (5)
hostile, ἐχθρός, -ά, -όν (7)
hostile, more, ἐχθίων, ἔχθιον (23)
hostile, most, ἔχθιστος, -η, -ον (23)
house, οἰκία, -ας, ἡ (3)
how (*interrogative*), πῶς (29)
how, ὅπως (30); ὡς (30)
how much / many (*interrogative*), πόσος, -η, -ον (30)
however (*relative*), ὅπως (30)
however much / many, ὁπόσος, -η, -ον (30)
human, ἄνθρωπος, -ου, ὁ (7)
hurry, σπεύδω (16)
husband, ἀνήρ, ἀνδρός, ὁ (11)

I, ἐγώ, ἐμοῦ / μου (18)
if, εἰ (12)
if only, εἴθε, εἰ γάρ (26)
illness, νόσος, -ου, ἡ (5)
immediately, εὐθύς⊠ (13)
in, ἐν (3)
in (*within, time expressions*), *gen. without preposition* (17)
in (*a point of time, time expressions*), *dat. without preposition* (17)
in order (to, that), ἵνα, ὡς, ὅπως (27)
injure, βλάπτω (6)
intend, μέλλω (+ *fut. inf.*) (13)
into, εἰς (+ *acc.*) (3)
invade, εἰσβάλλω (+ εἰς) (11)
island, νῆσος, -ου, ἡ (5)
it, *oblique cases of* αὐτό (9)
its, αὐτοῦ (9)
itself (*intensive*), αὐτό (9)
itself (*reflexive*), *oblique cases of* ἑαυτοῦ (24)

journey, πορεύομαι (17)
journey, ὁδός, -οῦ, ἡ (5)
judge, κριτής, -οῦ, ὁ (4)
justice, δικαιοσύνη, -ης, ἡ (4)

keep (someone) from, κωλύω ἀπό (+ *gen.*) (4)
kill, ἀποκτείνω (10)
killed, be, ἀποθνῄσκω (10)
kind, some, ποιός, -ά, -όν (*encl.*) (30)
kind, this, τοιοῦτος, τοιαύτη, τοιοῦτο (24)
kind, what (*interrogative*), ποῖος, -α, -ον (30)
kind, whatever, ὁποῖος, -α, -ον (30)
kind which, οἷος, -α, -ον (30)
king, be, βασιλεύω (+ *gen.*) (4)
king, βασιλεύς, -έως, ὁ (15)
king of Persia, βασιλεύς, -έως *without article* (15)
know, γιγνώσκω (27); οἶδα (27)

lake, λίμνη, -ης, ἡ (24)
land, γῆ, γῆς, ἡ (19)
land, by, κατὰ γῆν (28)
large, μέγας, μεγάλη, μέγα (16)
larger, μείζων, μεῖζον (23)
largest, μέγιστος, -η, -ον (23)
last, at, τέλος (32)
law, νόμος, -ου, ὁ (17)
lead, ἄγω (2)
lead away, ἀπάγω (13)
leader, ἡγεμών, -όνος (12)
learn, μανθάνω (21); πυνθάνομαι (27)
least, ἐλάχιστος, -η, -ον (23); ὀλίγιστος, -η, -ον (23)
leave, λείπω (14)
leave behind, καταλείπω (14)
Leonidas, Λεωνίδας, -ου, ὁ (11)
less, ἐλάττων, ἔλαττον (23); μείων, μεῖον (23)
letter, ἐπιστολή, -ῆς, ἡ (3)
life, βίος, -ου, ὁ (19)
lion, λέων, -οντος, ὁ (10)
listen to, ἀκούω (+ *acc.* thing, + *gen.* person) (11)
little, ὀλίγος, -η, -ον (13)
long, μακρός, -ά, -όν (7)
long ago, πάλαι (12)
long as, as, ἕως, μέχρι, ἔστε (34)
longer, no, οὐκέτι (31)
loose, λύω (2)
love, φιλέω (19)
love, ἔρως, -τος, ὁ (16)

majority, the, οἱ πλείονες (23); οἱ πλεῖστοι (23)
make, ποιέω (19)
make stand, ἵστημι (23)
man (*male*), ἀνήρ, ἀνδρός, ὁ (11); ὁ + *adj., etc.* (12)
man (*human*), ἄνθρωπος, -ου, ὁ (7); ὁ + *adj., etc.* (12)
man, old, γέρων, -οντος, ὁ (10)
man, young, νεανίας, -ου, ὁ (4)
manage, πράττω (11)
many, *plur. of* πολύς, πολλή, πολύ (16)
many as, as, *plur. of* ὅσος, -η, -ον (30); *plur. of* ὁπόσος, -η, -ον (30)
many, how (*interrogative*), *plur. of* πόσος, -η, -ον (30)
many, this, τοσοῦτος, τοσαύτη, τοσοῦτο (24)
many, very, πλεῖστος, -η, -ον (23)

march, στρατεύω (3); ἐλαύνω (15); πορεύομαι (17)
march away, ἀπελαύνω (15)
market-place, ἀγορά, -ᾶς, ἡ (3)
marsh, λίμνη, -ης, ἡ (24)
master (of a household), δεσπότης, -ου, ὁ (7)
may (*wishes*), εἰ γάρ, εἴθε (26)
meadow, λειμών, -ῶνος, ὁ (12)
messenger, ἄγγελος, -ου, ὁ (25)
mind, νοῦς, νοῦ, ὁ (19)
money, *plur. of* χρῆμα, -ατος, τό (8)
month, μήν, μηνός, ὁ (17)
more (*adj.*), πλείων, πλεῖον (23); πλέων, πλέον (23); *comparative adj.*
more (*adv.*), μᾶλλον (29); *comparative adv.* (29)
most (*adj.*), πλεῖστος, -η, -ον (23); *superlative adj.* (16)
most (*adv.*), μάλιστα (29); *superlative adv.* (29)
mother, μήτηρ, μητρός, ἡ (11)
mountain, ὄρος, -ους, τό, (13)
much (*adj.*), πολύς, πολλή, πολύ (16)
much (*adv.*), μάλα (29)
much as, as, ὅσος, -η, -ον (30)
much, how (*interrogative*), πόσος, -η, -ον (30)
much, however, ὁπόσος, -η, -ον (30)
much, so, τοσοῦτος, τοσαύτη, τοσοῦτο (24)
much, this, τοσοῦτος, τοσαύτη, τοσοῦτο (24)
much, very (*adj.*), πλεῖστος, -η, -ον (23); *superlative adj.* (16)
much, very (*adv.*), μάλιστα (29); *superlative adv.* (29)
Muse, Μοῦσα, -ης, ἡ (3)
my, ἐμός, -ή, -όν (18)
my own, ἐμαυτοῦ, -ῆς (24)
myself, *oblique cases of* ἐμαυτοῦ, -ῆς (24)

name, ὀνομάζω (17)
name, ὄνομα, -ατος, τό (8)
navy, ναυτικόν, -οῦ, τό (14)
near (*adv.*), ἐγγύς (17)
near, ἐγγύς (+ *gen.*) (17)
necessary, it is, δεῖ (13)
neither...nor, οὔτε...οὔτε (8); μήτε...μήτε (8)
never, οὔποτε (18)
night, νύξ, νυκτός, ἡ (10)
no (*adj.*), οὐδείς, οὐδεμία, οὐδέν (33); μηδείς, μηδεμία, μηδέν (33)
no longer, οὐκέτι (31)
no one, nothing, οὐδείς, οὐδεμία, οὐδέν (33); μηδείς, μηδεμία, μηδέν (33)
nor, οὔτε (8); μήτε (8)
not, οὐ, οὐκ (*before smooth breathing*), οὐχ (*before rough breathing*) (2); μή (6)
not one (*adj.*), οὐδείς, οὐδεμία, οὐδέν (33); μηδείς, μηδεμία, μηδέν (33)
not yet, οὔπω (31)
nothing, οὐδέν (33); μηδέν (33)
notice, escape (someone's), λανθάνω (32)
now, νῦν (10)

obey, πείθομαι (+ *dat.*) (17)
of (*possessive*), *gen. without preposition* (3)
of old, πάλαι (12)
old man, γέρων, -οντος, ὁ (10)
old woman, γραῦς, γραός, ἡ (15)
on, ἐν (+ *dat.*) (3); ἐπί (+ *gen.*) (26)
on (*time expressions*), *dat. without preposition* (17)
once, ποτέ (*encl.*) (30)
once, at, εὐθύς (13)
one, εἷς, μία, ἕν (33)
onto, εἰς (+ *acc.*) (3); ἐπί (+ *acc.*) (8)
or, ἤ (8)
orator, ῥήτωρ, -ορος, ὁ (11)
order, κελεύω (6)
order (to, that), in, ἵνα, ὡς, ὅπως (27)
other, ἄλλος, -η, -ο (16)
other, each, ἀλλήλων (24)
others, οἱ δέ (*with* οἱ μέν, 'some') (8)
our, ἡμέτερος, -α, -ον (18)
ourselves, *oblique cases of* ἡμῶν αὐτῶν (24)
out of, ἐκ, ἐξ (+ *gen.*) (3)
outside, ἔξω (+ *gen.*) (17)
own (*adj.*), ἑαυτοῦ, -ῆς, -οῦ (24)
ox, βοῦς, βοός, ὁ/ἡ (15)

peace, εἰρήνη, -ης, ἡ (4)
pelt, βάλλω (20)
people, ἄνθρωποι, -ων, οἱ (7); δῆμος, -ου, ὁ (19); οἱ + *adj., etc.* (12)
perceive, αἰσθάνομαι (27); γιγνώσκω (27)
Persian, a, Πέρσης, -ου, ὁ (4)
person, ὁ, ἡ + *adj., etc.* (12)
persuade, πείθω (3)
place, τίθημι (23)
plague, νόσος, -ου, ἡ (5)
plan, βουλεύω (18)
pleasant, ἡδύς, -εῖα, -ύ (20)
pleased with, be, ἥδομαι (32)
poet, ποιητής, -οῦ, ὁ (4)
Polycrates, Πολυκράτης, -ους, ὁ (21)
prepare, παρασκευάζω (13)
present, be, πάρειμι (εἰμί, 'be') (18)
prevent, κωλύω (2)
priest, ἱερεύς, -έως, ὁ (15)
prisoner (of war), αἰχμάλωτος, -ου, ὁ (17)
produce, παρέχω (6)
protect, σῴζω (10)
provide, παρέχω (6)
prudent, σώφρων, -ον (20)

pursue, διώκω (2)
put, τίθημι (23)

quick, ταχύς, -εῖα, -ύ (20)
quicker, θάττων, -ον (23)
quickest, τάχιστος, -η, -ον (23)
ransom, λύομαι (17)
reach, ἀφικνέομαι (+ εἰς) (26)
ready, ἑτοῖμος, -η, -ον (13)
receive, δέχομαι, (17)
reign, βασιλεύω (+ *gen.*) (4)
remain, μένω (5)
remember, μιμνήσκομαι / μιμνῄσκομαι (17)
remind, μιμνήσκω / μιμνῄσκω (17)
reply, ἀποκρίνομαι (27)
retreat, ἀποχωρέω (22)
ring, σφραγίς, -ῖδος, ἡ (21)
risks, run, κινδυνεύω (5)
river, ποταμός, -οῦ, ὁ (5)
road, ὁδός, -οῦ, ἡ (5)
rule, ἄρχω (+ *gen.*) (11)
run, τρέχω (20)
run risks, κινδυνεύω (5)

sacrifice, θύω (2)
safe, ἀσφαλής, -ές (20)
sail, πλέω (24)
sail away, ἀποπλέω (24)
sailor, ναύτης, -ου, ὁ (4)
same, the, αὐτός (*attributive*) (9)
save, σῴζω (10)
say, λέγω (7); φημί (14); *aor.* εἶπον (27)
sea, θάλαττα, -ης, ἡ (3)
sea, by, κατὰ θάλατταν (28)
sea battle, ναυμαχία, -ας, ἡ (15)
second, δεύτερος, -α, -ον (33)
see, ὁράω (19)
seek, ζητέω (19)
seem, φαίνομαι (17)
self, αὐτός, -ή, -ό (9)
send, πέμπω (2)
send away, ἀποπέμπω (25)
send forth, προπέμπω (11)
set, ἵστημι (23)
set free, λύω (2)
shepherd, ποιμήν, -ένος, ὁ (12)
shield, ἀσπίς, -ίδος, ἡ (9)
ship, ναῦς, νεώς, ἡ (15)
short, βραχύς, -εῖα, -ύ (20)
shorter, βραχίων, βράχιον (23); βραχύτερος, -α, -ον (22)
shortest, βράχιστος, -η, -ον (23); βραχύτατος (22)
shout, βοάω (19)
show, δηλόω (19); δείκνυμι (23)
silver, of, ἀργυροῦς, -ᾶ, -οῦν (19)
since, ὡς (19); ἐπειδή (30)
slave, δοῦλος, -ου, ὁ (5)
slow, βραδύς, -εῖα, -ύ (20)
small, μικρός, -ά, -όν (8)
smaller, ἐλάττων, ἔλαττον (23); μικρότερος, -α, -ον (16)
smallest, ἐλάχιστος, -η, -ον (23); μικρότατος, -η, -ον (16)
so, οὕτω(ς) (31)
so as to (*result*), ὥστε (31)
so great, τοσοῦτος, τοσαύτη, τοσοῦτο (24)
so many, *plur. of* τοσοῦτος, τοσαύτη, τοσοῦτο (24)
so much, τοσοῦτος, τοσαύτη, τοσοῦτο (24)
so that (*purpose*), ἵνα, ὡς, ὅπως (27)
so that (*result*), ὥστε (31)
Socrates, Σωκράτης, -ους, ὁ (13)
soldier, στρατιώτης, -ου, ὁ (4)
some amount, ποσός, -ή, -όν (30)
some...others, οἱ μὲν...οἱ δέ (8)
somehow, πως (*encl.*) (29)
someone, something, τις, τι (*encl.*) (29)
sometime, ποτέ (*encl.*) (30)
somewhere, που (*encl.*) (29)
somewhere, from, ποθέν (*encl.*) (29)
somewhere, to, ποι (*encl.*) (29)
sooner, πρόσθεν (34)
Sparta, Σπάρτη, -ης, ἡ (4)
Spartan, a, Λακεδαιμόνιος, -ου, ὁ (8)
speak, λέγω (7)
stand, ἵσταμαι, *with aor.* ἔστην (23)
stay, μένω (5)
steward, ταμίας, -ου, ὁ (4)
still, ἔτι (12)
stone, λίθος, -ου, ὁ (14)
stop, παύω (3)
storm, χειμών, -ῶνος, ὁ (12)
strange, δεινός, -ή, -όν (7)
strike, τύπτω (14)
strong, ἰσχυρός, -ά, -όν (7)
such, τοιοῦτος, τοιαύτη, τοιοῦτο (24)
such a kind, of, οἷος, -α, -ον (30)
suffer, πάσχω (29)
surely (*introducing questions*), ἆρα οὐ (24)
surely...not (*introducing questions*), ἆρα μή (24)
sweet, ἡδύς, -εῖα, -ύ (20)
sweeter, ἡδίων, ἥδιον (23)
sweetest, ἥδιστος, -η, ον (23)
swift, ταχύς, -εῖα, -ύ (20)
swifter, θάττων, θᾶττον (23)
swiftest, τάχιστος, -η, -ον (23)
sword, ξίφος, -ους, τό (23)

take, λαμβάνω (8); αἱρέω (22)
teach, παιδεύω (4)
tell, λέγω (7)

ten, δέκα, (17)
tend, θεραπεύω (5)
tenth, δέκατος, -η, -ον (17)
terrible, δεινός, -ή, -όν (7)
terrify, φοβέω (33)
than, ἤ (16)
thanks, χάρις, -ιτος, ἡ (9)
that (*relative*), ὅς, ἥ, ὅ (10)
that (*demonstrative*), ἐκεῖνος, -η, -ο (24)
that (*after verbs of saying*), ὅτι (*objective fact*); ὡς (*personal opinion*) (27)
that, so (*result*), ὥστε (31)
the, ὁ, ἡ, τό (4)
their, αὐτῶν (9)
their own, ἑαυτῶν (24)
them, *plur. oblique cases of* αὐτός (9)
Themistocles, Θεμιστοκλῆς, -έους, ὁ (14)
themselves (*intensive*), *plur. of* αὐτός (9)
themselves (*reflexive*), *plur. of* ἑαυτοῦ, -ῆς, -οῦ (24)
then, τότε (16)
there, ἐκεῖ (12); ἐνταῦθα (30)
there, be, πάρειμι (18)
there, from, ἐντεῦθεν (30)
there, to, ἐνταῦθα (30)
therefore, οὖν (*postpos.*) (8)
thing, χρῆμα, -ατος, τό (8); τό + *adj., etc.* (12)
think, νομίζω (14)
third, τρίτος, -η, -ον (33)
this, ὅδε, ἥδε, τόδε (24); οὗτος, αὕτη, τοῦτο (24)
this great, τοσοῦτος, τοσαύτη, τοσοῦτο (24)
this kind, τοιοῦτος, τοιαύτη, τοιοῦτο (24)
this many, *plur. of* τοσοῦτος, τοσαύτη, τοσοῦτο (24)
this much, τοσοῦτος, τοσαύτη, τοσοῦτο (24)
three, τρεῖς, τρία (33)
through, διά (+ *gen.*) (20)
throw, βάλλω (20); ἵημι (34)
throw away, ἀποβάλλω (24), ἀφίημι (34)
throw into, εἰσβάλλω (+ εἰς) (11)
throw into confusion, ταράττω (11)
thus, οὕτω(ς) (30)
time, χρόνος, -ου, ὁ (17)
to (*indirect obj., etc.*), *dative case* (3)\
to (*prep.*), εἰς (+ *acc.*) (3); πρός (+ *acc.*) (4); *with persons*, ὡς (+ *acc.*) (24)
torch, λαμπάς, -άδος, ἡ (9)
toward, πρός (+ *acc.*) (4)
town, ἄστυ, -εως, τό (14)
train, παιδεύω (4)
treat, ποιέω (19)
treat badly, κακῶς ποιέω (19)
treat well, εὖ ποιέω (19)
tree, δένδρον, -ου, τό (6)
trireme, τριήρης, -ους, ἡ (13)
true, ἀληθής, -ές (20)
trust, πιστεύω (+ *dat.*) (4); *perf.* πέποιθα *from* πείθω (32)
truth, the, τὰ ἀληθῆ (20)
tyrant, τύραννος, -ου, ὁ (19)

unjust, be, ἀδικέω (28)
until, ἕως, μέχρι, ἔστε, πρίν (34)
upon, ἐπί (+ *gen.*) (15)
useful, χρήσιμος, -η, -ον (22)

very (*adj.*), *superlative adj.* (16)
very (*adv.*), μάλα (29); *superlative adv.* (29)
very much / many (*adj.*), πλεῖστος, -η, -ον (23)
very much (*adv.*), μάλιστα (29); *superlative adv.* (29)
victory, νίκη, -ης, ἡ (7)
village, κώμη, -ης, ἡ (3)
voice, φωνή, -ῆς, ἡ (11)

wait for, μένω (13)
walk, βαίνω (21)
wall, τεῖχος, -ους, τό (13)
want, βούλομαι (20)
war, πόλεμος, -ου, ὁ (5)
water, ὕδωρ, ὕδατος, τό (15)
way (*road, journey*), ὁδός, -οῦ, ἡ (5)
we, ἡμεῖς, ἡμῶν (18)
weapons, ὅπλα, -ων, τά (6)
well, εὖ (12)
well-born, εὐγενής, -ές (20)
what (*interrogative*), τί (29)
whatever, ὅ τι (30)
whatever kind, ὁποῖος, -α, -ον (30)
when (*interrogative*), πότε (30)
when, ὅτε (30); ὁπότε (30)
whenever, ὁπότε (30)
where (*interrogative*), ποῦ (29)
where, οὗ (30); ὅπου (30)
where (*interrogative*), from, πόθεν (29)
where, from, ὅθεν (30); ὁπόθεν (30)
where, to (*interrogative*), ποῖ (29)
where, to, οἷ (30); ὅποι (30)
wherever, ὅπου (30)
wherever, from, ὁπόθεν (30)
wherever, to, ὅποι (30)
whether, εἰ (33); πότερον (33)
which, ὅς, ἥ, ὅ (10)
which (of two) (*interrogative*), πότερος, -α, -ον (33)
which, from, ὅθεν (28)
while, ἕως, μέχρι, ἔστε (34)
who, what (*interrogative*), τίς, τί (29)
who (*relative*), ὅς, ἥ, ὅ (10)
whoever, whatever, ὅστις, ἥτις, ὅ τι (30)
whole, πᾶς, πᾶσα, πᾶν (20)
why (*interrogative*), τί (29)

wide, εὐρύς, -εῖα, -ύ (20)
wife, γυνή, γυναικός, ἡ (15)
wild beast, θήρ, θηρός, ὁ (11)
willing, be, ἐθέλω (6); βούλομαι (20)
win, νικάω (19)
winter, χειμών, -ῶνος, ὁ (12)
wisdom, σοφία, -ας, ἡ (3)
wise, σοφός, -ή, -όν (7)
wish, ἐθέλω (6); βούλομαι (20)
with (*accompaniment*), μετά (+ *gen.*) (18); σύν (+ *dat.*) (11)
with (*means, instrument*), *dat. without preposition* (6)
within, *gen. without preposition* (12)
woman, γυνή, γυναικός, ἡ (15); ἡ + *adj., etc.* (12)
woman, old, γραῦς, γραός, ἡ (15)
wonder at, θαυμάζω (9)
wood (*forest*), ὕλη, -ης, ἡ (10)
word, λόγος, -ου, ὁ (5)
work, ἔργον, -ου, τό (6)
worse, κακίων, κάκιον (23); χείρων, χεῖρον (23)
worship, θεραπεύω (3)
worst, κάκιστος, -η, -ον (23); χείριστος, -η, -ον (23)
worthy, ἄξιος, -α, -ον (9)
would that, εἴθε, εἰ γάρ (26)
wretched, τάλας, τάλαινα, τάλαν (16)
write, γράφω (2)
wrong, ἀδικέω (28)
wrong, do, ἀδικέω (28)

Xenophon, Ξενοφῶν, -ῶντος, ὁ (10)
Xerxes, Ξέρξης, -ου, ὁ (4)

year, ἔτος, -ους, τό (16)
yet, ἔτι (12)
yoke, ζυγόν, -οῦ, τό (6)
you (*sing.*), σύ, σοῦ / σου (18)
you (*plur.*), ὑμεῖς, ὑμῶν (18)
young man, νεανίας, -ου, ὁ (4)
your (*sing.*), σός, σή, σόν (18)
your (*plur.*), ὑμέτερος, -α, -ον (18)
yourself (*reflexive*), *oblique cases of* σεαυτοῦ, -ῆς, -οῦ (24)
yourselves (*reflexive*), *oblique cases of* ὑμῶν αὐτῶν (24)

Zeus, Ζεύς, Διός, ὁ (15)

APPENDIX 1: PRINCIPAL PARTS

The following verbs appear in this book (excluding the readings). Principal parts are given for simple verbs, and for compounds when the uncompounded version is not in the chapter vocabularies. A dash preceding a form indicates that it only exists in compounds. A long dash indicates that no principal part is attested.

	1 PRESENT A/M	2 FUTURE A/M	3 AORIST	4 PERFECT A	5 PERFECT M/P	6 AORIST P
announce	ἀγγέλλω	ἀγγελῶ	ἤγγειλα	ἤγγελκα	ἤγγελμαι	ἠγγέλθην
lead	ἄγω	ἄξω	ἤγαγον	ἦχα	ἦγμαι	ἤχθην
be unjust	ἀδικέω	ἀδικήσω	ἠδίκησα	ἠδίκηκα	ἠδίκημαι	ἠδικήθην
take	αἱρέω	αἱρήσω	εἷλον, *stem* ἑλ-	ᾕρηκα	ᾕρημαι	ᾑρέθην
perceive	αἰσθάνομαι	αἰσθήσομαι	ᾐσθόμην	—	ᾔσθημαι	—
hear	ἀκούω	ἀκούσομαι	ἤκουσα	ἀκήκοα	—	ἠκούσθην
force	ἀναγκάζω	ἀναγκάσω	ἠνάγκασα	ἠνάγκακα	ἠνάγκασμαι	ἠναγκάσθην
die	(ἀπο)θνῄσκω	ἀποθανοῦμαι	ἀπέθανον	τέθνηκα	—	—
answer	(ἀπο)κρίνομαι	ἀποκρινοῦμαι	ἀπεκρινάμην	—	ἀποκέκριμαι	ἀπεκρίθην
kill	(ἀπο)κτείνω	ἀποκτενῶ	ἀπέκτεινα	ἀπέκτονα	—	—
go away	(ἀπο)χωρέω	ἀποχωρήσω	ἀπεχώρησα	ἀποκεχώρηκα	ἀποκεχώρημαι	ἀπεχωρήθην
rule	ἄρχω	ἄρξω	ἦρξα	ἦρχα	ἦργμαι	ἤρχθην
arrive	ἀφικνέομαι	ἀφίξομαι	ἀφικόμην	—	ἀφῖγμαι	—
go	βαίνω	-βήσομαι	-ἔβην	βέβηκα	—	—
throw	βάλλω	βαλῶ	ἔβαλον	βέβληκα	βέβλημαι	ἐβλήθην
be king	βασιλεύω	βασιλεύσω	ἐβασίλευσα	—	—	—
harm	βλάπτω	βλάψω	ἔβλαψα	βέβλαφα	βέβλαμμαι	ἐβλάβην / ἐβλάφθην
shout	βοάω	βοήσομαι	ἐβόησα	—	—	—
help	βοηθέω	βοηθήσω	ἐβοήθησα	βεβοήθηκα	βεβοήθημαι	—
plan	βουλεύω	βουλεύσω	ἐβούλευσα	βεβούλευκα	βεβούλευμαι	ἐβουλεύθην
want	βούλομαι	βουλήσομαι	—	—	βεβούλημαι	ἐβουλήθην
become	γίγνομαι	γενήσομαι	ἐγενόμην	γέγονα	γεγένημαι	—
know	γιγνώσκω	γνώσομαι	ἔγνων	ἔγνωκα	ἔγνωσμαι	ἐγνώσθην
write	γράφω	γράψω	ἔγραψα	γέγραφα	γέγραμμαι	ἐγράφην
show	δείκνυμι	δείξω	ἔδειξα	δέδειχα	δέδειγμαι	ἐδείχθην
receive	δέχομαι	δέξομαι	ἐδεξάμην	—	δέδεγμαι	—
show	δηλόω	δηλώσω	ἐδήλωσα	δεδήλωκα	δεδήλωμαι	ἐδηλώθην
give	δίδωμι	δώσω	ἔδωκα	δέδωκα	δέδομαι	ἐδόθην

	1 Present A/M	2 Future A/M	3 Aorist	4 Perfect A	5 Perfect M/P	6 Aorist P
pursue	διώκω	διώξω / διώξομαι	ἐδίωξα	δεδίωχα	—	ἐδιώχθην
enslave	δουλόω	δουλώσω	ἐδούλωσα	δεδούλωκα	δεδούλωμαι	ἐδουλώθην
wish	ἐθέλω	ἐθελήσω	ἠθέλησα	ἠθέληκα	—	—
be	εἰμί, *imperf.* ἦν	ἔσομαι	—	—	—	—
go (*fut.*)	εἶμι	—	—	—	—	—
drive	ἐλαυνω	ἐλῶ	ἤλασα	-ελήλακα	ἐλήλαμαι	ἠλάθην
free	ἐλευθερόω	ἐλευθερώσω	ἠλευθέρωσα	ἠλευθέρωκα	ἠλευθέρωμαι	ἠλευθερώθην
hope	ἐλπίζω	—	ἤλπισα	—	—	ἠλπίσθην
follow	ἕπομαι, *imperf.* εἱπόμην	ἕψομαι	ἑσπόμην	—	—	—
come	ἔρχομαι	ἐλεύσομαι	ἦλθον, *stem* ἐλθ-	ἐλήλυθα	—	—
ask	ἐρωτάω	ἐρωτήσω	ἠρώτησα / ἠρόμην	ἠρώτηκα	ἠρώτημαι	ἠρωτήθην
find	εὑρίσκω	εὑρήσω	ηὗρον / εὗρον	ηὕρηκα / εὕρηκα	ηὕρημαι / εὕρημαι	ηὑρέθην / εὑρέθην
have	ἔχω, *imperf.* εἶχον	ἕξω / σχήσω	ἔσχον	ἔσχηκα	—	—
seek	ζητέω	ζητήσω	ἐζήτησα	ἐζήτηκα	—	ἐζητήθην
enjoy	ἥδομαι	ἡσθήσομαι	—	—	—	ἥσθην
have come	ἥκω	ἥξω	—	—	—	—
wonder	θαυμάζω	θαυμάσομαι	ἐθαύμασα	τεθαύμακα	τεθαύμασμαι	ἐθαυμάσθην
honor	θεραπεύω	θεραπεύσω	ἐθεράπευσα	τεθεράπευκα	τεθεράπευμαι	ἐθεραπεύθην
sacrifice	θύω	θύσω	ἔθυσα	τέθυκα	τέθυμαι	ἐτύθην
throw	ἵημι	ἥσω	-ἧκα	-εἷκα	-εἷμαι	-εἵθην
stand	ἵστημι	στήσω	ἔστησα / ἔστην	ἕστηκα	ἕσταμαι	ἐστάθην
order	κελεύω	κελεύσω	ἐκέλευσα	κεκέλευκα	κεκέλευμαι	ἐκελεύθην
run risks	κινδυνεύω	κινδυνεύσω	ἐκινδύνευσα	κεκινδύνευκα	κεκινδύνευμαι	ἐκινδυνεύθην
cut	κόπτω	κόψω	ἔκοψα	-κέκοφα	κέκομμαι	-εκόπην
hide	κρύπτω	κρύψω	ἔκρυψα	—	κέκρυμμαι	ἐκρύφθην
acquire	κτάομαι	κτήσομαι	ἐκτησάμην	—	κέκτημαι	ἐκτήθην
hinder	κωλύω	κωλύσω	ἐκώλυσα	κεκώλυκα	κεκώλυμαι	ἐκωλύθην
take	λαμβάνω	λήψομαι	ἔλαβον	εἴληφα	εἴλημμαι	ἐλήφθην
(escape notice)	λανθάνω	λήσω	ἔλαθον	λέληθα	-λέλησμαι	—
say	λέγω	λέξω	ἔλεξα / εἶπον	εἴρηκα	λέλεγμαι	ἐλέχθην
leave	λείπω	λείψω	ἔλιπον	λέλοιπα	λέλειμμαι	ἐλείφθην
loose	λύω	λύσω	ἔλυσα	λέλυκα	λέλυμαι	ἐλύθην

	1 Present A/M	2 Future A/M	3 Aorist	4 Perfect A	5 Perfect M/P	6 Aorist P
learn	μανθάνω	μαθήσομαι	ἔμαθον	μεμάθηκα	—	—
fight	μάχομαι	μαχοῦμαι	ἐμαχεσάμην	—	μεμάχημαι	—
intend	μέλλω	μελλήσω	ἐμέλλησα	—	—	—
stay	μένω	μενῶ	ἔμεινα	μεμένηκα	—	—
remind	μιμνῄσκω / μιμνήσκω	μνήσω	ἔμνησα	—	μέμνημαι	ἐμνήσθην
conquer	νικάω	νικήσω	ἐνίκησα	νενίκηκα	νενίκημαι	ἐνικήθην
think	νομίζω	νομιῶ	ἐνόμισα	νενόμικα	νενόμισμαι	ἐνομίσθην
know	—	εἴσομαι	—	οἶδα	—	—
name	ὀνομάζω	ὀνομάσω	ὠνόμασα	ὠνόμακα	ὠνόμασμαι	ὠνομάσθην
arm	ὁπλίζω	—	ὥπλισα	—	ὥπλισμαι	ὡπλίσθην
see	ὁράω, *imperf.* ἑώρων	ὄψομαι	εἶδον, *stem* ἰδ-	ἑώρακα	ἑώραμαι	ὤφθην
teach	παιδεύω	παιδεύσω	ἐπαίδευσα	πεπαίδευκα	πεπαίδευμαι	ἐπαιδεύθην
prepare	(παρα)σκευάζω	παρασκευάσω	παρεσκεύασα	—	παρεσκεύασμαι	παρεσκευάσθην
suffer	πάσχω	πείσομαι	ἔπαθον	πέπονθα	—	—
stop	παύω	παύσω	ἔπαυσα	πέπαυκα	πέπαυμαι	ἐπαύθην
persuade	πείθω	πείσω	ἔπεισα	πέπεικα / πέποιθα	πέπεισμαι	ἐπείσθην
send	πέμπω	πέμψω	ἔπεμψα	πέπομφα	πέπεμμαι	ἐπέμφθην
fall	πίπτω	πεσοῦμαι	ἔπεσον	πέπτωκα	—	—
trust	πιστεύω	πιστεύσω	ἐπίστευσα	πεπίστευκα	πεπίστευμαι	ἐπιστεύθην
sail	πλέω	πλεύσομαι	ἔπλευσα	πέπλευκα	πέπλευσμαι	—
do	ποιέω	ποιήσω	ἐποίησα	πεποίηκα	πεποίημαι	ἐποιήθην
convey	πορεύω	πορεύσω	ἐπόρευσα	—	πεπόρευμαι	ἐπορεύθην
do	πράττω	πράξω	ἔπραξα	πέπραχα / πέπραγα	πέπραγμαι	ἐπράχθην
learn	πυνθάνομαι	πεύσομαι	ἐπυθόμην	—	πέπυσμαι	—
hasten	σπεύδω	σπεύσω	ἔσπευσα	—	—	—
march	στρατεύω	στρατεύσω	ἐστράτευσα	ἐστράτευκα	ἐστράτευμαι	—
save	σῴζω	σώσω	ἔσωσα	σέσωκα	σέσω(σ)μαι	ἐσώθην
throw into	ταράττω	ταράξω	ἐτάραξα	—	τετάραγμαι	ἐταράχθην
draw up	τάττω	τάξω	ἔταξα	τέταχα	τέταγμαι	ἐτάχθην
put	τίθημι	θήσω	ἔθηκα	τέθηκα	τέθειμαι	ἐτέθην
honor	τιμάω	τιμήσω	ἐτίμησα	τετίμηκα	τετίμημαι	ἐτιμήθην
run	τρέχω	δραμοῦμαι	ἔδραμον	-δεδράμηκα	-δεδράμημαι	—
happen	τυγχάνω	τεύξομαι	ἔτυχον	τετύχηκα	—	—
hit	τύπτω	τυπτήσω	—	—	—	—
appear	φαίνομαι	φανοῦμαι	—	—	πέφασμαι	ἐφάνην / ἐφάνθην

	1 PRESENT A/M	2 FUTURE A/M	3 AORIST	4 PERFECT A	5 PERFECT M/P	6 AORIST P
carry	φέρω	οἴσω	ἤνεγκον *stem* ἐνεγκ-	ἐνήνοχα	ἐνήνεγμαι	ἠνέχθην
flee	φεύγω	φεύξομαι	ἔφυγον	πέφευγα	—	—
say	φημί *imperf.* ἔφην	φήσω	ἔφησα	—	—	—
(do first)	φθάνω	φθήσομαι	ἔφθασα / ἔφθην	—	—	—
love	φιλέω	φιλήσω	ἐφίλησα	πεφίληκα	πεφίλημαι	ἐφιλήθην
frighten	φοβέω	φοβήσω	ἐφόβησα	—	πεφόβημαι	ἐφοβήθην
guard	φυλάττω	φυλάξω	ἐφύλαξα	πεφύλαχα	πεφύλαγμαι	ἐφυλάχθην

APPENDIX 2: USES OF CASES

The following uses of cases are covered in this book (excluding the readings). Chapter numbers are included in parentheses.

Nominative
- predicate (3)
- subject (3)

Genitive
- absolute (22)
- comparison (16)
- motion out of, away from (3)
- objective (16)
- partitive (16)
- personal agent (with ὑπό) (15)
- possession (3, 5)
- subjective (16)
- time within which (17)
- with prepositions: see Appendix 3
- with verbs: of ruling (ἄρχω, βασιλεύω), ἀκούω (person), παύομαι

Dative
- advantage and disadvantage (16)
- degree of difference (16)
- indirect object (to or for) (3, 5)
- manner (16)
- means and instrument (5)
- personal agent (31)
- place where (3)
- possession (7)
- time when (17)
- with prepositions: see Appendix 3
- with verbs: βοηθέω, ἕπομαι, ἥδομαι, μάχομαι, πείθομαι, πιστεύω, προσβάλλω, συμβουλεύω

Accusative
- direct object (3)
- duration of time (17)
- extent of space (17)
- motion toward, into (3)
- respect (17)
- subject of infinitive (6)
- two accusatives with one verb (17)
    - double object
    - internal and external
    - object and predicate
- with prepositions: see Appendix 3

Vocative
- direct address (3)

APPENDIX 3: PREPOSITIONS

The following prepositions appear in this book (including the readings). Those in chapter vocabularies have the chapter designation. The prepositions that appear only in the readings are also included. For prepositions that appear in this book *in composition* (as prefixes to compound verbs), the basic senses of the prefix are listed.

ἄνευ (+ *gen.*)	without
ἀντί (+ *gen.*)	instead of
ἄνω (+ *gen.*)	above
ἀπό (+ *gen.*)	from, away from (4)
in comp.	from, away, in return
διά (+ *gen.*)	through (20)
διά (+ *acc.*)	on account of (10)
in comp.	through, across, apart
ἐγγύς (+ *gen.*)	near (17)
εἰς (+ *acc.*)	into, onto, to (3); for (a purpose) (11)
in comp.	into, in, to
ἐκ, ἐξ (+ *gen.*)	out of, from (3)
in comp.	out, from, away
ἔμπροσθε(ν) (+ *gen.*)	in front of
ἐν (+ *dat.*)	in, on (3); *with pl.*, among (6)
in comp.	in, on, at, among
ἕνεκα (+ *gen*; *postpos.*)	for the sake of
ἔξω (+ *gen.*)	outside (17)
ἐπί (+ *gen.*)	on, upon (15)
ἐπί (+ *dat.*)	on
ἐπί (+ *acc.*)	against, onto (8)
in comp.	upon, over, to
κατά (+ *gen.*)	under
κατά (+ *acc.*)	by way of (28)
in comp.	down from, back, thoroughly
μετά (+ *gen.*)	with (18)
μετά (+ *acc.*)	after (11)
in comp.	among, after (time or purpose)
ὄπισθεν (+ *gen.*)	behind (11)
παρά (+ *gen.*)	from
παρά (+ *dat.*)	beside (17)
παρά (+ *acc.*)	to, to (the presence of)
in comp.	beside, beyond, aside
περί (+ *gen.*)	about, concerning (14)
περί (+ *acc.*)	around
in comp.	around, beyond, very much
πλήν (+ *gen.*)	except
πρό (+ *gen.*)	before, in front of (17)
in comp.	before, forward, on behalf of
πρός (+ *dat.*)	against; near, in the presence of; in addition to
πρός (+ *acc.*)	to, toward (4)
in comp.	to, toward, in addition, against
σύν (+ *dat.*)	with (11)
in comp.	together with, completely
ὑπέρ (+ *gen.*)	on behalf of, for (10)
in comp.	over, above, on behalf of, exceedingly
ὑπό (+ *gen.*)	by (*personal agent*) (15); by reason of, from (cause)
ὑπό (+ *dat.*)	under
in comp.	under, behind, secretly
ὡς (+ *acc.*)	to (a person) (24)

APPENDIX 4: SUMMARY OF FORMS

NOUNS

FIRST DECLENSION FEMININE

		honor	country	sea	bridge	Endings			
		a	b	c	d	a	b	c	d
Sing.	Nom.	τιμή	χώρα	θάλαττα	γέφυρα	-η	-ᾱ	-ᾰ	-ᾰ
	Gen.	τιμῆς	χώρας	θαλάττης	γεφύρας	-ης	-ᾱς	-ης	-ᾱς
	Dat.	τιμῇ	χώρᾳ	θαλάττῃ	γεφύρᾳ	-ῃ	-ᾱͅ	-ῃ	-ᾱͅ
	Acc.	τιμήν	χώραν	θάλατταν	γέφυραν	-ην	-ᾱν	-ᾰν	-ᾰν
	Voc.	τιμή	χώρα	θάλαττα	γέφυρα	-η	-ᾱ	-ᾰ	-ᾰ
Dual	N.A.V.	τιμά	χώρα	θαλάττα	γεφύρα	-ᾱ	-ᾱ	-ᾱ	-ᾱ
	G.D.	τιμαῖν	χώραιν	θαλάτταιν	γεφύραιν	-αιν	-αιν	-αιν	-αιν
Plur.	Nom.	τιμαί	χῶραι	θάλατται	γέφυραι	-αι	-αι	-αι	-αι
	Gen.	τιμῶν	χωρῶν	θαλαττῶν	γεφυρῶν	-ων	-ων	-ων	-ων
	Dat.	τιμαῖς	χώραις	θαλάτταις	γεφύραις	-αις	-αις	-αις	-αις
	Acc.	τιμάς	χώρας	θαλάττας	γεφύρας	-ᾱς	-ᾱς	-ᾱς	-ᾱς
	Voc.	τιμαί	χῶραι	θάλατται	γέφυραι	-αι	-αι	-αι	-αι

FIRST DECLENSION MASCULINE

		judge	young man	Endings	
		a	b	a	b
Sing.	Nom.	κριτής	νεανίας	-ης	-ᾱς
	Gen.	κριτοῦ	νεανίου	-ου	-ου
	Dat.	κριτῇ	νεανίᾳ	-ῃ	-ᾱͅ
	Acc.	κριτήν	νεανίαν	-ην	-ᾱν
	Voc.	κριτά	νεανία	-ᾰ	-ᾱ
Dual	N.A.V.	κριτά	νεανία	-ᾱ	-ᾱ
	G.D.	κριταῖν	νεανίαιν	-αιν	-αιν
Plur.	Nom.	κριταί	νεανίαι	-αι	-αι
	Gen.	κριτῶν	νεανιῶν	-ων	-ων
	Dat.	κριταῖς	νεανίαις	-αις	-αις
	Acc.	κριτάς	νεανίας	-ᾱς	-ᾱς
	Voc.	κριταί	νεανίαι	-αι	-αι

SECOND DECLENSION

		word (M)	island (F)	gift (N)	Endings M/F	Endings N
Sing.	Nom.	λόγος	νῆσος	δῶρον	-ος	-ον
	Gen.	λόγου	νήσου	δώρου	-ου	-ου
	Dat.	λόγῳ	νήσῳ	δώρῳ	-ῳ	-ῳ
	Acc.	λόγον	νῆσον	δῶρον	-ον	-ον
	Voc.	λόγε	νῆσε	δῶρον	-ε	-ον
Dual	N.A.V.	λόγω	νήσω	δώρω	-ω	-ω
	G.D.	λόγοιν	νήσοιν	δώροιν	-οιν	-οιν
Plur.	Nom.	λόγοι	νῆσοι	δῶρα	-οι	-ᾰ
	Gen.	λόγων	νήσων	δώρων	-ων	-ων
	Dat.	λόγοις	νήσοις	δώροις	-οις	-οις
	Acc.	λόγους	νήσους	δῶρα	-ους	-ᾰ
	Voc.	λόγοι	νῆσοι	δῶρα	-οι	-ᾰ

FIRST AND SECOND DECLENSION (Contract nouns)

		earth (F)		mind (M)	
Sing.	Nom.	γῆ	(γέ-α)	νοῦς	(νό-ος)
	Gen.	γῆς	(γέ-ας)	νοῦ	(νό-ου)
	Dat.	γῇ	(γέ-ᾳ)	νῷ	(νό-ῳ)
	Acc.	γῆν	(γέ-αν)	νοῦν	(νό-ον)
	Voc.	γῆ	(γέ-α)	νοῦ	(νό-ε)
Dual	N.A.V.			νώ	(νό-ω)
	G.D.			νοῖν	(νό-οιν)
Plur.	Nom.			νοῖ	(νό-οι)
	Gen.			νῶν	(νό-ων)
	Dat.			νοῖς	(νό-οις)
	Acc.			νοῦς	(νό-ους)
	Voc.			νοῖ	(νό-οι)

THIRD DECLENSION (Stems in -κ)

		herald (M)	**body** (N)	**Endings** M/F	N
Sing.	Nom.	κῆρυξ	σῶμα	-ς / none	—
	Gen.	κήρυκος	σώματος	-ος	-ος
	Dat.	κήρυκι	σώματι	-ῐ	-ῐ
	Acc.	κήρυκα	σῶμα	-ᾰ	as nom.
	Voc.	κῆρυξ	σῶμα	-ς / none	as nom.
Dual	N.A.V.	κήρυκε	σώματε	-ε	-ε
	G.D.	κηρύκοιν	σωμάτοιν	-οιν	-οιν
Plur.	Nom.	κήρυκες	σώματα	-ες	-ᾰ
	Gen.	κηρύκων	σωμάτων	-ων	-ων
	Dat.	κήρυξι(ν)	σώμασι(ν)	-σῐ(ν)	-σῐ(ν)
	Acc.	κήρυκας	σώματα	-ᾰς	as nom.
	Voc.	κήρυκες	σώματα	as nom.	as nom.

THIRD DECLENSION (Stems in dentals)

		torch (F)	**grace** (F)	**child** (M/F)
Sing.	Nom.	λαμπάς	χάρις	παῖς
	Gen.	λαμπάδος	χάριτος	παιδός
	Dat.	λαμπάδι	χάριτι	παιδί
	Acc.	λαμπάδα	χάριν	παῖδα
	Voc.	λαμπάς	χάρι	παῖ
Dual	N.A.V.	λαμπάδε	χάριτε	παῖδε
	G.D.	λαμπάδοιν	χαρίτοιν	παιδοῖν
Plur.	Nom.	λαμπάδες	χάριτες	παῖδες
	Gen.	λαμπάδων	χαρίτων	παίδων
	Dat.	λαμπάσι(ν)	χάρισι(ν)	παισί(ν)
	Acc.	λαμπάδας	χάριτας	παῖδας
	Voc.	λαμπάδες	χάριτες	παῖδες

THIRD DECLENSION (Stems in -κτ, -ντ)

		giant (M)	night (F)	lion (M)	Xenophon (M)
Sing.	Nom.	γίγας	νύξ	λέων	Ξενοφῶν
	Gen.	γίγᾰντος	νυκτός	λέοντος	Ξενοφῶντος
	Dat.	γίγαντι	νυκτί	λέοντι	Ξενοφῶντι
	Acc.	γίγαντα	νύκτα	λέοντα	Ξενοφῶντα
	Voc.	γίγαν	νύξ	λέον	Ξενοφῶν
Dual	N.A.V.	γίγαντε	νύκτε	λέοντε	
	G.D.	γιγάντοιν	νυκτοῖν	λεόντοιν	
Plur.	Nom.	γίγαντες	νύκτες	λέοντες	
	Gen.	γιγάντων	νυκτῶν	λεόντων	
	Dat.	γίγασι(ν)	νυξί(ν)	λέουσι(ν)	
	Acc.	γίγαντας	νύκτας	λέοντας	
	Voc.	γίγαντες	νύκτες	λέοντες	

THIRD DECLENSION (Stems in -ρ)

		orator (M)	wild beast (M)	mother (F)	father (M)	man (M)
Sing.	Nom.	ῥήτωρ	θήρ	μήτηρ	πατήρ	ἀνήρ
	Gen.	ῥήτορος	θηρός	μητρός	πατρός	ἀνδρός
	Dat.	ῥήτορι	θηρί	μητρί	πατρί	ἀνδρί
	Acc.	ῥήτορα	θῆρα	μητέρα	πατέρα	ἄνδρα
	Voc.	ῥῆτορ	θήρ	μῆτερ	πάτερ	ἄνερ
Dual	N.A.V.	ῥήτορε	θῆρε	μητέρε	πατέρε	ἄνδρε
	G.D.	ῥητόροιν	θηροῖν	μητέροιν	πατέροιν	ἀνδροῖν
Plur.	Nom.	ῥήτορες	θῆρες	μητέρες	πατέρες	ἄνδρες
	Gen.	ῥητόρων	θηρῶν	μητέρων	πατέρων	ἀνδρῶν
	Dat.	ῥήτορσι(ν)	θηρσί(ν)	μητράσι(ν)	πατράσι(ν)	ἀνδράσι(ν)
	Acc.	ῥήτορας	θῆρας	μητέρας	πατέρας	ἄνδρας
	Voc.	ῥήτορες	θῆρες	μητέρες	πατέρες	ἄνδρες

THIRD DECLENSION (Stems in -ν)

		Greek (M)	contest (M)	shepherd (M)	leader (M)
Sing.	Nom.	Ἕλλην	ἀγών	ποιμήν	ἡγεμών
	Gen.	Ἕλληνος	ἀγῶνος	ποιμένος	ἡγεμόνος
	Dat.	Ἕλληνι	ἀγῶνι	ποιμένι	ἡγεμόνι
	Acc.	Ἕλληνα	ἀγῶνα	ποιμένα	ἡγεμόνα
	Voc.	Ἕλλην	ἀγών	ποιμήν	ἡγεμών
Dual	N.A.V.	Ἕλληνε	ἀγῶνε	ποιμένε	ἡγεμόνε
	G.D.	Ἑλλήν	ἀγώνοιν	ποιμένοιν	ἡγεμόνοιν
Plur.	Nom.	Ἕλληνες	ἀγῶνες	ποιμένες	ἡγεμόνες
	Gen.	Ἑλλήνων	ἀγώνων	ποιμένων	ἡγεμόνων
	Dat.	Ἕλλησι(ν)	ἀγῶσι(ν)	ποιμέσι(ν)	ἡγεμόσι(ν)
	Acc.	Ἕλληνας	ἀγῶνας	ποιμένας	ἡγεμόνας
	Voc.	Ἕλληνες	ἀγῶνες	ποιμένες	ἡγεμόνες

THIRD DECLENSION (Stems in -σ, -ι, -υ)

		trireme (F)	wall (N)	city (F)	elder (M)	town (N)	fish (M)
Sing.	Nom.	τριήρης	τεῖχος	πόλις	πρέσβυς	ἄστυ	ἰχθύς
	Gen.	τριήρους	τείχους	πόλεως	πρέσβεως	ἄστεως	ἰχθύος
	Dat.	τριήρει	τείχει	πόλει	πρέσβει	ἄστει	ἰχθύϊ
	Acc.	τριήρη	τεῖχος	πόλιν	πρέσβυν	ἄστυ	ἰχθύν
	Voc.	τριῆρες	τεῖχος	πόλι	πρέσβυ	ἄστυ	ἰχθύ
Dual	N.A.V.	τριήρει	τείχει	πόλει	πρέσβει	ἄστει	ἰχθύε
	G.D.	τριήροιν	τειχοῖν	πολέοιν	πρεσβέοιν	ἀστέοιν	ἰχθύοιν
Plur.	Nom.	τριήρεις	τείχη	πόλεις	πρέσβεις	ἄστη	ἰχθύες
	Gen.	τριήρων	τειχῶν	πόλεων	πρέσβεων	ἄστεων	ἰχθύων
	Dat.	τριήρεσι(ν)	τείχεσι(ν)	πόλεσι(ν)	πρέσβεσι(ν)	ἄστεσι(ν)	ἰχθύσι(ν)
	Acc.	τριήρεις	τείχη	πόλεις	πρέσβεις	ἄστη	ἰχθύας, ἰχθῦς
	Voc.	τριήρεις	τείχη	πόλεις	πρέσβεις	ἄστη	ἰχθύες

THIRD DECLENSION (Stems in diphthong)

		king (M)	ox (M/F)	old woman (F)
Sing.	Nom.	βασιλεύς	βοῦς	γραῦς
	Gen.	βασιλέως	βοός	γραός
	Dat.	βασιλεῖ	βοΐ	γραΐ
	Acc.	βασιλέα	βοῦν	γραῦν
	Voc.	βασιλεῦ	βοῦ	γραῦ
Dual	N.A.V.	βασιλῆ	βόε	γρᾶε
	G.D.	βασιλέοιν	βοοῖν	γραοῖν
Plur.	Nom.	βασιλεῖς / -ῆς	βόες	γρᾶες
	Gen.	βασιλέων	βοῶν	γραῶν
	Dat.	βασιλεῦσι(ν)	βουσί(ν)	γραυσί(ν)
	Acc.	βασιλέας	βοῦς	γραῦς
	Voc.	βασιλεῖς / -ῆς	βόες	γρᾶες

THIRD DECLENSION (Irregular)

		woman (F)	ship (F)	water (N)	Zeus (M)
Sing.	Nom.	γυνή	ναῦς	ὕδωρ	Ζεύς
	Gen.	γυναικός	νεώς	ὕδατος	Διός
	Dat.	γυναικί	νηΐ	ὕδατι	Διΐ
	Acc.	γυναῖκα	ναῦν	ὕδωρ	Δία
	Voc.	γύναι	ναῦ	ὕδωρ	Ζεῦ
Dual	N.A.V.	γυναῖκε	νῆε	ὕδατε	
	G.D.	γυναικοῖν	νεοῖν	ὑδάτοιν	
Plur.	Nom.	γυναῖκες	νῆες	ὕδατα	
	Gen.	γυναικῶν	νεῶν	ὑδάτων	
	Dat.	γυναιξί(ν)	ναυσί(ν)	ὕδασι(ν)	
	Acc.	γυναῖκας	ναῦς	ὕδατα	
	Voc.	γυναῖκες	νῆες	ὕδατα	

ADJECTIVES

DEFINITE ARTICLE

		M	F	N
Sing.	Nom.	ὁ	ἡ	τό
	Gen.	τοῦ	τῆς	τοῦ
	Dat.	τῷ	τῇ	τῷ
	Acc.	τόν	τήν	τό
Dual	N.A.V.	τώ	τώ	τώ
	G.D.	τοῖν	τοῖν	τοῖν
Plur.	Nom.	οἱ	αἱ	τά
	Gen.	τῶν	τῶν	τῶν
	Dat.	τοῖς	ταῖς	τοῖς
	Acc.	τούς	τάς	τά

FIRST AND SECOND DECLENSION

		wise			friendly		
		M	F	N	M	F	N
Sing.	Nom.	σοφός	σοφή	σοφόν	φίλιος	φιλία	φίλιον
	Gen.	σοφοῦ	σοφῆς	σοφοῦ	φιλίου	φιλίας	φιλίου
	Dat.	σοφῷ	σοφῇ	σοφῷ	φιλίῳ	φιλίᾳ	φιλίῳ
	Acc.	σοφόν	σοφήν	σοφόν	φίλιον	φιλίαν	φίλιον
	Voc.	σοφέ	σοφή	σοφόν	φίλιε	φιλία	φίλιον
Dual	N.A.V.	σοφώ	σοφά	σοφώ	φιλίω	φιλία	φιλίω
	G.D.	σοφοῖν	σοφαῖν	σοφοῖν	φιλίοιν	φιλίαιν	φιλίοιν
Plur.	Nom.	σοφοί	σοφαί	σοφά	φίλιοι	φίλιαι	φίλια
	Gen.	σοφῶν	σοφῶν	σοφῶν	φιλίων	φιλίων	φιλίων
	Dat.	σοφοῖς	σοφαῖς	σοφοῖς	φιλίοις	φιλίαις	φιλίοις
	Acc.	σοφούς	σοφάς	σοφά	φιλίους	φιλίας	φίλια
	Voc.	σοφοί	σοφαί	σοφά	φίλιοι	φίλιαι	φίλια

FIRST AND SECOND DECLENSION (Contract)

silver

		M		F		N	
Sing.	Nom.	ἀργυροῦς	(-έ-ος)	ἀργυρᾶ	(-έ-α)	ἀργυροῦν	(-έ-ον)
	Gen.	ἀργυροῦ	(-έ-ου)	ἀργυρᾶς	(-έ-ας)	ἀργυροῦ	(-έ-ου)
	Dat.	ἀργυρῷ	(-έ-ῳ)	ἀργυρᾷ	(-έ-ᾳ)	ἀργυρῷ	(-έ-ῳ)
	Acc.	ἀργυροῦν	(-έ-ον)	ἀργυρᾶν	(-έ-αν)	ἀργυροῦν	(-έ-ον)
Dual	N.A.V.	ἀργυρώ	(-έ-ω)	ἀργυρᾶ	(έ-α)	ἀργυρώ	(-έ-ω)
	G.D.	ἀργυροῖν	(-έ-οιν)	ἀργυραῖν	(-έ-αιν)	ἀργυροῖν	(-έ-οιν)
Plur.	Nom.	ἀργυροῖ	(-έ-οι)	ἀργυραῖ	(-έ-αι)	ἀργυρᾶ	(-έ-α)
	Gen.	ἀργυρῶν	(-έ-ων)	ἀργυρῶν	(-έ-ων)	ἀργυρῶν	(-έ-ων)
	Dat.	ἀργυροῖς	(-έ-οις)	ἀργυραῖς	(-έ-αις)	ἀργυροῖς	(-έ-οις)
	Acc.	ἀργυροῦς	(-έ-ους)	ἀργυρᾶς	(-έ-ας)	ἀργυρᾶ	(-έ-α)

Note: No distinct vocative forms of contract adjectives are known.

THIRD DECLENSION

		prudent		true		sweeter			
		M/F	N	M/F	N	M/F		N	
Sing.	Nom.	σώφρων	σῶφρον	ἀληθής	ἀληθές	ἡδίων		ἥδιον	
	Gen.	σώφρονος	σώφρονος	ἀληθοῦς	ἀληθοῦς	ἡδίονος		ἡδίονος	
	Dat.	σώφρονι	σώφρονι	ἀληθεῖ	ἀληθεῖ	ἡδίονι		ἡδίονι	
	Acc.	σώφρονα	σῶφρον	ἀληθῆ	ἀληθές	ἡδίονα	ἡδίω	ἥδιον	
	Voc.	σῶφρον	σῶφρον	ἀληθές	ἀληθές	ἥδιον		ἥδιον	
Dual	N.A.V.	σώφρονε	σώφρονε	ἀληθεῖ	ἀληθεῖ	ἡδίονε		ἡδίονε	
	G.D.	σωφρόνοιν	σωφρόνοιν	ἀληθοῖν	ἀληθοῖν	ἡδιόνοιν		ἡδιόνοιν	
Plur.	Nom.	σώφρονες	σώφρονα	ἀληθεῖς	ἀληθῆ	ἡδίονες	ἡδίους	ἡδίονα	ἡδίω
	Gen.	σωφρόνων	σωφρόνων	ἀληθῶν	ἀληθῶν	ἡδιόνων		ἡδιόνων	
	Dat.	σώφροσι(ν)	σώφροσι(ν)	ἀληθέσι(ν)	ἀληθέσι(ν)	ἡδίοσι(ν)		ἡδίοσι(ν)	
	Acc.	σώφρονας	σώφρονα	ἀληθεῖς	ἀληθῆ	ἡδίονας	ἡδίους	ἡδίονα	ἡδίω
	Voc.	σώφρονες	σώφρονα	ἀληθεῖς	ἀληθῆ	ἡδίονες	ἡδίους	ἡδίονα	ἡδίω

FIRST AND THIRD DECLENSION

		wretched			all		
		M	F	N	M	F	N
Sing.	Nom.	τάλας	τάλαινα	τάλαν	πᾶς	πᾶσα	πᾶν
	Gen.	τάλανος	ταλαίνης	τάλανος	παντός	πάσης	παντός
	Dat.	τάλανι	ταλαίνῃ	τάλανι	παντί	πάσῃ	παντί
	Acc.	τάλανα	τάλαιναν	τάλαν	πάντα	πᾶσαν	πᾶν
	Voc.	τάλαν	τάλαινα	τάλαν	πᾶς	πᾶσα	πᾶν
Dual	N.A.V.	τάλανε	ταλαίνα	τάλανε			
	G.D.	ταλάνοιν	ταλαίναιν	ταλάνοιν			
Plur.	Nom.	τάλανες	τάλαιναι	τάλανα	πάντες	πᾶσαι	πάντα
	Gen.	ταλάνων	ταλαινῶν	ταλάνων	πάντων	πασῶν	πάντων
	Dat.	τάλασι(ν)	ταλαίναις	τάλασι(ν)	πᾶσι(ν)	πάσαις	πᾶσι(ν)
	Acc.	τάλανας	ταλαίνας	τάλανα	πάντας	πάσας	πάντα
	Voc.	τάλανες	τάλαιναι	τάλανα	πάντες	πᾶσαι	πάντα

		sweet		
		M	F	N
Sing.	Nom.	ἡδύς	ἡδεῖα	ἡδύ
	Gen.	ἡδέος	ἡδείας	ἡδέος
	Dat.	ἡδεῖ	ἡδείᾳ	ἡδεῖ
	Acc.	ἡδύν	ἡδεῖαν	ἡδύ
	Voc.	ἡδύ	ἡδεῖα	ἡδύ
Dual	N.A.V.	ἡδέε	ἡδεία	ἡδέε
	G.D.	ἡδέοιν	ἡδείαιν	ἡδέοιν
Plur.	Nom.	ἡδεῖς	ἡδεῖαι	ἡδέα
	Gen.	ἡδέων	ἡδειῶν	ἡδέων
	Dat.	ἡδέσι(ν)	ἡδείαις	ἡδέσι(ν)
	Acc.	ἡδεῖς	ἡδείας	ἡδέα
	Voc.	ἡδεῖς	ἡδεῖαι	ἡδέα

IRREGULAR

		big			much, many		
		M	F	N	M	F	N
Sing.	Nom.	μέγας	μεγάλη	μέγα	πολύς	πολλή	πολύ
	Gen.	μεγάλου	μεγάλης	μεγάλου	πολλοῦ	πολλῆς	πολλοῦ
	Dat.	μεγάλῳ	μεγάλῃ	μεγάλῳ	πολλῷ	πολλῇ	πολλῷ
	Acc.	μέγαν	μεγάλην	μέγα	πολύν	πολλήν	πολύ
Dual	N.A.V.	μεγάλω	μεγάλα	μεγάλω			
	G.D.	μεγάλοιν	μεγάλαιν	μεγάλοιν			
Plur.	Nom.	μεγάλοι	μεγάλαι	μεγάλα	πολλοί	πολλαί	πολλά
	Gen.	μεγάλων	μεγάλων	μεγάλων	πολλῶν	πολλῶν	πολλῶν
	Dat.	μεγάλοις	μεγάλαις	μεγάλοις	πολλοῖς	πολλαῖς	πολλοῖς
	Acc.	μεγάλους	μεγάλας	μεγάλα	πολλούς	πολλάς	πολλά

PARTICIPLES

REGULAR THEMATIC VERBS

		PRESENT ACTIVE			PRESENT MIDDLE/PASSIVE		
		M	F	N	M	F	N
Sing.	Nom.	λύων	λύουσα	λῦον	λυόμενος	λυομένη	λυόμενον
	Gen.	λύοντος	λυούσης	λύοντος	λυομένου	λυομένης	λυομένου
	Dat.	λύοντι	λυούσῃ	λύοντι	λυομένῳ	λυομένῃ	λυομένῳ
	Acc.	λύοντα	λύουσαν	λῦον	λυόμενον	λυομένην	λυόμενον
	Voc.	λύων	λύουσα	λῦον	λυόμενε	λυομένη	λυόμενον
Dual	N.A.V.	λύοντε	λυούσα	λύοντε	λυομένω	λυομένα	λυομένω
	G.D.	λυόντοιν	λυούσαιν	λυόντοιν	λυομένοιν	λυομέναιν	λυομένοιν
Plur.	Nom.	λύοντες	λύουσαι	λύοντα	λυόμενοι	λυόμεναι	λυόμενα
	Gen.	λυόντων	λυουσῶν	λυόντων	λυομένων	λυομένων	λυομένων
	Dat.	λύουσι(ν)	λυούσαις	λύουσι(ν)	λυομένοις	λυομέναις	λυομένοις
	Acc.	λύοντας	λυούσας	λύοντα	λυομένους	λυομένας	λυόμενα
	Voc.	λύοντες	λύουσαι	λύοντα	λυόμενοι	λυόμεναι	λυόμενα

		FIRST AORIST ACTIVE			SECOND AORIST ACTIVE (λείπω)		
		M	F	N	M	F	N
Sing.	Nom.	λύσας	λύσασα	λῦσαν	λιπών	λιποῦσα	λιπόν
	Gen.	λύσαντος	λυσάσης	λύσαντος	λιπόντος	λιπούσης	λιπόντος
	Dat.	λύσαντι	λυσάσῃ	λύσαντι	λιπόντι	λιπούσῃ	λιπόντι
	Acc.	λύσαντα	λύσασαν	λῦσαν	λιπόντα	λιποῦσαν	λιπόν
	Voc.	λύσας	λύσασα	λῦσαν	λιπών	λιποῦσα	λιπόν
Dual	N.A.V.	λύσαντε	λυσάσα	λύσαντε	λιπόντε	λιπούσα	λιπόντε
	G.D.	λυσάντοιν	λυσάσαιν	λυσάντοιν	λιπόντοιν	λιπούσαιν	λιπόντοιν
Plur.	Nom.	λύσαντες	λύσασαι	λύσαντα	λιπόντες	λιποῦσαι	λιπόντα
	Gen.	λυσάντων	λυσασῶν	λυσάντων	λιπόντων	λιπουσῶν	λιπόντων
	Dat.	λύσασι(ν)	λυσάσαις	λύσασι(ν)	λιποῦσι(ν)	λιπούσαις	λιποῦσι(ν)
	Acc.	λύσαντας	λυσάσας	λύσαντα	λιπόντας	λιπούσας	λιπόντα
	Voc.	λύσαντες	λύσασαι	λύσαντα	λιπόντες	λιποῦσαι	λιπόντα

		PERFECT ACTIVE			AORIST PASSIVE		
		M	F	N	M	F	N
Sing.	Nom.	λελυκώς	λελυκυῖα	λελυκός	λυθείς	λυθεῖσα	λυθέν
	Gen.	λελυκότος	λελυκυίας	λελυκότος	λυθέντος	λυθείσης	λυθέντος
	Dat.	λελυκότι	λελυκυίᾳ	λελυκότι	λυθέντι	λυθείσῃ	λυθέντι
	Acc.	λελυκότα	λελυκυῖαν	λελυκός	λυθέντα	λυθεῖσαν	λυθέν
	Voc.	λελυκώς	λελυκυῖα	λελυκός	λυθείς	λυθεῖσα	λυθέν
Dual	N.A.V.	λελυκότε	λελυκυία	λελυκότε	λυθέντε	λυθείσα	λυθέντε
	G.D.	λελυκότοιν	λελυκυίαιν	λελυκότοιν	λυθέντοιν	λυθείσαιν	λυθέντοιν
Plur.	Nom.	λελυκότες	λελυκυῖαι	λελυκότα	λυθέντες	λυθεῖσαι	λυθέντα
	Gen.	λελυκότων	λελυκυιῶν	λελυκότων	λυθέντων	λυθεισῶν	λυθέντων
	Dat.	λελυκόσι(ν)	λελυκυίαις	λελυκόσι(ν)	λυθεῖσι(ν)	λυθείσαις	λυθεῖσι(ν)
	Acc.	λελυκότας	λελυκυίας	λελυκότα	λυθέντας	λυθείσας	λυθέντα
	Voc.	λελυκότες	λελυκυῖαι	λελυκότα	λυθέντες	λυθεῖσαι	λυθέντα

CONTRACT THEMATIC VERBS

love

		Present Active M	Present Active F	Present Active N	Present Middle/Passive M	Present Middle/Passive F	Present Middle/Passive N
Sing.	Nom.	φιλῶν	φιλοῦσα	φιλοῦν	φιλούμενος	φιλουμένη	φιλούμενον
	Gen.	φιλοῦντος	φιλούσης	φιλοῦντος	φιλουμένου	φιλουμένης	φιλουμένου
	Dat.	φιλοῦντι	φιλούσῃ	φιλοῦντι	φιλουμένῳ	φιλουμένῃ	φιλουμένῳ
	Acc.	φιλοῦντα	φιλοῦσαν	φιλοῦν	φιλούμενον	φιλουμένην	φιλούμενον
	Voc.	φιλῶν	φιλοῦσα	φιλοῦν	φιλούμενε	φιλουμένη	φιλούμενον
Dual	N.A.V.	φιλοῦντε	φιλούσα	φιλοῦντε	φιλουμένω	φιλουμένα	φιλουμένω
	G.D.	φιλούντοιν	φιλούσαιν	φιλούντοιν	φιλουμένοιν	φιλουμέναιν	φιλουμένοιν
Plur.	Nom.	φιλοῦντες	φιλοῦσαι	φιλοῦντα	φιλούμενοι	φιλούμεναι	φιλούμενα
	Gen.	φιλούντων	φιλουσῶν	φιλούντων	φιλουμένων	φιλουμένων	φιλουμένων
	Dat.	φιλοῦσι(ν)	φιλούσαις	φιλοῦσι(ν)	φιλουμένοις	φιλουμέναις	φιλουμένοις
	Acc.	φιλοῦντας	φιλούσας	φιλοῦντα	φιλουμένους	φιλουμένας	φιλούμενα
	Voc.	φιλοῦντες	φιλοῦσαι	φιλοῦντα	φιλούμενοι	φιλούμεναι	φιλούμενα

honor

		M	F	N	M	F	N
Sing.	Nom.	τιμῶν	τιμῶσα	τιμῶν	τιμώμενος	τιμωμένη	τιμώμενον
	Gen.	τιμῶντος	τιμώσης	τιμῶντος	τιμωμένου	τιμωμένης	τιμωμένου
	Dat.	τιμῶντι	τιμώσῃ	τιμῶντι	τιμωμένῳ	τιμωμένῃ	τιμωμένῳ
	Acc.	τιμῶντα	τιμῶσαν	τιμῶν	τιμώμενον	τιμωμένην	τιμώμενον
	Voc.	τιμῶν	τιμῶσα	τιμῶν	τιμώμενε	τιμωμένη	τιμώμενον
Dual	N.A.V.	τιμῶντε	τιμώσα	τιμῶντε	τιμωμένω	τιμωμένα	τιμωμένω
	G.D.	τιμώντοιν	τιμώσαιν	τιμώντοιν	τιμωμένοιν	τιμωμέναιν	τιμωμένοιν
Plur.	Nom.	τιμῶντες	τιμῶσαι	τιμῶντα	τιμώμενοι	τιμώμεναι	τιμώμενα
	Gen.	τιμώντων	τιμωσῶν	τιμώντων	τιμωμένων	τιμωμένων	τιμωμένων
	Dat.	τιμῶσι(ν)	τιμώσαις	τιμῶσι(ν)	τιμωμένοις	τιμωμέναις	τιμωμένοις
	Acc.	τιμῶντας	τιμώσας	τιμῶντα	τιμωμένους	τιμωμένας	τιμώμενα
	Voc.	τιμῶντες	τιμῶσαι	τιμῶντα	τιμώμενοι	τιμώμεναι	τιμώμενα

show

		M	F	N	M	F	N
Sing.	Nom.	δηλῶν	δηλοῦσα	δηλοῦν	δηλούμενος	δηλουμένη	δηλούμενον
	Gen.	δηλοῦντος	δηλούσης	δηλοῦντος	δηλουμένου	δηλουμένης	δηλουμένου
	Dat.	δηλοῦντι	δηλούσῃ	δηλοῦντι	δηλουμένῳ	δηλουμένῃ	δηλουμένῳ
	Acc.	δηλοῦντα	δηλοῦσαν	δηλοῦν	δηιλούμενον	δηλουμένην	δηλούμενον
	Voc.	δηλῶν	δηλοῦσα	δηλοῦν	δηιλούμενε	δηλουμένη	δηλούμενον
Dual	N.A.V.	δηλοῦντε	δηλούσα	δηλοῦντε	δηλουμένω	δηλουμένα	δηλουμένω
	G.D.	δηλούντοιν	δηλούσαιν	δηλούντοιν	δηλουμένοιν	δηλουμέναιν	δηλουμένοιν
Plur.	Nom.	δηλοῦντες	δηλοῦσαι	δηλοῦντα	δηλούμενοι	δηλούμεναι	δηλούμενα
	Gen.	δηλούντων	δηλουσῶν	δηλούντων	δηλουμένων	δηλουμένων	δηλουμένων
	Dat.	δηλοῦσι(ν)	δηλούσαις	δηλοῦσι(ν)	δηλουμένοις	δηλουμέναις	δηλουμένοις
	Acc.	δηλοῦντας	δηλούσας	δηλοῦντα	δηλουμένους	δηλουμένας	δηλούμενα
	Voc.	δηλοῦντες	δηλοῦσαι	δηλοῦντα	δηλούμενοι	δηλούμεναι	δηλούμενα

PRONOUNS

PERSONAL AND INTENSIVE

		1st (I)	2nd (you)	3rd (he/she/it)		
				M	F	N
Sing.	Nom.	ἐγώ	σύ	αὐτός	αὐτή	αὐτό
	Gen.	ἐμοῦ μου	σοῦ σου	αὐτοῦ	αὐτῆς	αὐτοῦ
	Dat.	ἐμοί μοι	σοί σοι	αὐτῷ	αὐτῇ	αὐτῷ
	Acc.	ἐμέ με	σέ σε	αὐτόν	αὐτὴν	αὐτό
Dual	N.A.V.	νώ	σφώ	αὐτώ	αὐτώ	αὐτώ
	G.D.	νῷν	σφῷν	αὐτοῖν	αὐτοῖν	αὐτοῖν
Plur.	Nom.	ἡμεῖς	ὑμεῖς	αὐτοί	αὐταί	αὐτά
	Gen.	ἡμῶν	ὑμῶν	αὐτῶν	αὐτῶν	αὐτῶν
	Dat.	ἡμῖν	ὑμῖν	αὐτοῖς	αὐταῖς	αὐτοῖς
	Acc.	ἡμᾶς	ὑμᾶς	αὐτούς	αὐτάς	αὐτά

RECIPROCAL (each other)

		M	F	N
Dual	G.D.	ἀλλήλοιν	ἀλλήλοιν	ἀλλήλοιν
	A.	ἀλλήλω	ἀλλήλω	ἀλλήλω
Plur.	Gen.	ἀλλήλων	ἀλλήλων	ἀλλήλων
	Dat.	ἀλλήλοις	ἀλλήλαις	ἀλλήλοις
	Acc.	ἀλλήλους	ἀλλήλας	ἄλληλα

REFLEXIVE

		1st (myself)		2nd (yourself)		3rd (himself/herself/itself)		
		M	F	M	F	M	F	N
Sing.	Gen.	ἐμαυτοῦ	ἐμαυτῆς	σεαυτοῦ	σεαυτῆς	ἑαυτοῦ	ἑαυτῆς	ἑαυτοῦ
	Dat.	ἐμαυτῷ	ἐμαυτῇ	σεαυτῷ	σεαυτῇ	ἑαυτῷ	ἑαυτῇ	ἑαυτῷ
	Acc.	ἐμαυτόν	ἐμαυτήν	σεαυτόν	σεαυτήν	ἑαυτόν	ἑαυτήν	ἑαυτό
Plur.	Gen.	ἡμῶν αὐτῶν	ἡμῶν αὐτῶν	ὑμῶν αὐτῶν	ὑμῶν αὐτῶν	ἑαυτῶν	ἑαυτῶν	ἑαυτῶν
	Dat.	ἡμῖν αὐτοῖς	ἡμῖν αὐταῖς	ὑμῖν αὐτοῖς	ὑμῖν αὐταῖς	ἑαυτοῖς	ἑαυταῖς	ἑαυτοῖς
	Acc.	ἡμᾶς αὐτούς	ἡμᾶς αὐτάς	ὑμᾶς αὐτούς	ὑμᾶς αὐτάς	ἑαυτούς	ἑαυτάς	ἑαυτά

DEMONSTRATIVE

		this			that		
		M	F	N	M	F	N
Sing.	Nom.	οὗτος	αὕτη	τοῦτο	ἐκεῖνος	ἐκείνη	ἐκεῖνο
	Gen.	τούτου	ταύτης	τούτου	ἐκείνου	ἐκείνης	ἐκείνου
	Dat.	τούτῳ	ταύτῃ	τούτῳ	ἐκείνῳ	ἐκείνῃ	ἐκείνῳ
	Acc.	τοῦτον	ταύτην	τοῦτο	ἐκεῖνον	ἐκείνην	ἐκεῖνο
Dual	N.A.V.	τούτω	τούτω	τούτω	ἐκείνω	ἐκείνω	ἐκείνω
	G.D.	τούτοιν	τούτοιν	τούτοιν	ἐκείνοιν	ἐκείνοιν	ἐκείνοιν
Plur.	Nom.	οὗτοι	αὗται	ταῦτα	ἐκεῖνοι	ἐκεῖναι	ἐκεῖνα
	Gen.	τούτων	τούτων	τούτων	ἐκείνων	ἐκείνων	ἐκείνων
	Dat.	τούτοις	ταύταις	τούτοις	ἐκείνοις	ἐκείναις	ἐκείνοις
	Acc.	τούτους	ταύτας	ταῦτα	ἐκείνους	ἐκείνας	ἐκεῖνα

		this		
		M	F	N
Sing.	Nom.	ὅδε	ἥδε	τόδε
	Gen.	τοῦδε	τῆσδε	τοῦδε
	Dat.	τῷδε	τῇδε	τῷδε
	Acc.	τόνδε	τήνδε	τόδε
Dual	N.A.V.	τώδε	τώδε	τώδε
	G.D.	τοῖνδε	τοῖνδε	τοῖνδε
Plur.	Nom.	οἵδε	αἵδε	τάδε
	Gen.	τῶνδε	τῶνδε	τῶνδε
	Dat.	τοῖσδε	ταῖσδε	τοῖσδε
	Acc.	τούσδε	τάσδε	τάδε

INTERROGATIVE AND INDEFINITE

		who?/what?				someone/something			
		M/F		N		M/F		N	
Sing.	Nom.	τίς		τί		τις		τι	
	Gen.	τίνος	τοῦ	τίνος	τοῦ	τινός	του	τινός	του
	Dat.	τίνι	τῷ	τίνι	τῷ	τινί	τῳ	τινί	τῳ
	Acc.	τίνα		τί		τινά		τι	
Dual	N.A.V.	τίνε		τίνε		τινέ		τινέ	
	G.D.	τίνοιν		τίνοιν		τινοῖν		τινοῖν	
Plur.	Nom.	τίνες		τίνα		τινές		τινά	
	Gen.	τίνων		τίνων		τινῶν		τινῶν	
	Dat.	τίσι(ν)		τίσι(ν)		τισί(ν)		τισί(ν)	
	Acc.	τίνας		τίνα		τινάς		τινά	

RELATIVE

		who/what			anyone who				
		M	F	N	M		F	N	
Sing.	Nom.	ὅς	ἥ	ὅ	ὅστις		ἥτις	ὅ τι	
	Gen.	οὗ	ἧς	οὗ	οὗτινος	ὅτου	ἧστινος	οὗτινος	ὅτου
	Dat.	ᾧ	ᾗ	ᾧ	ᾧτινι	ὅτῳ	ᾗτινι	ᾧτινι	ὅτῳ
	Acc.	ὅν	ἥν	ὅ	ὅντινα		ἥντινα	ὅ τι	
Dual	N.A.V.	ὥ	ὥ	ὥ	ὥτινε		ὥτινε	ὥτινε	
	G.D.	οἷν	οἷν	οἷν	οἷντινοιν		οἷντινοιν	οἷντινοιν	
Plur.	Nom.	οἵ	αἵ	ἅ	οἵτινες		αἵτινες	ἅτινα	ἅττα
	Gen.	ὧν	ὧν	ὧν	ὧντινων	ὅτων	ὧντινων	ὧντινων	ὅτων
	Dat.	οἷς	αἷς	οἷς	οἷστισι(ν)	ὅτοις	αἷστισι(ν)	οἷστισι(ν)	ὅτοις
	Acc.	οὕς	ἅς	ἅ	οὕστινας		ἅστινας	ἅτινα	ἅττα

NUMBERS

CARDINAL AND ORDINAL

1.	εἷς, μία, ἕν	πρῶτος, -η, -ον
2.	δύο	δεύτερος, -α, -ον
3.	τρεῖς, τρία	τρίτος, -η, -ον
4.	τέτταρες, τέτταρα	τέταρτος, -η, -ον
5.	πέντε	πέμπτος, -η, -ον
6.	ἕξ	ἕκτος, -η, -ον
7.	ἑπτά	ἕβδομος, -η, -ον
8.	ὀκτώ	ὄγδοος, -η, -ον
9.	ἐννέα	ἔνατος, -η, -ον
10.	δέκα	δέκατος, -η, -ον
11.	ἕνδεκα	ἑνδέκατος, -η, -ον
12.	δώδεκα	δωδέκατος, -η, -ον
13.	τρεῖς καὶ δέκα	τρίτος, -η, -ον καὶ δέκατος, -η, -ον
14.	τέτταρες καὶ δέκα	τέταρτος, -η, -ον καὶ δέκατος, -η, -ον
15.	πεντεκαίδεκα	πέμπτος, -η, -ον καὶ δέκατος, -η, -ον
16.	ἑκκαίδεκα	ἕκτος, -η, -ον καὶ δέκατος, -η, -ον
17.	ἑπτακαίδεκα	ἕβδομος, -η, -ον καὶ δέκατος, -η, -ον
18.	ὀκτωκαίδεκα	ὄγδοος, -η, -ον καὶ δέκατος, -η, -ον
19.	ἐννεακαίδεκα	ἔνατος, -η, -ον καὶ δέκατος, -η, -ον
20.	εἴκοσιν	εἰκοστός, -ή, -όν
21.	εἷς καὶ εἴκοσι, εἴκοσι καὶ εἷς	πρῶτος, -η, -ον καὶ εἰκοστός, -ή, -όν
30.	τριάκοντα	τριακοστός, -ή, -όν
40.	τετταράκοντα	τετταρακοστός, -ή, -όν
50.	πεντήκοντα	πεντηκοστός, -ή, -όν
60.	ἑξήκοντα	ἑξηκοστός, -ή, -όν
70.	ἑβδομήκοντα	ἑβδομηκοστός, -ή, -όν
80.	ὀγδοήκοντα	ὀγδοηκοστός, -ή, -όν
90.	ἐνενήκοντα	ἐνενηκοστός, -ή, -όν
100.	ἑκατόν	ἑκατοστός, -ή, -όν
200.	διακόσιοι, -αι, -α	διακοσιοστός, -ή, -όν
300.	τριακόσιοι, -αι, -α	τριακοσιοστός, -ή, -όν
400.	τετρακόσιοι, -αι, -α	τετρακοσιοστός, -ή, -όν
500.	πεντακόσιοι, -αι, -α	πεντακοσιοστός, -ή, -όν
600.	ἑξακόσιοι, -αι, -α	ἑξακοσιοστός, -ή, -όν
700.	ἑπτακόσιοι, -αι, -α	ἑπτακοσιοστός, -ή, -όν
800.	ὀκτακόσιοι, -αι, -α	ὀκτακοσιοστός, -ή, -όν
900.	ἐνακόσιοι, -αι, -α	ἐνακοσιοστός, -ή, -όν
1000.	χίλιοι,-αι, -α	χιλιοστός, -ή, -όν

DECLENSION OF NUMBERS 1 to 4

	one			two	three		four	
	M	F	N	M/F/N	M/F	N	M/F	N
Nom.	εἷς	μία	ἕν	δύο	τρεῖς	τρία	τέτταρες	τέτταρα
Gen.	ἑνός	μιᾶς	ἑνός	δυοῖν	τριῶν	τριῶν	τεττάρων	τεττάρων
Dat.	ἑνί	μιᾷ	ἑνί	δυοῖν	τρισί(ν)	τρισί(ν)	τέτταρσι(ν)	τέτταρσι(ν)
Acc.	ἕνα	μίαν	ἕν	δύο	τρεῖς	τρία	τέτταρας	τέτταρα

REGULAR THEMATIC VERBS

PRESENT SYSTEM

		Active		Middle / Passive	
INDICATIVE		Present	Imperfect	Present	Imperfect
Sing.	1st	λύω	ἔλυον	λύομαι	ἐλυόμην
	2nd	λύεις	ἔλυες	λύῃ / -ει	ἐλύου
	3rd	λύει	ἔλυε(ν)	λύεται	ἐλύετο
Dual	2nd	λύετον	ἐλύετον	λύεσθον	ἐλύεσθον
	3rd	λύετον	ἐλυέτην	λύεσθον	ἐλυέσθην
Plur.	1st	λύομεν	ἐλύομεν	λυόμεθα	ἐλυόμεθα
	2nd	λύετε	ἐλύετε	λύεσθε	ἐλύεσθε
	3rd	λύουσι(ν)	ἔλυον	λύονται	ἐλύοντο
SUBJUNCTIVE					
Sing.		λύω		λύωμαι	
		λύῃς		λύῃ	
		λύῃ		λύηται	
Dual		λύητον		λύησθον	
		λύητον		λύησθον	
Plur.		λύωμεν		λυώμεθα	
		λύητε		λύησθε	
		λύωσι(ν)		λύωνται	
OPTATIVE					
Sing.		λύοιμι		λυοίμην	
		λύοις		λύοιο	
		λύοι		λύοιτο	
Dual		λύοιτον		λύησθον	
		λυοίτην		λυοίσθην	
Plur.		λύοιμεν		λυοίμεθα	
		λύοιτε		λύοισθε	
		λύοιεν		λύοιντο	

IMPERATIVE	Active Present	Active Imperfect	Middle / Passive Present	Middle / Passive Imperfect
Sing.	λῦε		λύου	
	λυέτω		λυέσθω	
Dual	λύετον		λύεσθον	
	λυέτων		λυέσθων	
Plur.	λύετε		λύεσθε	
	λυόντων		λυέσθων	
INFINITIVE				
	λύειν		λύεσθαι	
PARTICIPLE				
	λύων, λύουσα, λῦον		λυόμενος, λυομένη, λυόμενον	

FUTURE SYSTEM

INDICATIVE		ACTIVE	MIDDLE	PASSIVE
Sing.	1st	λύσω	λύσομαι	λυθήσομαι
	2nd	λύσεις	λύσῃ / -ει	λυθήσῃ / -ει
	3rd	λύσει	λύσεται	λυθήσεται
Dual	2nd	λύσετον	λύσεσθον	λυθήσεσθον
	3rd	λύσετον	λύσεσθον	λυθήσεσθον
Plur.	1st	λύσομεν	λυσόμεθα	λυθησόμεθα
	2nd	λύσετε	λύσεσθε	λυθήσεσθε
	3rd	λύσουσι(ν)	λύσονται	λυθήσονται
OPTATIVE				
Sing.		λύσοιμι	λυσοίμην	λυθησοίμην
		λύσοις	λύσοιο	λυθήσοιο
		λύσοι	λύσοιτο	λυθήσοιτο
Dual		λύσοιτον	λύσοισθον	λυθήσοισθον
		λυσοίτην	λυσοίσθην	λυθησοίσθην
Plur.		λύσοιμεν	λυσοίμεθα	λυθησοίμεθα
		λύσοιτε	λύσοισθε	λυθήσοισθε
		λύσοιεν	λύσοιντο	λυθήσοιντο
INFINITIVE				
		λύσειν	λύσεσθαι	λυθήσεσθαι
PARTICIPLE				
		λύσων, λύσουσα, λῦσον	λυσόμενος, λυσομένη, λυσόμενον	λυθησόμενος, λυθησομένη, λυθησόμενον

WEAK AORIST SYSTEM

INDICATIVE		ACTIVE		MIDDLE	PASSIVE	
Sing.	1st	ἔλυσα		ἐλυσάμην	ἐλύθην	
	2nd	ἔλυσας		ἐλύσω	ἐλύθης	
	3rd	ἔλυσε(ν)		ἐλύσατο	ἐλύθη	
Dual	2nd	ἐλύσατον		ἐλύσασθον	ἐλύθητον	
	3rd	ἐλυσάτην		ἐλυσάσθην	ἐλυθήτην	
Plur.	1st	ἐλύσαμεν		ἐλυσάμεθα	ἐλύθημεν	
	2nd	ἐλύσατε		ἐλύσασθε	ἐλύθητε	
	3rd	ἔλυσαν		ἐλύσαντο	ἐλύθησαν	
SUBJUNCTIVE						
Sing.		λύσω		λύσωμαι	λυθῶ	
		λύσῃς		λύσῃ	λυθῇς	
		λύσῃ		λύσηται	λυθῇ	
Dual		λύσητον		λύσησθον	λυθῆτον	
		λύσητον		λύσησθον	λυθῆτον	
Plur.		λύσωμεν		λυσώμεθα	λυθῶμεν	
		λύσητε		λύσησθε	λυθῆτε	
		λύσωσι(ν)		λύσωνται	λυθῶσι(ν)	
OPTATIVE						
Sing.		λύσαιμι		λυσαίμην	λυθείην	
		λύσειας	[λύσαις]	λύσαιο	λυθείης	
		λύσειε(ν)	[λύσαι]	λύσαιτο	λυθείη	
Dual		λύσαιτον		λύσαισθον	λυθείητον	[λυθεῖτον]
		λυσαίτην		λυσαίσθην	λυθειήτην	[λυθείτην]
Plur.		λύσαιμεν		λυσαίμεθα	λυθείημεν	[λυθεῖμεν]
		λύσαιτε		λύσαισθε	λυθείητε	[λυθεῖτε]
		λύσειαν	[λύσαιεν]	λύσαιντο	λυθείησαν	[λυθεῖεν]
IMPERATIVE						
Sing.		λῦσον		λῦσαι	λύθητι	
		λυσάτω		λυσάσθω	λυθήτω	
Dual		λύσατον		λύσασθον	λύθητον	
		λυσάτων		λυσάσθων	λυθήτων	
Plur.		λύσατε		λύσασθε	λύθητε	
		λυσάντων		λυσάσθων	λυθέντων	
INFINITIVE						
		λῦσαι		λύσασθαι	λυθῆναι	
PARTICIPLE						
		λύσας, λύσασα, λῦσαν		λυσάμενος, λυσαμένη, λυσάμενον	λυθείς, λυθεῖσα, λυθέν	

PERFECT SYSTEM

		Active		Middle / Passive	
INDICATIVE		Perfect	Pluperfect	Perfect	Pluperfect
Sing.	1st	λέλυκα	ἐλελύκη	λέλυμαι	ἐλελύμην
	2nd	λέλυκας	ἐλελύκης	λέλυσαι	ἐλέλυσο
	3rd	λέλυκε(ν)	ἐλελύκει(ν)	λέλυται	ἐλέλυτο
Dual	2nd	λελύκατον	ἐλελύκετον	λέλυσθον	ἐλέλυσθον
	3rd	λελύκατον	ἐλελυκέτην	λέλυσθον	ἐλελύσθην
Plur.	1st	λελύκαμεν	ἐλελύκεμεν	λελύμεθα	ἐλελύμεθα
	2nd	λελύκατε	ἐλελύκετε	λέλυσθε	ἐλέλυσθε
	3rd	λελύκασι(ν)	ἐλελύκεσαν	λέλυνται	ἐλέλυντο
SUBJUNCTIVE					
Sing.		λελυκὼς ὦ		λελυμένος ὦ	
		λελυκὼς ᾖς		λελυμένος ᾖς	
		λελυκὼς ᾖ		λελυμένος ᾖ	
Dual		λελυκότε ἦτον		λελυμένω ἦτον	
		λελυκότε ἦτον		λελυμένω ἦτον	
Plur.		λελυκότες ὦμεν		λελυμένοι ὦμεν	
		λελυκότες ἦτε		λελυμένοι ἦτε	
		λελυκότες ὦσι(ν)		λελυμένοι ὦσι(ν)	
OPTATIVE					
Sing.		λελυκὼς εἴην		λελυμένος εἴην	
		λελυκὼς εἴης		λελυμένος εἴης	
		λελυκὼς εἴη		λελυμένος εἴη	
Dual		λελυκότε εἶτον	[εἴητον]	λελυμένω εἶτον	[εἴητον]
		λελυκότε εἴτην	[εἰήτην]	λελυμένω εἴτην	[εἰήτην]
Plur.		λελυκότες εἶμεν	[εἴημεν]	λελυμένοι εἶμεν	[εἴημεν]
		λελυκότες εἶτε	[εἴητε]	λελυμένοι εἶτε	[εἴητε]
		λελυκότες εἶεν	[εἴησαν]	λελυμένοι εἶεν	[εἴησαν]
IMPERATIVE					
Sing.		λελυκὼς ἴσθι		λελυμένος ἴσθι	
		λελυκὼς ἔστω		λελυμένος ἔστω	
Dual		λελυκότε ἔστον		λελυμένω ἔστον	
		λελυκότε ἔστων		λελυμένω ἔστων	
Plur.		λελυκότες ἔστε		λελυμένοι ἔστε	
		λελυκότες ἔστων		λελυμένοι ἔστων	
INFINITIVE					
		λελυκέναι		λελύσθαι	
PARTICIPLE					
		λελυκώς, λελυκυῖα, λελυκός		λελυμένος, λελυμένη, λελυμένον	

PERFECT SYSTEM (RARE SIMPLE FORM)

SUBJUNCTIVE	Active		Middle / Passive (μιμνῄσκω)
Sing.	λελύκω		μεμνῶμαι
	λελύκῃς		μεμνῇ
	λελύκῃ		μεμνῆται
Dual	λελύκητον		μεμνῆσθον
	λελύκητον		μεμνῆσθον
Plur.	λελύκωμεν		μεμνώμεθα
	λελύκητε		μεμνῆσθε
	λελύκωσι(ν)		μεμνῶνται
OPTATIVE			
Sing.	λελύκοιμι	[λελυκοίην]	μεμνῄμην
	λελύκοις	[λελυκοίης]	μεμνῇο
	λελύκοι	[λελυκοίη]	μεμνῇτο
Dual	λελύκοιτον		μεμνῇσθον
	λελυκοίτην		μεμνῄσθην
Plur.	λελύκοιμεν		μεμνῄμεθα
	λελύκοιτε		μεμνῇσθε
	λελύκοιεν		μεμνῇντο

STRONG AORIST SYSTEM (λείπω)

INDICATIVE	ACTIVE	MIDDLE
Sing.	ἔλιπον	ἐλιπόμην
	ἔλιπες	ἐλίπου
	ἔλιπε(ν)	ἐλίπετο
Dual	ἐλίπετον	ἐλίπεσθον
	ἐλιπέτην	ἐλιπέσθην
Plur.	ἐλίπομεν	ἐλιπόμεθα
	ἐλίπετε	ἐλίπεσθε
	ἔλιπον	ἐλίποντο
SUBJUNCTIVE		
Sing.	λίπω	λίπωμαι
	λίπῃς	λίπῃ
	λίπῃ	λίπηται
Dual	λίπητον	λίπησθον
	λίπητον	λίπησθον
Plur.	λίπωμεν	λιπώμεθα
	λίπητε	λίπησθε
	λίπωσι(ν)	λίπωνται
OPTATIVE		
Sing.	λίποιμι	λιποίμην
	λίποις	λίποιο
	λίποι	λίποιτο
Dual	λίποιτον	λίποισθον
	λιποίτην	λιποίσθην
Plur.	λίποιμεν	λιποίμεθα
	λίποιτε	λίποισθε
	λίποιεν	λίποιντο
IMPERATIVE		
Sing.	λίπε	λιποῦ
	λιπέτω	λιπέσθω
Dual	λίπετον	λίπεσθον
	λιπέτων	λιπέσθων
Plur.	λίπετε	λίπεσθε
	λιπόντων	λιπέσθων
INFINITIVE		
	λιπεῖν	λιπέσθαι
PARTICIPLE		
	λιπών, λιποῦσα, λιπόν	λιπόμενος, λιπομένη, λιπόμενον

IRREGULAR STRONG AORIST SYSTEM (βαίνω, γιγνώσκω)

INDICATIVE	ACTIVE		MIDDLE	
Sing.	ἔβην		ἔγνων	
	ἔβης		ἔγνως	
	ἔβη		ἔγνω	
Dual	ἔβητον		ἔγνωτον	
	ἐβήτην		ἐγνώτην	
Plur.	ἔβημεν		ἔγνωμεν	
	ἔβητε		ἔγνωτε	
	ἔβησαν		ἔγνωσαν	
SUBJUNCTIVE				
Sing.	βῶ		γνῶ	
	βῇς		γνῷς	
	βῇ		γνῷ	
Dual	βῆτον		γνῶτον	
	βῆτον		γνῶτον	
Plur.	βῶμεν		γνῶμεν	
	βῆτε		γνῶτε	
	βῶσι(ν)		γνῶσι(ν)	
OPTATIVE				
Sing.	βαίην		γνοίην	
	βαίης		γνοίης	
	βαίη		γνοίη	
Dual	βαῖτον	[βαίητον]	γνοῖτον	[γνοίητον]
	βαίτην	[βαιήτην]	γνοίτην	[γνοιήτην]
Plur.	βαῖμεν	[βαίημεν]	γνοῖμεν	[γνοίημεν]
	βαῖτε	[βαίητε]	γνοῖτε	[γνοίητε]
	βαῖεν	[βαίησαν]	γνοῖεν	[γνοίησαν]
IMPERATIVE				
Sing.	βῆθι		γνῶθι	
	βήτω		γνώτω	
Dual	βῆτον		γνῶτον	
	βήτων		γνώτων	
Plur.	βῆτε		γνῶτε	
	βάντων		γνόντων	
INFINITIVE				
	βῆναι		γνῶναι	
PARTICIPLE				
	βάς, βᾶσα, βάν		γνούς, γνοῦσα, γνόν	

PERFECT MIDDLE SYSTEM (CONSONANT STEM VERBS)

INDICATIVE	Labial (γράφω)	Dental (πείθω)	Palatal (ἄγω)
Perfect			
Sing.	γέγραμμαι	πέπεισμαι	ἧγμαι
	γέγραψαι	πέπεισαι	ἧξαι
	γέγραπται	πέπεισται	ἧκται
Dual	γέγραφθον	πέπεισθον	ἧχθον
	γέγραφθον	πέπεισθον	ἧχθον
Plur.	γεγράμμεθα	πεπείσμεθα	ἥγμεθα
	γέγραφθε	πέπεισθε	ἧχθε
	γεγραμμένοι εἰσί(ν)	πεπεισμένοι εἰσί(ν)	ἠγμένοι εἰσί(ν)
Pluperfect			
Sing.	ἐγεγράμμην	ἐπεπείσμην	ἥγμην
	ἐγέγραψο	ἐπέπεισο	ἧξο
	ἐγέγραπτο	ἐπέπειστο	ἧκτο
Dual	ἐγέγραφθον	ἐπέπεισθον	ἧχθον
	ἐγεγραφθήν	ἐπεπείσθην	ἥχθην
Plur.	ἐγεγράμμεθα	ἐπεπείσμεθα	ἥγμεθα
	ἐγέγραφθε	ἐπέπεισθε	ἧχθε
	γεγραμμένοι ἦσαν	πεπεισμένοι ἦσαν	ἠγμένοι ἦσαν
INFINITIVE			
	γεγράφθαι	πεπεῖσθαι	ἧχθαι
PARTICIPLE			
	γεγραμμένος, -η, -ον	πεπεισμένος, -η, -ον	ἠγμένος, -η, -ον

LIQUID FUTURE

INDICATIVE	ACTIVE (μένω)	MIDDLE (πίπτω)
Sing.	μενῶ	πεσοῦμαι
	μενεῖς	πεσῇ / πεσεῖ
	μενεῖ	πεσεῖται
Dual	μενεῖτον	πεσεῖσθον
	μενεῖτον	πεσεῖσθον
Plur.	μενοῦμεν	πεσούμεθα
	μενεῖτε	πεσεῖσθε
	μενοῦσι(ν)	πεσοῦνται
INFINITIVE		
	μενεῖν	πεσεῖσθαι
PARTICIPLE		
	μενῶν, μενοῦσα, μενοῦν	πεσούμενος, πεσουμένη, πεσούμενον

LIQUID AORIST

INDICATIVE	ACTIVE
Sing.	ἔμεινα
	ἔμεινας
	ἔμεινε(ν)
Dual	ἐμείνατον
	ἐμεινάτην
Plur.	ἐμείναμεν
	ἐμείνατε
	ἔμειναν
INFINITIVE	
	μεῖναι
PARTICIPLE	
	μείνας, μείνασα, μεῖναν

CONTRACT THEMATIC VERBS

PRESENT SYSTEM (-έω)

	Active		Middle / Passive	
INDICATIVE	Present	Imperfect	Present	Imperfect
Sing.	φιλῶ	ἐφίλουν	φιλοῦμαι	ἐφιλούμην
	φιλεῖς	ἐφίλεις	φιλῇ / φιλεῖ	ἐφιλοῦ
	φιλεῖ	ἐφίλει	φιλεῖται	ἐφιλεῖτο
Dual	φιλεῖτον	ἐφιλεῖτον	φιλεῖσθον	ἐφιλεῖσθον
	φιλεῖτον	ἐφιλείτην	φιλεῖσθον	ἐφιλείσθην
Plur.	φιλοῦμεν	ἐφιλοῦμεν	φιλούμεθα	ἐφιλούμεθα
	φιλεῖτε	ἐφιλεῖτε	φιλεῖσθε	ἐφιλεῖσθε
	φιλοῦσι(ν)	ἐφίλουν	φιλοῦνται	ἐφιλοῦντο
SUBJUNCTIVE				
Sing.	φιλῶ		φιλῶμαι	
	φιλῇς		φιλῇ	
	φιλῇ		φιλῆται	
Dual	φιλῆτον		φιλῆσθον	
	φιλῆτον		φιλῆσθον	
Plur.	φιλῶμεν		φιλώμεθα	
	φιλῆτε		φιλῆσθε	
	φιλῶσι(ν)		φιλῶνται	
OPTATIVE				
Sing.	φιλοίην	[φιλοῖμι]	φιλοίμην	
	φιλοίης	[φιλοῖς]	φιλοῖο	
	φιλοίη	[φιλοῖ]	φιλοῖτο	
Dual	φιλοῖτον	[φιλοίητον]	φιλοῖσθον	
	φιλοίτην	[φιλοιήτην]	φιλοίσθην	
Plur.	φιλοῖμεν	[φιλοίημεν]	φιλοίμεθα	
	φιλοῖτε	[φιλοίητε]	φιλοῖσθε	
	φιλοῖεν	[φιλοίησαν]	φιλοῖντο	
IMPERATIVE				
Sing.	φίλει		φιλοῦ	
	φιλείτω		φιλείσθω	
Dual	φιλεῖτον		φιλεῖσθον	
	φιλείτων		φιλείσθων	
Plur.	φιλεῖτε		φιλεῖσθε	
	φιλούντων		φιλείσθων	
INFINITIVE				
	φιλεῖν		φιλεῖσθαι	
PARTICIPLE				
	φιλῶν, φιλοῦσα, φιλοῦν		φιλούμενος, φιλουμένη, φιλούμενον	

PRESENT SYSTEM (-άω)

	ACTIVE		MIDDLE / PASSIVE	
INDICATIVE	Present	Imperfect	Present	Imperfect
Sing.	τιμῶ	ἐτίμων	τιμῶμαι	ἐτιμώμην
	τιμᾷς	ἐτίμας	τιμᾷ	ἐτιμῶ
	τιμᾷ	ἐτίμα	τιμᾶται	ἐτιμᾶτο
Dual	τιμᾶτον	ἐτιμᾶτον	τιμᾶσθον	ἐτιμᾶσθον
	τιμᾶτον	ἐτιμάτην	τιμᾶσθον	ἐτιμάσθην
Plur.	τιμῶμεν	ἐτιμῶμεν	τιμώμεθα	ἐτιμώμεθα
	τιμᾶτε	ἐτιμᾶτε	τιμᾶσθε	ἐτιμᾶσθε
	τιμῶσι(ν)	ἐτίμων	τιμῶνται	ἐτιμῶντο
SUBJUNCTIVE				
Sing.	τιμῶ		τιμῶμαι	
	τιμᾷς		τιμᾷ	
	τιμᾷ		τιμᾶται	
Dual	τιμᾶτον		τιμᾶσθον	
	τιμᾶτον		τιμᾶσθον	
Plur.	τιμῶμεν		τιμώμεθα	
	τιμᾶτε		τιμᾶσθε	
	τιμῶσι(ν)		τιμῶνται	
OPTATIVE				
Sing.	τιμῴην	[τιμῷμι]	τιμῴμην	
	τιμῴης	[τιμῷς]	τιμῷο	
	τιμῴη	[τιμῷ]	τιμῷτο	
Dual	τιμῷτον	[τιμῴητον]	τιμῷσθον	
	τιμῴτην	[τιμῳήτην]	τιμῴσθην	
Plur.	τιμῷμεν	[τιμῴημεν]	τιμῴμεθα	
	τιμῷτε	[τιμῴητε]	τιμῷσθε	
	τιμῷεν	[τιμῴησαν]	τιμῷντο	
IMPERATIVE				
Sing.	τίμα		τιμῶ	
	τιμάτω		τιμάσθω	
Dual	τιμᾶτον		τιμᾶσθον	
	τιμάτων		τιμάσθων	
Plur.	τιμᾶτε		τιμᾶσθε	
	τιμώντων		τιμάσθων	
INFINITIVE				
	τιμᾶν		τιμᾶσθαι	
PARTICIPLE				
	τιμῶν, τιμῶσα, τιμῶν		τιμώμενος, τιμωμένη, τιμώμενον	

PRESENT SYSTEM (-όω)

	Active		Middle / Passive	
INDICATIVE	Present	Imperfect	Present	Imperfect
Sing.	δηλῶ	ἐδήλουν	δηλοῦμαι	ἐδηλούμην
	δηλοῖς	ἐδήλους	δηλοῖ	ἐδηλοῦ
	δηλοῖ	ἐδήλου	δηλοῦται	ἐδηλοῦτο
Dual	δηλοῦτον	ἐδηλοῦτον	δηλοῦσθον	ἐδηλοῦσθον
	δηλοῦτον	ἐδηλούτην	δηλοῦσθον	ἐδηλούσθην
Plur.	δηλοῦμεν	ἐδηλοῦμεν	δηλούμεθα	ἐδηλούμεθα
	δηλοῦτε	ἐδηλοῦτε	δηλοῦσθε	ἐδηλοῦσθε
	δηλοῦσι(ν)	ἐδήλουν	δηλοῦνται	ἐδηλοῦντο
SUBJUNCTIVE				
Sing.	δηλῶ		δηλῶμαι	
	δηλοῖς		δηλοῖ	
	δηλοῖ		δηλῶται	
Dual	δηλῶτον		δηλῶσθον	
	δηλῶτον		δηλῶσθον	
Plur.	δηλῶμεν		δηλώμεθα	
	δηλῶτε		δηλῶσθε	
	δηλῶσι(ν)		δηλῶνται	
OPTATIVE				
Sing.	δηλοίην	[δηλοῖμι]	δηλοίμην	
	δηλοίης	[δηλοῖς]	δηλοῖο	
	δηλοίη	[δηλοῖ]	δηλοῖτο	
Dual	δηλοῖτον	[δηλοίητον]	δηλοῖσθον	
	δηλοίτην	[δηλοιήτην]	δηλοίσθην	
Plur.	δηλοῖμεν	[δηλοίημεν]	δηλοίμεθα	
	δηλοῖτε	[δηλοίητε]	δηλοῖσθε	
	δηλοῖεν	[δηλοίησαν]	δηλοῖντο	
IMPERATIVE				
Sing.	δήλου		δηλοῦ	
	δηλούτω		δηλούσθω	
Dual	δηλοῦτον		δηλοῦσθον	
	δηλούτων		δηλούσθων	
Plur.	δηλοῦτε		δηλοῦσθε	
	δηλούντων		δηλούσθων	
INFINITIVE				
	δηλοῦν		δηλοῦσθαι	
PARTICIPLE				
	δηλῶν, δηλοῦσα, δηλοῦν		δηλούμενος, δηλουμένη, δηλούμενον	

ATHEMATIC VERBS: δείκνυμι, τίθημι, ἵστημι, δίδωμι

PRESENT SYSTEM (δείκνυμι)

	ACTIVE		MIDDLE / PASSIVE	
INDICATIVE	Present	Imperfect	Present	Imperfect
Sing.	δείκνυμι	ἐδείκνυν	δείκνυμαι	ἐδεικνύμην
	δείκνυς	ἐδείκνυς	δείκνυσαι	ἐδείκνυσο
	δείκνυσι(ν)	ἐδείκνυ	δείκνυται	ἐδείκνυτο
Dual	δείκνυτον	ἐδείκνυτον	δείκνυσθον	ἐδείκνυσθον
	δείκνυτον	ἐδεικνύτην	δείκνυσθον	ἐδεικνύσθην
Plur.	δείκνυμεν	ἐδείκνυμεν	δεικνύμεθα	ἐδεικνύμεθα
	δείκνυτε	ἐδείκνυτε	δείκνυσθε	ἐδείκνυσθε
	δεικνύασι(ν)	ἐδείκνυσαν	δείκνυνται	ἐδείκνυντο
SUBJUNCTIVE				
Sing.	δεικνύω		δεικνύωμαι	
	δεικνύῃς		δεικνύῃ	
	δεικνύῃ		δεικνύηται	
Dual	δεικνύητον		δεικνύησθον	
	δεικνύητον		δεικνύησθον	
Plur.	δεικνύωμεν		δεικνυώμεθα	
	δεικνύητε		δεικνύησθε	
	δεικνύωσι(ν)		δεικνύωνται	
OPTATIVE				
Sing.	δεικνύοιμι		δεικνυοίμην	
	δεικνύοις		δεικνύοιο	
	δεικνύοι		δεικνύοιτο	
Dual	δεικνύοιτον		δεικνύοισθον	
	δεικνυοίτην		δεικνυοίσθην	
Plur.	δεικνύοιμεν		δεικνυοίμεθα	
	δεικνύοιτε		δεικνύοισθε	
	δεικνύοιεν		δεικνύοιντο	
IMPERATIVE				
Sing.	δείκνυ		δείκνυσο	
	δεικνύτω		δεικνύσθω	
Dual	δείκνυτον		δείκνυσθον	
	δεικνύτων		δεικνύσθων	
Plur.	δείκνυτε		δείκνυσθε	
	δεικνύντων		δεικνύσθων	
INFINITIVE				
	δεικνύναι		δείκνυσθαι	
PARTICIPLE				
	δεικνύς, δεικνῦσα, δεικνύν		δεικνύμενος, δεικνυμένη, δεικνύμενον	

PRESENT SYSTEM (τίθημι)

	ACTIVE		MIDDLE / PASSIVE	
INDICATIVE	Present	Imperfect	Present	Imperfect
Sing.	τίθημι	ἐτίθην	τίθεμαι	ἐτιθέμην
	τίθης	ἐτίθεις	τίθεσαι	ἐτίθεσο
	τίθησι(ν)	ἐτίθει	τίθεται	ἐτίθετο
Dual	τίθετον	ἐτίθετον	τίθεσθον	ἐτίθεσθον
	τίθετον	ἐτιθέτην	τίθεσθον	ἐτιθέσθην
Plur.	τίθεμεν	ἐτίθεμεν	τιθέμεθα	ἐτιθέμεθα
	τίθετε	ἐτίθετε	τίθεσθε	ἐτίθεσθε
	τιθέασι(ν)	ἐτίθεσαν	τίθενται	ἐτίθεντο
SUBJUNCTIVE				
Sing.	τιθῶ		τιθῶμαι	
	τιθῇς		τιθῇ	
	τιθῇ		τιθῆται	
Dual	τιθῆτον		τιθῆσθον	
	τιθῆτον		τιθῆσθον	
Plur.	τιθῶμεν		τιθώμεθα	
	τιθῆτε		τιθῆσθε	
	τιθῶσι(ν)		τιθῶνται	
OPTATIVE				
Sing.	τιθείην		τιθείμην	
	τιθείης		τιθεῖο	
	τιθείη		τιθεῖτο	
Dual	τιθεῖτον	[τιθείητον]	τιθεῖσθον	
	τιθείτην	[τιθειήτην]	τιθείσθην	
Plur.	τιθεῖμεν	[τιθείημεν]	τιθείμεθα	
	τιθεῖτε	[τιθείητε]	τιθεῖσθε	
	τιθεῖεν	[τιθείησαν]	τιθεῖντο	
IMPERATIVE				
Sing.	τίθει		τίθεσο	
	τιθέτω		τιθέσθω	
Dual	τίθετον		τίθεσθον	
	τιθέτων		τιθέσθων	
Plur.	τίθετε		τίθεσθε	
	τιθέντων		τιθέσθων	
INFINITIVE				
	τιθέναι		τίθεσθαι	
PARTICIPLE				
	τιθείς, τιθεῖσα, τιθέν		τιθέμενος, τιθεμένη, τιθέμενον	

PRESENT SYSTEM (ἵστημι)

	Active		Middle / Passive	
INDICATIVE	Present	Imperfect	Present	Imperfect
Sing.	ἵστημι	ἵστην	ἵσταμαι	ἱστάμην
	ἵστης	ἵστης	ἵστασαι	ἵστασο
	ἵστησι(ν)	ἵστη	ἵσταται	ἵστατο
Dual	ἵστατον	ἵστατον	ἵστασθον	ἵστασθον
	ἵστατον	ἱστάτην	ἵστασθον	ἱστάσθην
Plur.	ἵσταμεν	ἵσταμεν	ἱστάμεθα	ἱστάμεθα
	ἵστατε	ἵστατε	ἵστασθε	ἵστασθε
	ἱστᾶσι(ν)	ἵστασαν	ἵστανται	ἵσταντο
SUBJUNCTIVE				
Sing.	ἱστῶ		ἱστῶμαι	
	ἱστῇς		ἱστῇ	
	ἱστῇ		ἱστῆται	
Dual	ἱστῆτον		ἱστῆσθον	
	ἱστῆτον		ἱστῆσθον	
Plur.	ἱστῶμεν		ἱστώμεθα	
	ἱστῆτε		ἱστῆσθε	
	ἱστῶσι(ν)		ἱστῶνται	
OPTATIVE				
Sing.	ἱσταίην		ἱσταίμην	
	ἱσταίης		ἱσταῖο	
	ἱσταίη		ἱσταῖτο	
Dual	ἱσταῖτον	[ἱσταίητον]	ἱσταῖσθον	
	ἱσταίτην	[ἱσταιήτην]	ἱσταίσθην	
Plur.	ἱσταῖμεν	[ἱσταίημεν]	ἱσταίμεθα	
	ἱσταῖτε	[ἱσταίητε]	ἱσταῖσθε	
	ἱσταῖεν	[ἱσταίησαν]	ἱσταῖντο	
IMPERATIVE				
Sing.	ἵστη	ἵστασο		
	ἱστάτω	ἱστάσθω		
Dual	ἵστατον	ἵστασθον		
	ἱστάτων	ἱστάσθων		
Plur.	ἵστατε	ἵστασθε		
	ἱστάντων	ἱστάσθων		
INFINITIVE				
	ἱστάναι	ἵστασθαι		
PARTICIPLE				
	ἱστάς, ἱστᾶσα, ἱστάν		ἱστάμενος, ἱσταμένη, ἱστάμενον	

PRESENT SYSTEM (δίδωμι)

	Active		Middle / Passive	
INDICATIVE	Present	Imperfect	Present	Imperfect
Sing.	δίδωμι	ἐδίδουν	δίδομαι	ἐδιδόμην
	δίδως	ἐδίδους	δίδοσαι	ἐδίδοσο
	δίδωσι(ν)	ἐδίδου	δίδοται	ἐδίδοτο
Dual	δίδοτον	ἐδίδοτον	δίδοσθον	ἐδίδοσθον
	δίδοτον	ἐδιδότην	δίδοσθον	ἐδιδόσθην
Plur.	δίδομεν	ἐδίδομεν	διδόμεθα	ἐδιδόμεθα
	δίδοτε	ἐδίδοτε	δίδοσθε	ἐδίδοσθε
	διδόασι(ν)	ἐδίδοσαν	δίδονται	ἐδίδοντο
SUBJUNCTIVE				
Sing.	διδῶ		διδῶμαι	
	διδῷς		διδῷ	
	διδῷ		διδῶται	
Dual	διδῶτον		διδῶσθον	
	διδῶτον		διδῶσθον	
Plur.	διδῶμεν		διδώμεθα	
	διδῶτε		διδῶσθε	
	διδῶσι(ν)		διδῶνται	
OPTATIVE				
Sing.	διδοίην		διδοίμην	
	διδοίης		διδοῖο	
	διδοίη		διδοῖτο	
Dual	διδοῖτον	[διδοίητον]	διδοῖσθον	
	διδοίτην	[διδοιήτην]	διδοίσθην	
Plur.	διδοῖμεν	[διδοίημεν]	διδοίμεθα	
	διδοῖτε	[διδοίητε]	διδοῖσθε	
	διδοῖεν	[διδοίησαν]	διδοῖντο	
IMPERATIVE				
Sing.	δίδου		δίδοσο	
	διδότω		διδόσθω	
Dual	δίδοτον		δίδοσθον	
	διδότων		διδόσθων	
Plur.	δίδοτε		δίδοσθε	
	διδόντων		διδόσθων	
INFINITIVE				
	διδόναι		δίδοσθαι	
PARTICIPLE				
	διδούς, διδοῦσα, διδόν		διδόμενος, διδομένη, διδόμενον	

SECOND AORIST SYSTEM (τίθημι)

INDICATIVE	ACTIVE		MIDDLE
Sing.	ἔθηκα		ἐθέμην
	ἔθηκας		ἔθου
	ἔθηκε(ν)		ἔθετο
Dual	ἔθετον		ἔθεσθον
	ἐθέτην		ἐθέσθην
Plur.	ἔθεμεν		ἐθέμεθα
	ἔθετε		ἔθεσθε
	ἔθεσαν		ἔθεντο
SUBJUNCTIVE			
Sing.	θῶ		θῶμαι
	θῇς		θῇ
	θῇ		θῆται
Dual	θῆτον		θῆσθον
	θῆτον		θῆσθον
Plur.	θῶμεν		θώμεθα
	θῆτε		θῆσθε
	θῶσι(ν)		θῶνται
OPTATIVE			
Sing.	θείην		θείμην
	θείης		θεῖο
	θείη		θεῖτο
Dual	θεῖτον	[θείητον]	θεῖσθον
	θείτην	[θειήτην]	θείσθην
Plur.	θεῖμεν	[θείημεν]	θείμεθα
	θεῖτε	[θείητε]	θεῖσθε
	θεῖεν	[θείησαν]	θεῖντο
IMPERATIVE			
Sing.	θές		θοῦ
	θέτω		θέσθω
Dual	θέτον		θέσθον
	θέτων		θέσθων
Plur.	θέτε		θέσθε
	θέντων		θέσθων
INFINITIVE			
	θεῖναι		θέσθαι
PARTICIPLE			
	θείς, θεῖσα, θέν		θέμενος, θεμένη, θέμενον

SECOND AORIST SYSTEM (ἵστημι)

INDICATIVE	ACTIVE	
Sing.	ἔστην	
	ἔστης	
	ἔστη	
Dual	ἔστητον	
	ἐστήτην	
Plur.	ἔστημεν	
	ἔστητε	
	ἔστησαν	
SUBJUNCTIVE		
Sing.	στῶ	
	στῇς	
	στῇ	
Dual	στῆτον	
	στῆτον	
Plur.	στῶμεν	
	στῆτε	
	στῶσι(ν)	
OPTATIVE		
Sing.	σταίην	
	σταίης	
	σταίη	
Dual	σταῖτον	[σταίητον]
	σταίτην	[σταιήτην]
Plur.	σταῖμεν	[σταίημεν]
	σταῖτε	[σταίητε]
	σταῖεν	[σταίησαν]
IMPERATIVE		
Sing.	στῆθι	
	στήτω	
Dual	στῆτον	
	στήτων	
Plur.	στῆτε	
	στάντων	
INFINITIVE		
	στῆναι	
PARTICIPLE		
	στάς, στᾶσα, στάν	

SECOND AORIST SYSTEM (δίδωμι)

INDICATIVE	Active		Middle
Sing.	ἔδωκα		ἐδόμην
	ἔδωκας		ἔδου
	ἔδωκε(ν)		ἔδοτο
Dual	ἔδοτον		ἔδοσθον
	ἐδότην		ἐδόσθην
Plur.	ἔδομεν		ἐδόμεθα
	ἔδοτε		ἔδοσθε
	ἔδοσαν		ἔδοντο
SUBJUNCTIVE			
Sing.	δῶ		δῶμαι
	δῷς		δῷ
	δῷ		δῶται
Dual	δῶτον		δῶσθον
	δῶτον		δῶσθον
Plur.	δῶμεν		δώμεθα
	δῶτε		δῶσθε
	δῶσι(ν)		δῶνται
OPTATIVE			
Sing.	δοίην		δοίμην
	δοίης		δοῖο
	δοίη		δοῖτο
Dual	δοῖτον	[δοίητον]	δοῖσθον
	δοίτην	[δοιήτην]	δοίσθην
Plur.	δοῖμεν	[δοίημεν]	δοίμεθα
	δοῖτε	[δοίητε]	δοῖσθε
	δοῖεν	[δοίησαν]	δοῖντο
IMPERATIVE			
Sing.	δός		δοῦ
	δότω		δόσθω
Dual	δότον		δόσθον
	δότων		δόσθων
Plur.	δότε		δόσθε
	δόντων		δόσθων
INFINITIVE			
	δοῦναι		δόσθαι
PARTICIPLE			
	δούς, δοῦσα, δόν		δόμενος, δομένη, δόμενον

IRREGULAR ATHEMATIC VERBS: ἵημι, εἰμί, εἶμι, φημί, οἶδα

PRESENT SYSTEM (ἵημι)

	ACTIVE		MIDDLE / PASSIVE	
INDICATIVE	Perfect	Imperfect	Perfect	Imperfect
Sing.	ἵημι	ἵην	ἵεμαι	ἱέμην
	ἵης	ἵεις	ἵεσαι	ἵεσο
	ἵησι(ν)	ἵει	ἵεται	ἵετο
Dual	ἵετον	ἵετον	ἵεσθον	ἵεσθον
	ἵετον	ἱέτην	ἵεσθον	ἱέσθην
Plur.	ἵεμεν	ἵεμεν	ἱέμεθα	ἱέμεθα
	ἵετε	ἵετε	ἵεσθε	ἵεσθε
	ἱᾶσι(ν)	ἵεσαν	ἵενται	ἵεντο
SUBJUNCTIVE				
Sing.	ἱῶ		ἱῶμαι	
	ἱῇς		ἱῇ	
	ἱῇ		ἱῆται	
Dual	ἱῆτον		ἱῆσθον	
	ἱῆτον		ἱῆσθον	
Plur.	ἱῶμεν		ἱώμεθα	
	ἱῆτε		ἱῆσθε	
	ἱῶσι(ν)		ἱῶνται	
OPTATIVE				
Sing.	ἱείην		ἱείμην	
	ἱείης		ἱεῖο	
	ἱείη		ἱεῖτο	
Dual	ἱεῖτον	[ἱείητον]	ἱεῖσθον	
	ἱείτην	[ἱειήτην]	ἱείσθην	
Plur.	ἱεῖμεν	[ἱείημεν]	ἱείμεθα	
	ἱεῖτε	[ἱείητε]	ἱεῖσθε	
	ἱεῖεν	[ἱείησαν]	ἱεῖντο	
IMPERATIVE				
Sing.	ἵει		ἵεσο	
	ἱέτω		ἱέσθω	
Dual	ἵετον		ἵεσθον	
	ἱέτων		ἱέσθων	
Plur.	ἵετε		ἵεσθε	
	ἱέντων		ἱέσθων	
IMPERATIVE				
	ἱέναι		ἵεσθαι	
PARTICIPLE				
	ἱείς, ἱεῖσα, ἱέν		ἱέμενος, ἱεμένη, ἱέμενον	

AORIST SYSTEM (ἀφίημι)

INDICATIVE	Active	Middle
Sing.	ἀφῆκα	ἀφείμην
	ἀφῆκας	ἀφεῖσο
	ἀφῆκε(ν)	ἀφεῖτο
Dual	ἀφεῖτον	ἀφεῖσθον
	ἀφείτην	ἀφείσθην
Plur.	ἀφεῖμεν	ἀφείμεθα
	ἀφεῖτε	ἀφεῖσθε
	ἀφεῖσαν	ἀφεῖντο
SUBJUNCTIVE		
Sing.	ἀφῶ	ἀφῶμαι
	ἀφῇς	ἀφῇ
	ἀφῇ	ἀφῆται
Dual	ἀφῆτον	ἀφῆσθον
	ἀφῆτον	ἀφῆσθον
Plur.	ἀφῶμεν	ἀφώμεθα
	ἀφῆτε	ἀφῆσθε
	ἀφῶσι(ν)	ἀφῶνται
OPTATIVE		
Sing.	ἀφείην	ἀφείμην
	ἀφείης	ἀφεῖο
	ἀφείη	ἀφεῖτο
Dual	ἀφεῖτον [ἀφείητον]	ἀφεῖσθον
	ἀφείτην [ἀφειήτην]	ἀφείσθην
Plur.	ἀφεῖμεν [ἀφείημεν]	ἀφείμεθα
	ἀφεῖτε [ἀφείητε]	ἀφεῖσθε
	ἀφεῖεν [ἀφείησαν]	ἀφεῖντο
IMPERATIVE		
Sing.	ἄφες	ἀφοῦ
	ἀφέτω	ἀφέσθω
Dual	ἄφετον	ἄφεσθον
	ἀφέτων	ἀφέσθων
Plur.	ἄφετε	ἄφεσθε
	ἀφέντων	ἀφέσθων
INFINITIVE		
	ἀφεῖναι	ἀφέσθαι
PARTICIPLE		
	ἀφείς, ἀφεῖσα, ἀφέν	ἀφέμενος, -η, -ον

	PRESENT SYSTEM (εἰμί, 'be')		PRESENT SYSTEM (εἶμι, 'go')		
INDICATIVE	Present	Imperfect	Present	Imperfect	
Sing.	εἰμί	ἦ / ἦν	εἶμι	ᾖα	[ᾔειν]
	εἶ	ἦσθα	εἶ(ς)	ᾔεισθα	[ᾔεις]
	ἐστί(ν)	ἦν	εἶσι(ν)	ᾔειν	[ᾔει]
Dual	ἐστόν	ἦστον	ἴτον	ᾖτον	
	ἐστόν	ἤστην	ἴτον	ᾔτην	
Plur.	ἐσμέν	ἦμεν	ἴμεν	ᾖμεν	
	ἐστέ	ἦτε	ἴτε	ᾖτε	
	εἰσί(ν)	ἦσαν	ἴασι(ν)	ᾖσαν	[ᾔεσαν]
SUBJUNCTIVE					
Sing.	ὦ		ἴω		
	ᾖς		ἴῃς		
	ᾖ		ἴῃ		
Dual	ἦτον		ἴητον		
	ἦτον		ἴητον		
Plur.	ὦμεν		ἴωμεν		
	ἦτε		ἴητε		
	ὦσι(ν)		ἴωσι(ν)		
OPTATIVE					
Sing.	εἴην		ἴοιμι	[ἰοίην]	
	εἴης		ἴοις		
	εἴη		ἴοι		
Dual	εἶτον	[εἴητον]	ἴοιτον		
	εἴτην	[εἰήτην]	ἰοίτην		
Plur.	εἶμεν	[εἴημεν]	ἴοιμεν		
	εἶτε	[εἴητε]	ἴοιτε		
	εἶεν	[εἴησαν]	ἴοιεν		
IMPERATIVE					
Sing.	ἴσθι		ἴθι		
	ἔστω		ἴτω		
Dual	ἔστον		ἴτον		
	ἔστων		ἴτων		
Plur.	ἔστε		ἴτε		
	ἔστων / ὄντων		ἰόντων		
INFINITIVE					
	εἶναι		ἰέναι		
PARTICIPLE					
	ὤν, οὖσα, ὄν		ἰών, ἰοῦσα, ἰόν		

	PERFECT SYSTEM (οἶδα)			PRESENT SYSTEM (φημί)		
INDICATIVE	Perfect	Pluperfect		Present	Imperfect	
Sing.	οἶδα	ᾔδη	[ᾔδειν]	φημί	ἔφην	
	οἶσθα	ᾔδησθα	[ᾔδεις]	φής	ἔφησθα	ἔφης
	οἶδε(ν)	ᾔδει(ν)		φησί(ν)	ἔφη	
Dual	ἴστον	[ᾖστον]	[ᾔδετον]	φατόν	ἔφατον	
	ἴστον	[ᾔστην]	[ᾐδέτην]	φατόν	ἐφάτην	
Plur.	ἴσμεν	ᾖσμεν	[ᾔδεμεν]	φαμέν	ἔφαμεν	
	ἴστε	ᾖστε	[ᾔδετε]	φατέ	ἔφατε	
	ἴσασι(ν)	ᾖσαν	[ᾔδεσαν]	φασί(ν)	ἔφασαν	
SUBJUNCTIVE						
Sing.	εἰδῶ			φῶ		
	εἰδῇς			φῇς		
	εἰδῇ			φῇ		
Dual	εἰδῆτον			φῆτον		
	εἰδῆτον			φῆτον		
Plur.	εἰδῶμεν			φῶμεν		
	εἰδῆτε			φῆτε		
	εἰδῶσι(ν)			φῶσι(ν)		
OPTATIVE						
Sing.	εἰδείην			φαίην		
	εἰδείης			φαίης		
	εἰδείη			φαίη		
Dual	εἰδεῖτον					
	εἰδείτην					
Plur.	εἰδεῖμεν	[εἰδείημεν]		φαῖμεν	[φαίημεν]	
	εἰδεῖτε	[εἰδείητε]		φαῖτε	[φαίητε]	
	εἰδεῖεν	[εἰδείησαν]		φαῖεν	[φαίησαν]	
IMPERATIVE						
Sing.	ἴσθι			φάθι, φαθί		
	ἴστω			φάτω		
Dual	ἴστον			φάτον		
	ἴστων			φάτων		
Plur.	ἴστε			φάτε		
	ἴστων			φάντων		
INFINITIVE						
	εἰδέναι			φάναι		
PARTICIPLE						
	εἰδώς, εἰδυῖα, εἰδός			φάς, φᾶσα, φάν		

APPENDIX 5: READING EXPECTATIONS

The following tables summarize constructions from the perspective of those wishing to recognize them (Greek to English). Chapter numbers are included in parentheses.

Conditions (12, 28)

Protasis (neg. μή)	Apodosis (neg. οὐ)	
ἐάν → subjunctive ↗	future indicative (or equivalent)	= future more vivid
↘	present indicative	= present general
εἰ → optative ↗	optative + ἄν	= future less vivid
↘	imperfect indicative	= past general
εἰ → indicative ↗	indicative	= simple condition
↘	indicative + ἄν	= contrary-to-fact

imperfect = present time
aorist = past time

Fearing clauses (33)

φοβοῦμαι μή →	present indicative	= present fear	I fear he does / is doing x.
φοβοῦμαι μή ↘	past indicative	= past fear	I fear he did / was doing x.
ἐφοβούμην μή ↗			I feared he had done x.
φοβοῦμαι μή →	subjunctive	= future fear	I fear he will do x.
ἐφοβούμην μή ↗	subjunctive	= vivid future fear	I feared he would do x.
↘	optative	= future fear	I feared he would do x.

Purpose clauses (27)

primary verb	↗ ἵνα + subjunctive ↘ future participle	= He goes *in order to do x.*
secondary verb	↗ ἵνα → optative ↘ future participle	= He went *in order to do x.*

Result clauses (31)

οὕτω(ς) → ὥστε ↗	indicative (neg. οὐ)	= actual result	He is so wise that he did x.
οὕτω(ς) → ὥστε ↘	infinitive (neg. μή)	= natural result	He is so wise as to do x.
comparative → ἤ ὥστε →	infinitive (neg. μή)	= natural result	He is too wise to do x.

Temporal clauses with ἕως, μέχρι and ἔστε (34)

secondary tense → ἕως, etc.	↗ indicative (neg. οὐ)	= definite past time
	↘ optative (neg. μή)	= indefinite past time OR time anticipated in the past
present tense → ἕως, etc.	↗ indicative (neg. οὐ)	= definite present time
	↘ ἄν + subjunctive (neg. μή)	= indefinite present time OR time anticipated in the present
future tense → ἕως, etc.	→ ἄν + subjunctive (neg. μή)	= indefinite future time

Temporal clauses with πρίν (34)

negative main clause	→ πρίν → finite verb (constr. as ἕως, etc.)	= 'until'
affirmative main clause	→ πρίν → infinitive	= 'before'

Wishes (26)

εἴθε / εἰ γάρ (neg. μή)	↗ optative	= future wish
	→ imperfect indicative	= present wish
	↘ aorist indicative	= past wish

APPENDIX 6: CONSTRUCTION SUMMARIES

The following tables summarize constructions from the perspective of those wishing to create them (English to Greek). Chapter numbers are included in parentheses.

Conditions (12, 28)

type of condition	Protasis (negative μή)	Apodosis (negative οὐ)
future more vivid:	ἐάν + subjunctive	future indicative
present general:	ἐάν + subjunctive	present indicative
future less vivid:	εἰ + optative	optative + ἄν
past general:	εἰ + optative	imperfect indicative
simple:	εἰ + indicative	indicative
contrary to fact:	εἰ + indicative	indicative + ἄν
	imperfect for present	imperfect for present
	aorist for past	aorist for past

Fearing clauses (33)

present fear:	φοβοῦμαι μὴ	+ present indicative	I fear he does / is doing x.
past fear:	φοβοῦμαι μὴ	+ past indicative	I fear he did / was doing x.
	ἐφοβούμην μὴ	+ past indicative	I feared he had done x.
future fear:	φοβοῦμαι μὴ	+ subjunctive	I fear he will do x.
	ἐφοβούμην μὴ	+ optative	I feared he would do x.
		+ subjunctive for vividness	

Purpose clauses (27)

primary verb:	+ ἵνα + subjunctive (negative μή)	He goes *in order to do x.*
	+ future participle	
secondary verb:	+ ἵνα + optative (negative μή)	He went *in order to do x.*
	+ future participle	

Result clauses (31)

οὕτω +	ὥστε + indicative (neg. οὐ):	actual result	He is so wise that he did x.
οὕτω +	ὥστε + infinitive (neg. μή):	natural result	He is so wise as to do x.
comp. +	ἢ ὥστε + infinitive (neg. μή):	natural result	He is too wise to do x.

Temporal clauses with ἕως, μέχρι and ἔστε (34)

definite past:	secondary tense	ἕως, etc. + indicative (neg. οὐ)
indefinite or anticipated past:	secondary tense	ἕως, etc. + optative (neg. μή)
definite present:	present tense	ἕως, etc. + indicative (neg. οὐ)
indefinite or anticipated present:	present tense	ἕως, etc. + ἄν + subjunctive (neg. μή)
indefinite future:	future tense	ἕως, etc. + ἄν + subjunctive (neg. μή)

Temporal clauses with πρίν (34)

until:	negative main clause	πρίν + finite verb (constr. as ἕως, etc.)
before:	affirmative main clause	πρίν + infinitive

Wishes (26)

future wish:	εἴθε / εἰ γάρ + optative (neg. μή)
present wish:	εἴθε / εἰ γάρ + imperfect indicative (neg. μή)
past wish:	εἴθε / εἰ γάρ + aorist indicative (neg. μή)

APPENDIX 7: REGULAR VERB TENSE MARKERS AND ENDINGS BY TENSE

PRESENT

	Indicative				Subjunctive		Optative	
	Present		Imperfect					
	A	M/P	A	M/P	A	M/P	A	M/P
Sing.	-ω	-ομαι	-ον	-ομην	-ω	-ωμαι	-οιμι	-οιμην
	-εις	-η/-ει	-ες	-ου	-ης	-η	-οις	-οιο
	-ει	-εται	-ε	-ετο	-η	-ηται	-οι	-οιτο
Plur.	-ομεν	-ομεθα	-ομεν	-ομεθα	-ωμεν	-ωμεθα	-οιμεν	-οιμεθα
	-ετε	-εσθε	-ετε	-εσθε	-ητε	-ησθε	-οιτε	-οισθε
	-ουσι	-ονται	-ον	-οντο	-ωσι	-ωνται	-οιεν	-οιντο
Infin.	-ειν	-εσθαι						
Part.	-ων	-ομενος						

FUTURE

	Indicative			Optative		
	A	M	P	A	M	P
Sing.	-σω	-σομαι	-θησομαι	-σοιμι	-σοιμην	-θησοιμην
	-σεις	-ση/-σει	-θηση/-ει	-σοις	-σοιο	-θησοιο
	-σει	-σεται	-θησεται	-σοι	-σοιτο	-θησοιτο
Plur.	-σομεν	-σομεθα	-θησομεθα	-σοιμεν	-σοιμεθα	-θησοιμεθα
	-σετε	-σεσθε	-θησεσθε	-σοιτε	-σοισθε	-θησοισθε
	-σουσι	-σονται	-θησονται	-σοιεν	-σοιντο	-θησοιντο
Infin.	-σειν	-σεσθαι	-θησεσθαι			
Part.	-σων	-σομενος	-θησομενος			

AORIST

	Indicative			Subjunctive			Optative		
	A	M	P	A	M	P	A	M	P
Sing.	-σα	-σαμην	-θην	-σω	-σωμαι	-θω	-σαιμι	-σαιμην	-θειην
	-σας	-σω	-θης	-σῃς	-σῃ	-θῃς	-σαις	-σαιο	-θειης
	-σε	-σατο	-θη	-σῃ	-σηται	-θῃ	-σαι	-σαιτο	-θειη
Plur.	-σαμεν	-σαμεθα	-θημεν	-σωμεν	-σωμεθα	-θωμεν	-σαιμεν	-σαιμεθα	-θειμεν
	-σατε	-σασθε	-θητε	-σητε	-σησθε	-θητε	-σαιτε	-σαισθε	-θειτε
	-σαν	-σαντο	-θησαν	-σωσι	-σωνται	-θωσι	-σαιεν	-σαιντο	-θειεν
Infin.	-σαι	-σασθαι	-θηναι						
Part.	-σας	-σαμενος	-θεις						

PERFECT

	Indicative		Subjunctive		Optative	
	A	M/P	A	M/P	A	M/P
Sing.	-κα	-μαι	-κως ὦ	-μενος ὦ	-κως εἴην	-μενος εἴην
	-κας	-σαι	-κως ῃς	-μενος ᾖς	-κως εἴης	-μενος εἴης
	-κε	-ται	-κως ῃ	-μενος ᾖ	-κως εἴη	-μενος εἴη
Plur.	-καμεν	-μεθα	-κοτες ὦμεν	-μενοι ὦμεν	-κοτες εἶμεν	-μενοι εἶμεν
	-κατε	-σθε	-κοτες ἦτε	-μενοι ἦτε	-κοτες εἶτε	-μενοι εἶτε
	-κασι	-νται	-κοτες ὦσι	-μενοι ὦσι	-κοτες εἶεν	-μενοι εἶεν
Infin.	-κεναι	-σθαι				
Part.	-κως	-μενος				

APPENDIX 8: REGULAR VERB TENSE MARKERS AND ENDINGS BY MOOD

INDICATIVE

	Present		Imperfect		Future			Aorist			Perfect	
	A	M/P	A	M/P	A	M	P	A	M	P	A	M/P
Sing.	-ω	-ομαι	-ον	-ομην	-σω	-σομαι	-θησομαι	-σα	-σαμην	-θην	-κα	-μαι
	-εις	-ῃ/-ει	-ες	-ου	-σεις	-σῃ/-ει	-θησῃ/-ει	-σας	-σω	-θης	-κας	-σαι
	-ει	-εται	-ε	-ετο	-σει	-σεται	-θησεται	-σε	-σατο	-θη	-κε	-ται
Plur.	-ομεν	-ομεθα	-ομεν	-ομεθα	-σομεν	-σομεθα	-θησομεθα	-σαμεν	-σαμεθα	-θημεν	-καμεν	-μεθα
	-ετε	-εσθε	-ετε	-εσθε	-σετε	-σεσθε	-θησεσθε	-σατε	-σασθε	-θητε	-κατε	-σθε
	-ουσι	-ονται	-ον	-οντο	-σουσι	-σονται	-θησονται	-σαν	-σαντο	-θησαν	-κασι	-νται

SUBJUNCTIVE

	Present		Imperfect		Future			Aorist			Perfect	
	A	M/P	A	M/P	A	M	P	A	M	P	A	M/P
Sing.	-ω	-ωμαι						-σω	-σωμαι	-θω	-κως ὦ	-μενος ὦ
	-ῃς	-ῃ						-σῃς	-σῃ	-θῃς	-κως ῃς	-μενος ᾖς
	-ῃ	-ηται						-σῃ	-σηται	-θῃ	-κως ῃ	-μενος ᾖ
Plur.	-ωμεν	-ωμεθα						-σωμεν	-σωμεθα	-θωμεν	-κοτες ὦμεν	-μενοι ὦμεν
	-ητε	-ησθε						-σητε	-σησθε	-θητε	-κοτες ἦτε	-μενοι ἦτε
	-ωσι	-ωνται						-σωσι	-σωνται	-θωσι	-κοτες ὦσι	-μενοι ὦσι

OPTATIVE

	Present		Imperfect		Future			Aorist			Perfect	
	A	M/P	A	M/P	A	M	P	A	M	P	A	M/P
Sing.	-οιμι	-οιμην			-σοιμι	-σοιμην	-θησοιμην	-σαιμι	-σαιμην	-θειην	-κως εἴην	-μενος εἴην
	-οις	-οιο			-σοις	-σοιο	-θησοιο	-σαις	-σαιο	-θειης	-κως εἴης	-μενος εἴης
	-οι	-οιτο			-σοι	-σοιτο	-θησοιτο	-σαι	-σαιτο	-θειη	-κως εἴη	-μενος εἴη
Plur.	-οιμεν	-οιμεθα			-σοιμεν	-σοιμεθα	-θησοιμεθα	-σαιμεν	-σαιμεθα	-θειμεν	-κοτες εἶμεν	-μενοι εἶμεν
	-οιτε	-οισθε			-σοιτε	-σοισθε	-θησοισθε	-σαιτε	-σαισθε	-θειτε	-κοτες εἶτε	-μενοι εἶτε
	-οιεν	-οιντο			-σοιεν	-σοιντο	-θησοιντο	-σαιεν	-σαιντο	-θειεν	-κοτες εἶεν	-μενοι εἶεν

INFINITIVE / PARTICIPLE

Present		Imperfect		Future			Aorist			Perfect	
A	M/P	A	M/P	A	M	P	A	M	P	A	M/P
-ειν	-εσθαι			-σειν	-σεσθαι	-θησεσθαι	-σαι	-σασθαι	-θηναι	-κεναι	-σθαι
-ων	-ομενος			-σων	-σομενος	-θησομενος	-σας	-σαμενος	-θεις	-κως	-μενος